Contextualising Difficulties in Literacy Development

Exploring politics, culture, ethnicity and ethics

Edited by Janet Soler, Janice Wearmouth and Gavin Reid

 **RoutledgeFalmer**
Taylor & Francis Group

LONDON AND NEW YORK

 The Open University

First published 2002
by RoutledgeFalmer
2 Park Square, Milton Park, Abingdon, Oxon OX14 4RN

Simultaneously published in the USA and Canada
by RoutledgeFalmer
270 Madison Avenue, New York, NY 10016

Reprinted 2007

RoutledgeFalmer is an imprint of the Taylor & Francis Group an informa business

Published by RoutledgeFalmer in association with The Open University and
the University of Edinburgh

Typeset in Goudy by
Florence Production Ltd, Stoodleigh, Devon
Printed and bound in Great Britain by
MPG Books Ltd, Bodmin, Cornwall

British Library Cataloguing in Publication Data
A catalogue record for this book is available from the British Library

Library of Congress Cataloging in Publication Data
A catalog record has been requested

ISBN 10: 0–415–28900–9 (hbk)
ISBN 10: 0–415–28901–7 (pbk)
ISBN 13: 978–0–415–28900–9 (hbk)
ISBN 13: 978–0–415–28901–6 (pbk)

Contents

Preface

Janet Soler

This volume brings together specially commissioned and previously published articles which examine the relationship between political, social and cultural contexts and the development of particular pedagogical responses to difficulties in literacy development. It is one of two readers compiled as part of the course *Difficulties in Literacy Development* (course module E801), which is one module of the (UK) Open University's MA in Education programme. The international contributors to this book provide ethical and policy discussions as well as contextualising individual and collective strategies to address difficulties in literacy development. The chapters break new ground by encompassing a wide range of perspectives related to socio-cultural, critical literacy, and cognitive and psychological viewpoints to help inform practice, policy and research into literacy difficulties. They also give their readers the ability to relate this timely collection of cross-disciplinary research in the area of difficulties in literacy development to current curriculum policies, controversies and ethical considerations.

Debates and concerns over how to address difficulties in literacy have become the focus of government and policy makers' attention in a number of countries, and have given rise to specific policy initiatives and political interventions in curriculum areas related to literacy teaching. The introductory chapter in this volume outlines the historical contexts of the debates over 'how to teach literacy' and examines the ways in which these debates have shaped recent literacy policy initiatives and interventions, in particular the NLS. This exploration of the contexts surrounding ways to address difficulties in literacy sets the background for the subsequent sections and chapters in this book.

The chapters in Part 1 explore the differing conceptualisations of literacy and address the question of 'What is literacy: a simple or complex process?' Rassool's chapter explores the ways in which theoretical conceptualisations of literacy have been shaped within and across disciplines in academic discourse and theory in recent decades. We can view literacy acquisition as the gaining of a neutral skill for economic advancement. We can also see it as an empowering, multi-faceted reflexive cultural activity which allows people to participate and make sense of the political and social aspects of their daily lives and redefine their links to the surrounding social world. Christie and Misson also investigate the complex and conflicting conceptualisations of literacy in the second chapter in this section. This chapter confronts the important issues that arise from differing conceptualisations of literacy for practitioners.

All the chapters in Part 2 address the question 'Are there increasing difficulties with literacy?' These chapters provide a closer examination of literacy standards and assessment which are associated with public debate and differing conceptions of literacy explored in the previous chapters. The Welch and Freebody chapter provides an overview and analysis and hypothetical explanations for the concerns about literacy standards, while the Stierer chapter investigates a particular episode of a literacy crisis in order to further our critical understanding of how such incidents impact upon policy makers' and practitioners' agendas for addressing difficulties in literacy. The Davis chapter examines the phonics versus whole language/whole book debate and attempts to find the 'one best method of teaching reading in response to public debates over declining literacy standards'. Murphy's chapter looks more closely at the politics of assessment that arise from the drive to increase literacy standards. This chapter examines the use of standardised tests as a form of literacy assessment and how the under-pinning assumptions can impact upon students, teachers and psychologists. The section concludes with the chapter by Green and Kostogriz which draws upon Vygotsky and New Literacy Studies to explore a view of literacy as a socio-cultural phenomenon and advocates approaches which stress socially inclusive ways of thinking about addressing difficulties in literacy.

Part 3 of this volume addresses the question of 'What political and historical considerations shape curricula and programmatic responses to literacy difficulties?' This section highlights the issues at the centre of particular pedagogical responses and approaches to teaching literacy. The Carson chapter provides a practitioner's perspective of the impact of the debates and the differing conceptualisations and models of reading over the span of an individual teacher's career. The Wearmouth and Soler chapter focuses upon Reading Recovery. The writers of this chapter highlight the issues and complexities associated with addressing literacy difficulties by comparing and contrasting the underpinning visions of Reading Recovery and the more recently developed Pause, Prompt, Praise initiative. The second Wearmouth and Soler chapter in this section addresses pedagogical issues associated with the Literacy Hour and raises the issue of how to address individual difference and cater for whole-class and whole-group teaching while working within this approach to teaching literacy. This section concludes with a chapter which illustrates the complex and contradictory issues that can arise from attempts to develop specific approaches which address literacy difficulties. Nicolson focuses upon the contexts and debates which have shaped the notion of dyslexia as a syndrome and associated approaches to addressing dyslexia as a specific cognitive-based learning disability.

The four chapters in Part 4 follow on from the concluding chapter of the previous section to focus specifically upon the social, cultural, gender and ethnic factors which impact upon difficulties in literacy development. The first chapter in this section focuses upon gender differences in literacy development. Moss concentrates upon literacy events in order to provide analytic tools to track the variation in literacy practices so as to gain a greater understanding of the literacy curriculum and its impact upon achievement levels. The following two chapters by Reed and Martin focus upon culturally related issues associated with English-as-Additional-Language (EAL) and bilingualism. Both of these chapters draw our attention to issues related to professional development and professional practice associated with literacy development for bilingual and multilingual students. The O'Connor and Pianta chapter takes a psychosocial focus in relation to the issues discussed in this section. It examines the cognitive impact of ethnic, geographic and demographic factors upon learning disabilities, in particular the impact such environmental factors may have upon behavioural and emotional disorders that can be associated with specific learning disabilities.

Part 5 takes the issues that have been covered in the previous sections into the realm of individual experiences and discusses the impact of the political, social and cultural upon individual difficulties with literacy and experiences of the school curricula. Eve Gregory discusses a study which investigates family and community experiences of home language and literacy traditions in a community encompassing ethnic minority groups from the viewpoint of individual community members who were interviewed for the study. Lankshear and Knobel explore 'commonsense assumptions' related to social–cultural factors and their impact upon (il)literacy and disadvantage. Their critique centres upon a discussion of particular invidualised programmes and assessment procedures and individual responses to these approaches.

The sixth and final section links all the previous sections together through an examination of the impact on individual students of the wider political and social issues examined in the previous sections and a consideration of ethical and social justice. Diorio's chapter returns to the conceptualisations of literacy and once again raises the issues associated with viewing literacy as a tool or a complex social phenomenon. He concludes with a discussion of the ethical issues associated with locating the source of literacy difficulties within the individual so that it becomes viewed as internal malfunction or a 'deficit' and the dangers of this view ruling out addressing literacy difficulties through external institutional and societal practices. The final chapter in this section and the book takes up the ethical issues of difference and equality raised by the previous chapter. Gerber addresses the issue of how to cater for individual difference, particularly extreme individual difference, and provide equal opportunities for all through a critical examination of the notion of 'inclusion'.

Acknowledgements

We are indebted to the following for allowing us to make use of copyright material:

Chapter 2: Rassool, N. (1999) 'Literacy: in search of a paradigm', in N. Rassool (ed.) *Literacy for Sustainable Development in the Age of Information* (pp. 25–53). Clevedon: Multilingual Matters. Reproduced by permission of Multilingual Matters Ltd.

Chapter 3: Christie, F. and Misson, R. (1998) 'Framing the issues in literacy education', in F. Christie and R. Misson (eds) *Literacy and Schooling* (pp. 1–17). London: Routledge. Reproduced by permission of Taylor & Francis Ltd, 11 New Fetter Lane, London, EC4P 4EE. www.tandf.co.uk.

Chapter 4: Welch, A. R. and Freebody, P. (1993) 'Explanations of the current international "literary crises"', in P. Freebody and A. R. Welch (eds) *Knowledge, Culture and Power: International Perspectives on Literacy as Policy and Practice* (pp. 6–22). London: RoutledgeFalmer. Reproduced by permission of Taylor & Francis Ltd, 11 New Fetter Lane, London, EC4P 4EE. www.tandf.co.uk.

Chapter 5: Stierer, B. (1994) 'Simply doing their job? The politics of reading standards and "real books"', in B. Stierer and J. Maybin (eds) *Language, Literacy and Learning in Educational Practice*. Clevedon: Multilingual Matters. Originally published in *Language Matters*, Vol. 3, pp. 2–8. London: CLPE. Reproduced by permission of the Centre for Language in Primary Education.

Chapter 6: Davis, O. L. (1999) 'When will the phonics police come knocking?', in *Journal of Curriculum and Supervision*, 14 (3), pp. 187–190. Alexandria, VA: ASCD. Reproduced by permission of the Association for Supervision and Curriculum Development. All rights reserved.

Chapter 7: Murphy, S. (1997) 'Literary assessment and the politics of identities', in *Reading and Writing Quarterly*, 13 (3), 261–278. Reproduced by permission of Taylor & Francis, Inc. www.routledge-ny.com.

Chapter 9: Carson, S. A. (1999) 'A veteran enters the reading wars: my journey', in *The Reading Teacher*, 53 (3), pp. 212–223. Newark: International Reading Association. Reproduced by permission of the International Reading Association.

Chapter 11: Wearmouth, J. and Soler, J. (2001) 'How inclusive is the Literacy Hour?', in *British Journal of Special Education*, 8 (3), pp. 113–119. Reproduced by permission of Blackwell Publishers Ltd.

Chapter 12: Nicolson, R. I. (2001) 'Developmental dyslexia: into the future', in A. Fawcett (ed.) *Dyslexia: Theory and Good Practice* (pp. 1–35). London: Whurr. Reproduced by permission of Whurr Publishers Ltd.

Chapter 13: Moss, G. (1999) 'Texts in context: mapping out the gender differentiation of the reading curriculum', in *Pedagogy, Culture and Society: Journal of Educational Discussion and Debate*, 7 (3), pp. 507–522. Reproduced by permission of Triangle Journals Ltd.

Chapter 14: Reed, T. (2000) 'The literary acquisition of Black and Asian "English-as-Additional-Language" (EAL) learners: anti-racist assessment and intervention challenges', in L. Peer and G. Reid (eds) *Multilingualism, Literacy and Dyslexia: A Challenge for Educators*. London: David Fulton. Reproduced by permission of David Fulton Publishers.

Chapter 15: Martin, D. (1999) 'Bilingualism and literacies in primary school: implications for professional development', in *Educational Review*, 51 (1), pp. 67–79. Reproduced by permission of Taylor & Francis Ltd, 11 New Fetter Lane, London, EC4P 4EE. www.tandf.co.uk.

Chapter 16: O'Connor, T. G. and Pianta, R. C. (2001) 'Psychosocial factors in the aetiology and course of specific learning disabilities', in K. Witmore, H. Hart and G. Willems (eds) *A Neurodevelopmental Approach to Specific Learning Disorders* (pp. 211–26). London: Mac Keith Press. Reproduced by permission of Mac Keith Press.

Chapter 17: Gregory, E. (1999) 'Myths of illiteracy: childhood memories of reading in London's East End', in *Written Language and Literacy*, 2 (1), pp. 89–111. Reproduced by permission of John Benjamins Publishing Company, Amsterdam/Philadelphia.

Chapter 18: Lankshear, C. and Knobel, M. (1998) 'New times! Old ways?', in F. Christie and R. Misson (eds) *Literacy and Schooling* (pp. 155–177). London: Routledge. Reproduced by permission of Taylor & Francis Ltd, 11 New Fetter Lane, London, EC4P 4EE. www.tandf.co.uk.

Chapter 20: Gerber, M. M. (1996) 'Reforming special education: beyond "inclusion"', in C. Christensen and F. Rizvi (eds) *Disability and the Dilemmas of Education and Justice*. Buckingham: Open University Press. Reproduced by permission of The Open University Press.

While the Publishers have made very effort to contact copyright holders of the material used in this volume, they would be grateful to hear from any they were unable to contact.

Introduction

Chapter 1

Policy contexts and the debates over how to teach literacy

Janet Soler

Introduction

Differing models for conceptualising literacy have resulted in conflicting views and diverse positions over how to teach reading which have often been energetically attacked and rigorously defended. The debates over the best way to teach a young child to read and how to overcome barriers to developing reading skills have consistently dominated the past fifty years. In the 1950s the focus of attention was on the Great Debate over Reading. From the 1950s until the 1970s experimental behavioural psychology with its claims to be a 'scientific' approach and an associated view of literacy as a neutral technology precipitated and shaped views of how to teach reading and prevent difficulties with reading (see Rassool, 1999).

Much of the research over literacy which surfaced in the Great Debate (Chall, 1967) and the more recent Reading Wars (see Goodman, 1998; Vacca, 1996) was generated by concerns over literacy standards. The over-riding and continual concern in these debates and the research they have generated has been the development and assessment of the most up-to-date and correct way of teaching. It has been claimed that recent legislative activity in the United States has opened up the potential for these research findings to be distorted or exaggerated in legislative advocacy campaigns seeking to justify the adoption of prescriptive top-down solutions to this issue (Allington and Woodside-Jiron, 1999).

In England international comparisons, national assessment evidence and results from literacy initiatives have also been used in a legislative advocacy campaign to justify the development of the National Literacy Strategy (NLS) during the 1990s. In order to explore the links between conflicting views and increasing concerns over difficulties in literacy development and related policy implications for practitioners, this chapter will discuss the historical contexts of the debates on the teaching of literacy and their impact upon the first two published policy documents related to the English NLS.

The Great Debate over Reading

Writing at the end of the 1960s and looking back on the previous two decades, Chall begins her influential book *Learning to Read: The Great Debate* (Chall, 1967) with a chapter on 'The crisis in beginning reading'. The Great Debate emerged at a time when psychometrics and experimental behavioural psychology were developing into major influences in literacy education through their claims to scientific validity. This debate rested upon claims of scientific validity for particular methods over others in order to establish the most efficient and effective way to teach reading. The conceptualisation of literacy as neutral and scientific helped foster a view in the media and political debates of an interpretation of literacy as the learning of 'basic' literacy skills of the 'Three Rs' through 'direct instruction and rote learning' (Rassool, 1999, p. 27). The promotion of this view of literacy and the resulting emphasis upon the correct method to teach reading in the 1950s and 1960s inevitably gave rise to a cycle of public debates and political concerns over literacy 'standards' in the following decades.

Claims backed up by 'objective data' and 'scientific findings' that standards of reading are declining and that the main cause of this decline in reading could be attributed to the methods of teaching reading began in the 1950s. If practices to promote literacy development are seen primarily to be a matter of finding the one best scientifically proven method to teach reading, it follows that literacy educators who do not utilise the 'best method' run the risk of lowering literacy standards. This was at the heart of the arguments put forward in the US and England in the 1950s and 1960s (see for example Flesch, 1955).

The Great Debate over literacy standards is inextricably linked to a particular view of literacy and reading which continued into the 1990s and underpins current concerns over literacy standards. Turner's (1990) arguments that there was a decline in reading standards and that this could be attributed to the widespread take-up of what he considered the ill-conceived method of teaching with 'real books' can be viewed as a continuation of the earlier debate and its associated conceptualisation of literacy.

The Literacy Wars

The Literacy Wars developed in the 1970s as an 'attack by experimental psychologists on the orthodoxy that evolved during the 1970s around the emphasis placed by psycholinguists on the reading process and the production of meaning through the use of contextual cues' (Rassool, 1999, p. 27). Rassool argues that, in the 1970s, psycholinguistic influences upon the conceptualisation of literacy resulted in a move from viewing literacy as the neutral decoding of print. Psycholinguists critiqued this behaviouristic, experimentally inspired view of literacy. They argued that it should be replaced with a view of literacy as a 'range of meanings produced at the interface of person and text, and the linguistic strategies and cultural knowledges used to "cue" into meanings embedded in the text' (Rassool, 1999, p. 28). This view formed the foundation for the 'whole-language' and 'real book' approaches that were advocated by literacy educators such as Kenneth Goodman and Frank Smith in the 1970s and 1980s (see for example Goodman, 1986 and Smith, 1971).

The whole-language or real book approach drew upon psycholinguistics and represented a 'top-down' approach to teaching literacy. In this approach meaning was seen to develop from 'whole to part [meaningful units of language], from vague to precise, from gross to fine, from highly concrete and contextualised to more abstract' (Goodman, 1986, quoted in Rassool, 1999, p. 28).

The Literacy Wars of the 1970s and 1980s resulted from behavioural, experimental psychologists such as Stanovich (see for example Stanovich, 2000) attacking this top-down, whole-language, real book approach. This group of psychologists viewed the whole-language, real book approach as lacking in scientific validity because it was to be based upon broad assumptions and insufficient empirical data. They argued for a 'bottom-up' model of reading, where children are seen to build their knowledge of words from part to whole. This approach leads to an emphasis on phonics and phonological awareness, common letter-strings and initial sound blendings in order to decode and write text. The conflicts between 'bottom-up' and 'top-down' approaches lie at the heart of the Great Debate, the Reading Wars and subsequent political storms over reading instruction. It is often referred to as the phonics versus whole-language debate, particularly in the United States, and as the phonics versus whole books or real books debate in the United Kingdom.

The literacy standards debate in England

In the 1990s the public debate over declining standards surfaced again in England when the *Times Educational Supplement* carried a front-page story reporting that educational psychologists had found that reading standards among seven-year-olds were falling rapidly in London LEAs. This story was subsequently reported in all the national English newspapers. Stierer describes the impassioned coverage of this claim as follows:

> On 29 June 1990, the *Times Educational Supplement* carried a front-page story reporting a claim made by nine unnamed educational psychologists that reading standards among seven-year-olds had declined dramatically in their LEAs. The story was picked up by all the national newspapers and by many television and radio news programmes, leading to emotive accusations of unstructured and uninformed teaching in schools, inflexible 'bandwagoning' amongst teacher-trainers and LEA inspectors and advisers, and lax control by politicians and policy-makers.
>
> (Stierer, 1994, p. 129)

During the 1990s concerns over declining standards arrived at through international comparisons, national assessment evidence and results from literacy initiatives have been used in a legislative advocacy campaign to justify the development of the National Literacy Strategy (NLS). The Preliminary Report of the United Kingdom Literacy Taskforce and subsequent explanations of the research base for their report cited international data and local data, as being influential in the development of 'best practices' in the NLS. The Taskforce drew upon this research base to help justify its use of a 'framework' to structure and sequence the pedagogic activities and specify the content that was to be taught during the 'Literacy Hour' (Beard, 1999a; Beard 1999b; Literacy Taskforce, 1997).

Attention to raising literacy standards has in turn led to recommendations for teacher development that focus upon training teachers and teacher trainees how to teach the Literacy Hour. This approach has been introduced against a background of an increasing external control exercised over the curriculum and teaching styles. During the late 1980s and 1990s, England revised the National Curriculum first introduced in the 1988 Education Reform Act. This act introduced a prescriptive and detailed curriculum with statutory national testing in the primary school at ages 7 and 11. It also initiated an inspection system which was controlled by the Office for Standards in Education (OFSTED).

The adoption of ability and whole-class teaching during this period also directly impacted upon the policies related to literacy instruction. In 1996 the Conservative government cut funding to the New Zealand-inspired Reading Recovery Scheme (Rafferty, 1996a) and set up the National Literacy Project (NLP) which promoted the development of 'a range of practical teaching strategies based on whole-class and group teaching' and the 'more effective use of time through the introduction of the daily Literacy Hour' as two of its main aims (National Centre for Literacy and Numeracy, 1997). This marked a significant move away from teacher-devised strategies to address literacy difficulties. The Reading Recovery Scheme targets poorer readers and provides one-to-one instruction and the training of the teacher to be an expert in early literacy learning (see for example Clay, 1985; Clay, 1990; Clay, 1994). The emphasis is on the specialist teachers training themselves to use systematic observation and records to probe their students' difficulties in learning and to assess quality of teaching in the classroom. The NLP's emphasis was upon the management of literacy at whole-school level through monitoring by senior staff and NFR-based researchers.

The introductory leaflet for the National Literacy Project outlined a framework of teaching objectives and set out 'clear expectations of what should be covered in each term'. It also introduced the concept of the Literacy Hour that was carefully structured to ensure a balance of whole-class and differentiated group teaching (National Centre for Literacy and Numeracy, 1997). As Labour education policy developed during 1997 it would be clear that many of the objectives and structures of the NLP would be kept and further developed by the new Labour government. The Literacy Taskforce initiated under the Labour government would gather 'together a range of initiatives, many of which have already taken on life under this, Conservative, government' (Editorial, TES, 28 February 1997).

In May 1996 the Labour Party announced a back-to-basics drive to improve literacy standards if it became the government in the election to be held the following year. David Blunkett noted that a recently published OFSTED report on the teaching of reading in 45 inner-London primary schools found that 40 per cent of Year 6 pupils had reading ages two or more years below their chronological ages. The Labour Party planned to raise standards through the introduction of a new literacy Taskforce and wanted to examine ways of ensuring 'that every child leaving primary school does so with a reading age of 11 by the end of the second term of office' (Rafferty, 1996a).

In the same announcement Blunkett, the shadow education secretary, stated that teachers were to 'use teaching methods which work and are not just the latest fashion'. The Labour Party dissatisfaction with the quality of newly trained teachers also resulted in a pledge to place greater emphasis on basic skills, classroom discipline and whole-class teaching. Blunkett stressed the use of phonics and stated that 'It is self evident that phonics are a crucial tool for teaching children in the early stages'. This statement, however, did not acknowledge the issues which surrounded the international debate over the use of phonics and whole language (Rafferty, 1996a).

The need to raise standards and skills was a key point in the 'New Life for Britain' document that was announced in July to lay the foundations for the Labour Party's election campaign. The document promised a 'radical improvement in primary standards through focusing on the basics, better testing and assessment with target-setting of results; value-added performance tables; the reform of teacher training and the sacking of inadequate staff'. It also announced that the newly formed taskforce on literacy would have its report and recommendations ready for an incoming government (Rafferty, 1996b).

The 1997 Literacy Taskforce report

On 28 February 1997 the Preliminary Report of the English Literacy Taskforce was released by the Labour government (Literacy Taskforce, 1997). The English Literacy Taskforce stated that literacy standards should be addressed by 'putting in place a coherent strategy rather than a series of fleeting and unconnected initiatives such as Reading Recovery, the Better English Campaign, and the National Literacy Project'.

Drawing upon international and local data and understandings of 'best practice', the English Literacy Taskforce claimed that 'a constant national strategic approach over five to ten years' is the only possible way to 'bring about a dramatic improvement in literacy standards'. They argued that this strategy 'combines what we now know about best practice in the teaching of reading with an appreciation of ten years of education reform'. Their analysis of the research base on 'best practice' stressed the need to develop a national strategy that decreases the professional autonomy to develop best practice:

The notion of professional autonomy was strongly embedded in the educational service yet there were insufficient mechanisms in place either within the profession itself or in the education service more generally to ensure either that practice was based firmly on evidence or that best practice was rapidly adopted or even adopted at all by others. As a result, practice varied hugely from school to school. At best it was excellent, at worst a matter of anything goes.

(Literacy Taskforce, 1997, paragraph 35, p. 4)

This emphasis upon 'best practice' appears to have led to an emphasis upon the education system rather than home or environmental factors as it located the failure to learn to read and a perceived drop in 'literacy standards' within the education system and the classroom. For example paragraph 21 of the document states that:

Whilst general societal factors (such as the status given to school learning or the prevalence of television viewing amongst adolescents) may be responsible for some of the poor British performance, most are agreed that the educational system bears the main responsibility.

(Literacy Taskforce, 1997, paragraph 21, p. 2)

Paragraph 32 also highlighted the location of failure to raise reading standards within British schools by pointing out that in 'British schools' the 'performance of lower ability pupils is substantially below that of other countries'. Paragraph 36 took the argument further by identifying:

a lack of a coherent strategy within these schools as mainly responsible for falling standards and failure to learn to read despite the fact that the National Curriculum had been implemented in 1988.

(Literacy Taskforce, 1997, paragraph 32, p. 4)

Overall the document tends to stress addressing literacy difficulties within the education system through the 'best method' and one particular strategy rather than allowing a diversity of approaches to cater for the socio-cultural and the cognitive complexities and individual diversity associated with literacy acquisition. The Taskforce wanted 'a coherent strategy' and wished to avoid 'fleeting and unconnected initiatives such as Reading Recovery' (Literacy Taskforce, 1997, paragraph 32, p. 4).

Beard's subsequent account of the 'influences on the Literacy Hour' also highlights the Report's emphasis upon the need for the school rather than society or family to address literacy development and links this focus upon the school as the main agent for improving literacy 'performance' to school effectiveness research. In his account Beard argued that the influences from the 'international school effective evidence' have 'consistently challenged earlier assumptions that pupils' social background largely determines their school performance' and argued that 'once pupils begin school, then the school itself can have a significantly greater influence on pupil progress' (Beard, 1999a, p. 8).

The Literacy Taskforce Report also appears to be ambiguous regarding its support for whole-class and/or individual approaches to teaching reading. For example at the beginning of the introduction the New Zealand strategy for addressing reading difficulties, which at the time focused upon Reading Recovery, was praised as the way forward for English literacy policy. Yet in paragraph 36, at the conclusion of the section, Reading Recovery was rejected as part of 'fleeting and unconnected initiatives' which are difficult to implement across the range of English schools.

In Section 3, in the sub-section on the 'Teaching of Reading', both whole-class and individual tuition appeared to be suggested for the proposed literacy strategy. For example Paragraph 45 suggests that the emphasis will be upon whole-class as well as individual tuition. It stresses 'carefully sequenced whole-class, group and individual work to focus upon strategies and skills, with the teacher combining instruction, demonstration, questioning and discussion, providing structure for subsequent tasks and giving help and constructive response' (Literacy Taskforce 1997, paragraph 45, p. 5).

The 1998 *Framework for Teaching* document and the 'Literacy Hour'

The *Framework for Teaching* document (DfEE, 1998) followed on from the release of the National Literacy Strategy which was launched in August 1997. The Framework came into operation under a quasi-statutory status in all state primary schools in England in September 1998. This document set out the teaching objectives in literacy for pupils from reception to Year 6. It was this document which set out the format of a Literacy Hour as a daily period of time throughout the school which would be dedicated to 'literacy teaching time for all pupils' (DfEE, 1998, p. 8). The Hour was intended to cover both reading and writing and was to take the form of an introduction of 30 minutes, 20 minutes' independent work and a 10-minute plenary (see DfEE, 1998, p. 9).

It has been argued the emphasis upon 'interactive whole-class teaching' can be seen to be derived from the school improvement literature which had been espoused by influential members of the Literacy Taskforce (Mroz *et al.*, 2000). This emphasis upon a particular form of whole-class teaching has raised issues associated with the need for individualised teaching in order to address literacy difficulties which, as we have seen, was recognised by the Literacy Taskforce's 1997 Report in its section related to children who have special needs in literacy (see Literacy Taskforce, 1997, paragraphs 105–106). It is not surprising, therefore, that *Framework for Teaching* was criticised for its lack of acknowledgement of individualised instruction and therefore a failure to cater successfully for children with special educational needs (Byers, 1999; Wearmouth and Soler, 2001).

The Framework advocates the pedagogical approaches of 'guided reading', 'shared writing', 'guided writing' and 'the plenary' and 'independent work'. The detailed account of these approaches given on pages 11–13 indicates that all of these approaches are to be carried out as whole-class or group activities apart from the 'independent work' which students undertake on their own while the teacher is supervising the 'guided group work'. This emphasis on whole-class teaching and group activities is supported by Beard (1999a) in his outline of the rationale underpinning the Literacy Hour:

> It stresses the importance of direct teaching by the use of the whole-class teaching in the first half of the literacy hour and the maintenance of direct teaching with groups, and then with the class again in the second half. It also maximises effective learning time by ensuring that there is a dedicated literacy hour each day, with further suggestions on providing additional literacy learning time during the rest of the day, including extended writing, reading to the class and independent reading.
>
> (Beard, 1999a, p. 8)

The lack of individualised programmes in the Framework has given rise to concerns about the ability of the Framework to address particular, complex individual needs of those students who may experience severe difficulties in learning to read. Mroz et al. (2000) have expressed concerns about whether or not 'interactive whole-class teaching' differs from 'whole-class teaching'. Byers (1999) has also expressed concerns about the ability of this form of teaching to address the needs of all students, particularly those who may experience difficulties in their literacy development.

The Framework also presents a particular solution to the issue of the adoption of 'top-down' or 'bottom-up' approaches to literacy. Its model for the teaching of reading is represented as 'a series of searchlights' each of which 'sheds light on the text' (DfEE, 1998, p. 3). In the outline of the 'searchlight approach', and in the diagram given on page 4 of the document, there appears to be recognition of the need to teach both the skills to decode phonics and strategies to use the context to make sense of the text. In the two pages dedicated to explaining this approach, however, most of the space is given to explaining the need for the teaching of phonics, as it was felt that 'most teachers know about these but have been over cautious about the teaching of phonics – sounds and spellings'.

Conclusion

Public concern and literacy crises over falling standards have a long history which stretch back through the Literacy Wars to the Great Debate over teaching reading in the 1950s and 1960s. A desire to implement the most efficient, up-to-date and universally correct method of conceptualising and teaching reading and other aspects of literacy are the hallmarks of such literacy crises. In the 1990s, concerns once again surfaced over 'declining standards' and 'poor performance'. These concerns are often seen to be backed up by international literacy comparison data and national assessments of reading.

An exploration of how such concerns have impacted upon English curriculum policy in recent decades highlights the tendency for literacy crises to encourage policy makers to produce simplistic solutions. The outcome is often a reduction of the complexities and issues surrounding literacy teaching. In England this has been achieved by adopting the top-down prescriptive policy solution which has introduced the Literacy Hour and a universal 'interactive whole-class teaching' approach to teaching literacy. Conflicting and diverse positions over how to teach reading have also been integrated into a single model which is outlined in the *Framework for Teaching* (DfEE, 1998) document. The tendency to confine and reduce the issues and conflicts generated by literacy debates and to find an efficient solution is also reflected in the tendency to try to raise literacy standards by focusing on the education system, in particular the teacher within the classroom.

Addressing the conflicting views and diverse positions that give rise to the debates over how to teach literacy by adopting a reductionist and prescriptive stance may appear to be an efficient, practical and effective solution to a literacy crisis for policy makers. It can offer a supportive, manageable framework for teachers, particularly newly qualified teachers, which evidence is suggesting (Earl *et al.*, 2000) has led to successful and widespread implementation. The examination of the literacy crisis and the resulting solutions advocated in the initial NLS policy documents reveal that while the strategy may solve some problems such a solution inevitably raises others and precludes an acknowledgement of the complexities that surround literacy development.

For example the Literacy Taskforce's view that the educational system can be held responsible for poor performance and assumptions that the solution is to prescribe particular classroom-based solutions through the school curriculum is not fully supported by research evidence. In the early years of schooling, research has shown that the needs of the curriculum and related teachers' agendas can hinder a child's disposition to learn (Wells, 1987). This research indicates that there is a need to take into account not only cognitive concerns, but also the social and affective needs of the young child.

A focus upon unitary, classroom-based solutions to raise literacy standards and address difficulties in literacy also poses problems when we seek to address diversity of family, cultural and linguistic backgrounds. Blackledge points out the apparent ambiguity and contradictions that have subsequently occurred in later National Literacy Strategy documents which seek to adhere to the National Literacy Strategy and claim to identify the value of 'an holistic view of pupil welfare which routinely incorporates their racial, cultural, religious and linguistic concerns' (Blackledge, 2001).

The reductionist aspects of the NLS are also coming to counter the positive aspects arising from its widespread implementation. More recent reports have shown teachers' inability to adapt the NLS (OFSTED, 2001).

The prescriptive, reductionist aspects of the NLS can lead to rapid uptake but they can also lead to inflexibility and restrictions on innovation, refinement and ownership by parents, children and the community as well as teachers (Hancock and Mansfield, 2002). There is also concern that the reductionist nature of the NLS may not support the flexibility, scope and wider vision of literacy that will be necessary for participation in the 'knowledge society' (Earl et al., 2000).

References

Allington, R. L. and Woodside-Jiron, H. (1999) The Politics of Literacy Teaching: How 'Research' Shaped Educational Policy. *Educational Researcher* 28(8): 4–12.

Beard, R. (1999a) Influences on the Literacy Hour. *Reading: A Journal about Literacy and Language in Education* 33(1): 6–12.

Beard, R. (1999b) *National Literacy Strategy: Review of Research and Other Evidence.* Leeds: School of Education, University of Leeds.

Blackledge, A. (2001) Literacy, Schooling and Ideology in a Multilingual State. *The Curriculum Journal*, 12(3): 291–312.

Byers, R. (1999) The National Literacy Strategy and Pupils with Special Educational Needs. *British Journal of Special Education*, 26(1): 8–11.

Chall, J. (1967) *Learning to Read: The Great Debate.* New York: McGraw-Hill.

Clay, M. M. (1985) *The Early Detection of Reading Difficulties.* Auckland: Heinemann.

Clay, M. M. (1990) The Reading Recovery Programme, 1984–1988: Coverage, Outcomes and Education Board District Figures. *New Zealand Journal of Educational Studies* 25(1): 61–70.

Clay, M. M. (1994) *Reading Recovery: A Guidebook for Teachers in Training.* Portsmouth, NH: Heinemann.

Department for Education and Employment (1998). *The National Literacy Strategy: Framework for Teaching.* London: DfEE.

Earl, L., Levin, B., Leithwood, K., Fullan, M., Watson, N., et al. (2000) *Watching and Learning: OISE/UT Evaluation of the Implementation of the National Literacy and Numeracy Strategies, Summary: First Annual Report*, Ontario Institute for Studies in Education, University of Toronto. London: DfES.

Flesch, R. F. (1955) *Why Johnny Can't Read – And What You Can Do About It* ([1st] edn). New York: Harper.

Goodman, K. S. (1986) *What's Whole in Whole Language?* (1st US edn). Portsmouth, NH: Heinemann.

Goodman, K. S. (1998) *In Defense of Good Teaching: What Teachers Need to Know About the 'Reading Wars'.* York, ME: Stenhouse Publishers.

Hancock, R. and Mansfield, M. (2002) The Literacy Hour: A Case for Listening to Children. *The Curriculum Journal* 13(1): 209–260.

Literacy Taskforce (1997) *A Reading Revolution: How We Can Teach Every Child to Read Well.* London: Institute of Education, University of London. http://www.leeds.ac.uk/educol/documents/000000153.html

Literacy Taskforce (1999) *Report of the Literacy Taskforce.* Wellington, NZ: Ministry of Education.

Mroz, M., Smith, F. and Hardman, F. (2000) The Discourse of the Literacy Hour. *Cambridge Journal of Education*, 30(3): 379–90.

National Centre for Literacy and Numeracy (1997) *The National Literacy Project*. London.

News and Opinion Editorial (1997) No More Quick Fixes. *Times Educational Supplement*, 28 February.

OFSTED (Office for Standards in Education) (2001) *The National Literacy Strategy: The Third Year* (HMI 332). London: OFSTED.

Rafferty, F. (1996a) Labour Gets Back to Basics. *Times Educational Supplement*, 31 May.

Rafferty, F. (1996b) The Road to Sanctuary Buildings. *Times Educational Supplement*, 12 July.

Rassool, N. (1999) Literacy: In Search of a Paradigm. In N. Rassool (ed.), *Literacy for Sustainable Development in the Age of Information* (pp. 25–53). Clevedon, UK; Philadelphia, PA: Multilingual Matters.

Smith, F. (1971) *Understanding Reading: A Psycholinguistic Analysis of Reading and Learning to Read*. New York: Holt, Rinehart & Winston.

Soler, J. (1999) Past and Present Technocratic Solutions to Teaching Literacy: Implications for New Zealand Primary Teachers and Literacy Programmes. *Curriculum Studies* 7(3): 521–38.

Stanovich, K. (1991) Discrepancy Definitions of Reading Disability: Has Intelligence Led us Astray? *Reading Research Quarterly*, 36(1): 7–29.

Stanovich, K. (2000) *Progress in Understanding Reading: Scientific Foundations and New Frontiers*. London: The Guilford Press.

Stierer, B. (1994) Simply Doing Their Job? The Politics of Reading Standards and 'Real Books'. In B. Stierer and J. Maybin (eds), *Language, Literacy, and Learning in Educational Practice: A Reader*. Clevedon, UK: Multilingual Matters.

Turner, M. (1990) *Sponsored Reading Failure: An Object Lesson*. Warlington, Surrey: IPSET Education Unit.

Wearmouth, J. and Soler, J. (2001) How Inclusive is the Literacy Hour? *British Journal of Special Education*, 28(3): 113–19.

Wells, C. G. (1987) *The Meaning Makers*. London: Hodder & Stoughton.

Vacca, R. T. (1996) Who Will Be the Winners? Who Will Be the Losers? *Reading Today*, 14(2): 3.

Young, S. (1997) Reading Standards Static for 50 Years. *Times Educational Supplement*, 11 July.

Source

This chapter was written especially for this volume.

Part 1

What is literacy: a simple or complex process?

Chapter 2

Literacy
In search of a paradigm

Naz Rassool

Literacy in academic discourse

Considerable developments have taken place in the broad area of literacy studies during the past two decades. Within this ongoing debate, the idea that literacy cannot be regarded as an autonomous set of technical skills is gaining support amongst many critical theorists. Literacy is now more generally regarded as a social practice that is integrally linked with ideology, culture, knowledge and power. Moreover, as is discussed in the previous chapter, reference is being made increasingly to different literacies or, as Gee (1996) and the NLG (1996) put it, 'multiliteracies' suited to a range of context-related situations. In consequence, the concept of literacy has lost much of the rigidity and linearity associated with it in the traditional, decontextualised, skills-oriented framework.

Instead literacy is perceived to be *organic* because it is seen as a cultural activity that involves people in conscious and reflexive action within a variety of situations in everyday life. Much of this has been reflected in various interpretations of Freire's approach to critical literacy, and its impact on adult literacy programmes internationally. Barton and Hamilton's (1998) description of community literacies provides another excellent account of the ways in which literacy practices shape people's lives. Community literacies as described by Barton and Hamilton (1998) illustrate the self-defining principles of literacy. They show how, through participating in literacy events, people can interrogate the narrative of everyday life and, in the process, redefine themselves in relation to the social world. Barton and Hamilton's ethnographic documentation of individual 'literacy histories and literacy lives' provides evidence of the ways in which people can change things in their everyday lives, and also transform the consciousness of others. Within this framework, emphasis shifts from concerns about *process*, or individual behaviours during reading, to that of *agency*, or active involvement, within a defined context.

Literacy is regarded also as being *multidimensional* because it is seen as serving a variety of social, economic, ideological and political purposes. The *social purposes*, referred to here, derive from the literacy practices that feature in everyday life, such as reading for information, learning, pleasure, recreation and religion. *Economic purposes* can be seen in relation to the literacy skills and knowledge demands made on people in the work-place. People seek to enhance their capabilities as workers as those who are literate are perceived to have better job opportunities in the labour market, and thus literacy obtains an exchange value. In this sense literacy is regarded as an investment in 'human capital'. Human capital theory emphasises the direct relationship between education, worker productivity and the economy, and is underscored by the principle that people need to invest in themselves in the acquisition of skills to make them more employable. . . . [T]his view of literacy has occupied a pivotal position in the discourse on societal development. Economic purposes can also be seen as relating to the specific value attached to 'formal' literacies associated with different professions and social roles.

Political *purposes* refer to the literacy practices in which people engage in their multiple roles as citizens, activists or community members allowing them to take up positions in relation to the social world. At the same time, they also describe the broader relationship between literacy and specific interests in society. These revolve around social structure and different power interests that shape definitions of literacy, and influence levels of access to the types and forms of literacy for different groups of people in society. *Ideological purposes* relate to the values, assumptions, beliefs and expectations that frame dominant literacy discourse within particular social contexts. Together, these different aspects and the criteria that define them frame the 'normal' levels of literacy 'competence' for everyday living, and thus they influence our common-sense understandings of 'personal efficacy'.

Literacy as a site of struggle over meaning/Literacy Wars in education

Alongside this dynamic debate we have had an ongoing critique within the educational terrain, from within the framework of experimental behavioural psychology (henceforth referred to as experimental psychology). Experimental psychology provides a view of literacy that is primarily concerned with the decoding of texts involving the perceptual process (phonological and graphic), word structure (morphological) and technical writing (spelling) skills. Of significance to this perspective are the *cognitive processes that underlie skilled reading and learning how to read* (Stanovich, 1986; Goswami and Bryant, 1990). For these writers 'teaching literacy is about teaching the skills of reading and writing' *per se* (Oakhill and Beard, 1995: 69). That is, teaching children 'how to analyse the sound in words [one word at a time] and how alphabetic letters symbolise these sounds' (Bryant, 1994), otherwise referred to as sound–symbol correspondences, or graphic–phoneme correspondences. Providing a 'scientific' approach to literacy, this presents literacy as a neutral technology. As Gough (1995: 80) puts it:

> I confess to subscribing to the autonomous model, 'a literacy narrowly conceived as individual, psychological skills'. I believe that literacy is a single thing ... that texts have independent meanings ... that readers can be separated from the society that gives meaning to their uses of literacy, and that their cognitive skills, importantly including their ability to read and write, can be assessed, and thus abstracted from social persons and cultural locations.

Experimental psychology represents the subject-discipline which, at least until the 1970s, influenced the dominant literacy meanings incorporated into educational policy frameworks. It is also the subject-discipline that has contributed greatly to discussions about literacy within the social terrain. When literacy is discussed in, for example, the media or in political rhetoric, reference is often made to the learning of 'basic' literacy skills or the 'three Rs', direct instruction and rote learning.

Literacy outcomes are measured in terms of skills acquisition, and the personal and social benefits derived from being literate. Being able to read and write is viewed as central to increasing or enhancing individuals' 'life chances'. Again, Gough (1995: 80) underlines this in his statement that, 'I believe that learning to read and write does contribute to social progress, to personal improvement and mobility, perhaps to better health, almost certainly to cognitive development'. This is in line with the views expressed by cognitive and social psychologists such as Goody and Watt (1968) and Ong (1982), regarding the intrinsic value of literacy to the development of the intellect and, relatedly, the development of society. Views of literacy as an 'autonomous' set of skills decontextualised from society and culture have been critiqued in considerable detail elsewhere (Street, 1984, 1993).

Experimental psychology versus psycholinguistics

What has been referred to polemically as the Literacy Wars (Stanovich and Stanovich, 1995) first started as an attack by experimental psychologists on the orthodoxy that evolved during the 1970s around the emphasis placed by psycholinguists on the reading *process* and the production of meaning through the use of contextual cues. Psycholinguists hold the view that:

> three language systems interact in written language: the graphophonic [sound and letter patterns], the syntactic [sentence patterns], and the semantic [meanings]. We can study how each one works in reading, and writing, but they can't be isolated for instruction without creating non-language abstractions.
>
> (Goodman, 1986: 38–9)

Readers construct meaning during reading by drawing on their prior learning and knowledge in order to make sense of texts (Goodman, 1986). As such, literacy is defined in terms of the range of meanings produced at the interface of person and text, and the linguistic strategies and cultural knowledges used to 'cue' into the meanings embedded in the text. I will return to this discussion later in the chapter.

A further critique was subsequently mounted against advocates of the 'whole language' and 'real book' approach who argue that children *learn to read by reading* (Goodman, 1986; Smith, 1971, 1979). The 'whole language' approach draws on key elements in the psycholinguistic perspective of reading discussed here, and research on writing within the broader framework of applied linguistics, notably the work of Britton (1975), Wells (1986) and Wilkinson (1965). Of significance is the 'language experience' approach that emerged within the Schools Council Initial Literacy Project, *Breakthrough to Literacy* (Mackay *et al.*, 1978), and the writing process. The 'language experience approach' and 'process writing' emphasise learners' active involvement in the construction of texts, as opposed to placing a reliance on textbooks. Overall emphasis is placed on the *meaning* that learners want to communicate.

This approach represents a top-down model of literacy development, that is, it is seen to develop 'from whole to part [meaningful units of language], from vague to precise, from gross to fine, from highly concrete and contextualised to more abstract' (Goodman, 1986: 39, information in brackets added). Goodman (1986: 26) summarises the principles of this approach in the argument that:

> language development is empowering: the learner 'owns' the process, makes the decisions about when to use it, what for and with what results . . . literacy is empowering too, if the learner is in control with what's done with it . . . language learning is learning how to mean: how to make sense of the world in the context of how our parents, families, and cultures make sense of it.
>
> (Quoted in Weaver, 1990: 5)

This philosophical approach to literacy, which involves both text and context, has been criticised within experimental psychology as operating on broad assumptions and not having sufficient empirical data. As such, it is viewed as lacking scientific validity (Stanovich and Stanovich, 1995).

A comparative analysis

Although the *foci* are different within the psycholinguistics and experimental psychology paradigms, they do share some similarities. For instance, their overall analyses are located within the individual child and developmental processes in which 'the child is seen as progressing through successively more complex stages, each building on the other, each characterised by a particular structuring of component cognitive and affective capabilities' (Cole and Scribner, 1981: 12). Similarly, literacy within both paradigms has an exclusively individual, child-focused, pedagogic orientation. Much of the emphasis in the psycho-linguistic approach to literacy also centres on perceptual skills and orthographic knowledge although this is approached from a different perspective.

But there are also differences. The one emphasises context and meaning, whilst the other stresses individual skills in isolation. Experimental psychologists have as their central goal:

> that children should learn how their writing system works. This means, for alphabetic writing systems, making sure [that] they learn the alphabetic principle, something that requires some attention to fostering students' phonemic awareness.
>
> (Perfetti, 1995: 112)

This involves a significant measure of direct teaching and skills reinforcement. It is only once basic literacy skills have been acquired that they can be 'applied and extended in a wealth of ways which might come within the remit of the broader definitions of reading' (Oakhill and Beard, 1995: 69). For psycholinguists, on the other hand:

> language learning is easy when it's whole, real, and relevant; when it makes sense and is functional; when it's encountered in the context of its use; when the learner chooses to use it . . . language is learned as pupils learn through language and about language, all simultaneously in the context of authentic speech and literacy events.
>
> (Goodman, 1986: 29)

Risk-taking involving readers in predicting and guessing as part of the meaning-making process, and writers in clarifying ideas and experimenting in spelling and punctuation, is seen as an essential part of the literacy process in this paradigm.

Stanovich and Stanovich (1995: 98) summarise the basis of the disagreement between the two camps as being:

> selectively focused around the necessity of explicit analytic instruction in word decoding in the early years of schooling. The current differences between the camps are all traceable to differing underlying assumptions about the process of reading that were present in the debates about top-down versus bottom-up models of reading that began over twenty years ago. Two decades of empirical research have largely resolved these debates in favour of bottom-up models.

Bottom-up models lay stress on the need for children to build 'word knowledge' proceeding from part-to-the-whole and thus would emphasise the need for children to know common letter-strings, initial sound blendings, phonics and to have phonological awareness as an integral part of learning to read and write.

This one-dimensional skills-based view is problematised by Hasan (1996) who, arguing from an applied linguistics perspective, suggests that reading and writing constitute complex processes that fundamentally involve the ability to grasp the principle of representation. She argues that:

> becoming literate in the sense of being able to read/write presupposes the ability to 'see' a phenomenon as 'standing for' something other than itself . . . the fundamental attribute for the onset of literacy is the ability to engage in acts of meaning: to be an initiate in literacy is to be able to make sense.
>
> (Hasan, 1996: 379)

In other words, children learn that words represent actions, emotions and concrete elements in the social world; they stand for something other than themselves. Literacy is integrally linked with a semiotic system that is grounded in language, culture and society. Signification is important in relation to making sense of any representational text. . . .

Experimental psychology versus the New Literacy Studies

Recently criticisms from experimental psychologists have also extended to the views expressed by adherents of the 'New Literacy Studies' (NLS) whose focus is on the *sociocultural aspects of literacy* (Street, 1993; Barton, 1994; Barton and Ivanic, 1991; Barton and Padmore, 1991). This paradigm argues against a universal concept of literacy and proposes an acceptance of different 'literacies' within various social and cultural contexts. The NLS draws on a range of conceptual–analytic frameworks including social anthropology, sociology, critical linguistics and discourse theory.

Of these, social anthropology has been very influential historically in shaping the overall literacy discourse. Social anthropology draws on key motifs in cognitive psychology but interpretations of the intellectual and social 'consequences' of literacy are related to large groups of people within particular societies. Thus they will include 'the study of kinship organisation, conceptual systems, political structures, economic processes' (Street, 1993: 14). Since literacy issues are discussed in relation to social and cultural practices within the context of social change, some anthropological analyses draw also on sociological concepts and sociolinguistics as well as historical relations. In this regard, the NLS draw on a range of research traditions and build on previous critical discussions on literacy. This includes the writings of Cole and Scribner (1981), Brice Heath (1983) and Scollon and Scollon (1979) whose work has challenged previous theories based on superficial and biased assumptions about literate and oral cultures. These writers stress the need to take account of the different ways of making sense of the world reflected within different cultures and communities.

To give an example, the approach advocated in the psycholinguistic paradigm is not applicable to the acquisition of Quranic literacy in non-Arabic speaking societies as described by Cole and Scribner (1981) in their study of the Vai in West Africa. Quranic literacy is learned initially 'by rote-memorisation since the students can neither decode the written passages nor understand the sounds they produce. But students who persevere learn to read [that is, sing out] the text and to write passages – still with no understanding of the language' (Scribner and Cole, 1988: 246). As a student of Quranic literacy myself in my early years, I recall that whilst we did not know the language (classical Arabic) we, nevertheless, did learn sound–symbol correspondence, we did learn to decode and we also learned about the rules and conventions of classical Arabic script. Technically then we *did* learn to read as described by experimental psychologists. But we learned really only to 'bark' at print. Our reading purpose (prayer) did not necessitate comprehension as textual interpretation is traditionally performed by the Ulamah (learned scholars) (see Rassool, 1995). This bears out Cole and Scribner's (1981) view that specific uses of literacy have specific implications, and that particular practices promote particular skills.

A comparative analysis

Many of the differences between the NLS and experimental psychology paradigms relate to the particular *focus* of the disciplines in which literacy is articulated. The latter's concern about the teaching of reading and writing skills relates to a significant extent to their primary involvement with the diagnosis of reading ability and the remediation of specific literacy problems amongst individual children in schools. Oakhill and Beard (1995: 72) summarise the differences in research approach between the subject-disciplines in their argument that:

> experimental research by psychologists adopts 'stipulative' [or operationalised] definitions, in order to facilitate 'controlled and circumscribed' studies. Ethnographic and other sociological studies tend to adopt or seek to establish 'descriptive' [or 'essentialist'] definitions, advancing particular constructs to enable them to discuss different 'literacies'. Thus the New Literacy Studies can be said to be developing new philosophical lines of enquiry, rather than seeking to replace 'old' notions of literacy.

There is some validity in this view and I return to this discussion again later in the chapter.

Literacy as a bounded discourse

Other subject-disciplines involved with theorisation and research into literacy include *cognitive psychology* which is concerned mainly with the impact of literacy on intellectual development – and, particularly, abstract thinking skills. Although there is some congruence with the views held in experimental psychology, the overall focus of research is different. Whilst emphasis within the latter is mainly on decoding skills, the former is concerned with the development of higher order reading skills and cognitive processes.

Social psychology, on the other hand, draws on elements of cognitive psychology, namely, the relationship between language and thought but locates its arguments within particular environments, cultures and societies. A variety of views of literacy prevail within this framework. Most influential has been the level of importance attached to the 'great divide' between literate and oral cultures by writers such as Goody and Watt (1968), Ong (1982) and Hildyard and Olson (1978). Others including Vygotsky (1962) and Luria (1979) emphasised the development of cognition and consciousness in relation to 'the social relations with the external world' (Luria, 1979: 43). Their emphasis was particularly on the cognitive consequences and the political and ideological dimensions of literacy acquisition during a period of social change in the USSR. This included the economic transition from a predominantly agrarian society to post-revolutionary industrialism as well as the sociocultural and ideological transition from the semi-feudalism of Tsarist Russia towards the modernist ideals of the new 'socialist' milieu. The underlying thesis was that 'sociocultural changes formed the basis for the development of higher memory and thinking processes and more complex psychological organisation' (Cole and Scribner, 1981: 10).

Overall, social psychology is primarily concerned with educational and cultural practices and the 'impact' and 'effects' of literacy on larger groups of people, and much emphasis is placed on the transference of cognitive literacy skills to the process of living in society. More recently social psychology has also focused on the uses to which basic literacy knowledges are applied and, accordingly, centres on '*what* people read, the *amount* of reading that is done, the *purposes* and *effects* of reading' (Edwards, 1997: 119, original emphases).

Literacy theorised within *sociolinguistics* generally takes account of the different forms and functions of written and spoken language within a variety of social and cultural contexts. Emphasis is placed on the communicative functions of speech and written language within different language communities. With regard to literacy, it also considers the communicative functions of 'text', including different textual forms and conventions, and their embeddedness in different language and cultural systems. As is the case with psycholinguistics, both readers and writers bring meaning to the text in terms of their knowledge of the language system as well as the sociocultural context. Stubbs (1980: 15) states that in order to:

> make sense of written material we need to know more than simply the 'linguistic' characteristics of the text: in addition to these characteristics we need to recognise that any writing system is deeply embedded in attitudinal, cultural, economic and technological constraints ... People

speak, listen, read and write in different social situations for different purposes.

Its focus on appropriateness in relation to context incorporates a consideration of 'communicative competence' in oral discourse. 'Communicative competence' is defined as:

> a synthesis of knowledge of basic grammatical principles, knowledge of how language is used in social settings to perform communicative func-tions, and knowledge of how utterances and communicative functions can be combined according to the principles of discourse
>
> (Canale and Swain, 1980; quoted in Verhoeven, 1994: 8)

Verhoeven (1994: 6) incorporated this notion of 'communicative competence' into the concept of 'functional literacy' which he appropriated from the UNESCO framework, reinterpreted and redefined in terms of 'the demands of literacy in the complex world'.

This redefined notion of functional literacy involves the development of different levels of competence including 'grammatical competence' relating to phonological, lexical and morpho-syntactic abilities; 'discourse competence' relating to cohesion and coherence within the text; 'decoding competence' involving code conventions and automisation, that is, 'grasping the essentials of the written language code itself'; 'strategic competence' centring on the meta-cognitive abilities involved in the planning, execution and evaluation of written texts; and 'sociolinguistic competence' revolving around understand-ing of literacy conventions, and cultural background knowledge (Verhoeven, 1994: 9).

The notion of 'grammatical competence' described here by Verhoeven shares similarities with the overall emphasis in the experimental psychology paradigm on developing linguistic awareness/competence as part of the process of learning to read. The model of communicative competence that he advances overall also includes knowledge of discourse and subject register. Discourse here refers to appropriate language use within a specific communicative event and thus involves role relationships, cultural norms and values, different textual conventions including content, form (schemata) and style as well as knowledge and understanding of the context. Subject register describes the language categories and forms of description particular to certain subjects or genre, for example, the language of science, history, music or art. . . .

On a different level, although multilingualism and issues of bi-literacy have been discussed within sociolinguistics, analysis has been limited to language policy and language programmes within particular societies. Issues related to local and subjugated literacies have not generally been theorised in this para-digm. Hymes (1974) and Labov (1972), concentrating mostly on speech communities, foregrounded the importance of going beyond the linguistic perspective in order to transcend inequalities between language and competence. These writers argued that linguistic inequalities needed to be analysed in relation to people and their location within the social structure. This perspective has been incorporated into the work of, *inter alia*, Kress et al. (1997), Fairclough (1992), Gee (1996), Halliday (1996) and Hasan (1996).

Research approaches

Within a macro-perspective, the research approaches adopted in social anthropology and sociolinguistics employ a variety of measurement instruments including descriptive interpretive approaches, participant observation, field notes and taped transcripts in ethnographic case studies and, in the instance of sociolinguistics, also textual analysis. In contrast, in the micro-perspective adopted by psycholinguistics and experimental psychology, the measurement of literacy includes, largely, psychometric testing, checklists, reading inventories, analysis of writing samples, observation quantification, interviewing and the classification of behaviour. Important emphases are reading diagnosis, instructional techniques and strategies, although these derive from very different views of the literacy process.

Definitions and models of literacy

Definitions of literacy relevant to teaching contexts tend to be implied rather than stated in the macro-perspective adopted in some of the paradigms. . . . [T]he issue of definition extends beyond the rhetorical. Indeed, Scribner (1984: 6) suggests that definitional problems have more than academic significance. She argues that:

> each formulation of an answer to the question 'What is literacy?' leads to a different evaluation of the scope of the problem (i.e. the extent of *il*literacy) and to different objectives for programs aimed at the formation of a literate citizenry. . . . A chorus of clashing answers also creates problems for literacy planners and educators.
>
> (Original emphasis)

Account needs to be taken also of the fact that research paradigms or theoretical frameworks that take the individual as the unit of analysis argue outside a consideration of the fact that literacy is a primary means of cultural transmission, which is essentially a social achievement (Scribner, 1984). Although the literacy act in itself is often a private experience as is suggested by experimental psychologists (Gough, 1995), it obtains its meaning ultimately within society and culture; it is a means of social communication, of knowledges, thoughts and ideas. As is argued by Hasan (1996: 378), 'the goals of literacy can hardly have a value in and of themselves: they need to be seen in the context of the wider social environment which is at once the enabling condition and the enabled product of literacy pedagogy'.

With the exception of psycholinguistics, and the Freirean approach . . . *models of literacy* are not clarified; they are understood at the level of common-sense, that is to say, they tend to feature as taken-for-granted variables in literacy analysis. Models of literacy refer to pedagogic frameworks in which theories about the literacy process are generated. They would therefore include the range of meanings produced in literacy practices as well as conceptions of how and what meanings can be obtained in texts – and contexts. Thus, models of literacy make explicit the range of knowledges or literacies that they frame – and the process through which they are accessed. Models of literacy do not constitute instructional techniques, although they may frame them. If we are to assess the value of literacy, we cannot do so effectively without taking account of the knowledges that they make available, and the contexts in which they are situated.

Many of these views also originate within different ideological frameworks. For example, literacy theorised as a sociocultural practice emphasises ideology, politics and power. In contrast, literacy theorised within the cognitive and behavioural psychology framework regards literacy as a value-free, autonomous set of skills, a neutral technology that can be applied to different literacy demands in everyday life. Similarly, literacy theorised within psycho-linguistics makes a variety of assumptions about what literacy *is* (e.g. print-text based). Its primary focus on the literacy *process* also implicitly underscores a de-ideologised view of literacy. According to Luke (1996: 311), in psycho-linguistics:

> language and literacy are theorised by reference to the internal states of human subjects – for example, . . . models of language acquisition, devel-opmental stage theories, schema theory, and humanist models of personal response and expression.

In other words, each perspective brings with it not only its own particular view of what literacy is and what it is for, but also a particular worldview.

Table 2.1 provides a brief and schematic outline of a selection of *subject-disciplines* in order to highlight the distinct nature of the literacy meanings produced within each framework.

What I am concerned with here are not the substantive or methodological differences between these perspectives *per se*. Rather, the point that I want to make is that, because the *foci* are different within these subject-disciplines, and because their research approaches differ, they yield a wide variety of infor-mation on literacy within a broad context. This discreteness supports Stubbs' view that each subject-discipline advances a particular analytical and research framework yielding different views on what constitutes important knowledge about literacy.

Table 2.1 Literacy as a bounded discourse

Subject-discipline	Literacy foci
Experimental behavioural psychology	Focus on the individual Perceptual process Logographic knowledge Phonological awareness Technical writing skills Decoding of texts Functional literacy Methods of instruction
Cognitive psychology	Focus on individuals and groups Impact of literacy on intellectual development Abstract thinking skills
Social psychology	Focus on groups Variety of positions taken: (a) great-divide theory – differences between oral and literate cultures (e.g. Goody and Watt; Hildyard and Olson) (b) emphasis on development of cognition and consciousness in relation to social relations within external world – ideological and political aspects of literacy (e.g. Luria; Vygotsky) (c) emphasis on need to understand various ways in which different societies and cultures make sense of their world – challenge great-divide theory (Scribner; Cole and Scribner)
Psycholinguistics	Focus on the individual Reading and writing *process* Internal relations between perceptual processes, orthographic systems and reader's knowledge of language Meaning production at interface of person and text
Sociolinguistics	Focus on individuals and groups Different forms and functions of written and spoken language within variety of social contexts Bilingualism and multilingualism Discourse and subject registers Communicative competence
Social anthropology	Focus on groups Interpretations of social consequences of literacy related to groups of people within their sociocultural context Social change

Boundaries, knowledge and power

With the exception of the integrated approach adopted by the New Literacy Studies and social anthropology, the divergent views on literacy discussed here lend support to Stubbs' contention that the field of literacy studies is marked by a lack of integration. The theorisation of literacy in different subject disciplines, he argues, has resulted in the development of a variety of conceptual–analytic frameworks. Stubbs (1980: 3) identified this problem in his argument that:

> one reason why the literature on reading is so vast and unintegrated is that topics have been approached from different directions from within disciplines, including psychology, education and linguistics. Often these approaches have been largely self-contained, making little reference to work within other approaches, and, in fact, putting forward contradictory definitions of *reading* and *literacy*.
>
> (Original emphases)

Whilst the sociocultural approach (NLS) and social anthropology derive their terms of reference across disciplinary boundaries, the rest of the views discussed here, to a large extent, rely on the frame and terms of reference of specific subject-disciplines as the basis of their interpretation and analysis.

Bernstein (1996: 156) defines a discipline as 'a specialised, discrete discourse, with its own intellectual field of texts, practices, rules of entry, modes of examination and principles of distributing success and privileges'; they are 'oriented to their own development rather than to applications outside themselves'. Each subject-discipline frames 'a domain of objects, a set of methods, a corpus of propositions considered to be true, a play of rules and definitions, of techniques and instruments' (Foucault, 1970: 59). and, as we could see in the different research approaches discussed earlier, each subject-discipline projects a particular view of what constitutes research, and different sets of variables operate within each frame of reference and arguments to arrive often at conclusions that, generally, are not integrated in a meaningful way within the educational terrain. This bears out Scribner's (1984) argument regarding difficulties in educational planning. It also bears out the views expressed by Oakhill and Beard (1995, referred to earlier), regarding the nature of the differences in the conceptual–analytic frameworks of NLS and experimental psychology.

Conceptual–analytical frameworks derive from the subject-discipline that provides the frame and terms of reference to the analysis. This includes subject-specific terminology, relational concepts as well as the range of assumptions, questions and problematics that can be engendered within this context. They refer also, at meta-level, to the ways in which discourses are structured as well as how meanings are produced and reproduced.

Conceptual–analytical frameworks grounded in subject-disciplines, according to Bernstein (1990), are not neutral; they are constituted in 'self interest' with their own subject-specific views of the 'truth' – which implicitly support a particular view of the world. Thus they constitute what Foucault (1980: 133) refers to as 'regimes of truth':

> 'truth' is to be understood as a system of ordered procedures for the production, regulation, distribution, circulation and operation of statements . . . [and] is linked in a circular relation with systems of power which produce and sustain it, and to effects of power which it induces and which extend it. A 'regime' of truth.

Together these frame what are legitimate knowledges and ways of knowing in research. Some of this professional interest is expressed in Oakhill and Beard's (1995: 69) argument that:

> [w]hilst acknowledging the undoubted contribution of language, motivation and cultural factors to literacy acquisition, *we should not forget the contribution of scientific experimental research to our understanding of reading and its development.*

> (Emphasis added)

Oakhill and Beard sought to reinforce the scientific validity of their 'language-as-system' and empirical research paradigm over and against the ethnographic and theoretical–analytical approaches adopted in what they term as 'sociological perspectives on literacy' (1995: 72), and the broad assumptions that they associate with psycholinguistic research.

Conceptual–analytic frameworks are ultimately embedded in particular ideologies and, as such, each represents a distinctive view of 'what is legitimate knowledge'. Without acknowledging the ideology with which their own perspective of literacy (reading) is imbued, Oakhill and Beard (1995: 72) call for counter-critiques of the 'ideological influences on how misplaced orthodoxies become so widely accepted', and why it takes so long for them to 'receive critical scrutiny'.

Literacy discourses in society

In addition to hierarchies constructed between subject-knowledges, different levels of importance are also attached to selected forms of knowledge within the social and political terrain. This relates, to a large extent, to prevailing (dominant) ideologies that underscore policy frameworks as well as particular hegemonic projects pursued by political and economic interest groups. Thus it is that some literacy knowledges are chosen for inclusion in educational policy frameworks, whilst others are marginalised, excluded or derided in social and political debate at specific moments in societal development.

For instance, the argument for *basic skills* and *rote learning* derives its scientific legitimacy largely from the positivism of behavioural psychology and, for a long time, constituted (and in many instances continues to be) the dominant view of 'what literacy is' in education. Moreover, . . . 'official' literacies are inscribed into national language policy. In Foucauldian terms, 'knowledge and power are inseparable, . . . forms of power are imbued within knowledge, and forms of knowledge are permeated by power relations' (Ball, 1990: 17). Ideologically, definitions of literacy can then be seen as constituting 'power/knowledge' discourses (Foucault, 1980). According to Foucault, discourse defined in terms of power/knowledge constitutes the means by which power is exercised through relations of dominance established within the social terrain. . . .

Border crossings

Some critiques of the unitary subject-discipline approach have come from what has become known as *critical literacy discourse* and include a diverse range of research approaches and conceptual frameworks.

Street (1984, 1993), one of the most significant contributors to the debate about adult literacy research in the UK during the past two decades, has made important inputs towards a re-conceptualisation of literacy within an inter-disciplinary framework. In his research conducted in Iran during the 1970s, Street analysed literate behaviours and the way meanings are produced in the reading process amongst the peasants of the village of Chesmeh. He identified two different forms of literacy that prevailed in Iran at the time, namely 'commercial' (economic) literacy and 'Maktab' (religious) literacy. Of major importance was the fact that Street was identifying different forms of literacy for specific social and economic purposes. Moreover, his critique of the 'autonomous' model of literacy adhered to by Goody (1968), and his identification of the 'ideological' model of literacy were major contributions to the way in which literacy has been theorised during the past decade.

The significance of this research in both methodological and conceptual terms was the way in which micro-social processes were linked with broader developments within society – whilst taking account also of historical relations. In his critique of the 'psychologistic' paradigm, Street (1984, 1993) challenges the claims made of the role of literacy in fostering rationality and abstract-thinking capabilities. Instead, he argues that literacy should be understood as a social practice in which there is an interplay of different ideologies. Street also stresses the importance of analysing literacy within its institutional as well as the wider sociopolitical and economic context. As such, it is argued that:

> the uses, consequences and meanings of literacy; the differences and similarities between written and spoken registers and inter-register variation with spoken and written modes; and the problem of what is culture specific and what [is] universal in literacy practices – must be answered

> with reference to close descriptions of the actual uses and conceptions of literacy in specific cultural contexts.
>
> (Street, 1993: 3)

Street's views on the theorisation of literacy have been central to the development of the New Literacy Studies discussed earlier. In pedagogical terms, this paradigm supports the development of different literacies, the centrality of the learner to the teaching and learning context, 'the politicisation of content in literacy instruction, and the integration of the voices and experiences of learners with critical social analysis' (Auerbach, 1992, quoted in Verhoeven, 1994: 7). This framework also takes account of the often neglected complex issue of literacy within multilingual social settings – the disappearance of minority languages, subjugated literacies and the importance of maintaining local literacies.

Critical linguists such as Skutnabb-Kangas an Phillipson (1995), similarly, carry this thread through their analysis of linguistic imperialism which refers to the imposition of colonial languages historically. These writers address the issue of linguistic human rights within which the concept of local literacies is grounded. Writers within this broad framework identify the inter-relationship between literacy, national language planning policies and power processes.

Social historians such as Graff (1979, 1987) and Williams (1961), analysing the political economy of literacy programmes, explore the importance attached in social policy to specific ideologies during different historical periods. Within a macro-perspective, these writers draw on sociological concepts in their emphasis on the sociocultural, political and structural variables that contribute to literacy inequalities and, *de facto*, sociocultural and economic inequalities. Significant contributions have come also from writers who focus on the political economy of textbooks and texts (De Castell *et al.*, 1989; Apple, 1982, 1986, 1993). In addition, important new developments have come from writers who locate their analyses within a *'postmodern' analytical framework*.

Border pedagogies

Drawing on Gramscian cultural theory centred on the role of language in maintaining hegemonic relations – and the contestation and resistance that this intrinsically generates, writers such as Giroux (1987, 1993) and McLaren (1995) emphasise the links between knowledge, ideology and power. These writers extend the concept of 'conscientisation' advanced within the Freirean framework and propose concepts that they term *'critical pedagogy'* and *'border pedagogies'*. Outlining a 'postmodern' framework which borrows concepts from feminist research and cultural theory, Giroux (1993: 75) stresses the need for a language:

> that allows for competing solidarities and political vocabularies that do not reduce the issues of power, justice, struggle, and inequality to a single

script, a master narrative that suppresses the contingent, the historical, and the everyday as serious objects of study.

This approach emphasises agency, difference, contestation and the relationship between these and social structures and ideological forces. Giroux argues further that 'critical pedagogy needs to create new forms of knowledge through its emphasis on breaking down disciplinary boundaries and creating new spheres in which knowledge can be produced' (Giroux, 1993: 76).

Critical pedagogies or 'border' pedagogies draw on aspects of feminist theory, cultural studies and the sociology of knowledge and, in this sense, constitute politicised discourses. Most of the writers within the cross-disciplinary paradigm ground their analyses in the 'specificities of people's lives, communities, and cultures' (Giroux, 1993: 67) and place relative emphasis on the time–space dimensions of specific literacy knowledges. Significantly though, only a few (McLaren, 1995; Giroux, 1993) embed their analyses in an exposition of the complexity of social theory that incorporates the variables of gender, 'race' and social position as analytic categories.

As was the case with the discussion on subject-disciplines earlier, at the level of practice, the views of literacy highlighted in the critical literacy paradigm continue to raise qualitative questions about: (a) definitions of literacy, (b) models of literacy, (c) criteria for and, relatedly, the level of importance attached to local variables in the measurement of societal literacy levels, (d) what literacy in relation to human rights means in concrete terms and (e) the real and symbolic impact and effects of particular forms of literacy on individual 'empowerment' and social development. Account also needs to be taken of the fact that literacy meanings are in a constant state of flux – and thus are subject to alteration within different social milieux. Scribner (1984: 8) underlines this point in her argument that:

> since social literacy practices vary in time and space, what qualifies as individual literacy varies with them. At one time, ability to write one's own name was the hallmark of literacy; today in some parts of the world, the ability to memorise a sacred text remains the modal literacy act. Literacy has neither a static nor a universal essence.

This issue is highly pertinent at the moment as new technologies and, relatedly, new ways of living evolve within society. . . .

Summary

The different perspectives outlined here illustrate that, conceptually, literacy is multifaceted and thus requires different *levels* of analysis within a broad and flexible framework that incorporates complexities. These include, *inter alia*, historical relations, social practices and institutions, locality as well as individual and group subjectivities, and the tension that exists between agency and specific state-sanctioned political and hegemonic projects.

Luke (1996), for instance, arguing from a sociological perspective, critiques socially based models of literacy pedagogy including the Freirean approach ... and the new 'genre-based' literacies within sociolinguistics (Veel and Coffin, 1996; van Leewen and Humphrey, 1996). He contends that these approaches 'stop short of coming to grips with their assumptions about the relationship between literacy and social power' (Luke, 1996: 309). These views, he suggests, define agency as an individual property which is 'neither collective or inter-subjective, nor necessarily connected with political ideology or cultural hegemony' (p. 311). Luke maintains that the history of literacy education is about power and knowledge:

> But it is about power not solely in terms of which texts and practices will 'count' and which groups will have or not have access to which texts and practices. It is also about who in the modern state will have access to a privileged position in specifying what will count as literacy ... Schooling and literacy are used to regulate and broker not just access to material wealth, but as well access to legally constituted 'rights', to cultural and subcultural histories and archives, to religious virtue and spiritual rewards, and to actual social networks, gendered desires and identities.
>
> (Luke, 1996: 310)

For Luke, a critical literacy approach extends beyond issues related to textual biases and representation, 'it is nothing less than a debate over the shape of a literate society, its normative relations to textual and discourse exchange, and the relative agency and power of the literate in its complex and diverse culture and communities' (Luke, 1996: 145). Luke's perspective is central to the view of literacy in the information age. . . .

Literacy as a field of inquiry: levels, contexts and definitions

Since literacy spans such a broad terrain within various subject-disciplines, to address the complexities that surround literacy in the modern world necessitates an approach that incorporates many of the literacy meanings discussed earlier. In order to do so, I will explore the conceptualisation of literacy as a *regionalised field of inquiry*. A regional field of study according to Bernstein (1990: 156) represents a 'recontextualising of disciplines which operate both in the intellectual field of disciplines and in the field of practice'. Because literacy interpenetrates a wide range of subject-disciplines, we can argue that regions are the interface between subject-disciplines, and the literacy knowledges that are thus made available. These are illustrated in Figure 2.1.

The degree of overlap indicated in Figure 2.1 signifies the dialogical relationship between literacy knowledges and subject disciplines. These overlaps, or interstices, represent the regionalised field of inquiry. . . .

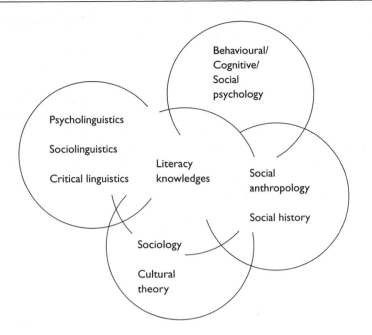

Figure 2.1 Literacy as a regionalised field of study

The range of literacy meanings identified in the earlier critical paradigm highlight the fact that literacy constitutes, simultaneously, a *social practice*, an *ideological practice*, a *cultural practice* and an *educational practice*. Within the regionalised field identified here, discussion of these inter-related aspects would be able to draw on concepts and analytical categories across the disciplines. It would also be able to draw on analytic categories used in cross-disciplinary frameworks such as feminism and cultural studies. Crossing boundaries in this way provides opportunity to analyse the dynamic interplay that exists between specific literacy practices and the social, cultural, economic and political structures in which they are grounded, as is suggested by Luke (1996). Thus it would be possible to address educational meanings, whilst at the same time, take account of the fact that meaning production takes place organically within the complex power relations that traverse the social terrain. Moreover, it can take account also of agency, contestation and struggle which make possible the production of alternative meanings and practices as highlighted in the critical literacy framework.

The different interlocking aspects of literacy [that can] be explored as a regionalised field of study. . . are summarised in Table 2.2, and will be discussed in more detail below.

Table 2.2 Interlocking levels at which literacy needs to be theorised

Literacy as:	Variables
A social practice	Social life Institutions: state, industry, commerce, finance, media, education Social processes e.g. national language policy, educational policy, social policy (health, employment, economic) Social system: models of governance, social roles Structures e.g. social policy, language rights, ethnicity, gender, social position Religious–cultural practices
An ideological practice	Meanings produced in social discourse e.g. policy, media, political interest groups, industry, funding bodies Censorship Textual and contextual meanings Critical literacies/counter-discourses
A cultural practice	Historical relationships Work-place literacy requirements Leisure/interest literacy requirements Literacy requirements to function in everyday life e.g. technologies, banking, health, social services, housing, civic engagement Range of cultural meanings produced and reproduced e.g. values, beliefs, expectations, aspirations Impact of religious–cultural beliefs on levels of access to literacy for particular groups e.g. women, religious minorities, ethnic groups
An educational practice	Models and forms of knowledge Technical literacy skills Technological skills and knowledges Theories of knowledge Pedagogical models Teaching methodologies Teaching and learning resources (including staffing, multimedia) Democratisation of sociopolitical structures and processes Literacy for democratic participation, e.g. decision-making, knowledge of rights and obligations, freedom of expression, freedom of access to information, knowledge of social system, citizenship, critical knowledges

Literacy as a social practice

Working towards concretising this framework and identifying analytic categories, I start with the argument that literacy defined as a *social practice* has to be contextualised within a general theory of society. As is argued earlier, its permeation into the social body requires that literacy as a social practice needs to be analysed in terms of its relationship with institutions, structures and processes and the social system in which they are grounded. The importance of this lies in the fact that these contexts constitute the key defining sites of what literacy is, who it is for and what purposes it should serve for the individual, specific groups of people and society as a whole. Scribner (1984: 8) concretises the intrinsic link between literacy and structures in the argument that:

> grasping what literacy 'is' inevitably involves social analysis: What activities are carried out with written symbols? What significance is attached to them, and what status is conferred on those who engage in them? Is literacy a social right or a private power? . . . Does the prevailing distribution of literacy conform to standards of social justice and human progress? What social and educational policies might promote such standards?

Such considerations should inform policy frameworks. Clearly then, the interrelationship between literacy and knowledge needs to be concretised and theorised in relation to specific conditions that exist within particular societies – and the diverse uses of literacy within different societies. In positioning literacy within the context of societal relations, analysis would draw on sociological concepts and theories to explain the complex interactions in which literacy meanings are shaped – as well as what their concrete effects are on the lives of people. In terms of the latter, analyses of societal literacy levels should therefore also include a consideration of sociocultural factors such as ethnicity, languages, religious–cultural practices, gender and social position. Transferred to practice, this means that within culturally and linguistically plural societies issues of national language policy have to be considered in analysis of societal literacy levels.

It also means that literacy levels need to be discussed in relation to the role of women in society as is highlighted in the work of Stromquist (1990) and Rockhill (1987). These studies identify the fact that the social position of women and their differential levels of access to particular forms of literacy – or literacy *per se* – need to be addressed in relation to the social relations that inhere in particular religious–cultural practices within different societies. In relation to this, the emphasis in the UNESCO discourse currently on the need for higher literacy rates amongst women needs to be examined with regard to the particular value attached to the role of women in different societies.

Literacy defined in terms of 'individual empowerment' and 'social transformation' and literacy defined as a 'fundamental human right' can only really be understood within the context of specific cultural formations and the diverse and complex power relations that traverse the social terrain. This incorporates political processes including models of governance and social policy (see Table 2.2). Ultimately, literacy policy and provision arise within the organisation of particular social systems, forms of governance as well as economic, social and political priorities identified within the context of the state. Related to this are issues that revolve around, for example:

- migration and the language rights of asylum seekers and refugees;
- routes of access to participation in the democratic process;
- fiscal policy as this affects approaches adopted to public expenditure – and thus funding for educational and/or language provision;
- social change related to technological developments;
- the linguistic and cultural rights of settled minority groups;
- the role and influence of external funding bodies.

Alongside these variables are issues that revolve around exclusion, subjugation and control exercised over particular forms of literacy – and the struggles and possibilities for transformation that these inequalities generate within the context of everyday life. Again, these multifaceted and interlocking variables highlight the fact that, because literacy is rooted in both the social and material world, discussions of societal literacy levels cannot be reduced to the level of discourse alone. To do so would be to present only a partial view of literacy as a dynamic social practice.

Literacy and technology issues

This is particularly important in the current period of technological change and rapid social transformation. Indeed, the organic links between microelectronics and, especially, information technology and economic, social and political processes raise important questions regarding the conceptualisation of literacy as a social practice. The gains made in terms of time and space, facilitated by the new technologies, have resulted not only in the fact that the world is rapidly becoming smaller because of mass communication practices, but in the emergence of multifaceted networks of unequal social relations on a global scale. The new 'flexible accumulation' made possible by 'flexible' technologies enable not only speedier capital transfer to take place across the world but also contribute to new forms of control emerging within the restructured work-place. New realities are in the process of being constructed with the evolution of ever-newer, more adaptable and faster technologies. Thus, literacy defined as a social practice has also to address the effects of the uses of the new technologies on the social experience of people in their everyday social roles – as well as their quality of life as workers. This includes not only skills and knowledge requirements but also a consideration of the relationship between levels of technological literacy and broader social factors such as unemployment, intermittent or sporadic employment such as 'yearly work-time' and seasonal work – in addition to the variables of gender, race, their position as workers in the work-place as well as their everyday experiences as workers.

In definitional terms then, other than the necessary technical skills and knowledges required to function on an everyday basis, we need to move towards a re-conceptualisation of, *inter alia*, how we interpret the world, think of our lived realities and analyse the essence of power and control inherent in the technologies themselves – and the social processes through which they operate.

Literacy as an ideological practice

Literacy defined as an *ideological practice* needs to address the multiple meanings ascribed to literacy by different interest groups. First, this refers to not only the views of literacy legitimated in policy discourse, but also those articulated within other defining sites such as funding bodies, social institutions and political interest groups within society. For instance, UNESCO's current concerns with the breakdown of moral values in society and its growing emphasis on the role of education in inculcating 'those principles which are conducive to peace, human rights and democracy that finally must constitute the fabric of the "intellectual and moral solidarity of mankind"' (UNESCO, 1995: 17) signify a clear move towards re-establishing a link between literacy and a moral economy. This, in turn, has to be seen in juxtaposition with the overall emphasis within the UNESCO framework, at least since the 1970s, on the principles of technological modernisation. It also includes a consideration of the mechanisms of control of information or censorship and the subjugation of local and critical literacies. Examples here can be taken from the particular forms of censorship that prevailed in pre-revolutionary Iran in the Shah's modernisation programme during the 1970s (see Street, 1984; Rassool, 1995). Within that context at the time, whilst the mass literacy programme launched by the Shah sought to increase literacy rates amongst the peasants, different forms of censorship affected those who could read and write. According to Kamrava (1992: 138–9) in Iran at that time '[p]eople were encouraged to read and write the alphabet, but reading and trying to understand books that were suspected of being threatening to the state was punishable by long sentences'. Oppositional literature, film, novels and essays were banned and the literati came under state surveillance by the notorious secret police, the SAVAK (Rassool, 1995).

Elsewhere, in Eastern Europe, Bulgaria pursued the same model of literacy that prevailed in the UNESCO framework; that is, literacy as a central part of societal modernisation, despite the fact that it was grounded in a different ideological framework. Yet alongside this process of rapid modernisation, the rights of ethnic Turkic and Roma people to become literate in their own languages were systematically repressed under the Zhivkov regime's policy of

'Bulgarisation' (Rassool and Honour, 1996). Again, what is highlighted here, first, is the overall ideological 'package' in which literacy is inscribed into state policy and practices – and the specific purposes that dominant forms of literacy served within these contexts within a specific time-frame – and as part of a specific hegemonic project of the state to assimilate minority cultural groups.

Second, the case of pre- and post-revolutionary Iran illustrates the point made earlier that literacy meanings are contingent; that they are subject to change within different sociohistorical frameworks – as well as in relation to the emergence of new technologies within the social terrain. Analysis thus has to draw on social history as well as the political economy of literacy programmes. Third, account has to be taken of the fact that literacy is also a signifier of cultural, social and individual aspirations – some of which may conflict with one another – as is the case for women in post-revolutionary Iran, and the empowering meanings inscribed into the revolutionary Nicaraguan literacy programme. . . .

Literacy and technology issues

Fourth, the impact of the new technologies on the reconstruction of our social reality requires a re-conceptualisation of the literacy process. Apple (1987: 171), for example, argues that the new technologies are not only 'an assemblage of machines and their accompanying software', they also have potent symbolic power. Embedded within the communications industry, the new technologies make possible the construction of – and, relatedly, they have the capacity to sustain – 'second order universes that increasingly are our experience of the cultural and social world' (Hall, 1989: 43). Applied to literacy this refers to the reality that we live today in a world dominated by the television advert defining our consumer needs, wants and desires; computer games in homes, shops, pubs and amusement arcades; and video equipment in family homes having access to video libraries providing boundless popular entertainment. Alongside this is the power of communication contained in the almost unlimited textual interaction possibilities provided by the Internet as well as the multiple realities that inhere in CD-ROM facilities. Computers form part of the taken-for-granted values, beliefs, material aspirations and expectations that we have of our everyday lives and thus they have been incorporated as hegemonic cultural capital. That is to say, technology has become an unquestioned, taken-for-granted 'must have' in order to function in everyday life.

In real terms then we have already moved beyond a one-dimensional view of text within our experience of everyday life. Indeed, because of the organic links between the new technology, the state and other power processes such as corporate business and the microelectronics industry, the concept of literacy today transcends written and other representational texts such as visual art, television, information technologies and photography to include also the social and political contexts in which communication practices are grounded. In other words, to be a literate citizen in the age of high technology means to be able read not only the word and image, but as is argued by Freire and Macedo (1987), also the world in its fullest sense.

Literacy as a cultural practice

As a *cultural practice* literacy has to be theorised in a conceptual–analytic framework that makes it possible to consider the subordinating meanings, values and beliefs that inhere not only in dominant discourse but also in traditional cultural practices. This refers to the maintenance of gender and political power elites legitimated in religious–cultural beliefs and practices, through which access to literacy can be controlled to exclude women and minority groups from acquiring particular forms of literacy. Dominant literacy practices also serve to subjugate local cultural literacies. The current rise of religious fundamentalism in countries such as Algeria, Egypt, Turkey and Afghanistan has implications for the range and types of literacy that would be made available to women within these societies.

In a more general sense literacy as a cultural practice also refers to the relative importance attached to particular types and forms of literacy within the culture. These comprise not only religious–cultural literacies, but also the range of social literacies required within everyday life including the work-place and leisure. Collectively, these influence the literacy knowledges that people would aspire to have in order to survive and become 'useful' citizens. Analyses should therefore also include the ways in which cultural meanings are produced and reproduced within and through literacy practices.

Literacy as an educational practice

As an *educational practice*, literacy has to be theorised in terms of definitions, models including pedagogy, assessment and measurement. Moreover, literacy as an educational practice cannot, reasonably, be conceptualised outside a theory of knowledge, or the function that it will serve in terms of the multifaceted purposes in people's everyday lives within society. As has already been suggested earlier, this extends beyond a direct link between literacy and the functional skills and knowledges required within the workplace to include also social and political purposes.

Scribner (1984: 8), emphasising the fact that literacy is a 'many-meaninged thing', tries to overcome this difficulty by identifying three metaphors, namely, 'literacy as adaptation, literacy as power, and literacy as a state of grace' around which to articulate the multiple and multifaceted meanings that surround literacy for the individual. *Literacy as adaptation* involves the skills needed to function in a 'range of settings and customary activities' such as jobs, training and benefits, civic and political responsibilities. In this sense, she argues, literacy as adaptation is pragmatic and involves a range of competencies which should be broad enough to encompass new systems of literacy as are represented here in the new technologies. In this regard, account needs to be taken of the fact that literacy needs will not be the same for everyone; they may increase for some and reduce for others. *Literacy as power* is articulated around the 'relationship between literacy and community advancement' (Scribner, 1984: 11) and highlights the association between illiteracy and disempowerment grounded in the Freirean view of literacy. Scribner advocates mobilisation for literacy around local needs and small-scale activism. *Literacy as a state of grace* is defined in terms of the liberal tradition of intellectual, aesthetic and spiritual enhancement. Not all uses of literacy have a practical end. All these views of literacy, she argues, are inter-related and have validity for educational planning. Thus although there are obvious boundaries between these metaphors, they are not inflexible.

Another integrated view of what literacy is, pertinent to the discussion here, can be derived from the range of discourses described by the Russian literary theorist Mikhail Bakhtin. According to Bakhtin, discourse is not a fixed communication; it is intertextual (Todorov, 1984: x). That is to say, it exists in a dialogical relationship with previous discourses on the same subject; meanings are transferred from one discourse to another within a particular social context. Emphasising language and communication thus in relation to the social world, he argues that 'language is not an abstract system of normative forms but a concrete heterological opinion on the world' (quoted in Todorov, 1984: 56). In other words, it is constituted in a diversity of languages and a diversity of voices. Thus, both plurality and difference are intrinsic to discourse.

Bakhtin identifies a typology of socially located discourses essential to functioning in everyday life:

> (1) the communication of production [in the factory, ship etc.]; (2) the communication of business [in offices, in social organisation etc.]; familiar communication [encounters and conversations in the street, cafeteria, at home etc.]; (4) artistic communication (in novels, paintings etc.]; and finally (5) ideological communication in the precise sense of the term: propaganda, school, science, philosophy, in all their varieties.
>
> (Bakhtin; quoted in Todorov, 1984: 57;
> information in brackets added)

To this we can add communication of the classroom defined in terms of learning processes. Literacy located within this framework of socially-based communication practices becomes linked with discursive sets of interaction in which a diversity of social and individual meanings are negotiated within the social terrain. What does this mean for education? I argue . . . that, first, in definitional terms, it would include a range of subject-registers in order to function within a variety of contexts – extending beyond those identified earlier in the OECD survey. Second, it also includes levels of access to adequate literacy provision which revolves around different forms of knowledge, cultural traditions, beliefs and values, resources, integrated teaching approaches as well as freedom of access to different forms of information. . . .

Third, with regard to pedagogy, it includes a consideration of goal-directed learning and the specification of criterion-referenced learning outcomes. . . . [L]iteracy for citizenship within a democratic framework is intrinsically bound up with access to different knowledges as well as with concepts of individual empowerment and social progress. Fourth, literacy defined in terms of its role in facilitating social transformation needs to extend to the democratisation of sociopolitical structures and processes. This, implicitly, includes a contextualisation of literacy within models of governance, the nature of decision-making and the possibilities that they provide for bottom-up influences on policy frameworks. Collectively, these factors impact on the range and levels of literacies that can be made available to different groups of people within society – and, relatedly, influence the assessment and measurement of literacy levels in terms of the range of competencies required to function within society. Thus literacy as an educational practice is integrally linked with literacy defined as social and ideological practices.

Conclusion

Using these categories as guiding principles, literacy theorised within the regionalised field suggested here draws on all the major subject disciplines without confining itself to the parameters of knowledge inscribed into them. Within this flexible and integrated framework, constituted in a dynamic interchange of concepts, criteria and registers, literacy can be analysed and theorised in relation to both individual and broader contextual issues. These refer to social and individual development in relation to complex political cultural, educational and ideological processes and practices. . . .

References

Apple, M. W. (1982) *Education and Power*. London: Routledge.

Apple, M. W. (1986) National reports and the construction of inequality. *British Journal of Sociology of Education* 7 (2), 171–90.

Apple, M. W. (1987) Mandating computers: The impact of the new technology on the labour process, students and teachers. In S. Walker and L. Barton (eds) *Changing Policies and Changing Teachers*. Milton Keynes: Open University Press.

Apple, M. W. (1993) *Official Knowledge: Democratic Education in a Conservative Age*. London: Routledge.

Ball, S. J. (1990) *Politics and Policy Making in Education: Explorations in Policy Sociology*. London: Routledge.

Barton, D. (1994) *Literacy: An Introduction to the Ecology of Written Language*. Oxford: Blackwell.

Barton, D. and Hamilton, M. (1998) *Local Literacies: Reading and Writing in One Community*. London: Routledge.

Barton, D. and Ivanic, R. (1991) *Writing in the Community*. London: Sage.

Barton, D. and Padmore, S. (1991) Roles, networks and values in everyday writing. In D. Barton and R. Ivanic (eds) *Writing in the Community*. London: Sage.

Bernstein, B. (1990) *Pedagogy, Symbolic Control and Identity: Theory, Research, Critique*. London: Taylor & Francis.

Britton, J. (1975) *Language and Learning*. Harmondsworth, Middlesex: Penguin Books.

Bryant, P. (1994) Reading research update. *Child Education* (Oct.), 13–19.

Cole, M. and Scribner, S. (1981) *The Psychology of Literacy*. Boston, MA: Harvard University Press.

De Castell, S., Luke, A. and Luke, C. (1989) *Language, Authority and Criticism: Readings on the School Textbook*. Lewes: The Falmer Press.

Edwards, J. (1997) The social psychology of reading. In V. Edwards and D. Corson (eds) *Encyclopedia of Language and Education, Volume 2: Literacy* (pp. 119–26). Amsterdam: Kluwer.

Fairclough, N. (ed.) (1992) *Critical Language Awareness*. London: Longman.

Foucault, M. (1970) The order of discourse. Inaugural Lecture at the College de France, given 2 December 1970. In R. Young (ed.) *Untying the Text: A Post-Structuralist Reader* (pp. 48–78). London: Routledge & Kegan Paul (1987).

Foucault, M. (1980) *Power/Knowledge: Selected Interviews and Other Writings 1972–1977*. Colin Gordon, Leo Marshall, John Mepham and Kate Soper (trans.). Brighton: The Harvester Press.

Freire, P. and Macedo, D. (1987) *Literacy: Reading the Word and the World*. Massachusetts: Bergin and Garvey.

Gee, J. P. (1996) *Social Linguistics and Literacies: Ideology in Discourses* (2nd edn). London: Taylor & Francis.

Giroux, H. A. (1993) *Border Crossings: Cultural Workers and the Politics of Education*. London and New York: Routledge.

Goodman, K. (1986) *What's Whole in Whole Language?* London: Scholastic.

Goody, J. (ed.) (1968) *Literacy in Traditional Societies*. Cambridge: Cambridge University Press.

Goody, J. and Watt, I. (1968) The consequences of literacy. In J. Goody (ed.) *Literacy in Traditional Societies* (pp. 27–68). Cambridge: Cambridge University Press.

Goswami, U. and Bryant, P. (1990) *Phonological Skills and Learning to Read*. London: Lawrence Erlbaum.

Gough, P. B. (1995) The New Literacy: Caveat emptor. *Journal of Research in Reading* 18 (2), 79–86.

Graff, H. J. (1979) *The Literacy Myth: Literacy and Social Structure in Nineteenth Century Canada*. New York and London: Academic Press.

Graff, H. J. (1987) *The Labyrinths of Literacy: Reflections on Literacy Past and Present*. London: The Falmer Press.

Halliday, M. A. K. (1996) Literacy and linguistics: A functional perspective. In R. Hasan and G. Williams (eds) *Literacy in Society* (pp. 339–76). London and New York: Longman.

Hasan, R. (1996) Literacy, everyday talk and society. In R. Hasan and G. Williams (eds) *Literacy in Society* (pp. 377–424). London and New York: Longman.

Heath, S. B. (1983) *Ways with Words*. Cambridge: Cambridge University Press.

Hildyard, A. and Olson, D. (1978) Literacy and the specialisation of language. Unpublished MS, Ontario Institute for Studies in Education.

Hymes, D. (1974) *Foundations in Sociolinguistics*. London: Tavistock.

Kress, G., Leite-Garcia, R. and van Leewen, T. (1997) Discourse semiotics. In T. Van Dijk (ed.) *Discourse as Structure and Process* (pp. 257–91). London: Sage.

Labov, W. (1972) *Language in the Inner City: Studies in Black English Vernacular.* Philadelphia: Philadelphia Press.

Luke, A. (1996) Genres of power? Literacy education and the production of capital. In R. Hasan and G. Williams (eds) *Literacy in Society* (pp. 308–38). London and New York: Longman.

Luria, A. (1979) The making of mind. In M. Cole (ed.) *Soviet Developmental Psychology.* Boston, MA: Harvard University Press.

Mackay, D., Thompson, B. and Schaub, P. (1978) *Breakthrough to Literacy: The Theory and Practice of Teaching Initial Reading and Writing.* London: Longman for the Schools Council.

McLaren, P. (1995) *Critical Pedagogy and Predatory Culture: Oppositional Policies in a Postmodern Era.* London: Routledge.

Oakhill, J. and Beard, R. (1995) Guest editorial. *Journal of Research in Reading* 18 (2), 69–73.

Ong, W. (1982) *Orality and Literacy: The Technologizing of the Word.* London: Routledge.

Perfetti, C. A. (1995) Cognitive research can inform reading education. *Journal of Research in Reading* 18 (2), 106–15.

Phillipson, R. and Skutnabb-Kangas, T. (1995) Language rights in postcolonial Africa. In T. Skutnabb-Kangas and R. Phillipson (eds) *Linguistic Human Rights: Overcoming Linguistic Discrimination* (pp. 335–46). Berlin: Mouton de Gruyter.

Rassool, N. (1995) Language, cultural pluralism and the silencing of minority discourses in England and Wales. *Journal of Education Policy* 10 (3), 287–302.

Rassool, N. and Honour, L. (1996) Cultural pluralism and the struggle for democracy in post-communist Bulgaria. *Education Today* 46 (2), 12–23.

Rockhill, K. (1987) Gender, language and the politics of literacy. *British Journal of Sociology of Education* 8 (2), 153–67.

Scollon, R. and Scollon, S. (1979) *Linguistic Convergence: An Ethnography of Speaking at Fort Chipwyan, Alberta.* New York: Academic Press.

Scribner, S. (1984) Literacy in three metaphors. *American Journal of Education* (Nov.), 6–21.

Scribner, S. and Cole, M. (1988) Unpackaging literacy. In N. Mercer (ed.) *Language and Literacy from an Educational Perspective Vol. I: Language Studies* (pp. 241–55). Milton Keynes: Open University Press.

Skutnabb-Kangas, T. (1990) *Language, Literacy and Minorities.* London: Minority Rights Group.

Skutnabb-Kangas, T. and Phillipson, R. (eds) (1995) *Linguistic Human Rights: Overcoming Linguistic Discrimination.* Berlin: Mouton de Gruyter.

Smith, F. (1971) *Understanding Reading: A Psycholinguistic Analysis of Reading and Learning to Read.* London: Holt, Rinehart & Winston.

Smith, H. (1991) Revolutionary diplomacy Sandinista style: Lessons and limits. *Race and Class: Configurations of Racism in the Civil Service* 33 (1), 57–70.

Stanovich, K. (1986) Mathew effects in reading: Some consequences of individual differences in the acquisition of literacy. *Reading Research Quarterly* (Fall), 360–406.

Stanovich, K. and Stanovich, P. J. (1995) How research might inform the debate about early reading acquisition. *Journal of Research in Reading* 18 (2), 87–105.

Street, B. V. (1984) *Literacy in Theory and Practice.* Cambridge: Cambridge University Press.

Street, B. V. (ed.) (1993) Introduction. *Cross-cultural Approaches to Literacy* (pp. 1–21). Cambridge: Cambridge University Press.

Stromquist, N. P. (1990) Women and illiteracy: The interplay of gender subordination and poverty. *Comparative Education Review* 34 (1), 95–111.

Stubbs, M. (1980) *Language and Literacy: The Sociolinguistics of Reading and Writing*. London: Routledge.

Todorov, T. (1984) *Mikhail Bakhtin: The Dialogical Principle*. Wlad Godzich (trans.). Manchester: Manchester University Press.

UNESCO (1995) *World Education Report*. Paris: UNESCO.

Van Leewen, T. and Humphrey, S. (1996) On learning to look through a geographer's eyes. In R. Hasan and G. Williams (eds) *Literacy in Society* (pp. 29–49). London and New York: Longman.

Veel, R. and Coffin, C. (1996) Literacy learning across the curriculum: Towards a model of register for secondary school teachers. In R. Hasan and G. Williams *Literacy in Society* (pp. 191–231). London and New York: Longman.

Verhoeven, L. (1994) Modeling and promoting functional literacy. In L. Verhoeven (ed.) *Functional Literacy: Theoretical Issues and Educational Implications* (pp. 3–34). Amsterdam: John Benjamins.

Vygorsky, L. S. (1962) *Thought and Language*. Cambridge, MA: MIT Press.

Weaver, C. (1990) *Understanding Whole Language: From Principles to Practice*. Portsmouth, NH: Heinemann.

Wells, G. (1986) *The Meaning Makers*. London: Hodder & Stoughton.

Wilkinson, A. (ed.) (1965) *Spoken English*. With contributions by A. Davies and D. Atkinson. Educational Review Occasional Publications, No. 2, University of Birmingham.

Williams, R. (1961) *The Long Revolution*. Harmondsworth: Penguin Books in association with Chatto & Windus.

Source

This is an edited version of a chapter previously published in N. Rassool (ed.) *Literacy for Sustainable Development in the Age of Information*. 1999. Reproduced by permission of Multilingual Matters Ltd.

Chapter 3

Framing the issues in literacy education

Frances Christie and Ray Misson

The concept of literacy

Until very recent times, the custom in educational theory and discussion was to talk of the teaching of reading and writing, rather than the teaching of literacy. Reading and writing were seen as separate skills. Time-honoured practice, going back some centuries, required that students learn to read first, moving on to learn writing much later on. In practice, in the nineteenth century and even in the early years of [the twentieth] century, many educational programmes for children, particularly at the elementary level, concentrated on the teaching of reading only, requiring no more than that the children also learned to pen their names. There was a sense in which, in much educational practice, reading was often seen as the more significant skill. Writing gained more significance for those students fortunate to stay on at school for the secondary years.

From the fifteenth century on, a 'literate person' has been one who was acquainted with letters or with literature. The juxtaposition of the two terms is interesting: to be familiar with literature, one needed to know the alphabet, and this was a measure of one's status as an educated person. One who was 'illiterate' was necessarily ignorant of letters, and hence also of literature. But though the terms 'literate' and 'illiterate' were known and in use for several centuries, the term 'literacy' was not widely used. Teaching was understood to be about reading and writing, where these were seen as somewhat separate skills. Teacher education dates from the second half of the nineteenth century, and the first teacher training programmes in the English-speaking world attached a great deal of importance to preparing their trainee teachers for instructing the young in their letters. Instruction in one's letters for the greater majority of children in the elementary schools of the nineteenth century was about learning to recognise the alphabet, to be able to read improving works, including religious tracts, and perhaps to write one's name. But the term 'literacy' was not a term much in use, nor was it widely used in educational discussions for much of the first half of this century.

After the Second World War, a great many former colonies around the world became newly launched independent nations, and a priority for such nations very early on was to provide adequate educational opportunity for their children. Education was closely linked to the building of economic security. Bodies like the United Nations, and related agencies such as UNICEF and UNESCO have, in the postwar period, devoted large amounts of resources to educational provision in the developing countries. After the 1960s, international agencies began to develop programmes in 'functional literacy' – a term intended to capture a sense of a basic competence in reading and writing of a kind held to be sufficient for fostering efficient and informed workers.

The year 1990 was declared the International Literacy Year (ILY), sponsored by the United Nations. The fact that such a year was instituted speaks in itself for the worldwide significance that had come to be attached to possession of literacy. The ILY led to the development of many literacy programmes in the developing world, but it also had an impact in developed countries such as the UK, Australia and the USA, where additional money was spent on developing new policies to promote literacy.

Stimulated in part by initiatives like the ILY, the English-speaking countries have increasingly come to use the term 'literacy', both in official policy statements prepared by governments and in a great deal of educational theorising.

To take the issue of official government policy first, it is notable that, during the election that saw Blair lead the British Labour Party into office in 1997, he and his colleagues made educational provision, including provision of literacy programmes, a major electioneering theme. A Literacy Taskforce, appointed while the party was still in opposition, went to work on developing policies, and a new government White Paper, launched in 1997, stressed the importance of literacy teaching as a means of bringing about a renewal of purpose and commitment in British schools. In Australia, the Liberal Party came to office in 1996, and it too began to develop a range of policies intended to enhance the teaching of literacy in Australian schools. These included adoption of so-called 'literacy benchmarks' for gauging children's performance at different levels of schooling. Politicians of all political parties regularly allude to the importance of literacy, often linking success in it to the development of enhanced national prosperity.

Often, in fact, the apparent connection suggested between literacy and economic well-being is too simple. Possession of literacy will not in itself guarantee any individual the certainty of work, and it is naive to suggest that it will. However, it is also true that, in the contemporary world, any individual without literacy will probably be unemployed or, at best, obliged to take up one of the few, probably poorly paid, remaining occupations available that don't require literacy. The latter observation is important for a number of reasons, not least that it points to the profound social changes brought about this century because of the extension of literacy.

Literacy has genuinely changed the world, and it continues to change it in ways about which we are often not even very conscious. The sheer volume of printed materials available now in the world is of a size greater than at any time in human history. More and more information, knowledge, ideas, advice, literature and entertainment are available in the printed word. Add to this the awesome impact of information technology, the fact that we often don't even use the printed word at all these days, instead relying on digital means, and we begin to understand the remarkable changes to literacy in the modern world. The work of modern businesses, governments, educational systems, legal systems, health systems, and so on, is made possible because of our capacity to generate information in writing and to communicate it at speed both within our own communities, and around the world.

It is because of the profound changes in literacy this century, and because of the exciting possibilities many scholars see in discussing literacy and its role in pedagogy, that we have seen the upsurge in theorising about it, alluded to above. Literacy has proved to be a fertile field for a great deal of educational theory, leading to the publication of many books and journal articles about literacy, ways to define it, and ways to teach it. Many theorists have resisted notions of 'functional literacy', arguing instead for models of literacy that are in some sense more empowering of the individual. Hence the term 'critical literacy', associated with writers such as Giroux, Luke, Lankshear and Fairclough. This is a term we will look at in a little more detail below.

A number of other, increasingly metaphorical ways of using the term 'literacy' have appeared. When E. D. Hirsch, for example, writes about 'cultural literacy', he is referring to knowledge of particular valued cultural 'facts' (names of authors, names of places, basic philosophical terminology, etc.) that might be referred to in a text, and which writers should be able to expect the normally 'cultured' person to know. For his project of cultural literacy, these snippets of knowledge are seen almost as the equivalent of the letters in the alphabet in older notions of learning how to read, and schools are castigated for not having taught them to students. Others write of 'visual literacy', drawing attention to the facts (i) that the act of responding to and interpreting images of various kinds is itself a skill requiring tuition and cultivation, and (ii) that in a world of increasingly easy access to computers, students will all learn to create texts that exploit and blend the resources of verbal texts and images of many kinds. Other writers write of 'computer literacy', which is of course increasingly significant, given the growing impact of computers in schools, homes and workplaces, and the consequent need for most people nowadays to be able to understand and work with computer technology.

Overall, we would argue that the increasing frequency with which teachers and educational theorists have come to use the term 'literacy' in the second half of this century is both useful and important. It is a measure of the fact that they have come to see reading and writing as so intimately interrelated that we cannot understand the one without the other. Reading and writing are not discrete, isolable skills. Theorists and teachers alike have come to realise increasingly that the most successful teaching programmes will encourage students to move freely between reading and writing. The most successful reader is often also the most successful writer, and the best teaching programmes will guide students to draw on their skills in the one to develop their skills in the other. No doubt in any teaching programme there will be points at which teachers and students will need to give greater emphasis to either reading or writing, but it will be development of proficiency in both which is the measure of educational success.

Literacy truly is a remarkable phenomenon. Like oral language as well, we can think of literacy as a technology, as a kind of tool humans have learned to exploit in order to serve their many purposes. The advent of literacy many centuries ago began to change the very nature of the human societies that used it, opening new ways of constructing and ordering information, and making possible the development of new discoveries of many kinds. Literacy both changes the nature of human societies and is changed by them. As we fast approach the twenty-first century, it is already clear that literacy is again rapidly changing, bringing about other changes in the ways we construct and order information. In the process literacy change will no doubt open the way to many as yet unimagined means of constructing and communicating information. Whether all the changes made possible will be desirable is itself a very important question. So important is this question that it requires that teachers do all they can to develop students able to question, and able to discriminate between those developments worth preserving and those that should be challenged.

In a world in which change is commonplace, and rapid change apparently the norm, it is clear that education systems will need to assist students of the future to anticipate and deal with change. Among the many possible strategies needed to assist students to prepare will be the development of programmes that will equip them to understand literacy, its relationship to oral language, its infinite capacity for adaptation to make new meanings, and its significance as a social phenomenon. This last notion is particularly significant and deserves consideration in itself.

Literacy as a social phenomenon

If there is one major idea that colours the field of literacy in the late 1990s, it is that all language and literacy are social. In many ways, there is nothing new about this. Language is a social phenomenon through and through and has always been recognised as such. It obviously developed from a need to communicate, which necessarily presupposes some primitive social interactions. Language is a *sine qua non* of any human society. One would not want to deny our apelike ancestors, gibbering and gesturing in their caves, the dignity of having formed communities, but one cannot conceive of any genuinely human society that is not based on language. Language gives the ability to make absent things present for contemplation and discussion, the ability to manipulate ideas in subtle ways. It gives the capacity to execute communal actions on a large and complex scale that requires the means to plan, divide up responsibilities and monitor progress.

Literacy, like oral language, has always been seen as concerned with community too. Through the power of literacy to reach across time and space, society is all the more powerfully maintained and developed: innovation can be more easily shared, trade transactions can be recorded, a huge range of knowledge can be accessed, laws more easily enforced. Literacy is, rather more than language in general, particularly concerned with the reproduction of a society that is suitably skilled and/or properly moral.

Given all this, it may seem strange to insist that the distinctively new feature of literacy education in the past decade or so is a recognition of the social nature of language and literacy. The difference, of course, lies in the kind of social theory being used to frame the phenomenon. Sociology began to influence linguistic research strongly from the 1960s, providing a focus on such things as the importance of language in the building of social life, its role in the development of children as social beings, and the significance of language in institutions of socialisation such as schools. Social theorists as diverse as Berger and Luckmann, Mary Douglas, Basil Bernstein and Michael Halliday all drew attention to the significance of language in structuring and maintaining social life. During the 1980s, this awareness of the social nature of language flooded into the mainstream of literacy education, having been given tremendous impetus by influences as diverse as the writings of Paolo Freire, the rise of poststructuralist theory (perhaps particularly in its feminist uses), the work of later social theorists such as Michel Foucault and Pierre Bourdieu, and the development of cultural studies as a favoured model in many tertiary English departments. By now we have had almost a decade of conceptualising literacy within this sociocultural framework, and the influence of this framing is in no danger of waning. . . .

In popular discourse, literacy is important because it provides an educated workforce who can further the economic goals of the nation. Literacy, it is believed (however erroneously, as discussed above), gets one a job. While still dominant in the minds of many politicians and indeed much of the general public, this concern with the utilitarian skills of basic reading and writing tends, in the discourse of English teaching at least during a great deal of the century, to have taken second place to the concern with literacy as an instrument of self-improvement. Whereas in earlier centuries the aim of teaching literacy had frequently been seen as aiding moral development through enabling people to read the Bible, from Matthew Arnold on a similar moral work was considered to be being done by enabling people to read (or later write) creative texts.

The utilitarian and developmental traditions were often at swords drawn, but they had one thing in common: neither was working within a social theory that could illuminate what literacy teaching was doing as a social practice. With the explosion of social and cultural theory in the 1970s and 1980s the way education, and particularly literacy teaching, worked to reproduce the dominant society became apparent and, to many, a matter of concern. Rather than just being concerned with literacy as a social phenomenon, literacy teaching gained a political edge. There came to be a real concern for using literacy teaching as a means to influence society, and particularly to overcome social inequity, whether by trying to ensure that all students had equal access to the kinds of literacy that mattered, or by exposing the workings of ideology in language.

Whereas language and literacy had previously been seen as being produced from an essential private self, the very existence of a self outside language and society was now being questioned. This stemmed from a much fuller theory of how language and texts operate to position people in a certain ideology and way of seeing the world. This led to the notion that, in fact, people might be constituted out of these ways of seeing the world, and so, in a very real sense, might be constructed within language. Our very identity, it appeared, might be made up of the language we used, the texts we produced and read.

If language was seen as central to making human beings what they are, it was also fundamental to the development of society and to keeping the society functioning smoothly, which, depending on one's political persuasions, might or might not be a good thing. The way in which power circulated in society through language became clearer. The complex ways in which social institutions depended on language, and the ways in which they shaped language to their particular purposes, became apparent.

Thus, while language could still certainly be seen as an instrument of empowerment that enabled people to operate productively in their social and personal lives, it could also be seen as the very thing that was constricting them into certain ways of thinking and being, and so seen as the shackles keeping them bound. Literacy teaching had suddenly become problematic. In terms of literacy 'skills', the work of teachers could be seen as fundamentally important in providing students with the means whereby they would have choices and could take their wished-for, valued and ideally remunerative place in the workforce and in society. On the other hand, it could simply be seen in the rather unflattering light of providing the next batch of fodder for offices and factories, with a few more able students being prepared for the heights of management, or at least of being the manager's secretary. In terms of inner self-development, teachers could be seen as giving students the means of independent thought and a richer understanding of the complexities of how their social world, indeed their very being, is constituted, but they could also be seen as simply reproducing in students the dominant ideologies of the society with the effect of making them docile and compliant cogs in the social machine.

Much of the theorising about literacy teaching in the last decade or so has been concerned to ensure that the positive outcomes are achieved and the negative ones avoided. Thus teachers often see themselves as trying to give all students access to the kinds of language and literacy that are the instruments of power, thereby enabling the less fortunate to overcome their disadvantage and achieve success. They also often see themselves as trying to expose the social limitations and the constrictions of thinking imposed by language, enabling the students to see how they are being positioned and limited, thereby hopefully enabling them to resist their enslavement.

Fundamental to both ways of working is the aim of making explicit how texts are working both in themselves and as instruments of social purposes. However, the very notion of a text has itself become problematic, and before we can look at some major current traditions of working with texts, we need to examine the question of what exactly a text might be.

Text and context

The term 'text' actually comes from the Latin word for weaving: it refers to words and sentences woven together to create a single whole, one with 'texture'. We can see then that, even in its origins, the term is metaphorical. Just as a piece of cloth or a tapestry can be said to be woven together to create the finished piece, so too we can think of sets of language items working together to create the coherent thing we call a text. The word 'context' has an equally interesting and metaphorical history. It meant originally 'being woven together', where the prefix 'con' carried the sense of being together. Over the passage of the centuries it has come to refer to those elements that accompany a text, giving it meaning. The elements may be partly a feature of the physical setting in which language is used; but more importantly, they are also social and psychological, and part of the shared understandings that people need to have in order to create and/or comprehend a text and its purpose.

Putting together what all this suggests about text and context, we can see that any text is said to be comprehensible only in terms of the context which gives rise to it. Strictly, many linguists at least would say, context is known only because of the text which gives it life. Conversely, text is only known because of the context which makes it relevant.

Overall, we can say that a text is identifiable because it is meaningful: that is to say, it is a coherent passage of language in which some meaning is made. Texts may be of very variable lengths. Thus, a public notice saying 'Keep off the grass' is as much a text as a very long novel. The criterion for judging a text its always its coherence: does it 'hang together' in some way to build meaning?

While all that has been said so far relates to the notion of text as linguists use the term, it is important to note that today the term is used in many other related ways. This is of interest because it suggests that metaphor is again at work, as scholars and literacy theorists adopt the term to serve their purposes in the advancement of knowledge. Quite commonly today, for example, theorists write of visual images as texts. A visual text is said to differ from a verbal text, and this can be of interest for educational reasons. . . .

All these many ways of thinking about texts today arise from a related interest in another study: namely the study of semiotics. This is, literally, the study of the signs and symbols with which meanings are made. When we study meaning-making in humans, we study their semiosis: the various symbolic systems they use in order to construct their sense of the world, the multitude of relationships in which they engage, and the many forms of knowledge available to them. There are in fact many semiotic systems found in the contemporary world. Language itself is the principal semiotic system available to humans, but it always operates along with many other semiotic systems, such as music, dance, the visual arts, film, photography, dress and so on. All these semiotic systems can be said to involve the creation of texts in which significant meanings are made.

Frameworks for literacy teaching

The writers [referred to in this chapter] all work from a close consideration of the texts students read and write, just as they all subscribe to the notion that the most pertinent insights into literacy learning come from acknowledging its sociocultural framing. However, they are largely working within two different traditions. The one operates within a linguistic framework largely supplied by systemic functional (SF) linguistics developed by Halliday, Hasan, Martin and Matthiessen, to name a number of theorists. The other tradition works within a framework of poststructuralist cultural and social theory drawing on a range of theorists such as Foucault, Bourdieu, Althusser and Kristeva as filtered through the work of educationists such as Freire, Giroux and James Paul Gee. This latter tradition can be given the loose name of critical literacy. The two traditions are very far from opposed to each other. . . . They can be linked together, and have been in the work of such writers as Fairclough, Kress and Lemke, and most significantly in Australia in the report of the team that made recommendations to government on strategies for the preservice preparation of teachers to teach English literacy (Christie *et al.*, 1991).

Systemic functional linguistics

The crucial aspect of SF linguistics for educational purposes lies in its functional nature. Rather than think of language as rules, as some traditions of language study have proposed, SF theory proposes that we think of language as offering systems of choices for making meaning. The choices we learn to make are functional in that they are relevant to building different kinds of meanings. The choices are not conscious (though some of them can be brought to consciousness in teaching–learning activities) and the choices are to do with the particular contexts of use in which people operate. Thus, for example, if one is in a job interview, the language choices one employs are rather different from those made, say, with family and friends over the dinner table, or perhaps with one's colleagues in a work situation. The language choices made in any context of use are said to be choices with respect to register. Just as a singer changes register from time to time, so too, metaphorically, a language user is said to change register depending upon the context.

The choices with respect to register are to do with the particular social activity (*field*), the relationship between the participants in the interaction (*tenor*), and the manner of communication (*mode*). For example, the language differs depending on whether it is spoken or written, whether it is face to face, or distant, whether it accompanies pictorial information or not, and so on. In the late twentieth century the modes of language construction have become very various indeed. Language choices with respect to register are said to be made in terms of the ideational metafunction (i.e. choices that build the social activity and/or 'content' being constructed), the interpersonal metafunction (i.e. the choices that build the relationship), and the textual metafunction (i.e. the choices that organise the language into messages).

The educational relevance claimed for all this is that it is argued that when students in schools learn to use language they are learning to make relevant language choices for the construction of important kinds of meaning. The various school subjects or 'disciplines' represent ways of building information and ways of reasoning with that information. In order to understand the different kinds of information and their associated methods of reasoning, students must learn the language patterns in which these things are encoded. They must also learn the various text types or genres in which the knowledge is constructed.

A great deal of recent work in the SF tradition has been devoted to identifying the text types or genres students learn to read and write in order to be successful in their school learning. Genres are said to be structured in particular ways to achieve their purposes. In fact, a genre is said to be a 'staged, goal-oriented social process'. As it unfolds, its various stages all have a role in the organisation of information and experience. A procedural genre, of the kind found in a recipe book, for example, represents experience in a different set of stages from, say, an argumentative genre about the causes of pollution. Stories – and there are many kinds of stories – can also be shown to have particular sets of stages through which they unfold, entertaining and enlightening their readers or their listeners.

Genres can be said to be prototypical. They represent particular ways of organising and communicating meaning. Once people are familiar with them and competent in manipulating them, they can play around with them, often making subtle changes. Good writers in fact often play with the genre, but they do it, of course, against a background of the reader's expectations of the more standard pattern. Like other social phenomena, genres change over time, though perhaps written genres are more conservative than are spoken ones, so that they may change more slowly. Genres are not culture free, so whatever may be said of genres in English has no necessary relationship to what might be said of genres in other languages. Even within the international community of English speakers, different cultures will use the linguistic and textual resources available to them in somewhat different ways.

Genre theorists argue that it is because genres are so important for the building and communication of written information in particular, especially in educational settings, that they need to be the subject of overt teaching and learning. Some consciousness of the genre and its structure assists the student to become more competent in its uses. Such consciousness is also said to be an important step towards developing students able to critique a genre and the values and ideas it represents. It is in the latter sense that genre theory can connect with and, indeed, learn from, many of the perspectives drawn from critical literacy.

Critical literacy

Critical literacy is a pedagogy largely concerned with making explicit the ideological workings of texts. It is probably true that its analytical techniques are less specific and precise than those of the genre theorists, but it is probably also true that the theorisation of how ideology works through texts and how it creates the mind-set or subjectivity of the reader is more subtle and complex than that found in most genre theory. Indeed the subtlety and complexity of a great deal of the thought underlying critical literacy may well be something of a liability to it (just as the complexities of systemic functional grammar may prove inhibiting to those approaching work on texts within that tradition). Poststructuralist thought is not easy, particularly since much of it is counterintuitive and asks us to be suspicious of the obvious and natural. Even more difficult is its refusal to take the self as a single, stable grounding for experiential knowledge. However, the insights into the nature of textuality and its close connections with how we are constituted as social beings provide a powerful agenda for classroom work.

Ideology, in much current thinking stemming largely from the work of Louis Althusser, works through representing the world to us in certain ways. Texts give us representations of the world that we acquiesce in because they correspond to our desires or because they show us our place in the larger scheme of things. It is thus we become the subject of ideology. We are the subject in two ways: the first in that we are subjected to the ideology of the representation, the second in that the ideology comes to constitute our subjectivity, our way of experiencing the world subjectively. We see an advertisement for coffee with an obviously well-off couple sitting down in their beautifully designed, warmly lit apartment, enjoying a quiet moment at the end of the day as they sip their coffee. Not only do we see this image as desirable, but we see ourselves as potentially inhabiting the image, being offered the image through the product. We consent to the kind of society and belief systems that aim at and produce these images of middle-class consumerist, heterosexual contentment.

The main thrust of much work in critical literacy is towards analysing representations to make apparent the inherent ideology. Its aim is to render explicit the belief systems inscribed in the text and so negate their power. Since it is thought that ideology is at its most powerful when the representations through which it is being transmitted seem most natural, to denaturalise the naturalised image and show its constructedness and its tendentiousness is thought to defuse the ideology and make the student safe from its imposition. This does undoubtedly genuinely happen in some cases, but there must be some considerable doubt that the process is usually quite as simply effective as that. Ideology infiltrates our minds in particularly subtle and multifarious ways, and making explicit some of its workings does not necessarily free us from its multiplicitous grasp.

People are seen as being largely defined by their positioning in terms of class, ethnicity and gender. Much of the work in the classroom therefore is concerned to teach against limitations imposed on people in terms of one or other of these systems. This is done through analysis of the ideological implications of texts, examining how disadvantage is reproduced by constructing images that assume that certain qualities or ways of life are 'natural' to a certain group, or by looking at what is excluded from or not acknowledged in the way that a text is talking about a particular phenomenon. Excellent work has been done on teaching against discrimination, although it is worth noting that this, like anything else in the classroom, can become a rather empty routine. The students can produce the expected answer and mouth the appropriate sentiments without any notable impact on their actual attitudes.

The aim of critical literacy, in a phrase that stems from the work of Paolo Freire, is to enable students to 'read the word and the world' (Freire and Macedo, 1987). By doing this, they will come to a greater state of consciousness of how their lives are being limited by the society in which they are living, and there will thus be opened up for them the possibility of transforming, indeed liberating, both themselves and the society. The view thus baldly stated is undoubtedly both overly idealistic and rather simplistic in its conception of individual psychology and of how society works, but in its essential thrust it does provide a serious, attractive and challenging vision of what literacy teaching might achieve.

References

Christie, F. et al. (1991) Teaching English Literacy: A Project of National Significance on the Preservice Preparation of Teachers for Teaching English Literacy, Darwin: Centre for Studies of Language in Education.

Freire, P. and Macedo, D. (1987) Literacy: Reading the Word and the World, Massachusetts: Bergin and Garvey.

Source

This is an edited version of a chapter previously published in F. Christie and R. Misson (eds) *Literacy and Schooling*. 1998. Reproduced by permission of Taylor & Francis Ltd.

Part 2

Are there increasing difficulties with literacy?

Chapter 4

Explanations of the current international 'literacy crises'

Anthony R. Welch and Peter Freebody

Introduction

The almost archetypal innocence of a scene in which one person helps another learn to read or write is matched by the ideological innocence claimed by the disciplines that once exclusively informed that scene – Psychology, Human Development, and Educational Measurement. But the study of reading and writing has become a political pursuit. The most significant events in recent theorizing about reading and writing have been the applications of critical perspectives from sociology, anthropology, history, politics, linguistics, and economics to the study of literacy and literacy education. These perspectives, exemplified in anthologies edited by Baker and Luke (1991), Street (1993), and Wagner (1987), have not only contextualized but have often countered the three traditionally dominant accounts of literacy: the growth-through-heritage account, the cognitive-psychological account, and the skills-and-measurement account (Gilbert, 1989, see especially Chapter 1).

The perspectives on literacy arising from this comparatively new cross-disciplinary attention in turn provide the grounds for critiques of both technicist and progressivist accounts of literacy education. The Great Debate between so-called skills and meaning approaches to literacy teaching (presented by Chall, 1967) has been put into its historical and ideological context (Christie, 1990), and the ways in which it has blinkered the exploration of literacy practices are beginning to be documented (Gee, 1990).

The increasingly prevalent use of the term 'literacy practices' instead of the massifying term 'literacy' reflects the variety of social activities to which literacy is crucial, and the interconnections of literacy activities with other cultural practices in specific settings such as schools, factories, and churches (Grillo, 1989). The term 'literacy practices' also signifies that it is daily material activities that are the topics of literacy study, rather than abstractions drawn from psychological or institutional theorizing.

It is fast becoming commonplace, therefore, to assert that literacy practices are not ideologically innocent. They do not merely meet cultural and individual needs: rather they shape both the ways in which cultures develop socio-economic arrangements and the ways in which literate individuals develop 'adaptive' psychological dispositions and cognitive strategies (Ong, 1982, presents the strongest case for the influence of literacy on conscious-ness). In a literate culture, neither inter- nor intra-personal conditions are unaffected by the technologies of literacy. This idea – which may be expressed by the slogan that literacy practices are culturally and psychologically emer-gent – is a central scaffold that is taken for granted by a growing number of scholars, educators, and policy-makers. The aim . . . is simply to give body to that scaffold. . . .

Understanding the process by which literacy practices come to be the matter of ideology, as much as they are its vehicle, depends partly on understanding the idea of 'selective tradition' (Williams, 1977). Of the many possible forms in which literacy activities could develop and be put to work (in schools, offices, factories, churches, government departments, homes, and so on), some are recruited by a culture and others are ignored or marginalized. The successful forms themselves, by the psychological attributes and interpersonal relations they encourage, highlight and value some ways of behaving, using language, and knowing, and marginalize others. It is this understanding . . . that most directly challenges the assumption that literacy is exhaustively defined as a set of psychological skills, and is thus measurable, transportable, and packagable.

Connecting literacy and power through 'standards'

Literacy education is at the centre of debates about society and instruction, in and out of school. As such it is a site from which to view the shifting fortunes of contesting interests: public and private, working class and bour-geois, male and female, host communities and ethnic minorities, and, increasingly, school, work-place, and market-place. Further, these contests often target the issue of standards of literacy, rather than, say, the methods or materials of literacy education. Over many decades, perhaps most forcefully in Western nations, there have recurred assertions that school and community standards in literacy are falling and that this decline has direct consequences for economic performance and cultural levels as a starting point, then, it seems important to explore and critique the major hypothetical explanations for these assertions about literacy standards, as a way of providing the broad context for the contributions that follow.

Many arguments about literacy standards can be seen as inflections of one or more of the following four hypotheses:

1. *The Slide Hypothesis*: That the rhetoric of concern about literacy standards is indeed a result of genuinely declining standards in the recent past in the literacy competence of school students or perhaps of nations or sub-national groups.
2. *The Demands Hypothesis*: That, while competences have not declined, the requisite literacy competences for effective civil, social, and cultural func-tioning have increased and diversified in our society.

3. *The Credentials Hypothesis*: That, while neither competences nor cultural demands may have changed significantly, the increased competitiveness of the labour market, and/or the decline in work-force numbers of low-literacy occupations in a society have led to an increase in the necessary formal credentials for any given job. And

4. *The Invention Hypothesis*: That the rhetoric of concern about literacy standards is, like the concept of 'standards' itself, a confection, designed or at least functioning to undermine certain progressive or socially powerful educational trends that have developed in the recent past.

We will now deal with each of these hypotheses briefly. . . .

The Slide Hypothesis

What empirical support is there for the hypothesis that there has been a recent and general decline in literacy competences in recent years? We need first to consider some methodological issues involved in possible answers to this question. It turns out that serious problems arise for researchers aiming to document generalizations about changes over time in literacy competence. Attempts to plot performance rates for groups of people over a period of time must deal with a shifting average. The establishment over time of stable levels of literacy performance with changing samples of people becomes possible only in the most abstract terms.

Comparing the performance levels, for example, of a certain group of same-aged students over a long period assumes that the composition of the samples on the multiple occasions has remained stable on variables other than age that may relate to literacy performance (such as socio-economic status or ethnicity), such that all samples in fact represent the same hypothetical population. Assessing over time the literacy activities of a group standardized by the fact that they have successively worked at the same job calls into play similar questions about the stability of the work-force (first language status or educational levels) in that position at differing points in the economic or cultural history of that society. It is clear that in periods of migration or economic change the critical assumptions cannot be made safely in either of these cases. In addition, statistical and analytic capabilities and fashions among the research community change over time. Confidence in item reliability, scoring reliability, comparability in testing conditions, and the nature of the statistical analyses applied are all issues which bear directly on the ability to compare literacy performance across extensive periods of time. These issues assume particular importance when it is considered that the sample sizes used in such survey test programmes are usually sufficiently large to allow small absolute differences in performance levels to assume statistical significance.

These are some of the doubts arising just on the grounds of sampling and measurement that trouble the Slide Hypothesis. There are further significant theoretical questions that could be pursued: about the relevance of test materials to the actual literacy practices that have developed in the school or the work-place, and about the attendant difficulties and biases introduced by the incursion of the school's form of 'read-remember-comment' literacy into contexts other than school (Heap, 1987).

All of these constraints upon reliability and validity of empirical studies about standards of literacy over time need to be kept in mind when considering the available research, in particular on the matter of the onus of proof. In a statistical sense, the null hypothesis is that standards of literacy performance among comparable groups of people have not changed. In the light of changing school clienteles, changing pedagogies, and changing methods of performance assessment, the difficult task of proving that standards have either increased or decreased lies squarely with those who wish to argue for an observable change in performance levels. That is, until proven wrong, we need to assume that general standards of literacy have remained precisely stable over time.

In addition, some account needs to be offered that would describe the network of factors functioning to cause a genuine decline in text-management competences among members of a society or groups within it. These accounts themselves can then be interrogated for evidence of recruitment in ideological agenda. The following are a sample of such accounts:

1. Certain class-reproductive or ethnocentric pedagogical methods may become prevalent which, in subsequent times of economic contraction or in times in which previously disenfranchised groups come to be offered more complete educational access, result in overall sample decline (see Berstein, 1975).
2. Governments may allow salaries and conditions of teachers to decline in comparison with comparable occupations such that the literacy experiences and competences of beginning teachers change, and/or available literacy materials for school and work-place literacy programs diminish.
3. Political pressure may be placed upon teachers and school authorities to respond to certain apparent market forces by emphasizing areas of curriculum that are, again apparently, less demanding of literacy competence in their study and assessment.
4. A process of migration of traditional groups to urban, Westernized commercial centres may initially bring with it an increase in the proportion of the population engaged in white-collar occupations. Thus these migrants encounter increased textual demands, and subsequently more of their children attend school. Later, this migration may subside or in fact be reversed such that a rural reconstruction is attempted and earlier increases in overall community literacy competences are halted or reversed.

All of these accounts implicate genuinely changing socio-economic conditions, or changing perceptions in the relationship between literacy education and cultural and economic development. However, the Slide Hypothesis is generally presented in a functional vacuum, as if teachers or students were wilfully derelict either in their appreciation of the value of literacy or in their competence to teach and learn it. Such characterizations hail the ideologies of both class and generation, and 'literacy', as an unquestioned commodity, comes to be used as a legitimator of class and generational privilege.

Thus there are serious empirical problems in substantiating the Slide Hypothesis, and the explanations that are generally called upon to account for this slippery phenomenon are generally ideologically motivated. In the face of a lack of reliable empirical support, the methodologically appropriate move is to 'fail to reject the hypothesis of no change'. Nonetheless, the point is worth making that, as this 'no change' discourse finds its way into debates about literacy standards, it does itself have ideological significance and practical consequences, especially for groups traditionally marginalized by educational practices.

In the light of the difficulties of establishing a 'slide', a case can be reconstituted in terms of a 'gap': the apparently increasing gap between the literacy competences of many people and the genuine and proper demands that societies are coming to place on those competences. That line of argument can now be developed.

The Demands Hypothesis

The Demands Hypothesis states that, while literacy performance standards may or may not have decreased, it is the social and cultural expectations of literacy performance that have increased markedly in recent times. That is, society demands increasing levels of literacy performance and the school system is increasingly missing this moving target.

Useful summaries of the historical changes in literacy expectations over time have been attempted by, for example, Graff (1986, 1987) and Resnick and Resnick (1977). As an example, Resnick and Resnick identified three major models relating to literacy expectations evident in European history: the Protestant-religious model, in which literacy skills were developed primarily for the memorization of religious writing; the elite-technical model, which emphasized the use of literacy for the development of theoretical knowledge and technical problem-solving; and the civic-national model in which literacy was used primarily to instil civic goals and national identity and pride, and which demanded understanding of familiar and routine textual material. Drawing upon historical policy documents in the United States, Resnick and Resnick claimed that it is only within the context of a growing civic-national model following the First World War that the demand for understanding and the use of textual information in new contexts developed. With reference to the USA, they claimed (p. 379) that to the extent that people are disturbed about literacy levels it is because they are applying an inappropriately demanding criterion and construing the problem not in that light but as less capable student performance. Compared with previous generations, increasingly sophisticated pedagogical techniques are required before the goal of having all students and workers 'fully literate' in these comparatively new terms can be attained.

It is useful to identify two inflections of the Demands Hypothesis. First this hypothesis may be taken to mean that the functional demands on literacy performance have increased because individuals need to cope with increasingly complex bureaucracies and job specifications, both of which call upon increasingly complex and specialized forms of dealing with written texts. A second version of the hypothesis is that many societies are demanding or at least aspiring to a more culturally literate community than previously – a community that reads 'good literature', that perhaps writes in a greater diversity of genres, and that can respond more sensitively to literary works.

With respect to the first version of the Demands Hypothesis mentioned above, the civil-functioning aspect, the research of Mikulecky (1981) is pertinent. He examined the literacy demands placed upon industrial workers and high school students, concluding that technical workers faced more difficult job-related literacy demands than did students in technical schools; further that workers reported reading more for job-related tasks than did students for school-related tasks, with workers reading an average of 143 minutes per day compared to 98 minutes for high school students and 135 minutes for technical school students (pp. 408–409). Mikulecky also revealed that the workers read more difficult materials than did the students, with even blue collar manuals and directions averaging a Year 10 level of difficulty.

So the civil-functional Demands Hypothesis may not apply evenly across various levels of the work-force. That is, we would have expected in the past that white collar jobs as well as professional employment would necessarily entail Year 10 or better levels of literacy performance, but we might not have expected in the past that semi-skilled, unskilled or blue collar workers would necessarily face these demands. Similarly, the cultural version of the Demands Hypothesis has a social-class dimension: current notions concerning the benefits of literacy in terms of personal enrichment have led to pressure on teachers (of children and adults) to believe that all members of the community should appreciate literary works acceptable in the canon of the ruling culture, when the function of that canon is to set itself in contradistinction to mass culture. The ensuing community 'disappointment' becomes a public feature of class-reproductive discourse (Bourdieu, 1983).

The Demands Hypothesis is difficult to establish empirically over the short term. Resnick and Resnick and, in a less direct way, Eisenstein (1979) have documented literacy demands and expectations that have increased dramatically and changed in their nature over the centuries. But it has yet to be documented that the genuine demands on literacy practices, either in civil-functional or cultural terms, have shifted radically in the recent past. What may be more readily documented is the phenomenon that formal credentials for attaining jobs of various kinds in any given society have increased. A most common impression, at least in many Western nations, seems to be that many of the so-called unskilled jobs that lower school achievers formerly filled are disappearing or have come to require formally some enhanced literacy and numeracy competences, especially in urban centres. This is in part then a matter of credentialing, a different kind of explanation.

The Credentials Hypothesis

This third thesis draws attention to the influence of rising expectations in the job market. The point of this hypothesis is that some societies may allow or encourage their school systems to become closely articulated to literacy criteria driven by competitive industrial selection. That is, this hypothesis draws attention to the economic and cultural conditions (market forces and cultural aspirations) that lead to increases in the formal requirements of certain occupations, independently of the degree to which changing job demands genuinely call for more or different forms of literacy competence.

Dore (1976), for example, has cited cases in which students pursue increasingly higher credentials in order to keep one step ahead of competitors for job places. He argued that in Third World nations this can be catastrophic for certain groups; but that it continues to form a popular option to large numbers of people drawn by the notion of earning more in the 'modern', commercial sector of the economy than could otherwise be earned in the traditional sectors.

> In the late sixties, the Ugandan graduate just entering the civil service could expect his (sic) income to be fifty times the average income in Uganda. Even in India, after a much longer period of independence under governments with a much more explicitly egalitarian philosophy, the ratio was twelve to one.
>
> (Dore, 1976, p. 3)

Increases and change in literacy practices, among individuals and social groups, have featured prominently in movements into commercial sectors. In some nations a job in the civil service calls for competence in selective literacy practices; at a national level, research in the 1960s appeared to give added strength to the simple 'human capital' position – that increases in literacy performance were causally and directly involved in increases in general affluence. In Bowman (1968), for example, it is shown that, in a purely correlational sense, the richest countries showed the highest literacy levels, and the poorest the lowest.

The outcomes of a belief in the human-capital model of literacy (and education generally) in promoting Third World economic development have been in some cases damaging. It has been used to legitimate the substantial growth of educational systems, often well in excess of the capacity of economies to absorb 'school-educated' labour in these quantities. Further, it has been argued that the economic advantages that accrue to individuals or groups as a result of increased or broadened literacy competences can, depending on other socio-economic conditions, be discriminatory: that the most advantaged groups in society gain most from rising standards of literacy, and that this further widens the social and economic gap between, perhaps, rich and poor, or rural and urban, or male and female (Soltow and Stevens, 1981; Fuller, Edwards and Gorman, 1987).

Especially, but not only in the Third World, employers were witness to a process whereby increased levels of education were called upon to secure particular jobs. Where previously a primary education certificate was adequate, now several years of secondary schooling became necessary. Even in nations that attempted to deal explicitly with this problem, such as Sri Lanka, India, and some parts of Africa and Latin America, the competition for credentials has increased. Because Western-style schooling has in these nations grown faster than the 'modern' commercial sector, an educated and no doubt frustrated cohort of unemployed has developed (Oxenham, 1984, p. 11). The issue then compounds: in both Third World and developed nations a surplus of educated individuals has meant that, in an increasingly competitive labour market, employers can afford to be more and more selective. There has grown an increasing divergence between the level of competence that is appropriate for a particular job and that which could be commanded. Thus some people with adequate competences are pushed out of a given level of the job market, with the necessary justification that their literacy competences are inadequate. In this way the credential market, independently of any documentable increases in the demands attached to a job, creates a rhetoric of falling literacy standards.

Viewed from this perspective, the literacy crisis may be something of a confection. Certain groups in all societies have been ill-served by formal schooling since its development, partly because of the comparative cultural and economic position of teaching as a job, and the consequent ready recruitment of educational practices as displays of ruling culture. The literacy competences of these groups have always been different from and lower than more privileged groups, and these competences in turn become a pivotal concept in student-centred legitimations of class reproduction. In this view the most parsimonious and powerful explanation for current concerns in many societies about literacy competences is not to do with job demands genuinely requiring increased credentials, but rather with the shifting configuration of cultural, economic, and political factors that give rise to the occasional need to confect a literacy crisis.

The Invention Hypothesis

It has been suggested that the contemporary 'literacy crisis', particularly as it is enacted in advanced industrial states, is largely an invention, at least in its most common inflections. If so, what might be its origins? Why has talk of a crisis surfaced at this time in many societies, and what does it signify? Are there correlative arguments about the nature of schooling and society which are associated with particular interest groups? What sort of 'standards' and 'crises' are these?

Using Canada as an example, Willinsky (1988) has pointed to the ways in which the discourse of literacy crisis has been constructed in recent years. His example is worth some close consideration. In Canada an important stimulus for 'crisis' discourse was the Southam Literacy Survey, sponsored by a group of newspapers and given prominence in 1987. This survey, claiming much higher rates of illiteracy than had been found previously, was sensationalized in the press with front-page headlines such as 'Survey Rates Five Million Canadians Illiterate'. The outcomes of the survey included the establishment of a Secretariat of Illiteracy by the Canadian Government, a formal, institutional statement of the 'problem of illiteracy'. Commenting on the Southam survey, Willinsky (p. 9) claimed that, among the panel selected as representing the community, which was to devise a standard test for literacy, there was no consensus as to how literacy was to be defined or assessed. A supposedly liberal standard nonetheless resulted in one in four Canadians being labelled illiterate, although the vast majority of respondents reported spending time each day reading the newspaper. The survey did not feel shy in allocating blame for the allegedly large numbers of Canadian illiterates it discerned. Some journalists in reporting the results imputed the poor levels to both liberal immigration policies and a 'flawed education system' (p. 12). The schools were accused of adding 100,000 extra illiterates to the Canadian population each year.

What is remarkable here is the ready ascription of the causes of the 'crisis' to areas of societal policy and practice about which there was long-standing debate in Canadian society, notably about workers, immigrants, and the 'Back to Basics' school curriculum. In these ways research programmes can be recruited to further marginalize certain segments of society, and to legitimate reactionary educational agenda. In the Southam case, the survey's results functioned to reaffirm nostalgic and reactionary industrial and educational values, evoking a past age in which curricular knowledge was supposedly more certain and social structures were more stable.

The recruitment of such surveys in these agendas is facilitated by the fact that typically the survey developers, as in the Southam example, have tended to adopt a technicist definition of literacy as that minimum level of competence necessary for 'public efficiency and civic function' (Heap, 1987; Willinsky, 1988). De Castell, Luke and Egan (1986) have shown how technicist approaches have underpinned the principal models of literacy in North America this century. Such models allow only an analytic, reductive notion of universal literacy competences. Thus they afford not only standardized and contextually transportable tests but also close and apparently objective monitoring by teachers, government departments and employer bodies. In much of the discourse . . . technical and economic progress are seen to demand rising standards of these particular forms of literacy for all.

As a further example, in the USA the discourse of 'literacy crisis' displays features of invention and recruitment in reactionary agenda. The publication of A Nation at Risk (National Commission on Excellence in Education, 1983) did more than assert that educational standards were falling: it also used the device of literacy standards to position the schools as scapegoats for perceived national failings in the international economic stakes. The focus is placed unproblematically but squarely on the schools at the outset of the book at which point they are described as the 'cause' that 'undergirds American prosperity, security and civility' (p. 5).

So part of the explanation for the appearance of this powerful rhetorical device of literacy standards is the changing economic and political contexts. The current American rhetoric is similar to that which arose there in the late 1950s. Then there was a widespread fear that the USA was about to lose its technological lead to the USSR, a fear symbolized by the successful launch of the first Soviet spacecraft in 1957. There was considerable media attention given to the superiority of the Soviet educational system, widely assumed to be the principal reason for the new-found technological superiority of that nation. Much of the criticism for the alleged failure of the American scientific and technological communities was levelled at the American schooling system, which was charged with producing a nation of illiterates and innumerates (Barzun, 1959).

In the 'Sputnik era' publications with titles such as *Why Johnny Can't Read* (Flesch, 1955), *Teaching Johnny to Read* (Flesch, 1956), *Educational Wastelands* (Bestor, 1953), *Crisis in Education* (Bell, 1949) and *What Ivan Knows that Johnny Doesn't* (Trace, 1961) enjoyed high public profile. In the early and mid 1980s Cold War rhetoric was once more prevalent in the USA, but on this occasion the focus of American economic anxiety was Japan. The effect of this apprehension, however, was the same – an increase in the use of the icon of literacy and numeracy standards, in reductive terms, to attack American schools.

None of this is to deny the individual, social and economic costs of illiteracy. It is rather to assert that analysis of and discourse about 'standards' cannot be divorced from contemporary social and economic changes. . . . It is not uncommon for a crisis of the state to be exported onto schooling systems, such that they are, at all levels from elementary school to university, under pressure from governing ministries, industry, and the general public. (This phenomenon has been pointed out by others, such as Apple, 1986, and Welch, 1991, in different cultural contexts.) Ironically this pressure has often been accompanied by the withdrawal of funding support for public education, thus widening the gap in educational levels between bourgeois and working class, host and minority, and rural and urban sectors of society. . . . [T]here are parallels in the disparities between nations, in that the literacy gap between First and Third World countries is likely to widen.

[There are many] different ways in which nations deal with internal and external pressures to enhance their 'literacy education effort' in the schools and work-places. Much discursive work is put, in some cases, into apportioning fault for inadequate performance levels, elsewhere into convincing communities of a simple version of the human-capital view of literacy practices, and yet elsewhere into offsetting claims about the destructive effects of imported literacy education campaigns on indigenous ways of social and intellectual life. The common element in these various efforts draws attention to the principal motif . . . that is the motivation to develop a critical understanding of literacy practices through an analysis of their material and visible relations to knowledge, culture, and power.

References

Apple, M. (1986) *Teachers and Texts: Political Economy and Class and Gender Relations in Education*, London, Routledge and Kegan Paul.

Baker, C.D. and Luke, A. (1991) *Toward a Critical Sociology of Reading Pedagogy*, Amsterdam/Philadelphia, John Benjamins.

Barzun, J. (1959) *The House of Intellect*, New York, Harper and Brothers.

Bell, B. (1949) *Crisis in Education: A Challenge to American Complacency*, New York, Whittlesey House.

Bernstein, B. (1975) *Class, Codes and Control*, Vol. 3, London, Routledge and Kegan Paul.

Bestor, A. (1953) *Educational Wastelands*, Urbana, University of Illinois Press.

Bourdieu, P. (1983) *Distinction: A Social Critique of the Judgement of Taste*, London, Routledge and Kegan Paul.

Bowman, M. (ed.) (1968) *Readings in the Economics of Education*, Paris, UNESCO.

Chall, J.S. (1967) *Learning to Read: The Great Debate*, New York, McGraw Hill.

Christie, F. (1990) 'The changing face of literacy', in Christie, F. (ed.) *Literacy for a Changing World*, Hawthorn, Victoria, Australian Council for Educational Research, pp. 1–25.

Davis, A. (1981) *Women, Race and Class*, New York, Random House.

De Castell, S., Luke, A. and Egan, K. (eds) (1986) *Literacy, Society and Schooling*, Cambridge, Cambridge University Press.

Dore, R. (1976) *The Diploma Disease: Education, Qualification and Development*, London, Allen and Unwin.

Eisenstein, E. (1979) *The Printing Press as an Agent of Change*, 2 Vols., Cambridge, Cambridge University Press.

Flesch, R. (1955) *Why Johnny Can't Read*, New York, Harper and Brothers.

Flesch, R. (1956) *Teaching Johnny to Read*, New York, Grosset and Dunlap.

Fuller, B., Edwards, J. and Gorman, K. (1987) 'Does rising literacy spark economic growth? Commercial expansion in Mexico', in Wagner, D. (ed.) *The Future of Literacy in a Changing World*, New York, Pergamon Press, pp. 319–40.

Gee, J.P. (1990) *Social Linguistics and Literacies: Ideology in Discourses*, London, Falmer Press.

Gilbert, P. (1989) *Writing, Schooling, and Deconstruction: From Voice to Text in the Classroom*, London, Routledge and Kegan Paul.

Graff, H. (1986) *The Legacies of Literacy*, Bloomington, Indiana University Press.

Graff, H. (1987) *The Labyrinths of Literacy*, London, Falmer Press.

Grillo, R. (1989) *Social Anthropology and the Politics of Language*, Cambridge, Cambridge University Press.

Heap, J. (1987) *Effective Functioning in Daily Life: A Critique of Concepts and Surveys of Functioning Literacy*. Paper presented to the National Reading Conference, Arizona.

Luke, A., McHoul, A. and Mey, J. (1990) 'On the limits of language planning: Class, state and power'. In R. Baldauf and A. Luke (eds) *Language Planning and Education in Australia and the South Pacific*, Clevedon, UK, Multilingual Matters, pp. 25–44.

Mikulecky, L. (1981) 'The mismatch between school training and job literacy demands', *Reading Research Quarterly*, 16, pp. 400–17.

National Commission on Excellence in Education (1983) *A Nation at Risk: The Imperative for Educational Reform*, Washington, US Government Printing Office.

Ong, W. (1982) *Orality and Literacy: Technologizing the Word*, London, Methuen.

Oxenham, J. (ed.) (1984) *Education Versus Qualifications: A Study of the Relationship between Education, Election for Employment and Labour Productivity*, London, Allen and Unwin.

Resnick, D. and Resnick, L. (1977) 'The nature of literacy: An historical exploration', *Harvard Educational Review*, 47, pp. 370–85.

Soltow, L. and Stevens, E. (1981) *The Rise of Literacy and the Common School in the United States*, Chicago, The University of Chicago Press.

Street, B.V. (1993) *Cross-cultural Approaches to Literacy*, Cambridge, Cambridge University Press.

Trace, A. (1961) *What Ivan Knows that Johnny Doesn't*, New York, Random House.

Wagner, D. (1987) *The Future of Literacy in A Changing World*, New York, Pergamon.

Welch, A.R. (1991) 'Education and legitimation in comparative education', *Comparative Education Review*, 34, p. 3.

Williams, R. (1977) *Marxism and Literature*, Oxford, Oxford University Press.

Willinsky, J. (1988) *The Construction of a Crisis: Literacy in Canada*, unpublished manuscript, University of Calgary.

Source

This is an edited version of a chapter previously published in P. Freebody and A. R. Welch (eds) *Knowledge, Culture and Power: International Perspectives on Literacy as Policy and Practice*. 1998. Reproduced by permission of Taylor & Francis Ltd.

Chapter 5

Simply doing their job? The politics of reading standards and 'real books'

Barry Stierer

Yet the New Literacy finds that even the limited case it makes on its own behalf is dismissed, not because its claims are unfounded, but for failing to use the measures currently governing education. The predominant discourse of quantitative studies and standardized measures makes it difficult for New Literacy programmes to gain a national hearing . . . By dominating the form, as well as the substance, of educational discourse, this reading tradition, in effect, suppresses the spread of new programmes seeking to overstep the governing cartel in reading of researchers, professional associations and publishers . . .

John Willinsky, *The New Literacy*, p. 164

At school and local authority level, discussion [of different methods for teaching reading] is nasty, brutish and short . . . So much talk about today's methods, modern ways, is mesmerizing. In fact it is possible to get people to do almost anything if you can convince them they are carrying forward the banner of progress . . .

But in fact there is no discussion, no criticism or counter-criticism, no attempt at effective argument. If clear and expert advice, targetted at highly relevant 'quality' and 'standards' committees, together with unequivocal evidence of serious decline, can safely be ignored in Conservative-led councils, then there is only the question of whose education system is it, who is in control . . .?

Martin Turner, *Sponsored Reading Failure*, p. 15

These two conflicting observations, each alleging that the world of early reading has been commandeered, through various forms of ideological influence, by the opposing factional interest group, provide the starting point for this chapter. The last few months have seen sustained media interest in the subject of early reading, fuelled by reports of declining reading standards among seven-year-olds. Teachers adhering to certain philosophies and using certain practices have been identified as culprits. Teacher-trainers, LEA advisers and inspectors, and so-called reading 'gurus' have been savagely criticised. Indeed in some quarters this has been an opportunity to question the very political and cultural basis of state education. The purpose of this chapter is two-fold:

to analyse this episode in order to gain a more critical understanding of it, and to propose an agenda for research and evaluation which might enable a more informed and rational debate.

'Progressivism' under attack

On 29 June 1990, the *Times Educational Supplement* carried a front-page story reporting a claim made by nine unnamed educational psychologists that reading standards among seven-year-olds had declined dramatically in their LEAs. The story was picked up by all the national newspapers and by many television and radio news programmes, leading to emotive accusations of unstructured and uninformed teaching in schools, inflexible 'bandwagoning' amongst teacher-trainers and LEA inspectors and advisers, and lax control by politicians and policy-makers. The press (and by no means exclusively the tabloids) had a field day: 'Children's reading ability plummets' (*Guardian*, 29.6.90); 'MacGregor to investigate reading crisis' (*Daily Telegraph*, 30.6.90); 'Scandal of our young illiterates' (*Daily Mail*, 30.6.90); and 'More dunces' (*Daily Mirror*, 29.6.90).

This was an extraordinary episode in the history of educational opinion-formation, since within a matter of days these unsubstantiated allegations by unnamed individuals had assumed the status of self-evident fact. The press referred to 'objective data', 'rigorous investigation by experts' and so on, when in fact no evidence had been made available. The political climate of opinion was clearly receptive to alarmist reports.

This episode was followed in the early autumn by the publication of *Sponsored Reading Failure: An Object Lesson* by Martin Turner, Senior Educational Psychologist in the London Borough of Croydon and one of the nine who had been behind the earlier furore. In fact, Turner's pamphlet is an attempt to publish, analyse and explain the 'findings' which had been anonymously promulgated in June. It is therefore the nearest thing we have to a presentation of the evidence purporting to document a decline in standards and an explanation of the alleged link between this apparent decline and the so-called 'real books' approach. The pamphlet deserves to be taken seriously – not as a research report, but as an expression of a particular ideological position, as well as for the disproportionate impact it has had on public opinion.

The 'evidence'

Turner's main points are these:

- Educational psychologists in nine LEAs pooled their reading test data for seven-year-olds going back in some cases ten years or more.
- The mean reading score in eight of the nine LEAs had declined in the period 1985–89, on average by 3.12 points of standard score.

- Again in these eight LEAs, the proportion of pupils with reading scores in the lowest band increased by about 50 per cent.
- Changes in teaching and curriculum appear to Turner to be the most compelling explanation for the decline – in particular, the (allegedly) widespread take-up of the 'real books' approach.

Two points are worth noting here. First, of the nine LEAs taking part, one did not show a decline. The validity of this result is dismissed by Turner on the grounds that the LEA in question uses an unorthodox approach to annual comparison (it readjusts its norm each year). It has been excluded from the analysis. So, although it was widely reported that nine LEAs were involved in the survey, only the eight which found a decline were included in the analysis.

Second, the figure of 347,000 children involved in the survey, which was widely quoted in the press (Turner himself refers to 'affected populations reaching towards half a million' children), is based on the numbers of children for whom test data are available going back 10 years, for all nine LEAs. In fact the number of children tested each year by the eight LEAs involved in the analysis would probably have been less than 30,000. Turner does not in fact specify the size of the annual cohorts tested.

The claim by Turner is therefore based upon a fairly small number of children chosen only from those authorities which showed a decline. Most people reading the press reports at the time would be forgiven for concluding that the claim was based upon a large and representative sample, but this may merely have been the result of press misrepresentation.

Assumptions

For Turner to move from these sketchy data, to a claim that reading standards have declined, requires acceptance of a number of crucial assumptions, none of which he makes explicit. The first assumption is that *a decline in scores on conventional reading tests is synonymous with a decline in reading standards.* Nowhere in the pamphlet is the validity of the tests used in the survey scrutinised. In fact, all of the tests mentioned by Turner are outdated and have been widely discredited, since they only provide a crude measure of children's ability to decipher decontextualised print, or to comprehend unseen text which is read for no real purpose (see, for example, Levy & Goldstein, 1984; Barrs & Laycock, 1989; Cato & Whetton, 1991). Even the government's Assessment of Performance Unit has acknowledged that tests of this kind produce unreliable results. Nevertheless, press treatment of the claims consistently referred to 'objective data' and 'scientific findings'.

A second assumption is that *using a wide range of available reading tests prevents the weaknesses of a single test from distorting the data.* The decline was, according to Turner, observable across a range of tests: the Young, the Edinburgh, the Neale, the Macmillan, the Suffolk and tests developed in-house by some of the (unnamed) authorities. He writes: 'The effect is strikingly independent of the tests used' (p. 20). In fact, at an overarching level of analysis they are all the same, since they are all based on the same conceptions of reading and the same principles of psychometrics.

A third assumption is that *the methods used by the psychologists to analyse their data followed established canons of scientific rigour*. In fact, many of the psychologists' procedures are suspect, if not actually improper. In order for the psychologists to compare scores from different LEAs, they had to aggregate scores from widely differing scales (e.g. reading ages, reading quotients, error counts, etc.). They converted scores from all of them to a standard currency, using a form of statistical manipulation, as if all the tests were technically comparable, which they are not. They also excluded inconvenient cases from the analysis, as described above, which violated principles of statistical analysis to which the psychologists themselves would normally subscribe. Indeed Professor Asher Cashdan, writing in *Education* on 28 September 1990, observed that Turner's analysis 'would not have been allowed to appear in its present form in any publication of standing', and that we should treat it with great caution since it 'has not gone through the normal process of peer examination such as would be the case if it were a journal article'.

A final assumption is that *educational psychologists have no particular educational axe to grind*. Melanie Phillips, writing about this case in the *Guardian* on 6 July 1990, exemplifies this attitude when she praises 'the experts [the educational psychologists] who are *simply doing their job* in providing the information' (my emphasis). 'The psychologists', she writes, 'owe no allegiance to educational theories but simply observe children in the classroom and record their findings in a scientific manner.' In fact, educational psychologists, like any other professional grouping, subscribe to a set of values and perspectives which reflect the history of their discipline and their positioning within the education system. Most educational psychologists have strong views about the way in which children should be taught to read, how reading should be assessed, and how poor readers should be helped. Any analysis by them is bound to be guided by their assumptions and preconceptions. Curriculum and pedagogy are highly contested areas, and no-one can legitimately claim impartiality.

Hence, although Turner's allegations were popularly accepted as unambiguous evidence which demonstrated that standards had declined, they are simply too selective and open to too many interpretations to be taken as proof one way or the other. In a democratic society we all have a right to know how effective schools are in helping children to become literate, but we shan't know this until new kinds of research and evaluation are carried out, linked to new thinking about suitable methods and valid evidence, as I shall discuss at the end of this chapter.

Declining standards and 'real books'

Having demonstrated to his own satisfaction that reading standards among seven-year-olds showed a marked and alarming decline in the 1980s, Turner then considers possible explanations for this worrying trend. He rejects a whole range of possible causes: demographic changes; socio-economic factors; the effects of the 1984–86 pay dispute; the rise in single-parent families; the mortgage interest rate; low teacher morale and high staff turnover; hyperactivity and distractability of children at school entry; lessening of parental involvement in pre-school activity; the influence of television. These kinds of factors, he claims, would have taken their toll indiscriminately across the range of children's learning, whereas the only evidence of significant decline is in the area of reading. The only explanation which remains credible, he claims, centres upon the allegedly widespread take-up of 'real books' philosophies and practices through the 1980s.

The section of Turner's pamphlet dealing with possible causes of his alleged decline is pure polemic: he produces no evidence whatever which would enable us to evaluate the validity of his assertions. In particular, he provides no evidence to substantiate his claim that 'real books' approaches were widely taken up in the LEAs featuring in his analysis. In fact, he fails even to offer an unambiguous definition of the 'real books' approach which would enable us to identify those classrooms guided by such principles. To Turner, 'real books' is synonymous with 'no teaching'.

An alternative interpretation of Turner's evidence is that it demonstrates the rapidly accelerating obsolescence of standardised reading tests, since models of teaching and learning no longer reflect the psychometric conceptions of reading built into the tests. It's plausible to assume that children taught to read in traditional ways perform well on traditional tests. We may discover that children who are introduced to print through their experience of language and literacy, rather than through the teaching of deciphering skills, outperform other children on a whole range of literacy competences, provided the assessment procedures used are sufficiently sensitive, but that they do not acquire the specific narrow skill of 'sounding out' individual decontextualised words until later in childhood.

Motives

It is possible to consider two theories to account for the decision by Turner and his colleagues to publish their 'findings' and to release them to the press prior to publication. On the one hand, we could consider that they were honestly surprised and genuinely concerned at their unexpected discovery, and simply felt a responsibility to share their findings with the educational community. Martin Turner invites us to view him and his colleagues in this light:

> The data reported on here have come to light as a result of quite casual enquiries. I do not claim more than a *prima facie* case for the general argument. As yet there may be a suspect, even a smoking gun, but not culprit.

(pp. 24–5)

He implies that they did not wish to induce a moral panic over standards, or to trigger an emotive series of press attacks on particular approaches to early reading in schools, but merely to 'draw attention' and 'call for investigation'.

On the other hand, there is evidence to suggest rather more calculating motives. Many of the press reports in the summer used identical or very similar phraseology in their reports (e.g. 'the sharpest decline in reading standards in more than 40 years', 'secret data', 'bound to fuel concern over methods', 'trend discovered by accident at an informal meeting' etc.), suggesting that press correspondents were carefully briefed or that the press-release went far beyond the psychologists' evidence. In his own pamphlet, Turner makes no effort to disguise his own conviction that the decline has been caused by the moral and professional pressure which LEA advisers and inspectors have brought to bear upon otherwise reasonable classroom teachers to abandon their 'tried and tested' and 'commonsense' methods in favour of 'real books'.

Educational psychologists have in recent months displayed growing professional anxiety over what they perceive as their increasing marginalisation. In particular, they have witnessed a gradual erosion of their previously unchallenged expertise in the province of reading. A large proportion of them are disturbed by, among other things:

- the way in which reading was formulated in the report of the national curriculum English working group (DES, 1989), which reflected an essentially psycholinguistic view ('Reading is much more than the decoding of black marks upon a page: it is a quest for meaning and one which requires the reader to be an active participant . . . meaning should always be in the foreground' [para 16.2]);
- the approach to assessing reading adopted by the consortia developing SATs for seven-year-olds, which is essentially a diagnostic one and not a conventional test of reading ability;
- the growing shift away from traditional approaches to meeting special educational needs (holistic as opposed to skills-based);
- changing models of learning, e.g. social constructivist models replacing behaviourist and cognitive psychological models;
- the uncertain funding base for educational psychological services as LEAs devolve increasing proportions of their budgets to schools;
- the signs that headteachers might be prepared to 'make do' with national curriculum assessment results, however crude, rather than 'buy in' the assessment services of educational psychologists.

In this light, it is not fanciful to speculate that the psychologists who released this explosive information on the public will have had a number of implicit messages they wished to communicate. They may, for example, have wished us to conclude that SATs will not deliver diagnoses of individual children's reading competence, and that only educational psychologists can do this. Moreover, there is the implicit message that if it weren't for the testing done by educational psychologists, if it weren't for their conscientiousness in pooling their data for the purposes of comparison, and if it weren't for their courage in making their 'findings' available, *we would never have known about this alarming trend*. Certainly SATs and other forms of national curriculum assessment will not be able to deliver data on reading standards over time. Educational psychologists therefore have a demonstrably valuable role to play.

Turner and his colleagues must have known that their report would be accepted on trust by the media. They must have known that it wouldn't matter whether their evidence was valid, or whether their speculations about possible causes were responsible and informed. This was, I suspect, a well-orchestrated media campaign, carefully timed and planned. The psychologists have capitalised on the scientific mystique which surrounds their profession, and the high esteem in which they are generally held (as Melanie Phillips's *Guardian* article revealed), to create an atmosphere which would quickly restore them to what they consider to be their rightful place within the education system.

It must also be appreciated that Martin Turner, in his pamphlet, goes well beyond the 'standards and methods' debate, and attempts to articulate a more overarching ideological position which employs the familiar discourse of 'New Right' polemic. In particular, he claims that the allegedly widespread take-up of 'real books' is the result of a strangle-hold which has been achieved on all aspects of the teaching of reading by 'paladins of the educational establishment' (i.e. LEA advisers and inspectors, teacher-trainers), and that 'real books' reflects an attempt by this group to promulgate a wider political programme of left-wing causes. His proposed solution is to dismantle the institutions of state education in order to free schools from the shackles of LEA control: if 'real books' had to compete in an educational free market with other approaches its irrelevance to the concerns of parents would soon become apparent, since schools offering a 'real books' approach would quickly go to the wall. These portions of his pamphlet demonstrate that Turner's attack on 'real books' is ultimately a platform from which to argue a New Right educational manifesto.

In a telling remark, Turner bemoans the 'politicisation' of the teaching of reading:

> Something irrevocably silly has happened in the educational world when wives of aspiring Labour prime ministers announce to the media that they are very left wing about teaching reading! What, on a commonsense view, could possibly be political about teaching young children to read?
>
> (p. 27)

In this reference to Glenys Kinnock, Turner reveals his 'paradigm blindness'. He appears to be unaware of the fact that *all* approaches to the development and use of literacy will reflect cultural values. Whilst Turner's own caricature of the 'real books' movement is simplistic and ill-informed, it is nevertheless true that 'progressive' methods are 'biased' in that they stem from a pluralist intellectual root. Turner's perspective is *equally* ideological, but because it conforms to dominant values in education and society it appears to him to be politically neutral. Turner repeatedly underscores the need for structure and discipline in education, the importance of deferring to 'scientists' (psychologists) on matters of children's learning, the necessity of separating reading from other language experiences, and the vital assimilating function of schooling. His numerous references to the 'classics' of British philosophy and literature reflect his privileging of enduring elitist traditions. These views help us to draw a map of his ideological terrain. Turner would have been more intellectually honest had he declared his own ideological colours and argued his corner accordingly. Instead, he claims ideological neutrality in an area of the school curriculum as hotly contested as literacy, and accuses his opponents of dragging politics into the argument.

Towards a reading research agenda for the 1990s

The mainstream professional response to Turner's position has been to ignore its wider professional and ideological underpinnings, and to treat the debate as an unnecessarily polarised comparison of two techniques for teaching reading. 'Moderates' quoted in the press refuted Turner by reporting that most teachers use a combination of methods, and that the world of reading is not as fraught a battleground as Turner would have us believe.

This response appears in one sense to be appealing, since it promises to introduce commonsense into the argument and reconcile the growing polarisation. However, in its claim to impartiality, this response falls into the same trap that Martin Turner does: it is blind to its own ideological underpinnings. As Carole Edelsky (1990) writes, 'There can be no eclecticism at the level of deep underlying beliefs' (p. 7). So, this kind of response seems to me to be a spurious attempt to reconcile fundamentally irreconcilable philosophical positions, under the guise of impartiality, by reducing the debate to one of techniques and by accepting implicitly all of the assumptions about teaching, learning and schooling underpinning Turner's stance. It leaves unanswered the really crucial questions about literacy, which stand at the frontiers of practice, crying out to be investigated.

Another problem inherent in responding to Turner relates to the dilemma summarised by John Willinsky in the quote at the beginning of this chapter: the traditional psychometric methodologies which might be used to compare competing approaches to early reading are artefacts of the dominant perspective rejected by New Literacy adherents. In short, in their rejection of quantitative measures of reading, and quantitative procedures for evaluation and comparison, progressives leave themselves open to this kind of attack.

There are therefore several related questions which urgently need to be addressed:

1. Are studies which compare traditional methods with progressive methods worth supporting? The Leicestershire Literacy Initiative Evaluation Project and the ILEA Hackney Literacy Study were modest beginnings at such comparison, but they did not begin to explore the deeper questions raised by competing notions of literacy, such as the effect of different approaches on disadvantaged and lower-ability children and the relationship between effectiveness and teachers' personal styles. Is further research and evaluation in these areas worthy of support, or would it simply perpetuate the sense of inquisition felt by progressives?

2. Is the issue of standards in reading across large populations of children a legitimate concern? If so, what kinds of evidence would progressives accept?

3. Are qualitative methods of recording and assessment such as the *Primary Language Record* (Barrs *et al.*, 1988), which are embedded in the processes of teaching and learning, suitable for larger-scale assessment purposes, such as monitoring standards over time, allocating resources, facilitating transfer, identification of children for special help, etc.? If so, what kinds of work need to be done in order to promote this extension of the use of qualitative methods into previously unexplored areas? If *not*, are conventional quantitative methods being implicitly condoned for these purposes?

4. Are progressives prepared to define the essential features of a 'real books' methodology in sufficient detail to enable it to be distinguished from traditional approaches for the purposes of comparative research and evaluation?

5. Might one unanticipated result of 'New Literacy' programmes be that children will tend to develop the ability to decipher unseen decontextualised print at a later age than children introduced to reading through the acquisition of decoding skills? Would this matter?

I suggest here a few fruitful areas for research and evaluation, which might arise from the process of answering the above questions, or might alternatively help to answer them:

*   Small-scale descriptive studies of the *Primary Language Record* in use, including use of the two five-point 'reading scales'.
*   Small-scale descriptive studies of teacher assessment and moderation in the area of children's reading.
*   Analyses of *PLR*-type teacher–pupil conferences and teacher–parent conferences.
*   Small-scale descriptive studies of any existing attempts to use the *PLR* for assessment purposes such as monitoring, transfer, resources allocation, referral, etc.
*   Analyses of the attitudes of parents in relation to issues such as national standards in reading, competing methodologies for teaching reading, etc.

References

Barrs, M. and Laycock, L. (1989) *Testing Reading*. London: Centre for Language in Primary Education.

Barrs, M., Ellis, S., Hester, H. and Thomas, A. (1988) *The Primary Language Record: Handbook for Teachers*. London: Centre for Language in Primary Education.

Bird, M. and Norton, N. (1988) *The Hackney Literacy Study*. London: ILEA Research and Statistics Branch.

Bridge, M. (1988) *Learning to Read: Literacy Initiative Evaluation Project – 1986–87*. Leicester: Leicestershire Literacy Support Service.

Cashdan, A. (1990) The great unproven failure. *Education*, 28 September 1990.

Cato, V. and Whetton, C. (1991) *An Enquiry into LEA Evidence on Standards of Reading of Seven-year-old Children*. London: Department of Education and Science (with NFER).

Department of Education and Science (1989) *English for Ages 5 to 16*. London: DES.

Edelsky, C. (1990) Whose agenda is this anyway? A response to McKenna, Robinson and Miller. *Educational Researcher* 19(8), 7–11.

Levy, P. and Goldstein, H. (eds) (1984) *Tests in Education*. London: Academic Press.

Phillips, M. (1990) Commentary. *The Guardian*, 6 July 1990.

Turner, M. (1990) *Sponsored Reading Failure: An Object Lesson*. Warlingham, Surrey: IPSET Education Unit.

Willinsky, J. (1990) *The New Literacy: Redefining Reading and Writing in the Schools*. London: Routledge.

Source

This is an edited version of a paper previously published in B. Stierer and J. Maybin (eds) *Language, Literacy and Learning in Educational Practice*. Clevedon: Multilingual Matters. Originally published in *Language Matters*, Vol. 3, pp. 2–8. London: CLPE. Reproduced by permission of the Centre for Language in Primary Education.

Chapter 6

When will the phonics police come knocking?

O. L. Davis Jr

Phonics is 'in'. This reality is no longer news. Indeed, advocates promote phonics as the 'one best system' in American education for the initial teaching of reading. They seek more than the replacement of the whole-word approach. Phonics also serves as the emblem of the increasingly aggressive crusade to rid schooling of the alleged blights of a polluted and rancid progressivism. This movement's anthem well might be 'The World Turned Upside Down'.

To be sure, teachers and educational leaders in the United States have weathered previous political storms over reading instruction. They have resisted the simplistic folly of either-or instructional proposals. As a matter of fact, they have continued their steady work amidst strident charges of failure from rival opposition forces.

These previous tempests mainly were rhetorical. The work of education continued to be practical. For example, advocates of phonics and whole-word approaches have competed for rhetorical dominance for more than a century. At various times, one or another approach became fashionable, even popular, at conference sessions, in journal accounts, and even in textbooks and teachers' lounges. By and large, teachers mainly ignored the swirling winds of advocacy or temporarily coopted the new slogan to describe their practice. They continued to teach individual children as they believed most appropriate and adopted as their own some elements of the 'new' procedures that made sense to them. No matter which advocacy group claimed victory, most teachers of reading continued to teach in the very best ways they knew. Their 'best' continually improved. A wealth of solid educational research across the entire century has informed their practice.

Even so, not all children have learned to read well. Many, certainly too many, have failed to learn to read. Even after mindful diagnosis and the use of carefully crafted, individually designed programmes, some individuals read only haltingly or not at all. No teacher, no administrator – at least, none in my experience – remains unmoved by such results. They want their pupils to learn to read. They want to do more. Typically, they try some other procedure, invent or adapt another approach. The existence of nonreading children and adults constitutes a monumental frustration and loss to those individuals – as well as to their teachers.

The great majority of US teachers of reading are likely to continue to use both of the major contested approaches – and others – as they seek to help children with different talents and backgrounds to learn to read. To be sure, individual teachers prefer one or some approaches over others. Nevertheless, teachers follow the general pattern of generations of their predecessors. They use whatever procedures they know or can devise or have at hand to help their students learn to read. Significantly, most administrators have supported their teachers' intense and balanced efforts.

The current contest over reading continues to be rhetorical, of course, but it differs from earlier reading wars. It is more an intense political campaign of ideological zealots than it is a controversy. Several changed features dominate its landscape. Most importantly, the present controversy is *not* professional; it is *not* about influence. It is public, impressively political and bureaucratic, and about absolute ideological control.

Proponents of phonics-only instruction appear to have captured the attention and power of several key state governors and state boards of education. Consequently, they have dominated these states' new standards for reading instruction not only about specific goals. They are now working to mandate that phonics be the standard instructional procedure to teach reading throughout the state. Among their tactics is legislation that mandates phonics-only reading instruction in a state's public schools. Their influence over the bureaucratic links between state-mandated standards and professional teacher and administrator licensure already has produced a nightmarish vision of government intrusion into higher education. This horrid spectre erupts from serious proposals that all accredited educator preparation programmes in a state must employ common syllabi that feature phonics-only reading instruction. In the current situation, phonics proponents appear to be following a 'take no prisoners' position. Already real are early casualties: they are responsible, serious teachers.

Can the phonics police be far behind? When will they come knocking at schoolhouse doors? Will they handcuff errant teachers as pupils watch? Or will they apprehend the teacher or administrator at home in the darkness of the night?

This dismal vision of the near future appears at once to be outrageous and monumentally bizarre. On the other hand, it could happen and it could occur soon. Legislated phonic instruction must define legal and illegal instructional practice and establish punishments for violations of the law. Some agency (and it could be a new 'Corps of Phonics Police') must be the enforcers of the law. Violators – in this case, teachers and college professors, perhaps administrators, school systems, and universities – must be prosecuted. What might be the penalties for the use of an illegal procedure to teach reading? Public censure? Suspension or revocation of teaching licence? Dismissal? Fines? Imprisonment?

Less possibly imagined would be proposals to legislate practice in other professions. For example, a legislative requirement that defence attorneys employ a prescribed strategy without regard to the specifics of the alleged crime, its circumstances, and the defendant seems unthinkable. Similarly, legislation that would require surgery as the only treatment for all cancers, no matter the type of their cells or their spread or the patient's individual history, is ludicrous. For the teaching of reading, however, politicians appear eager to accept as appropriate the selection of just one procedure for all children in every situation.

In the present tortured uncertainty, phonics-only advocates usually influence politicians and bureaucrats behind public view. Therefore, most Americans, including most education professionals, remain 'out of the loop' until agencies announce freshly written administrative mandates. The legislative process, however, remains more open than are the labyrinths of bureaucratic operations. The political takeover of educational practice, even at this late hour, still can be frustrated. The chilling prospects of the phonics police can be avoided, but not without responsible action.

Obviously, the situation is grave, and easy answers are unavailable. On the other hand, American citizens and, especially, the nation's educational leaders and teachers must recognize the certain perils of inaction. Not just reading programmes and reading teachers are in peril. Emboldened by success in the phonics-only battles, the proponents surely will target additional school subjects. Little imagination is required to wonder what legislation may follow for the teaching of other school subjects; surely, biology, history, and literature are among several patently obvious selections. Appropriately cautionary in this regard is the postwar confession of Lutheran pastor Martin Niemoeller, called Hitler's favourite concentration camp prisoner. He remembered:

> First, they came for the Jews and I did not speak out – because I was not a Jew. Then, they came for the communists and I did not speak out – because I was not a communist. Then, they came for the trade unionists and I did not speak out – because I was not a trade unionist. They came for me – and there was no one left to speak out for me.[1]

The time for speaking out – by all teachers and educational leaders and other citizens – is now.

Reasonable first steps are possible. Educational leaders must regain their now silent voice. Superintendents and building principals can offer vigorous public support of the balanced efforts of their school's and system's teachers. They can help illuminate the plague of consequences of a 'one size fits all' teaching procedure for reading to their community and to the nation. University administrators and professors across the campus must speak out against legislative and bureaucratic intrusion into university course content, not just in education courses, but in courses that teacher candidates take – such as history and English and mathematics. Too, as companions rather than adversaries, teachers and administrators can describe at various venues their committed practices to improve the teaching of reading. They also can draw public attention to their use of a number of research-based procedures to teach reading. This kind of joint enterprise might tout, for individual pupils and for differing lengths of time, the Success for All programme for some children, Reading Recovery for others, a strictly phonics-only programme for others, a whole-word approach for another group, a literature-based programme for still other pupils, and combinations of emphases for other children. These actions, by themselves, may help, but they likely will not be sufficient; they are beginning steps. Educators must also align themselves with other citizens for concerted political action to influence governors, legislators, and bureaucrats.

To be silent and to do nothing in this current situation is to welcome a monstrous disaster. Then, only one of the concerns will be the question: When will the phonics police come knocking?

Note

1   The University of the State of New York State Education Department, *Teaching About the Holocaust and Genocide: The Human Rights Series*, vol. 2 (Albany: New York State Education Department, Bureau of Curriculum Development, 1985), p. 313.

Source

This is an edited version of an article previously published in *Journal of Curriculum Supervision*, 14(3). 1999. Reproduced by permission of the Association for Supervision and Curriculum Development.

Chapter 7

Literacy assessment and the politics of identities

Sharon Murphy

To ask people to read or write is to ask them to engage in an act of self-identification that echoes biography, history, and a sense of place. To engage in the assessment of that reading and writing is to mark that biography, history, and sense of place within a larger landscape of pasts, possible futures, and the recognized or unrecognized politics of the assessment situation. School assessment has a particular impact on identities because it not only deals with identities revealed through the acts of reading or writing, it also creates them. Any assessment situation, such as the assessment of reading and writing, can lead to such unwanted identities as giftedness, averageness, illiterateness, and learning disabledness identities that intersect with already held visions of self, system, and state. But the identities of the assessed are not the only ones at stake in school-based assessment. School-based assessment also participates in the construction of the identities of those who are not assessed but who are complicit in the act of assessment by their oblique or active participation – parents, psychologists, teachers, school and school district officials, the media, and the state-governed institution of schooling itself. This chapter will indicate how some of these identities are bypassed, constructed, and constrained by assessment; it will also raise questions about how the politics of identity construction work for or against the concepts of professionalism, democratic education, and the interplay between individual and collective self-determinism.

Setting the backdrop for contemporary test use

Any argument about the way in which tests contribute to the construction of identities is moot unless it can be demonstrated that tests are actually used. Even though grounds for new conceptualizations of assessment have been laid both in the psychometric community (e.g., Bennett and Ward, 1993) and in the literacy community (e.g., Farr and Beck, 1991; Goodman, 1991; Valencia and Pearson, 1987), standardized achievement tests have been and will continue to be indicators of literacy in the United States. Estimates of general standardized test use vary (e.g., Coley and Goertz, 1990; Mehrens, Phillips and

Schram, 1993; Perrone, 1991); however, every year millions of tests are administered at a cost of multi-millions of dollars (even without factoring in the personnel costs for administration, public relations, and interpretation). Perrone (1991) estimated that students graduating in 1991 would have taken 18 to 21 standardized tests across their schooling, compared with an average of 3 tests for graduates before 1950.

The case for readers and writers who struggle with literacy usually means a further intensification of testing practices. This intensification occurs in several ways. First, these students may be subject to the same frequency of testing as the regular students in the system (Steele and Meredith, 1991). However, Steele and Meredith (1991) also reported that the most commonly used measures for placement in Chapter 1 and learning-disabled classes are individualized standardized tests (even though many of these are widely viewed as technically problematic). This individualization of assessment means that students who have difficulty with literacy are assessed more frequently and with a greater variety of measures than is the regular student. An example of intense testing was reported by Taylor (1991), who documented 4 group tests and 26 individual tests administered to a student in the first 3 years of schooling alone.

Finally, readers and writers who experience difficulty can become the victims of tests they have never taken because of the consequence of high-stakes achievement testing in some jurisdictions. McGill-Franzen and Ailington (1993) provided evidence that the high-pressure environment requiring schools to have high scores on district or statewide achievement tests means that some students get shunted off for placement even before they take the tests, for fear that these students' potentially low scores will be detrimental to the school's ranking.

Identity metamorphosis and testing

This abundance of testing in contemporary American society is just one more manifestation of the desire to control, to be 'scientific', and to leave nothing to chance. Indeed, as the philosopher Ian Hacking (1990) argued, this desire to 'take chance' has historical antecedents that go back well beyond the turn of the twentieth century, a time generally attributed to the advent of standardized testing. By re-examining social history, Hacking (1990) presented a credible case for the manner in which statistics came to be used to overcome the argument that our lives are controlled by chance or fate. Because society could be described statistically, it seemed that somehow this imbued the describers with control over chance. This was particularly the case with deviancy. By saying, for example, that 2 per cent of the population would commit suicide, it seemed that this aspect of society was somehow knowable in a way that it had not been before (even though exactly which 2 per cent was involved could not be specified). Nevertheless, the power of knowing through statistics came to dominate bureaucratic institutions in Western society.

Standardized testing is, perhaps, a prototypical exemplar of this broader desire to control chance. Hacking (1990) argued that 'enumeration requires categorization, and defining new classes of people for the purposes of statistics has consequences for the ways in which we conceive of others and think of our own possibilities and potentialities' (p. 6). This he referred to as the 'making up of people' (Hacking, 1990, p. 6). The reach of standardized testing in the making up of people was captured by Mercer (cited in Milofsky, 1989), who observed that most of those whom schools identify as handicapped are not so identified outside the school context. Milofsky (1989) argued that this does not necessarily invalidate the handicap; rather, it means 'that the social biases built into schools will be expressed in these handicaps' (p. 233). These, then are the immediate questions: What are the social biases of schools such that they can create identities of failure, and how are such biases enacted by standardized testing?

The concept of the meritocracy

Education, and testing in particular, have been deeply influenced by merito-cratic principles (Gifford, 1989). In a meritocracy, the talented are identified and moved ahead based on their achievement. Enfolded within this view is usually a rhetoric of being fair, allocating rewards to the deserving, and treating all within the system equally. As the development of standardized testing demonstrates, these seemingly harmonious goals are far from compatible.

Histories of standardized reading tests reveal that, like most of the assessment tools in education and psychology, these tests are portrayed as objective, scientifically constructed devices (e.g., Willis, 1991). As such, they seemed to appeal to fairness. Because of the development of dichotomously scored multiple-choice items, the past criticisms of the subjectivity of teacher-constructed examinations, the influence peddling of high-status society members, and the carelessness of teacher-examiners (e.g., Brooks, 1920, 1921) could be put to rest.

Brooks (1920, 1921) provided examples of how standardized tests seemed to involve scientific precision that would yield educational benefits to all. Claims were implied or directly made to the effect that standardized tests would let teachers definitely know 'what a child of his age and grade really ought to know in order to be as well informed as other children of his age and grade in other schools' (Brooks, 1921, p. 161). The ultimate reward for using standardized tests, then, was that education could be made more efficient and effective. Students in this envisioned system would be rewarded by participating in classes that would not be too difficult or too easy, but just right. Teaching and learning were viewed as highly precise and controllable processes. The past century of testing has perpetuated this legacy. In fact, the culture of American schooling has made the rewards for test performance tangible ones that relate to the provision of funding and resources for schools (McGill-Franzen and Ailington, 1993).

But one person's 'achievement' in standardized testing turns out to be another's 'failure', Although it has taken nearly a century of testing to demonstrate, it is becoming clear, at least to some, that standardized tests are flawed. In the area of literacy, the fairness of standardized tests is being questioned on both technical and sociopolitical grounds (Murphy, Shannon, Johnston, and Hansen, manuscript in preparation). Recent comments by psychometrists and literacy theoreticians alike acknowledge that, as assessment devices, standardized tests remain frozen in time – relics of turn-of-the-century conceptualizations of reading, writing, thinking, and learning (e.g., Chittenden, 1987; Gardner, 1993; Linn, 1986; Mislevy, 1993; Valencia and Pearson, 1986). The technical flaws and sociopolitical biases of tests have left in their wake students who name themselves as failures in school even though the failure may not be theirs, but rather is contained in the instruments designed to serve them.

At a general level, standardized tests prove to be unfair in several ways.

- Standardized tests treat high-scoring and low-scoring students differently. A low scorer's performance is judged on a relatively small sample of items in comparison with others who take the test (Bradley, 1976). This low sampling has negative implications for test reliability with low-scoring populations. In addition, those items on which such students would have done well are likely to have been dropped from the test because of their failure to discriminate among students (Tierney, 1990).

- Standardized tests more often than not discriminate against those who have part of the knowledge required to complete an item but not quite enough to complete it successfully. Students receive no credit for being in possession of partial knowledge (Tierney, 1990). They are treated as though they had no knowledge at all. They receive zero credit.

- Summary scores can mask the quite varying performances that underlie them (Bradley, 1976; Tierney, 1990). If a test is not broken down into subtests, it is quite conceivable for two students to achieve the same summary score when one student performs uniformly on a set of different tasks while another performs poorly on one task but well on the others. Their comparability as readers is questionable. Compounding this problem is the low reliability of subtests on which students score poorly.

- Knowledge of test-taking skills positively influences test scores (e.g., Scruggs, White, and Bennion, 1985). This proves an unfair disadvantage to those who do not have such skills. For instance, knowledge about the format of items on standardized tests has been found to affect performance (e.g., O'Connor, 1989; Scruggs and Mastropieri, 1988; Scruggs, Mastropieri, and Tolfa-Veit, 1986). Given that the formats of some standardized tests have been found to change as frequently as every 1.2 minutes or, by comparison, as seldom as every 21.3 minutes (Tolfa, Scruggs, and Bennion, 1985), the influence of this element in masking literacy abilities must be considered.

- The limited generalizability of reading comprehension test tasks to the construct of reading raises questions about the appropriateness of their use as reading assessment instruments. For example, the ability of students to answer the questions on reading comprehension tests without reading the text upon which they are based (e.g., Johnston, 1983) leaves suspect the inferences made from such tests. These suspicions are added to by in-depth studies (e.g., Farr, Pritchard, and Smitten, 1990; Freedle and Kostin, 1994) revealing that, even though college students do make use of text in standardized reading tests, it is doubtful that performance on these tests generalizes to the general construct of reading comprehension because the tests task is a very specific type of task.
- Standardized reading tests tend to treat both students and teachers as responders; literacy involves both responding and initiating (Tierney, 1990). Besides 'assuming a lowest common denominator view of readers' (Tierney, 1990, p. 255), this stance reflects only a tiny part of the demands of reading in the non-school world. . . . As a consequence, students may be penalized by school-based tests of limited relevance to non-school reading tasks.
- Standardized tests tend to glorify a kind of competitiveness that exists only in schools. This is not to say that competitiveness does not exist outside of schools. Rather, the nature of the competitiveness differs. As Haertel (1989) argues, assessments outside of school are complex – 'people have some latitude in choosing the goals toward which they will strive; and a large proportion of individuals are likely to excel by at least some standards' (p. 30). In contrast, required tests 'offer only one narrow way to succeed, and that may seem unfair to those whose particular strengths are hard to demonstrate on written examinations' (Haertel, 1989, p. 30).

There are numerous other examples of the ways in which standardized tests corrupt the concept of fairness. The descriptions above, with one or two exceptions, are general – they are not confined to specific populations of test takers. Consequently, these injustices are available to all. Their contribution to identity formation is that of the general depression of the concept of self as literate and as competent. This is no small contribution, as its shelf-life for the individual may be quite enduring. As Hanson (1993) argued, the very act of testing can bring about a transformation, but in schools the transformation is 'played out in the negative, in that tests prevent changes or developments in individuals that would otherwise take place' (p. 292).

However, there is a more insidious way in which standardized tests contribute to the creation, dismissal, or eradication of identities. It is insidious because, on the one hand, the standardization tests is being used as the instrument of the meritocratic sorting, and there seems to be an inherently egalitarian aura to the testing. Students seemingly all have the opportunity to 'prove their worth'. Yet, these 'egalitarian' ends become moot when it is demonstrated that tests are systematically biased against some children.

The recognition that denies identities

Children enter schools raw. They are available to institutional knowledge in a way that is at once wonderful and frightening. But children's rawness is not synonymous with a lack of knowledge or a lack of identity. In fact, part of children's rawness upon entering schools is the way in which their identities and knowledge are so readily manifest and available to others. The folklore of schooling is replete with stories of children who seemingly do not discover their own racialness or poverty until they enter school (e.g., Baxter, 1993). These stories evidence children's total identification with their worlds outside of school – worlds that are full of the successes and failures of everyday living, worlds that are defined by economic, racial, cultural, and gendered patterns of interaction and of making sense.

Ironically, standardized testing is very successful at recognizing these identities. Unfortunately, however, some of these identities are, to all intents and purposes, negated, dismissed, and ultimately eradicated within the confines of standardized tests and schooling. Tests are portrayed as vehicles by which to treat everyone the same, but they do not. Standardized tests themselves have long been criticized on the grounds of systematic bias (e.g., Fowles and Kimple, 1972). Racial and linguistic minorities, in particular, have long been over-represented in classes for the below-average and under-represented in classes for the above-average (e.g., Figueroa, 1989; Palmer, Olivarez, Willson, and Fordyce, 1989; Serwatka, Deering, and Stoddard, 1989). This bias has often been brought to the attention of the organized psychometric community. For instance, in 1975, George Jackson, Chair of the Association of Black Psychologists, in responding to a report of the Ad Hoc Committee of Educational Uses of Tests with Disadvantaged Students, not only referred to the report as racist and asked for a moratorium on testing, but also asked for 'government intervention and strict legal sanctions' (Jackson, 1975, p. 92). Even so, studies continue to demonstrate that the biases inherent in testing have not been eradicated (e.g., Crocker, Schmitt, and Tang 1988; O'Connor, 1989), and requests for moratoriums (Perrone, 1991) or independent auditing mechanisms (Madaus, 1992) seem to go unheard.

The recognition of identity by tests is all the more devastating because it becomes the instrument of denial – denial of resources, denial of respect, denial of dignity, and denial of the discriminatory subjectivity inherent within tests. This paradox of the recognition of identities by denying them receives much support in the research literature on standardized testing in studies of the effects of race, culture, class, and gender on testing.

Testing is a social event, replete with participants, a context, and rules that govern the behaviour that occurs during the event. At the most fundamental and human level of interpersonal interaction within the social event of testing, the effects of the individual's biography are revealed in the research on testing (Emihovich, 1990). First of all, there is the interaction between the examiner and the examinee, each of whom is a gendered, raced, and classed individual. While some studies have reported mixed results (e.g., Bursztyn, 1992), Anastasi (1982) concluded that 'there is considerable evidence that test results may vary systematically as a function of the examiner' (p. 39). Added to this evidence is research reported by Sadker and Sadker (1994) on gender biases in schools. Milofsky's (1989) study of the practice of school psychology in urban and suburban Chicago also homed in on the over-testing and inappropriately rapid testing (i.e., speed of testing was not in accordance with suggested test administration procedures) of African-American children.

Besides examiner/examinee effects, testing in and of itself may cause feelings of anxiety that impact on performances (e.g., Nolen, Haladyna, and Haas, 1992; Scruggs et al., 1986). Given the long history of standardized testing and its documented and undocumented negative effects on African-Americans, it is no wonder that African-American males have been found to be less encouraged by tests and more anxious and negative about taking them (Henry, Bryson, and Henry, 1989). It is also not surprising that low achievers, such as readers and writers who struggle, have more negative feelings towards tests (Karmos and Karmos, 1984), as do students from low socioeconomic backgrounds (Herman and Golan, 1993). This is further evidence of 'the recognition that denies'. Students who have grounds for fearing the biases inherent in tests become unwilling and fearful participants in a process that sorts them by race or class but refuses to admit to such biases.

This theme of recognition and denial is played out over and over again for many different sociocultural groups. From the Indochinese (Trueba, Jacobs, and Kirton, 1990) to the Amerindians (Brescia and Fortune, 1989), testing appears to be very effective at recognizing cultural difference. Differences such as socioeconomic status (Herman and Golan, 1993; Guskey and Kifer, 1990) and gender (Miller, 1990) are also persistently recognized by tests. These and numerous other studies reiterate the fact that tests are very good at identifying, but they leave much doubt that the grounds of such identification are strictly academic.

The culture of the denial of identity is so strong that, even in the case of students whose first language is not English or whose dialect is not 'standard', the mythology of testing is not eroded. O'Connor (1989) provided numerous examples of the impact of language, including (a) the fact that the frequency of specific word use differs across languages and therefore, even if tests are translated to the student's first language, a student's familiarity with certain words may be advantaged or disadvantaged; (b) the use of multiple-choice items often requires subtle syntactic knowledge that disadvantages ESL examinees; and (c) in cases where translation is used for ESL speakers, the resultant tasks are not necessarily equivalent – for instance, remembering numbers for digit span in Spanish requires holding in short-term memory twice as many syllables as remembering numbers in English.

In short, studies of testing reveal that tests are like magic mirrors – they actually reflect many identities, but they reward only one, and that one is likely to be white, male, middle-class, and American. These studies reveal the complexity of human interaction and learning. They reveal that some categorizations of illiteracy may be more findings of cultural difference than anything else. The recognition of the complexities of learning has led to changes in large-scale group assessment (e.g., Koretz, Stecher, Klein, and McCaffrey, 1994; Valencia, Hiebert, and Afflerbach, 1994); however, individualized assessment has been relatively stagnant, and even in new models of large-scale assessment, there has been a blindness to such issues as the privileging of some forms of knowledge over others (Murphy, 1995). This blindness cannot occur without the complicity of adults within the institution of schooling, adults whose identities are also shaped by testing.

School-based professionals: the changers and the changed[1]

Adults who participate in schooling through their employment are already at a disadvantage when it comes to establishing identities in relation to schools. After all, at least for those who work in the school system, it must be remembered that theirs are the 'success stories' of that system. They are the ones who either were recognized by the system or whose identities were transformed into something the system could recognize through instruments such as standardized tests. Even if these school-based professionals imagine new identities, the influence of standardized tests within the culture of schooling often interrupts these possibilities. The cases of teachers and psychologists are exemplars of this point.

Teachers as unwilling servants of testing

Much of the action of schooling takes place in the classroom. The profession of teaching is dedicated to the thoughtfulness and care of that action; however, locating teaching within the framework of thoughtfulness and care is subverted through standardized testing. What is even worse is that testing can replace thoughtfulness with managing (Galagan, 1985) and care with unnecessary anxiety (Herman and Golan, 1993). The evidence for the shift in the idealized identity of teacher as pedagogue to teacher as a worried manager is evidenced throughout the research on testing. Tests are implicated as one of the forces in this change.

First of all, teachers are put in the unenviable position of explicitly denying their own judgment. Despite expressed doubts about the efficacy of testing (Herman and Golan, 1993), teachers not only participate in the administration of tests or the referral of students for testing services, but they are often placed in the position of giving up 'real teaching time' to focus on improving test scores (Hall and Kleine, 1992; Nolen *et al.*, 1992; Smith and Rottenberg, 1991). As numerous researchers have pointed out, these efforts to beat the odds at the high-stakes game of testing result in a narrowing of curriculum and, ironically, the further elevation of the tests and the culture that supports them – much to the detriment of struggling students.

Teachers are also placed in subservient positions in identifying children in need of support services. They refer students to others, such as psychologists, who know the students less well but whose judgments are given more weight than theirs. As a further irony, it is often the case that psychologists end up confirming the recommendations of teachers even when the data are ambiguous (O'Reilly, Northcraft, and Sabers, 1989). It is as though the psychologists must speak in order for the teacher to be heard.

The use of widespread, high-stakes achievement testing can also alter the way the teacher defines the job of teaching. Teaching becomes identified as working with or around the testing tools that control rewards rather than as engaging children's minds. For example, teachers end up focusing their attention on students who will make gains on the tests and improve the school average (Haertel, 1989), sometimes with the encouragement of their principals (Shannon, 1986).

With respect to teacher identity, then, maximizing scores in the high-stakes environment of the testing culture takes on an air of unwilling submission. Teachers not only teach to maximize scores but, to achieve this end, they engage in numerous other behaviours that pervert teaching, learning, assessment, and the institution of schooling. Teachers reportedly engage in such behaviours as teaching to the test, using actual items from the test in their teaching, editing answers, clarifying 'stray marks', coaching students, and timing the tests inaccurately (Mehrens *et al.*, 1993; Wodtke *et al.*, 1989). This failure to follow the instructions of test developers might be considered a form of resistance to a technology that is not respected or valued. However, this resistance never parallels the direct resistance of, for instance, high school students who simply randomly fill in the bubbles of what they perceive to be inconsequential tests (Paris *et al.*, 1991). Instead, teachers feel pressured by administrators and parents to somehow make students achieve on instruments that they doubt in the first place (Smith and Rottenberg, 1991). This kind of influence can only lead to the hollowing of the identity of teacher as pedagogue, since the ethics of care and thoughtfulness in teaching are replaced by false imperatives – imperatives toward which teachers claw while struggling in vain to preserve professional dignity.

Psychologists as testing automatons

Teachers are not the only ones transformed by testing. Psychologists may also become victims of a culture more powerful than any vision they may have held of the possibilities of their practice. The relative autonomy psychologists have in school districts, combined with the appearance of choice in selecting instruments for assessment (see Milofsky, 1989), seems to make psychologists willing participants in the amount and frequency of testing that occurs. However, what appears to be autonomy or independence can soon be revealed to be related to a host of other factors that illustrate the manner in which the culture of testing reproduces itself.

When people enter the profession of school psychology, they often have been trained to take the view that learning can be broken down into discrete and sequenced skills (Shepard, 1991). But they also enter schools with other kinds of expertise about the influence of organizational or systemic contexts for schooling (Milofsky, 1989). This knowledge could allow them to look at the school as an organizational whole and to construct problems in terms of how the school as an entity works. This new conceptualization might result in problems being located in organizational structures rather than in individual children and in their collective identities. Psychologists might also partner with those who know about curriculum in order to thoughtfully engage in assessment questions (e.g., Griffin, Smith, and Burrill, 1995).

In fact, in her research, Milofsky (1989) found that psychologists working in the suburbs very selectively and very carefully allowed themselves to pursue this type of practice, while urban psychologists were not much more than testing automatons – involved in a loop of working through piles of referrals, administering tests, writing reports, and repeating the cycle (see Milofsky, 1989). Because tests represent an archaic psychology, this latter practice of school psychology is regressive and ensures the reproduction of the culture of testing.

Why, then, would some psychologists choose to spend time spewing out documentation required by federal laws and 'compiling and maintaining records rather than working with children and trying to solve their problems' (Milofsky, 1989, p. 16)? Milofsky's work offers several explanations: (a) gathering diverse data on children requires time – time that the allocation of services across several schools does not allow; (b) diverse data are contestable, unlike standardized test data, which can be used to mystify and ultimately subordinate others through technological obfuscation; (c) the seeming objectivity of tests provides a legitimacy and, ironically, a way for psychologists to gain the trust of others whom they see infrequently; (d) psychologists do not feel competent to collect diverse data; and (e) the legal pressures created by federal laws emphasize the leaving of an audit trail rather than the education of children. Milofsky (1989) argued that 'by managing an image and choosing cases carefully, psychologists can wield influence out of proportion to their marginal role in the whole enterprise' (p. 103).

In short, many psychologists knowingly or unknowingly create their identities out of the soil of testing. Fear and the desire for a sense of place within the school system seem to motivate their tendency to reproduce the practices of those who have preceded them. Their moving from school to school does not allow them to build trust, to know students, or to have the time to engage in opening up conversations about new assessment or school psychology practices. And so it becomes easy to become legitimated, empowered, and ultimately identified by testing, even though psychologists may suspect that the tests they administer are not the objective instruments people imagine (Milofsky, 1989). Indeed, the more this identification becomes entrenched, the more difficult it becomes to imagine any role other than testing for psychologists. However, this failure to dream of possibilities need not be the case.

Conclusion: recourses to the collective and self-determination of school identities

Testing has a pervasive effect on identities. By recognizing cultural difference in students while denying it, tests set students on a trajectory of school-based failure that may be more an artefact of the tests than of the abilities of students. Tests influence the identities of teachers, who often doubt the knowledge that tests offer but who must engage in subterfuge to ensure that their students will succeed. The culture of testing in schools limits the possibilities within the professional practice of school psychologists and, instead, turns them into testing machines.

So, if testing has such an overwhelming influence on both individual and collective identities, what recourses are left for change? How can the identification of reading and writing failure, based on either systematic biases or inadequacies in tests, be redressed in the face of the culture of testing in schools? The current moment of the destabilization of large-scale, multiple-choice testing creates an opportunity to reinvent possibilities for individualized assessment and for all those who participate in the action of these assessments. It creates moments for teachers and psychologists to reinvent themselves as professionals by reaching out beyond the limitations of the past, since the grounds of multiple-choice testing are, at least, shaky.

New models for what it means to assess can only redress the problems of the past if they take into account the very diversity they have ignored, and the real-life contexts in which literacy is to be used. In essence, then, the certainty of assessment must be replaced by considering assessment as a problem that requires of its participants 'defensible' practices (Sizer, 1995). Furthermore, in the spirit of Moss (1994), what would be required

> would involve holistic, integrative interpretations of collected performances that seek to understand the whole in light of its parts, that privilege readers [interpreters] who are most knowledgeable about the context in which the assessment occurs, and that ground those interpretations not only in the textual and contextual evidence available, but also in rational debate among the community of interpreters.
>
> (p. 7)

Such steps are beginning to be taken in a variety of schools throughout the United States (e.g., Darling-Hammond, Ancess, and Falk, 1995; Valencia *et al.*, 1994). These alternative projects make room for the exercise of teacher judgment; they seem to be targeted somewhat more toward what are being called 'authentic' tasks; and in cases such as the Australian project by Griffin *et al.* (1995), there is room for a psychometry – although the practices of some of the suburban psychologists in Milofsky's (1989) study might be a better aspiration. However, there still must be safeguards put in place against the racial, class, and gender prejudices of the past. These new assessments require teachers, in particular, to recognize their own positionality and to seek out those who would help them see and value the myriad identities of the children entering school. It means building upon identities rather than destroying them. It means recognizing that the politics of identities must acknowledge the shadows of the past as well as the possibilities for the future, so that the enrichment that diverse identities offer is revalued as schools strive to learn what it means to offer education in a diverse society.

Note

1 The latter phrase is borrowed from the song title 'Changer and the Changed' by C. Williamson.

References

Anastasi, A. (1982). *Psychological Testing* (5th ed.). New York: Macmillan.

Baxter, S. (1993). *A Child is not a Toy: Voices of children in poverty*. Vancouver, BC: New Star Books.

Bennett, R. E., and Ward, W. C. (eds) (1993). *Construction versus Choice in Cognitive Measurement: Issues in constructed response, performance testing, and portfolio assessment*. Hillsdale, NJ: Lawrence Erlbaum.

Bradley, J. M. (1976). Evaluating reading achievement for placement in special education. *Journal of Special Education*, 10, 237–245.

Brescia, W., and Fortune, J. C. (1989). Standardized testing of American Indian students. *The College Student Journal*, 2, 98–104.

Brooks, S. S. (1920). Getting teachers to feel the need for standardized tests. *Journal of Educational Research*, 2, 425–435.

Brooks, S. S. (1921). Measuring the progress of pupils by means of standardized tests. *Journal of Educational Research*, 4 (3), 161–171.

Bursztyn, A. M. (1992). The effects of judgmental heuristics on the psychoeducational assessment of language minority children. Unpublished doctoral dissertation, Columbia University, New York.

Chittenden, E. A. (1987). Styles, reading strategies and test performance: A follow-up study of beginning readers. In R. O. Freedle and R. P. Duran (eds), *Cognitive and Linguistic Analyses of Test Performance* (pp. 369–390). Norwood, NJ: Ablex.

Coley, R. J., and Goertz, M. E. (1990). *Educational Standards in the 50 States*. Princeton, NJ: Educational Testing Service.

Crocker, L., Schmitt, A., and Tang, L. (1988). Test anxiety and standardized achievement test performance in the middle school years. *Measurement and Evaluation in Counselling and Development*, 20 (4), 149–157.

Darling-Hammond, L., Ancess, J., and Falk, B. (1995). *Authentic Assessment in Action: Studies of schools and students at work*. New York: Teachers College Press.

Emihovich, C. (1990). Ask no questions: Sociolinguistic issues in experimental and testing contexts. *Linguistics and Education*, 2, 165–183.

Farr, R., and Beck, M. (1991). Formal methods of evaluation. In J. Flood, J. M. Jensen, D. Lapp, and J. R. Squire (eds), *Handbook of Research on Teaching the English Language Arts* (pp. 489–501). New York: Macmillan.

Farr, R., Pritchard, R., and Smitten, B. (1990). A description of what happens when an examinee takes a multiple-choice reading comprehension test. *Journal of Educational Measurement*, 27, 209–226.

Figueroa, R. A. (1989). Psychological testing of linguistic-minority students: Knowledge gaps and regulations. *Exceptional Children*, 56, 145–152.

Fowles, B. A., and Kimple, J. A. (1972). Language tests and the 'disadvantaged' reader. *Reading World*, 11 (3), 183–195.

Freedle, R., and Kostin, I. (1994). Can multiple-choice reading tests be construct-valid? A reply to Katz, Lautenschlager, Blackburn, and Harris. *Psychological Science*, 5, 107–110.

Galagan, J. E. (1985). Psychoeducational testing: Turn out the lights, the party's over. *Exceptional Children*, 52, 288–299.

Gardner, H. (1993). *Frames of Mind: The theory of multiple intelligences* (2nd ed.). New York: Basic Books.

Gifford, B. R. (1989). The allocation of opportunities and the politics of testing: A policy analytic perspective. In B. R. Gifford (ed.), *Test Policy and the Politics of Opportunity Allocation* (pp. 3–32). Boston: Kluwer Academic Publishers.

Goodman, Y. M. (1991). Informal methods of evaluation. In J. Flood, J. M. Jensen, D. Lapp, and J. R. Squire (eds), *Handbook of Research on Teaching the English Language Arts* (pp. 502–509). New York: Macmillan.

Griffin, P., Smith, P. G., and Burrill, L. E. (1995). *The American Literacy Profile Scales: A framework for authentic assessment*. Portsmouth, NH: Heinemann.

Guskey, T. R., and Kifer, E. W. (1990). Ranking school districts on the basis of statewide test results: Is it meaningful or misleading? *Educational Measurement: Issues and Practice*, 9 (1), 11–16.

Hacking, I. (1990). *The Taming of Chance*. Cambridge: Cambridge University Press.

Haertel, E. (1989). Student achievement tests as tools of educational policy: Practices and consequences. In B. R. Gifford (ed.), *Test Policy and the Politics of Opportunity Allocation* (pp. 25–50). Boston: Kluwer Academic Publishers.

Hall, J. L., and Kleine, P. F. (1992). Educators' perceptions of NRT misuse. *Educational Measurement: Issues and Practice*, 11 (2), 18–22.

Hanson, F. A. (1993). *Testing Testing: Social consequences of the examined life*. Berkeley: University of California Press.

Henry, P., Bryson, S., and Henry, C. A. (1989). Black student attitudes toward standardized tests: Does gender make a difference? *College Student Journal*, 23, 346–354.

Herman, J. L., and Golan, S. (1993). The effects of standardized testing on teaching and schools. *Educational Measurement: Issues and Practice*, 12 (4), 20–25 and 41.

Jackson, G. D. (1975). On the report of the ad hoc committee on educational uses of tests with disadvantaged students: Another psychological view from the Association of Black Psychologists. *American Psychologist*, 30, 88–93.

Johnston, P. H. (1983). *Reading Comprehension Assessment: A cognitive basis*. Newark, DE: International Reading Association.

Karmos, A. H., and Karmos, J. S. (1984). Attitudes toward standardized achievement tests and their relation to achievement test performance. *Measurement and Evaluation in Counselling and Development*, 17 (2), 56–66.

Koretz, D., Stecher, B., Klein, S., and McCaffrey, D. (1994). The Vermont portfolio assessment programme: Findings and implications. *Educational Measurement: Issues and Practice*, 13 (3), 5–16.

Linn, R. L. (1986). Educational testing and assessment: Research needs and policy issues. *American Psychologist*, 41.

Madaus, G. F. (1992). An independent auditing mechanism for testing. *Educational Measurement: Issues and Practice*, 11 (1), 26–29 and 31.

McGill-Franzen, A., and Ailington, R. L. (1993). Flunk 'em or get them classified: The contamination of primary grade accountability data. *Educational Researcher*, 22 (1), 19–22.

Mehrens, W. A., Phillips, S. E., and Schram, C. M. (1993). Survey of test security practices. *Educational Measurement: Issues and Practice*, 12 (4), 5–9 and 19.

Miller, S. K. (1990). Interaction effects of gender and item arrangement on test and item performance. *Dissertation Abstracts International*, 51 (6), 1959-A.

Milofsky, C. (1989) *Testers and Testing: The sociology of school psychology*. London: Rutgers University Press.

Mislevy, R. J. (1993). Foundations of a new test theory. In N. Frederiksen, R. J. Mislevy, and I. I. Bejar (eds), *Test Theory for a New Generation of Tests* (pp. 19–39). Hillsdale, NJ: Lawrence Erlbaum.

Moss, P. A. (1994). Can there be validity without reliability? *Educational Researcher*, 23 (2), 5–12.

Murphy, S. (1995). Revisioning reading assessment: Remembering to learn from the legacy of reading tests. *Clearing House*, 68 (4), 235–239.

Nolen, S. B., Haladyna, T. M., and Haas, N. S. (1992). Uses and abuses of achievement test scores. *Educational Measurement: Issues and Practice*, 11 (1), 9–15.

O'Connor, M. C. (1989). Aspects of differential performance by minorities on standardized tests: Linguistic and sociocultural factors. In B. R. Gifford (ed.), *Test Policy and Test Performance: Education, language, and culture* (pp. 121–181). Boston: Kluwer Academic Publishers.

O'Reilly, C., Northcraft, G. B., and Sabers, D. (1989). The confirmation bias in special education eligibility decisions. *School Psychology Review*, 18 (1), 126–135.

Palmer, D. J., Olivarez, A., Willson, V. L., and Fordyce, T. (1989). Ethnicity and language dominance – influence on the prediction of achievement based on intelligence test scores in nonreferred and referred samples. *Learning Disability Quarterly*, 12, 261–274.

Paris, S. G., Lawton, J. C., Turner, J. C., and Roth, J. L. (1991). A developmental perspective on standardized achievement testing. *Educational Researcher*, 20, 12–30.

Perrone, V. (1991). On standardized testing. *Childhood Education*, 67, 132–142.

Sadker, M., and Sadker, D. (1994). *Failing at Fairness: How our schools cheat girls*. New York: Touchstone.

Scruggs, T. E., and Mastropieri, M. A. (1988). Are learning disabled students 'test-wise'?: A review of recent research. *Learning Disabilities Focus*, 3 (2), 87–97.

Scruggs, T. E., White, K. R., and Bennion, K. (1985). Teaching test-taking skills to elementary-grade students: A meta-analysis. *Elementary School Journal*, 87, 69–82.

Scruggs, T. E., Mastropieri, M. A., and Tolfa-Veit, D. (1986). The effects of coaching on the standardized test performance of learning disabled and behaviorally disordered students. *Remedial and Special Education*, 7 (5), 37–41.

Serwatka, T. S., Deering, S., and Stoddard, A. (1989). Correlates of the underrepresentation of black students in classes for gifted students. *Journal of Negro Education*, 58, 520–530.

Shannon, P. (1986). Consensus or conflict: Views of reading curriculum and instructional practice. *Reading Research and Instruction*, 26, 31–49.

Shepard, L. A. (1991). Psychometricians' beliefs about learning. *Educational Researcher*, 20 (7), 2–16.

Shepard, L. A. (1993). The place of testing reform in educational reform: A reply to Cizek. *Educational Researcher*, 22 (4), 10–13.

Sizer, T. R. (1995). Foreword. In L. Darling-Hammond, J. Ancess, and B. Falk, *Authentic Assessment in Action: Studies of schools and students at work* (pp. vii–ix). New York: Teachers College Press.

Smith, M. L., and Rottenberg, C. (1991). Unintended consequences of external testing in elementary schools. *Educational Measurement: Issues and Practice*, 10 (4), 7–11.

Steele, J. L., and Meredith, K. (1991). Standardized measures of reading achievement for placement of students in Chapter I and learning disability programmes: A nationwide survey of assessment practices. *Reading Research and Instruction*, 30 (2), 17–31.

Taylor, D. (1991). *Learning Denied*. Portsmouth, NH: Heinemann.

Tierney, R. J. (1990). Verbocentrism, dualism, and oversimplification: The need for new vistas for reading comprehension research and practice. In R. Beach and S. Hynds (eds), *Developing Discourse Practices in Adolescence and Adulthood* (pp. 246–260). Norwood, NJ: Ablex.

Tolfa, D., Scruggs, T. E., and Bennion, K. (1985). Format changes in reading achievement tests: Implications for learning disabled students. *Psychology in the Schools*, 22, 387–391.

Trueba, H. T., Jacobs, L., and Kirton, E. (1990). *Cultural Conflict and Adaptation: The case of Hmong children in American Society*. New York: Falmer.

Valencia, S. W., and Pearson, P. D. (1986). New models for reading assessment. *Reading Education* NO. 71. Champaign, IL: Center for the Study of Reading, University of Illinois at Urbana-Champaign.

Valencia, S. W., and Pearson, P. D. (1987). Reading assessment: Time for a change. *The Reading Teacher*, 40, 726–732.

Valencia, S. W., Hiebert, E. H., and Afflerbach, P. P. (1994). *Authentic Reading assessment: Practices and possibilities*. Newark: DE: International Reading Association.

Willis, A. I. (1991). Panorama: A narrative history of standardized elementary reading comprehension test development and reading test authors in the United States, 1914–1919. Volumes I and II. *Dissertation Abstracts International*, 51 (10), 3374-A.

Wodtke, K. H., Harper, F., Schommer, R. M., and Brunelli, P. (1989). How standardized is school testing? An exploratory observational study of standardized group testing in kindergarten. *Educational Evaluation and Policy Analysis*, 11 (3), 223–235.

Source

This is an edited version of an article previously published in *Reading and Writing Quarterly*, 13(3). 1997. Reproduced by permission of Taylor & Francis Inc.

Chapter 8

Learning difficulties and the New Literacy Studies

A socially-critical perspective

Bill Green and Alex Kostogriz

Introduction

'Learning difficulties', and more broadly 'learning disabilities' (LD), are commonly understood within the orthodox frames of cognitive and developmental psychology. For literacy education, this means all too often conceptualising them as terms of deficit or deficiency, or as deviations from a Norm. This latter is the so-called 'normal child' – that is, a normative literate subject, capable of reading and writing easily and readily, and of learning, without any unusual or unexpected hassles or problems. Such work all too often is characterised by a totalising normative judgement, and it is one that much be recognised accordingly as intensely problematical. An alternative stance is that of the New Literacy Studies (NLS), which sees literacy pedagogy and literate practice alike expressly in socio-cultural terms, and as organised around the notion of socially-situated textual practice. This chapter first introduces the work of the New Literacy Studies, with the focus being on the links with critical pedagogy and, relatedly, the notion of 'critical literacy'. It then presents an account of a different, more socially-oriented psychology, as a resource for understanding learning difficulties in literacy practice and development. This is the cultural–historical tradition, originally associated with and stemming from Lev Vygotsky but drawing subsequently on work such as that of Alexei N. Leont'ev and Yrjö Engeström, and also James Wertsch and Michael Cole. However, our particular focus here is on Vygotsky's work, with a view to providing the basis of what we see as a more productive, socially-inclusive way of thinking about classrooms, learning and teaching.

How do 'learning difficulties' figure in new understandings of literacy studies and literacy education? How might literacy teachers most usefully and appropriately engage the learning continuum – specifically, from 'difficulties' to 'disabilities' – in managing classroom literacy programmes and working, as inevitably they do, with 'mixed-ability' student cohorts? How to understand the notion of 'disability', as a distinctive social category? What might be the possibilities here for rethinking 'LD' issues within a socially-critical frame? These are key organising questions, although obviously far too broad in their scope and reference to deal with adequately here. Our more limited ambition is to provide a brief account of the implications and challenges of new work in literacy pedagogy, with a view to informing the issue of student learning difficulties in school practice.

The New Literacy Studies

The focus of this chapter is the New Literacy Studies. A growing body of trans-disciplinary work in literacy studies and literacy education, it is distinctive in being expressly organised and energised by what has been called 'the social turn' (Gee, 2000). Work of this kind and orientation is distinguished by:

- an emphasis on literacy as sociocultural practice;
- a keen awareness of the importance of social context, as well as of the reciprocal relationship between meaning and context; and
- renewed interest therefore in issues of history, culture and power.

Such work has been gathering in both momentum and explanatory value for over two decades now, and is to be conceived as in fundamental opposition to mainstream scientific–cognitivist positions in curriculum and literacy work in schools, as elsewhere. At the same time it is arguably still relatively marginal in educational policy and practice, attesting to the persistence of significant inequities and ideologies in education and society alike. Moreover, it is still far from being an integral part of *literacy* policies and programmes – although it must be said, in this regard, that the trends and signs may well be more positive in Australia than in other anglophone countries (Luke, 2000).

As noted, the past two decades have brought together a number of complementary perspectives in the field of literacy studies focusing on the sociocultural nature of literacy learning and, associated with this, our understanding of and approach to literacy learning difficulties. Revolutionary changes in our understanding of literacy as social practice have occurred in times of massive postindustrial transformations, among other things fuelling debates over what counts as literacy and learning. Sociocultural researchers of literacy have cogently emphasised that literacy learning is not just about print-processing 'skills', occurring in individual 'minds' – the 'autonomous' model (Street, 1993). Rather, it must be conceived as a socially and culturally crafted set of practices, within which individuals are mutually dependent as they participate in activities with and around texts. People learn and use literacy in specific sociocultural contexts, and the ways they use texts are associated with relations of power and ideology as these inform and underlie contextual meaning-making. What Street (1993) calls the 'ideological' model of literacy, in contrast, highlights a sociocultural view of learning as scaffolded apprenticeship to particular 'ways of behaving, interacting, valuing, thinking, believing, speaking, and often reading and writing' (Gee, 1996, p. viii; Rogoff, 1995). From this perspective, literacy learning is embedded in the practices and discourses of social groups and, as such, literacy learners are conceived as in the course of becoming knowledgeable and capable participants in and of communities of literacy practice.

In this regard, the studies of literacy practices come to constitute a distinctive 'interdisciplinary' approach interested in many issues related to the process of becoming literate in society. In contrast to the 'autonomous' model of literacy learning, the New Literacy Studies (Gee, 2000; Street, 1993) emphasise the role of social interaction and networks of cultural practices in the social construction of meaning. Literacy learning is seen as occurring in multiple localities, involving particular cultural and political practices which enable some 'ways with words' and disenable others. Furthermore, literacy practices are constitutive of people's identities, as they are constantly evaluated against social constructions of normativity, correctness, and proficiency. Literacy learners experiencing difficulties of one kind or another are characteristically labelled (e.g., 'at risk', 'struggling', 'incompetent', etc.), marked out as Other. This among other things has the effect of helping *produce* those who are different as, in fact, 'disabled'. When literacy is understood as a set of autonomous skills, it is easy to focus on brain disorders and the like and to explain deviancy from the norm as a matter of individual defect. But when we conceive literacy as a matter of *social practices* and indeed, even more so, as *multiple literacies*, any notion of 'mental deviation' becomes problematic. The very existence of LD phenomena, from this perspective, is closely related to the availability of cultural technologies of identity construction and also to various 'disabling' contexts of literacy learning that are, in effect, intolerant of difference (McDermott and Varenne, 1995).

Hence, literacy practices in schools constitute a specific sociopolitical context for learning and development. Fundamental to this context is the *classification* of students – as 'normal' and 'abnormal', 'competent' and 'incompetent', 'gifted' and 'disabled', etc. This classificatory work needs to be understood accordingly as an aspect of a generalised technological apparatus working to differentiate and classify as well as to normalise or exclude (Foucault, 1977). This is what Gee (2000, p. 191) calls 'enactive' and 'recognition' work, realised as it is through textually-mediated social activity. The nature of such classifications and their consequences for students' developing identities and future life-trajectories is increasingly being recognised as problematic and contested, however and clearly it is crucial to find ways and resources to help in better understanding these issues.

Within the broad context of the NLS, there are two matters we want to highlight. The first is the concept and the practice of *critical literacy*. This is a challenging and innovative development in literacy pedagogy, firmly emphasising its political and socially critical character but – importantly, and increasingly – doing so via the mainstream medium of classroom practice. In essence, critical-literacy practice involves the programmatic articulation of literacy education and critical pedagogy, with literacy teaching and learning located at the centre of a socially-critical curriculum. Key issues of debate in such work include

- the amelioration of educational disadvantage, in all its forms;
- the active promotion of social justice in and through education;
- the pursuit and furtherance of democratic principles and practices; and indeed
- a practical-pedagogic project of possibility, with regard to social transformation and change.

In this regard, it has links with the work in the critical sociology of education, although it also draws upon a wider field of reference than this, being significantly shaped and informed by a long tradition of 'practical progressivism' in classroom pedagogy. This latter point is quite crucial.

The second matter to observe here is that there has been a tendency in such work to refuse, or at least to downplay, the value and significance of *psychology*. This is partly because of the felt need, historically, to give more room on the agenda of literacy pedagogy to sociology – to sociological questions and issues, such as context or power. An associated matter is the historical contextualisation of the educational field within what has been called the *psy-complex*: those sciences of subjectivity and government that are organised around the regulation of individuals and the organisation of populations, and the care of the Soul. As well, there has been a growing scepticism in the field as to the meta-narrative claims and pretensions of scientific psychology.

More recently, however, there have been signs of an important movement, beyond a constraining 'from . . . to' logic (i.e., *from* psychology *to* sociology . . .) to one that is much more usefully organised by a 'both–and' way of seeing things. That is, rather than being held within a limited and limiting binary logic, the focus in literacy research has shifted now to a more complex and accommodating concern with *both* psychology and sociology. More generally, this is to be understood as a *transdisciplinary* focus, the shift in question constituting a new position which seeks to include the two without being captured by either of them. The effect is, potentially at least, quite liberating.

Apropos of the new Literacy Studies, Gee (2000) has written of sociocultural ('cultural–historical') psychology as one of a set of what might be called adjacent fields, all of which are characterised by a new engagement with social practice and cultural politics. His reference is both to what he calls 'socio-historical psychology', 'following Vygotsky and later Wertsch', and to 'closely related work in situated cognition [and] activity theory' (Gee, 2000, p. 181). Although less clear about this, here at least, it would appear a logical and productive move for such work to be increasingly, organically incorporated into literacy pedagogy *per se*. In this way, opportunity is provided to problematise and critically transcend the 'individual–society' dichotomy that bedevils much educational debate.[1] This is the context for the following section, then, which addresses more directly the issue of LD from a reconceptualised critical-literacy perspective.

Rethinking 'LD'

While we are witnessing drastic changes in reconceptualising literacy, how-ever, shifts in our understanding of literacy learning difficulties and disabilities are much less dynamic. Literacy 'disability' is a relatively recent construction, and one that should always be contextualised by a scrutiny at both 'literacy' and 'disability', as concepts. A direct connection may be posited between the kinds of literacy most valued in society and a presumption of literacy deficiencies – that is, (in)competence of (dis)ability. To understand what counts as (dis)ability means, then, to address what counts as literacy as well as what counts as (in)competence.

Literacy education has been historically constructed on the basis of a stan-dardised norm, linked with rules, grammar and correctness, and hence driven by an overarching logic of unification, measurement, and comparison with regard to students' competence and performance. Competence in literacy has been generally defined in curriculum documents as a set of 'skills' enabling students' reading, writing, composition and spelling. In this definition, acquiring 'cognitive skills' constitutes the basic competence needed to perform literacy tasks – either to decode print in order to gain access to information or to encode one's own thoughts in written-textual form so as to communi-cate information to others. In this regard, literacy competence becomes socially defined, inscribed and entrained. It is not in doubt until someone exhibits evidence of failure, of failed or flawed performance. To be *seen* as a literacy-'abled' person, then, one should always strive to speak, read and write correctly and indeed appropriately, 'properly'. Otherwise, any sign of incorrect or in-appropriate performance may be constructed as a marker of difference, an interruption in the normal flow of things, a 'disability'. Attribution of LD thus rests upon a social construction of what counts as 'correctness', generating classificatory fields of both ability and disability, and marking them as a key 'dividing practice'.

In this sense, the basic orientation of traditional literacy education has been to teach the 'canon', on the one hand, and to detect and correct 'error', on the other hand. Emphasising correctness and normativity has provided a rationale for commonsensical judgements that deviations in reading or writing are related to individual deficiency, either perceptual or cognitive. However, a positivist logic of 'correctness' does not leave space to reflect self-critically on what might be problematical about the normative structure itself (Giroux, 1997). Instead, the focus on error shifts all responsibility onto those whose performance has been already 'disabled', whose problems and diffi-culties may be bio-physiological in nature but also of a social and cultural kind. It is important to bear in mind that the standardisation/canonisation of literacy is always based on dominant cultural values and reflects relations of power in broader society that are clearly disenabling for many socially dis-advantaged and minority students (Alvermann, 2001). The positivist logic of correctness in literacy education – a key means for maintaining and reinforcing social order – thus contributes to our structured incapacity to see multiple reasons for poor performance and literacy learning difficulties. Hence, when the construction of 'disabling' environments for literacy learning is not questioned *critically*, then the problem of 'LD' itself is relegated solely to the domain of clinical research.

At this point we want to briefly posit two models of literacy learning difficulties and disabilities, one 'clinical' in its orientation and the other 'cultural'. The latter we shall go on to describe at greater length below. For the moment it is sufficient to highlight what we describe as *the clinical model* here, noting its pervasiveness and persistence as an explanatory and executive framework for thinking about LD aspects of literacy pedagogy. In essence this model entails a deficiency view of literacy learning and literacy learners alike, and is based on what might be called scientised forms of normative judgement. There is, if course, a long heritage of clinical work in dyslexia and related to this literacy problems, understood 'medically' (e.g., Hinshelwood, 1917; Orton, 1937; Galaburda, 1991). Importantly, there are links to be observed between 'clinical' perspectives of this kind and 'autonomous' models of literacy, between logics of deficiency and neuropsychological deviancy and the politics of testing and classification in literacy studies (Cook-Gumperz, 1986). The over-representation of minority and socially disadvantaged students in the category of 'disability' attests to the incapacity of clinical models to take into account the sociocultural complexity of literacy learning difficulties (Artiles and Trent, 2000). With that in mind, we turn now to what we call cultural models of LD, and in particular Vygotsky's legacy in this regard.

Vygotsky's legacy: towards a cultural model of LD

Vygotsky's ideas about the social origin of the mind, the role of language and social interaction in the formation of psychological functions, and the importance of a 'practice' account of learning, constitute now a significant conceptual component within new sociocultural approaches to literacy learning (Lee and Smagorinsky, 2000; Scribner and Cole, 1981; Wertsch, 1998; etc.). However, his work in the area of teaching children with special needs is less known, even though this makes up a substantial part of his overall theoretical legacy (Gindis, 1995). In fact, Vygotsky started his intellectual–psychological career in the mid 1920s (in the Moscow Institute of Psychology) while being simultaneously involved in practical work with disabled children – specifically, the blind, deaf-mute and mentally handicapped. For him, this was the main empirical domain for conceptualising the principles of his cultural–historical theory of learning and psychological development (Luria, 1979).

The most fundamental concept of cultural–historical theory is that the human mind is *mediated*. Vygotsky (1978) argued that people in their practical life do not act directly on the world or on other people but rely, instead, on tools and signs. We use tools to transform the material world and conditions in which we live, as well as using signs to mediate and regulate our relationships with each other and with ourselves in social activities. Tools and signs are cultural–historical artefacts which afford as well as constrain specific practices and hence shape particular ways of doing and meaning-making. Among a multiplicity of semiotic artefacts, within which Vygotsky included written signs, symbols, graphs, maps, systems for counting, mechanical drawings, works of art, etc., language is the most powerful means used by people. During participation in social activities with others, a child internalises social language(s), funds of knowledge, cultural–technical artefacts as well as norms and modes of acting. It is then in cultural practices, in our engagement with others, that human mind evolves as cultural and social from the outset owing to its semiotic mediation by cultural artefacts.

From the cultural–historical perspective, these mediating means – multimodal literacy resources, as they might be called – function as 'psychological tools' changing the natural, or biological properties of mind. 'By being included in the process of behaviour', Vygotsky (1981, p. 137) argues, 'the psychological tool alters the entire flow and structure of mental functions'. A child learns how to use semiotic means of culture first in social practices, in communication with others, and later these social ways with words and signs become internalised and used by the child as psychological tools. Therefore, Vygotsky (1978) concluded that psychological development transpires on two planes. First, it appears *interpsychologically*, in interaction between people, and secondly, as an *intrapersonal* category within the child. By differentiating these two intersecting planes of psychological development, Vygotsky emphasises the role of society, learners' participation in collective practices, and cultural mediating resources in shaping children's consciousness and thinking.

These ideas enabled Vygotsky (1993) a way of looking differently at the disabled child, and disability in general. Before Vygotsky, the main focus of 'defectology'[2] was on the organic or biological nature of a handicap: deafness, blindness, etc. He turned this approach on its head, arguing that the problem is not the handicap itself but rather its effect on the sociocultural development of the child. While an organic or 'primary' disability has in many cases a biological origin, the main problem for education becomes how to compensate it *culturally*. Focusing only on biological compensation, such as by training sharpness of hearing or smell in a blind child, means for Vygotsky a training *in* disability. He calls this the production of a 'secondary' disability, one that increasingly separates a handicapped child from social life and its cultural resources, leading to her distorted psychological development and social deprivation. Vygotsky likens such clinical models of disability to the actions of a doctor who, relying exclusively on drugs, denies a patient normal food (Vygotsky, 1983, p. 71). In order to overcome the production of 'secondary' disability in children and their 'disontogenesis' in disabling practices of special education, Vygotsky proposes a culturally inclusive model of pedagogy. This new and – at that time – revolutionary position on disability was based on the idea that the cultural line of development transforms the natural–

biological one. In the process of interaction between these two lines, individuals' consciousness and behaviour can no longer be explained solely in biological terms. Rather, active participation of the handicapped children in social practices is a key to the *cultural* compensation of disability.

Inclusion of a disabled child in broader social practices, for Vygotsky, is both a complex problem and a contradictory process. This requires a positive approach which focuses on a child's capacities and proficiencies and what he/she can do, rather than a negative one which concentrates on weaknesses and defects. In this regard, he criticises those trends in special education that, while emphasising weaknesses, design a curriculum of lowered expectations. However, any attempt to assimilate the disabled child into the 'abled' mainstream through normalisation is also misleading. Disability, as any form of difference, requires the construction of new social relationships in a collective of peers and an active search for alternative, non-marginalising ways of promoting the cultural development of the disabled. Vygotsky was convinced that conventional practices of 'mainstreaming' are not able to positively accommodate difference. Therefore, the inclusion of physically disabled persons needs a third way, which he calls a 'positive differential approach'. This implies the construction of specific learning environments, facilitating and building on the strengths and potential of disabled children.

Designing such environments requires close attention, first, to *multimodality* – that is, the availability of a range of means of semiotic mediation – something which would enhance internalisation of cultural knowledge, while simultaneously compensating for a particular disability. Secondly, it requires attention to the patterning of social activities in educational settings. With regard to the education of blind and deaf-mute children, for example, Vygotsky (1993) argues that the mode of interpersonal communication, be this Braille, a sign language (mimicry) or lip-reading, should not be conceived as the only means of communication, so constraining the cultural development of disabled children. These sign systems must be complemented by several forms of communication or speech modes (polyglossia). What is important here is the focus on *meaning* and not on the sign system. Inclusion of a disabled child and her acculturation can be reached, then, by multiple means of semiosis and by the quality and quantity of communication. Vygotsky (1993, 1997) put particular emphasis on the development of new technological means, which had the potential, as he saw it, to facilitate communication between disabled persons and also between the disabled and their more capable peers. With the advent of new computer technologies, literacy education of physically disabled persons through software development is more compelling then ever (see Bujarski *et al.*, 1999).

With regard to the second concern – the patterning of social practices in educational settings – Vygotsky (1993) argued that a physical handicap not only altered the child's relationship with the world but also affects her interaction with other people. For a disabled child, blindness or deafness represent normality – not a condition of illness. The child experiences the handicap only indirectly or secondarily, as a result of living and communicating with social others. In this sense, a disability becomes socially interpreted and constructed *from the point of view of the abled*. The ways in which a disabled child's identity is constructed originate out of the particular environments, and may differ according to the specific sociocultural conditions, in which a child is living. For instance, a peasant child's blindness is likely to have different social consequences for her personhood from how blindness is conceived in a rich family (Vygotsky, 1993). But notwithstanding those sociocultural differences, the general stance is often paternalistic and damaging.

In this regard, Vygotsky (1997, p. 287) describes a story of a blind musician conceived from the point of view of a sighted person as a constant 'suffering from an instinctive striving toward light and from the consciousness of his disability'. This perception is entirely incorrect from the blind person's point of view, as he notes, because 'blind people lack any sense of living in some kind of darkness'. What is true, however, in this story is the description of self-centred suffering as a result of social construction of the blind musician's identity. Vygotsky argues that to overcome this damaging effect on consciousness, social attitudes to a disabled person should change from a paternalistic model to a broad social experience model. By accepting disability as a difference in a social person, instead of an overshadowing defect, a programme of inclusion implies the removal of those social-discursive barriers that are hindering the cultural development of students different from the mainstream.

A cultural model of disability invites literacy researchers and practitioners to focus more on the cultural construction and configuration of a 'disabled' person, and less on his/her clinically perceived 'mental' condition. To be literacy-disabled is a complex sociocultural problem, extending far beyond physical, sensory, psychological and cognitive explanations of print-processing impairments. A cultural model also involves engagement with the 'contemporary politics of difference, or the various complex ways in which exclusion and discrimination are now practiced', in order to formulate more inclusive programmes and practices compatible with the principles of social justice and democratic education (Rizvi and Lingard, 1996, p. 15). Such inclusive and enabling strategies cannot be realised, however, without the re-distribution of resources for students defined as 'literacy-disabled' and the local redesign of learning environments.

Large-scale attempts to resolve the problem of literacy disability have been largely unsuccessful because both the mainstreaming-through-normalisation and the segregation-through-exclusion strategies in special education only produce further disability. The former insists on a way of literacy learning convenient or familiar to the middle-class mainstream and does not tap into the multiplicity of cultural resources in the classroom. Many 'disabilities' have come about because of a hegemonic insistence on the literacy canon and correctness, inadequate measures of IQ and intolerance to difference. The latter enhances disability by teaching to a watered-down curriculum based on the 'breakthroughs' of 'the bad science that hurts children' (Coles, 2000). In disability-centric learning environments, students' potential remains largely underutilised.

Therefore, we argue for the local redesign of learning environments, something that would *re-able* socially disadvantaged and culturally different students currently diagnosed as 'disabled'. In so doing, we call for a shift of focus from the individual's-need-to-change to assessment of what needs to be changed in what are effectively dysfunctional learning environments. Redistribution of cultural–semiotic resources is needed to create new literacy pedagogic patterns which, by reciprocating with consciousness of students, will re-able their learning. What semiotic resources should be incorporated in local literacy learning environments may become clear as we begin to ask what might be 'normal' for the classroom community of difference and what keeps many students from becoming multi-literate. We should also change our logic of correctness to see students' errors not only as a cognitive failure but as a struggle for meaning, occurring in liminal positions imposed by a disability label and often in relation to poverty, gender, race and ethnic labelling. We need to step back and consider relations of power, and to step forward and see the challenges of living with difference. And lastly, we need a revised view of literacy success, one that rewards and celebrates the plurality of students' achievements in everyday classroom literacy events. At heart, we need a new guiding set of principles that do not encourage us to dis-able, but rather, move us to see students' potential and, by building on this, to re-able.

Implications and challenges for literacy educators

Bringing together a critical-literacy perspective and cultural–historical psychology, within the reconceptualised context of the New Literacy Studies, has enormous potential for literacy educators engaged with the issue of learning difficulties in their classrooms. In this concluding section, we outline briefly some of the key implications and challenges of such an articulated view, as we see them.

First, as McDermott and others have argued, there is an important sense in which we produce LD through our own actions and attitudes. This is not to deny that some children experience genuine learning difficulties, or that others live with significant disabilities, whether these be physical in nature or intellectual–emotional. Postmodern social life is characterised by difference and diversity, and most classrooms are always 'mixed-ability' in their composition. Managing differences, working with diversity, is a fact of teaching for many educators today – and certainly not just those working in multicultural conditions or with 'special needs' children. However, the important point is that *culture itself produces disability*. Or rather, disability is *functional* for the cultural contexts and practices that our advanced (post)industrial societies seem to value. Hence:

> [E]very culture, as an historically evolved pattern of institutions, teaches people what to aspire to and hope for and marks off those who are to be noticed, handled, mistreated, and remediated as falling short.
>
> (McDermott and Varenne, 1995, p. 336)

It is one thing to look out for LD, especially in such circumstances, and to be prepared to provide whatever forms of compensation or supplementation are deemed necessary or desirable. It is quite another to accede to the logic and politics of such a circumscribed and fundamentally divisive vision of the social world. In this regard, it is necessary that we become attentive to the various forms of enactive and recognition work we engage in, as literacy educators, and that happens all around us – even *to* us. What Discourses do we help to build and sustain, in the course and context of our literacy work? (Gee, 2000).

Second, if our goal is to help *all* students learn literacy, we need to understand that sociocultural difference is to be seen as a *resource* rather than a liability. In today's 'mixed ability' classrooms, there is an increasing need to reconsider, and re-value, difference in this way. This is an important aspect in the reconstruction of rich literacy learning environments, in which teachers and students engage in collaborative and even 'distributed' learning, mediating and assisting each other in a variety of ways. In sociocultural terms, effective literacy learning involves utilising the full social, cultural and linguistic resources of *all* participants in classroom communities-of-difference.

What does this mean for literacy educators more specifically working with what we have called here the LD continuum? How are 'learning difficulties' to be understood? How to take account of 'disability' in ways that fully acknowledge its status and significance as a sociocultural category but nonetheless provide for classroom practice that is both inclusive and productive, in learning terms? Acknowledging these particular difference-dynamics is crucial, but that does not mean pathologising them. Rather, it means generating tasks and environments that are richly predicated on difference, and that value the full range of educational outcomes, including those associated with active and critical citizenship. In this way, working with the LD continuum needs to be understood in terms both of cultural–linguistic diversity and of civic pluralism, as a practical project of critical pedagogy.

A further matter to consider here concerns the need for an adequate and congruent theory of learning and development, one that clearly and firmly emphasises their social dimension and allows for heterogeneity and difference. The New Literacy Studies is accordingly most appropriately supplemented with the sociocultural framework outlined here – that is, with specific reference to cultural–historical psychology and the Vygotskian legacy. In particular, we have only just begun to explore the full implications and challenges associated with 'tool-and-sign' mediation as a key organising principle, especially with regard to LD phenomena in classrooms and the educational possibilities of new technologies.

And last, living with and within differences calls for widening the frame of learning difficulties and literacy education, and for viewing literate practice differently and more generatively. This is not just a matter of 'meaning-making' versus 'skills development', although there is certainly something important in that formulation, however simplistic it is. Rather, we need a richer understanding of literacy itself, reconceptualised in terms of events and practices, artefacts and environments, networks and mediators, repertoires and resources. How might literacy classrooms look if we were to work more explicitly and systematically with sociocultural and critical–democratic perspectives and agendas? And how might we re-think the problem of learning difficulties accordingly, in such a re-imagined world of difference and possibility?

Notes

1 Linked to which is a whole set of such dichotomies and dualisms: 'mind–body', 'inside–outside', 'concrete–abstract', 'process–product', etc.
2 'Defectology' in Vygotsky's time was a field of studies focusing on the development, upbringing and education of physically and mentally handicapped children (Gindis, 1995). It included four disciplines: *surdo*-pedagogy (education of the deaf and hard of hearing children), *tiflo*-pedagogy (education of the blind and visually impaired), *oligophreno*-pedagogy (education of the mentally handicapped children) and *logopedia* (education of speech and language impaired children).

References

Alvermann, D. (2001) Reading adolescents' reading identities: Looking back to see ahead, *Journal of Adolescent & Adult Literacy*, 44 (8), 676–609.
Artiles, A. and Trent, S. (2000) Representation of culturally/linguistically diverse students, in C. R. Reynolds and E. Fletcher-Jantzen (eds) *Encyclopedia of Special Education*, vol. 1, pp. 513–517. New York: John Wiley & Sons.
Bruner, J. (1990) *Acts of Meaning*. Cambridge: Harvard University Press.
Bujarski, M., Hildendrand-Nilshon, M. and Kordt, J. (1999) Psychomotor and socioemotional processes in literacy acquisition: Results of an ongoing case study involving a nonvocal cerebral palsic young man, in Y. Engeström, R. Miettinen, and R. Punamäki (eds) *Perspectives on Activity Theory*, pp. 206–227. Cambridge: Cambridge University Press.
Coles, G. (2000) *Misreading Reading*. Portsmouth: Heinemann.
Cook-Gumperz, J. (1986) Literacy and schooling: An unchanging equation?, in J. Cook-Gumperz (ed.) *The Social Construction of Literacy*, pp. 16–44. Cambridge: Cambridge University Press.
Foucault, M. (1977) *Discipline and Punish: The Birth of the Prison*, A. Sheridan (trans.). London: Allen Lane.
Galaburda, A. (1991) Anatomy of dyslexia: Argument against phrenology, in D. Duane and D. Gray (eds) *The Reading Brain: The Biological Basis of Dyslexia*, pp. 119–131. Pankton: York Press.
Gee, J. (1996) *Social Linguistic and Literacies: Ideology in Discourses*, 2nd edn. London: Taylor & Francis.

Gee, J. (2000) The New Literacy Studies: From 'socially situated' to the work of the social', in D. Barton, M. Hamilton and R. Ivanic (eds) *Situated Literacies*, pp. 180–196. London: Routledge.

Gindis, B. (1995) The social/cultural implications of disability: Vygotsky's paradigm for special education, *Educational Psychologist*, 30 (2), 77–81.

Giroux, H. (1997) *Pedagogy and the Politics of Hope: Theory, Culture, and Schooling.* Boulder: Westview Press.

Hinshelwood, J. (1917) *Congenital Word Blindness*. London: Lewis.

Lee, C. and Smagorinsky, P. (eds) (2000) *Vygotskian Perspective on Literacy Research. Constructing Meaning through Collaborative Inquiry.* Cambridge: Cambridge University Press.

Luke, A. (2000) Critical literacy in Australia: A matter of context and standpoint, *Journal of Adolescent & Adult Literacy*, 43 (5), 448–461.

Luria, A. R. (1979) *The Making of Mind: A Personal Account of Soviet Psychology.* Cambridge: Harvard University Press.

McDermott, R. and Varenne, H. (1995) Culture as disability, *Anthropology and Education Quarterly*, 26 (3), 324–348.

Orton, S. (1937) *Reading, Writing and Speech Problems in Children.* New York: Norton.

Rizvi, F. and Lingard, B. (1996) Disability, education and the discourses of justice, in C. Christensen and F. Rizvi (eds) *Disability and the Dilemmas of Education and Justice*, pp. 9–26. Buckingham: Open University Press.

Rogoff, B. (1995) Observing sociocultural activity on three planes: Participatory appropriation, guided participation, apprenticeship', in J. Wertsch, P. del Rio and A. Alvarez (eds) *Sociocultural Studies of Mind*, pp. 139–164. Cambridge: Cambridge University Press.

Scribner, S. and Cole, M. (1981) *The Psychology of Literacy*. Cambridge: Harvard University Press.

Street, B. (1993) Introduction: The New Literacy Studies, in B. Street (ed.) *Cross-Cultural Approaches to Literacy*, pp. 1–21. Cambridge: Cambridge University Press.

Vygotsky, L. S. (1978) *Mind in Society: The Development of Higher Psychological Processes.* Cambridge: Cambridge University Press.

Vygotsky, L. S. (1981) The instrumental method in psychology, in J. Wertsch (ed.) *The Concept of Activity in Soviet Psychology*, pp. 134–143. Armonk: M. E. Sharpe.

Vygotsky, L. S. (1983) *Sobranie Sochinenii, Osnovy Defektologii* (Collected Works, The Fundamentals of Defectology), vol. 5. Moscow: Pedagogika.

Vygotsky, L. S. (1993) *The Collected works of L. S. Vygotsky, The Fundamentals of Defectology*, vol. 2 (Abnormal Psychology and Learning Disabilities), R. Rieber and A. Carton (eds). New York: Plenum Press.

Vygotsky, L. S. (1997) *Educational Psychology*, R. Silverman (trans.). Boca Raton: St Lucie Press.

Wertsch, J. (1998) *Mind as Action*. New York: Oxford University Press.

Source

This chapter was written especially for this volume.

Part 3

Political and historical considerations

Curricula and programmatic responses to literacy difficulties

Chapter 9

A veteran enters the Reading Wars

My journey

Shirley A. Carson

As a teacher of reading and as a college professor, I have had the opportunity to hear several noted authors speak about their reading experiences, growing up reading real literature. Unlike most of these authors and advocates of literature, my family had few books, but those we had Mama read over and over to my siblings and me. I attribute Mama's repeated reading of *Little Women*, *Heidi*, the Anne of Green Gables books, and classic stories from the Bible to the moulding of who I am. I fondly recalled values from them when I made important decisions in childhood and adult life. Through repeated readings of these classics, I developed a concept of story as I saw those dynamic literature characters, with whom I identified, struggle through obstacles toward their goals in life.

My brother, sister, and I played out scenes from those beloved classics on the front porch. Sometimes we dramatized scenes with paper dolls we had made from pictures in catalogues. I can still see Mama sitting on the floor with us as we pretended Heidi and Peter were driving the goats up the Swiss Alps. As an adult, I ate ice cream in front of a tiny church in Switzerland. As I looked at a picture of Heidi and looked at the mountains, I thought of the lessons that Heidi learned. I looked at some problems of my own life at the time, and I used those deeply embedded lessons to solve them, allowing me to enjoy the rest of my vacation.

In 1941, when my family was sharecropping and had little money, I received an alphabet book for my 5th birthday. I constructed my own learning as I watched Mama and Daddy read it to me. I remember distinctly how I progressed through levels of emergent reading (Sulzby, 1991). I remember progressing from reading pictures to mixing pictures and text and, finally, to actually reading text. As I sought meaning and as Mama helped, I learned the names of the letters, the sound–symbol relationships, and how to read the book with comprehension. I remember that I started pretending to read the 'funny papers' in Grandma's Sunday newspaper. I could move left to right reading world-word-word. Others in the family called what I was doing 'reading the paper', and it thrilled me. At about age 4, while adults played dominoes and other games, they gave me paper to 'keep score', write messages, draw, and to emulate adults' writing. I would fill many pages with my 'cursive and manuscript' writing.

When I started first grade at age 5½ during the 'sight-word era', I already made sense of print in every environmental opportunity possible, and I could easily read the preprimer. However, reading with the sight-word method alone was not so easy for a large number of children in my class. We first-grade students were introduced to isolated words out of meaningful context, and we read from charts with no word identification strategies or search for meaning. My sister has always talked about how much she wanted to read the story instead of working with sight words first and how she wished to turn the page and *read* in books instead of having to sit, waiting until others caught up with her.

In spite of the 'see-and-say' beginning reading experience that my siblings and I had in the school classroom, we were successful readers because we had already made sense of communication and possessed word identification and comprehension strategies we, ourselves, had constructed. Our literacy-rich home was apparently a prime factor in our reading success. We often gathered around the wood cookstove to read, talk, play finger games, and tell stories. Those early underpinnings of the love of literature and literacy stood us well. My siblings and I later earned advanced degrees in college and have been involved with educating others about the joys of reading.

As a mother, I shared these stories of my childhood as I read to my own children and grandchildren. I also shared them with students in the public schools and continue to share them as I help train future teachers. I did not stay with those early reading techniques, but gradually moved toward an integrated approach to teaching reading. I did so because I had vivid memories of how I learned to read and the success that I had in using those self-learned techniques and print-rich environments with my own children and grandchildren. I tried to create that same literate environment in my classroom. My youngest granddaughters have learned to read and write at an early age in my home while playing with me and while I did assisted reading (Tompkins, 1998) with classic literature. My grandchildren and my students were read literature, and they all responded to that literature in many wonderful ways.

The legitimacy of my memories, methods, and advocates was reaffirmed as I heard Charlotte Huck, one of my favourite literature advocates, speak at an International Reading Association Southwest Regional Conference in Tucson, Arizona, in 1997. She told about her childhood reading and how we could become advocates for methods that will bring children and books together. In addition to sharing childhood memories of the value of literature and experience, I want to share chronologically the path I have taken as a first- and second-grade teacher and a teacher educator, using quality literature and experiences to lead children to reading and writing.

My purpose will be to respond to the challenge in the editorial in the May 1998 issue of *The Reading Teacher*. The journal's editors asked us, as teachers, to respond to the Reading Wars so that legislators and the public would support our use of teaching methods we have found to be the most productive. We were challenged to consider our own experiences and resulting philosophies, to share the stories of our students, and to validate our methods with research.

I also want to validate the Lapp and Flood (1998) case for integrated code instruction. I particularly want to share how I finally came to lead children to learn basic word identification and comprehension strategies while reading and while responding to literature and experiences through play, drama, and writing. This holistic method of teaching, using literature and response, coupled with an early systematic teaching of phonics information within meaningful contexts, empowers children, especially those for whom reading might be difficult. Recent professional literature and the current philosophy of the reading community validate these methods as an integrated, balanced, transactional, comprehensive approach to reading instruction (Cecil, 1999; Lapp and Flood, 1997; Silkebakken, 1996; Weaver, 1988).

Like a majority of public school teachers in the US, I do not assume a polar position, but use eclectic methods, or a balanced instructional diet (Baumann, Hoffman, Moon, and Duffy-Hester, 1998). My 40-year journey of teaching, observing, and assessing how individual children learn has led me to adopt a constructivist theory. I realize that children must construct their own learning and meaning as they are scaffolded by a more knowledgeable person. I further understand that children have varying preferred modes of learning and that the teacher must use, even within a holistic environment, many comprehension and word identification strategies. Personal and educational experiences have led me to implement and to advocate multidimensional curricula that provide multiple empowering learning strategies to children (Joyce, 1999).

Family experiences and formal education gave mixed signals

As I noted earlier, I learned to read, completed school, and studied to become a school teacher during the 'look-and-say' reading era, which reigned supreme from the 1930s until the early 1970s (Berrybill, 1997). But I was also very impressed by the early reading experiences of my mother and by the stories of a grandmother who had taught school in Indian Territory (later Oklahoma), using phonics and *The Blue Back Speller*. Spelling bees (s-a-t, sat; i-s, is; f-a-c, fac; t-i-o-n, tion; satisfaction) were a regular part of my family memories and experience. My grandma and her brothers were the best in spelling bees; my mother's generation was next best; and my generation was the poorest. If we younger ones could pronounce a word in the dictionary, Grandma said she could spell it. At age 95, she could still beat all of her very academic offspring in Scrabble or any other word game. It seemed that there was something unique about the analytical skills the older generation possessed. I kept in mind these skills as teaching phonics within children's own spelling later became so important to me.

But another fact about Grandma impressed me. With initial help from parents and older siblings, she had read most of the adult novels in a very literate home by age 8, *before* she started school. My mother, also raised in a literacy-rich home, started school at age 5 and learned to read a long version of 'The Little Red Hen' the first day of school (before having any phonics) and said it was easy for her.

I received mixed signals from my preservice training and from members of my family who had become successful readers, but I began to see a common denominator for the generations who learned to read in different eras. Regardless of methods used in school, those good readers in previous generations had constructed their own learning in a literacy-rich environment and had been scaffolded by members of the family from an impressionable early age.

In my grandmother's waning years, I talked with her often about her successes and interactions with the 16 children that she raised in her home. She talked of wanting to show them the beauties of nature, of their imaginative play, of being determined to have books and magazines regardless of poverty and hard times, and of her determination to perpetuate the literate traditions of her family. I think that I learned to read because I discovered many wonderful books and magazines at Grandma's; because I wanted to imitate her reading habits; and because Mama told and shared stories, played with us, and talked about letters and sounds. I remember that I searched for environmental print to read. I tried to make sense of the printed text on Sunday School scripture cards long before we were supposed to read them for ourselves. I know that I decoded words and used the analogy strategy of onsets and rimes (Gunning, 1995) when I was in first grade, though I was not taught to do so with the sight-word method. When new sight words or sentence strips were introduced, I could figure out what they said, even out of context, by comparing and contrasting new words to words I already knew.

While I was training to be a teacher in the 1950s, our professors still advocated teaching reading by the sight-word method, and writing was not encouraged until after children were reading and spelling well. Writing, spelling, and grammar were very separate from reading. Reading in library books was separate from regular classroom reading instruction and was hardly mentioned in language arts and reading methods classes. Contradictions existed between my own literacy experience and methods learned in preservice training. I think my movement toward the integrated, transactional, balanced approach began when I started teaching in 1959.

Moving toward the integrated approach to teaching primary grades

I taught second grade my first year as a teacher. I think I did a good job teaching the analytical students for whom reading was easy. I was constantly told by the parents (both university professors) of one of my students that they were very impressed with my self-made work sheets and with the unusual progress beyond grade level made by their daughter. My great enthusiasm for teaching and reading led many of the students in my class to become very fluent readers. Introducing vocabulary, sight words, and flashcards before reading and out of context was successful for some of the children. But I do not congratulate myself for what I did for those for whom reading was difficult. I did do some individualized instruction around children's interests. But most of what I did was whole-group instruction or round-robin reading. I gave most students the same diet of basal instruction. I did not fully assess what each child knew and did not use assessment to direct individual instruction.

I think I did do one thing right those first 3 years, but I was later talked out of continuing it by more experienced teachers. I read many stories to my second graders, and they responded with drama and writing or summarized main ideas from the plot, using their own invented spelling. As I thrilled to their wonderful spellings and stories, other teachers said, 'But don't you think they should learn the skills first, then be allowed to write when they can write correctly?' Against my own better judgement, but with instruction from teachers who had been at the game far longer, I stopped their writing in response to stories.

I then taught intermediate grades and junior high English for the next few years. On my first day in junior high, I asked seventh graders to write an essay during class (in one draft) about themselves so I would know more about them. I took the papers home to read. My husband looked at the first paper I marked. It was filled with my corrections and comments in red, as I responded to the structural, grammatical, and spelling errors. He said, 'If you did that to my paper, I wouldn't want to write for you again. I thought you told me you were going to have them write so you would know about their interests and strengths.' Enough said! That paper 'got lost' and I responded in *oral* conversation the next day to what that student wrote. I responded to the *communication* on others' papers and took notes for myself about the skills my new students needed.

In 1969, I returned to teaching first and second grades. I taught a new series using the reading readiness, phonics first approach. The pendulum does swing! I was amazed that I was teaching much the way Grandma was taught in school and by the method she used to instruct students beginning in 1899. Again, many first and second graders loved the analytical readiness skills and the explicit, direct, systematic, intensive, comprehensive phonics information (Groff, 1998). But those who were possibly dyslexic or who focused on wholes rather than analysis of parts (Carbo, 1981; Carbo, Dunn, and Dunn, 1986; Weaver, 1988) did not thrive on it. The lower reading group did more reading readiness and more drill and decoding. When at-risk readers couldn't figure out a word, I would say, 'Sound it out.' I would tell members of the top group to figure out a new word by using semantic and syntactic cueing systems, supplying a new word that made sense in the context. The good readers had time to do enrichment activities, to read, dramatize, and orally retell folk tales and library books during their reading instruction time. In retrospect, I think I should have appealed to meaning first with the lower level reading students.

As the years went by, I gradually learned from my own children's emergent literacy at home and also built on my own precious childhood memories, so I began to read more and more literature to all my students. I gave opportunities for all children to retell stories orally, dramatize, dictate their own stories, and do art in response to the literature. My students did these activities mostly during storytime and fun times. I continued teaching nearly all the phonics rules during first grade so that students would do well on achievement tests and because I knew its value. I waited until the last 9 weeks of first grade to have children retell stories in writing or to write about experiences – after they had learned phonics, the mechanics of grammar, sentence structure, and spelling.

My introduction to the emergent literacy perspective

In 1988, I was exposed to the emergent literacy perspective of whole language, the writing process, and invented spelling by Gail Tompkins (Hoskisson and Tompkins, 1987; Tompkins, 1998), my teacher and mentor at the University of Oklahoma. In February of that year, she gave me two types of assignments to do in the first-grade class that I was teaching. One was an assignment in oral language and the other in written communication. The oral language assignment validated my past practice of using directed listening/thinking activities (DLTA), oral retellings, and drama (which I learned was called 'thematic fantasy play') in response to literature.

While completing the assigned written communication project, I learned that first graders could write sooner than I thought. Students did their own spelling, progressing through stages of invented spelling (Read, 1975). They learned phonics and other word identification strategies, spelling, and mechanics of writing while they wrote. Their early attempts were real writing, not just precursors to writing (Tompkins, 1990). My first graders each wrote and published a long book containing many stories that year. I was especially thrilled with books that were written by an ESL student, by a student who had much trouble with her eyes, and by other students for whom reading was difficult. I decided that the next year I would risk starting first graders writing the first day of class.

Empowering students to take risks

The year of 1989–1990, I gave first graders opportunities to become truly empowered by taking risks (Schulz, 1991). On the first day of school, following discussion, I asked students to draw and write about one thing they had done that summer. My first grandson was in my class. His mother had always spelled all words for him when he wrote in a journal or when he wrote lists and letters at home. He cried because he wanted words spelled correctly. Another very bright but rather shy little girl cried also. I thought I was off to a bad beginning. I knew they had not been exposed to writing like this in kindergarten.

But they saw others drawing and writing in various forms, and they soon joined in. They all 'read' to me what they had written. This began my experiment of teaching phonics from 'day one' of first grade through the students' writings. Children drew in response to literature and did written retellings from 'day one to June one' of first grade. I did my doctoral research (Carson, 1991) in my classroom that year to see whether first graders could, in the spring, independently retell literature in writing, including the important elements of story.

Writing and the writing process

This same year, I chose writing and the writing process as my focus for change. (Au, 1997). I determined to have an authentic writing programme, having children write for real purposes every day. As a part of the writing process, I gave topics for children to write about. Students learned to read from their own writing (Karnowski, 1989) and kept daily journals and portfolios (Tierney, Carter, and Desai, 1991), which I used to determine the instruction they were ready for next. Students responded to literature in many ways, and some writings progressed through the whole writing process. When we were preparing to write books as a culminating experience, the first graders and I made the discovery that stories from the personal journals gave them many ideas and were good first drafts from which revisions could be made and put into a 'dummy'. Students edited dummies and published their own books. I am still amazed and ecstatic as I look at progress made throughout that year as documented with journals, portfolio entries, and published books. My grandson and a majority of those first-grade students had shown that they could revise, edit, and publish!

Clear goals for first graders' learning

I kept in mind the skills mandated by state law that should be taught in first grade. But I disposed of four of the workbooks previously used – spelling, writing, language, and one of the phonics workbooks. I wanted my students to learn all skills that were previously emphasized in these workbooks through their own writing and reading. It did not come naturally. I did lots of teaching of phonics, spelling, mechanics of writing, and grammar within the context of our reading and writing. My goal was to build on children's knowledge of environmental print and on their concept of how print works and communicates, and then to teach from whole to part all the phonics rules and word identification strategies that I had previously taught through workbooks when I used the phonics first, reading readiness approach. I developed a method for doing this.

I began with whole-to-part phonics instruction within shared reading of a predictable story (Moustafa and Maldonado-Colon, 1999). Students spontaneously read aloud with the teacher. As I did assisted reading, the children saw themselves as readers. The predictable story established a basis for making phonics lessons memorable and meaningful in context. I directly taught the consonants because they mainly have dependable sounds. Phonemic awareness and language skills also developed as the students explored environmental print, played in learning centres, talked about things they brought from home, dictated to me, and read the morning message (Morrow, Tracey, Woo, and Pressley, 1999). I taught mnemonics from 'Talking Phonics Cards' that made remembering sounds easy. Children were soon using beginning and ending sounds in their own writing.

Puppets helped with developing phonics and spelling and also gave motivation for library time and reading. My puppets introduced new units and books and taught important rules to develop the classroom community. One character, with whom some could identify, had trouble with phonics, didn't understand, and often made mistakes. Another, the antagonist, challenged children and told them things were too hard and were not attainable. The children argued and proved her wrong. I also made 32 puppets whose names began with each of the consonants, vowels, and digraphs. Each was introduced with a literature story, poetry, or skit. Each day, children brought objects from home with the same initial sounds as the puppets' names. They talked for the puppets at the puppet stand as we communicated about the objects brought from home and the initial sounds their objects and the puppet represented.

Also, in small reading and writing groups, we would use the puppets to help us learn to spell words. Students each held several puppets. If I gave the word *came* as a word to spell, students who had Clarabelle Cow, Annie Ant, Mickey Moose, and Ellie Elephant held up these puppets in the correct order to spell *came*. First graders gradually added middle sounds and silent vowels to words in their own writing. Assessment of invented spelling showed me when children were ready to hear long and short vowels, blends, and digraphs, and when they were ready to learn the rules for them.

During the year, children learned to use the many phonics rules effectively and correctly, in meaningful context that had been taught in previous years through workbooks. After exploring and using the rules through the language-experience method, the rules were introduced in the basal reader. I would then do systematic teaching of them, and first graders would do a worksheet and verbalize how to use the rule. In order to develop automatic word recognition skills quickly so children could devote their attention to meaning and enjoyment (Stahl, 1992), I concentrated on acquisition of a sight-word vocabulary. After basic sight words were first introduced and learned in the context of reading and writing, I would add them to our sight-word flashcard list. My goal was for children to learn the 220 Dolch Basic Sight Words by the end of first grade. Usually about 80 per cent of my first graders could do this.

Beginning with Dr Seuss's *Hop on Pop* (1963) we did much work with word families and the analogy strategy (Gunning, 1995; Stahl, 1992) using onsets and rimes (h-op, p-op, t-op; f-ight, n-ight) to make, spell, and read words. While the utility of phonics rules and generalizations for vowels are not dependable (Clymer, 1996), letter–sound correspondences in rhymes are dependable. Students were able to verbalize many strategies for word identification and word spellings, using the analogy strategy of compare and contrast. Quality phonics instruction was integrated and relevant to the literacy programme and was based upon first graders' experiences with text (Stahl, 1992).

Movement through the stages of invented spelling toward conventional spelling

During the first-grade year, most students move from semiphonetic, to phonetic, and to transitional spelling (Read, 1975). Transitional spelling is the stage in which students begin to use the rules of orthography. I educated parents about the stages of invented (emergent or developmental) spelling and asked them to observe the children as they progressed, assuring them that they would move to correct spelling and would learn phonics more quickly and meaningfully this way. I promised visible proof to parents. In addition to regularly sending writings home and showing portfolios, at the end of the year I sent home eight writings collected throughout the year that clearly showed irrefutable progress. Contributing to success was the fact that words for spelling tests were taken from their writings; from the 100 most-used words; and from literature, themed units, and high-interest challenge words. Before summer vacation, I asked parents to provide journals and topics about which children could write and to take part in the public library summer reading programme so they would not regress before second grade.

Developing a love for and comprehension of literature

Reading literature to children and allowing them to learn to do shared reading of Big Books allows them to enjoy reading and to read for 'meaning first'. Within this shared reading, semantics, syntax, and graphophonemic clues could be taught as word identification strategies, and the use of all three result in comprehension. First graders began the year by reading literature and responding to it by drawing a picture and labelling it or telling about it. Soon they were writing the main idea of the story. As we developed the concept of story and learned the elements found in the beginning, middle, and end (Tompkins, 1998), first graders retold stories orally and began drawing and labelling each part. By the latter part of March, first graders were retelling in writing the beginning, middle, and end of stories that were read to them and were writing their own stories with beginnings, middles, and ends using their own emergent spelling. Even the most challenged students could do this if they had an opportunity to dramatize the story before writing.

In March and April of the school year, I conducted experimental research to see the effect a form of dramatic play, called thematic fantasy play (Christie, 1987), would have upon first graders' writing of story elements as they responded to literature (Carson, 1991). First graders from this holistic environment were able to independently retell in writing the characters, setting, precipitating event, problem, attempt to solve the problem, and the solution. They wrote, using their invented spelling, in response to a picture story book that was read to them, after they participated in directed listening/thinking activities (DLTA) and dramatized the story. Independent raters said they could easily read their invented spelling.

Assessment using Mandler and Johnson's (1977) basic elements of story grammar showed that drama affected the statistical and educational significance of writings of story elements and affected the use of richer language, better sequencing, and coherence. First graders from a holistic classroom can retell the elements of story, following thematic fantasy play, using their invented spelling. When comparing writing responses with and without drama, I decided that drama was worth the extra time needed in the curriculum. Statistical results showed dramatizing stories to be especially effective for developing concept of story and writing for at-risk readers. Dramatizing stories helped children comprehend story.

That year of allowing children to write from the first day and dispensing with some of the workbooks resulted in slightly higher scores on the phonics and reading comprehension sections of the year-end achievement test and much better scores on the grammar, sentence structure, punctuation, and spelling tests than in past years. This kind of success continued for the next 3 years that I taught first grade.

During that first year of taking risks, I started cooperative writing groups and cooperative reading groups. Within the reading/writing group, students learned to write and to read from their independent writings. Students shared the first drafts of their writings, and we exchanged compliments and suggestions for revisions. We discussed word identification strategies within students' own writing. My concept of developing literacy in the circle expanded, but I did not move from homogeneous to mixed groupings for these reading and writing circles until the 1991–1992 class school year.

Heterogeneous reading and writing groups

For the last 2 years that I taught first grade, I took the risk of having heterogeneous small-group instruction and collaborative learning and made many wonderful discoveries:

- I didn't have to struggle through reading readiness and drill in decoding with a lower level group that was not interested. I experimented with Weaver's (1988) conclusions for teaching dyslexics and readers who are not analytic. They need to be taught with meaning first, be taught the most basic of phonics (consonants), and learn phonics in context of reading literature and of their own writing. Those for whom reading was difficult were the ones who thrived on enrichment.

- All children looked forward to seeing what buddies would be in their groups each day, and all felt great about their groups.
- Gifted students and less able students learned from one another. The slow learners learned much faster than they had in previous years.
- Good literature, using rhythm, rhyme, and repetition, can be read on many levels. One book, such as a Dr Seuss book or *Chicka Chicka Boom Boom* (Martin, 1989) can be used to teach nonreaders and better readers together, and each gets what he or she needs from it. Each can respond on his or her own level.
- On occasion, I had homogeneous groups for giving minilessons for those ready for a skill or for conducting a complete circle time, using ability-level materials, without students being aware of the grouping arrangement.
- I still had individualized reading of literature, individual conferences, and buddy reading in which students could progress to their own potential.
- The children who were working independently or collaboratively with classmates while I was in the circle were much more successful with mixed grouping.
- I was required to go through the basal readers. I presented these to the full class, and I had to do it only once, rather than three or four times with each reading circle. That gave more time for small group and individual reading of literature. Again, word identification strategies and sight words from the basal were introduced in small-groups in meaningful contexts *before* encounters with them in the basal. Basic skills taught in the basal were more meaningful after being learned in holistic ways.

Themed units, integrating reading and writing with the content areas

During my last 5 years teaching first grade, moving to a balanced approach, I facilitated more themed units and integrated reading and writing with the content areas. First graders also covered all the chapters in the science and social studies texts, though not always in the order in which they were arranged. Student interests and planned themed units determined chapters to be used from the basal texts. Children met knowledge of content area objectives required for first grade but learned much more as the project method (Katz and Chard, 1989) was employed. The project method enables teachers to guide children's learning of skills, content, and processes across various subject areas in the primary grades. My first graders wrote across the curriculum, explored trade books to complement science and social studies texts, and incorporated fine arts with content area learning. Children and their families supplied many of the information books for units to supplement those from our school and public libraries. High-interest words for spelling tests were taken from literature and unit themes.

First graders can learn reading comprehension strategies for expository texts. Nowhere is there a better place for the use of schema theory (connecting new material to existing schema) than in the content areas. When preparing to give texts to students, I asked them, 'What is science?' I wrote on charts everything they said. When we finished, we had 'words of wisdom' for all the science disciplines, which were published in the school newspaper. The children did an overview of the texts and shared predictions of what we would learn this year and what they wanted to learn. I had objectives for what they must learn, but they could learn much more through building upon interests from past experiences.

When introducing a new theme and chapter, even young children can use comprehension strategies such as K-W-L (What I *know*, what I *want* to learn, and, later, what I *learned*; Ogle, 1986). They can even survey a chapter, looking at pictures, illustrations, and headings to predict what they will learn, and they can question, read, recite, and review, as in SQ3R (Vacca and Vacca, 1999). I truly believe I used the best of eclectic choices, as I used both the science and social studies texts and information books and literature while facilitating themed units and reading and writing across the curriculum. I had the opportunity to directly teach valuable content and factual objectives; children explored and constructed their own learning with reading and writing and developed comprehension strategies.

Articulation of my own theory and philosophy

I was fortunate to initially teach university education classes in reading while I was still teaching first graders. I was able to test with children the lofty concepts that I espoused to future teachers. Then, leaving first-grade students to teach early childhood education classes full time was an exciting step because I felt I could share from personal experience how I facilitated literacy. But I did not initially tell university students how to teach. I began by first putting my university students into disequilibrium as I introduced the methods of developmentally appropriate and inappropriate practices of teaching, various definitions of the reading process, the polar philosophies, and the debates on theory and process. Future teachers were challenged to use broad educational philosophies, such as maturationist, constructivist, and behaviourist theories to construct their own philosophies, methods, and strategies for teaching comprehension and word identification strategies and for creating the environment in which children would love to read and write. I wanted them to move to at least a temporary equilibrium by the end of the semester.

After instructing future teachers through questioning; allowing them to research, examine, and model methods; and viewing classrooms exemplifying excellent teaching, I shared more of my own discoveries and methods for a balanced approach. I shared overhead transparencies and portfolio examples of first graders' writings from the beginning to the end of first grade. The class assessed these writings of children in various stages of emergent spelling, and students were to use this assessment to determine what step of instruction in phonics and other encoding and decoding strategies the children were ready for next. We used a word identification strategies book as one of our texts and learned the phonics rules, as well as other methods of word identification. In this way, future educators saw opportunities to teach the phonics rules and word identification strategies within students' writings.

Future teachers went to elementary schools, read literature to primary children, and had them respond using their own independent spelling. The university students then assessed responsive writings and analyzed how to assess emergent spelling and writing and how to use that assessment to teach skills within context. Strickland's (1995) balanced approach and Adams's (1990) history of the debate and research over approaches to reading instruction confirmed that phonics and direct instruction are a part of the whole language approach.

I encourage students to learn to articulate theory, philosophy, and methods and strategies for practice and to be able to share this when interviewed for a teaching position and when interacting with parents, the professional community, and legislators. I now warn future teachers to be ready for the question 'Will you teach phonics *or* whole language?' They must be ready to tell how they will teach and assess word identification strategies and comprehension strategies within the meaningful, holistic environment. The assessment must be used to plan the next step of instruction to benefit the student.

During the last 6 years, while struggling with better ways of teaching future educators, I was also working on *verbalizing* my own theory, with its eclecticism of methods, of how children become literate. I was very interested in New Zealand's success in developing literacy. Though I knew the Reading Recovery programme was designed for use with individual students, I wondered how certain practices from it could be used in reading conferences and small groups within the regular classroom. I had the opportunity to go to New Zealand in 1996 to visit the College of Education at The University of Auckland and its laboratory school, the Epsom Normal Primary School. The visits to primary classrooms and departments in the College of Education were very enlightening.

My visit with the Head of the Centre for Language and Languages, Libby Limbrick, rendered some surprising insights for me. Though I knew the term *whole language* was coined in the United States, I expected only a pure, holistic theory to be espoused in New Zealand. Limbrick and I exchanged syllabi for several courses, and as we discussed them, she gave me a copy of her article, 'Literacy: Why the great debate?' (1995). In this article, she explained the great debate centring around the two theoretical stances at opposite ends of a continuum. She thoroughly described the 'bottom-up theory' and the 'top-down theory'. She then answered the question, 'So where does New Zealand lie on this continuum?' Limbrick said that the answer is 'somewhere in between'. She described this intermediate position as an 'interactive view'. Syllabi showing training for reading instruction emphasized Balanced Language Programmes and Balanced Reading Programmes. Reutzel (1999) urges us to remember our 'reading past', to remember the success of the Balanced Reading

Programmes of New Zealand, and to implement them fully in a comprehensive, seamless blend of factors related to reading success, rather than to swing with the pendulum, defining anew what balanced literacy means. I was quite sure that I embraced the interactive, balanced approach to developing literacy in children, and I was even more sure when I observed a class in the Epsom Normal Primary School.

As I observed classes of 5-year-olds through 10-year-olds in the laboratory schools at Auckland College of Education, I found individual conferences used extensively with children as they read from writings in their portfolios and from literature. Much bottom-up instruction (part to whole) was done in the conferences as specific skills were taken from children's own writing and reading and then taught in isolation, just as I had always done with first graders. But the specific skills instruction was also used in the top-down (whole-to-part) experiences. Students' response to literature covered the walls of classrooms and halls, and artwork painted on the outside of school buildings distinguished community schools from each other. Collaborative learning was taking place within a mixture of the indigenous Maori population, white New Zealanders, and new immigrants from China and Japan as children did shared reading and interactive writing. Oral language acquisition was stressed, and the reading and writing processes were addressed. It seemed to me that New Zealand teachers embraced constructivism and the teaching of basic skills within the students' own reading and writing.

I also observed Reading Recovery in action and saw a focus on comprehension of connected text, writing as an integral part of reading instruction, students being made aware of goals and of their own strategies, and direct instruction within the meaningful whole. Though Reading Recovery is focused upon success only for targeted, identified, at-risk students, I, like Spiegel (1995), see these factors as guidelines for success for all programmes.

After I returned from New Zealand, and as I continued preparing future early childhood and elementary reading teachers, my university students and I continued visiting primary classrooms. We have been concerned about the ways politics and public opinion are influencing teaching in our state of Oklahoma. Though whole language improperly employed may contribute to reading problems for children, there are many other contributing factors to illiteracy. Very recently, teachers have had new 'phonics first' programmes thrust upon them, and are teaching kindergarteners and beginning first graders the many phonics rules outside of meaningful context. Our legislators and some publishing companies are influencing great change in Oklahoma, from the complete redesign of teacher education to methods used to develop literacy in beginning reading. The pendulum is swinging drastically to a phonics first, bottom-up method. As a member of the university academic community and as a past public school teacher, I feel an obligation to refine my own rhetoric as I share stories of my own reading experiences and those of my students, back them with research, and join in the reading methods debates. We teachers need to do this not only at professional meetings, but also in the public forum.

References

Adams, M.J. (1990). *Beginning to read: Thinking and learning about print*. Cambridge, MA: MIT Press.

Au, K.H. (1997). Literacy for all students: Ten steps toward making a difference. *The Reading Teacher, 51*, 186–194.

Baumann, J.F., Hoffman, J.V., Moon, J., and Duffy-Hester, A.M. (1998). Where are teachers' voices in the phonics/whole language debate? Results from a survey of US elementary classroom teachers. *The Reading Teacher, 51*, 636–650.

Berrybill, A. (1997). Whatever happened to Dick and Jane? The debate between whole language and phonics. *Better Homes and Gardens*, February, 50–54.

Carbo, M. (1981). *Reading style inventory manual*. Raslyn Heights, NY: Learning Research Associates.

Carbo, M., Dunn, R., and Dunn, K. (1986). *Teaching students to read through their individual reading styles*. Reston, VA: Prentice Hall.

Carson, S.A. (1991). The effect of thematic fantasy play upon the understanding of beginning, middle, and end as first graders write in response to literature. Doctoral dissertation, The University of Oklahoma. *Dissertation Abstracts International, 52*, 1237–A.

Carson, S.A. (1999). Whole language and risk taking: Meeting the needs of at-risk students. *The Missouri Reader, 23*, 29–33.

Cecil, N.L. (1999). *Striking a balance: Positive practices for early literacy*. Scottsdale, AZ: Holcomb Hathaway.

Christie, J. (1987). Play and story comprehension: A critique of recent training research. *Journal of Research and Development in Education, 21*, 36–43.

Clymer, T. (1996). The utility of phonic generalizations in the primary grades. *The Reading Teacher, 50*, 182–187.

Glazer, S.M. (1995). Do I have to give up phonics to be a whole language teacher? *Reading Today, 12*, February/March, 37–43.

Groff, P. (1998). Where's the phonics? Making a case for its direct and systematic instruction. *The Reading Teacher, 52*, 138–141.

Gunning, T.G. (1995). Word building: A strategic approach to the teaching of phonics. *The Reading Teacher, 48*, 484–489.

Hoskisson, K., and Tompkins, G. (1987). *Language arts: Content and teaching strategies*. Columbus, OH: Merrill.

Joyce, B.R. (1999). Reading about reading: Notes from a consumer to the scholars of literacy. *The Reading Teacher, 52*, 662–671.

Karnowski, L. (1989). Using LEA with process writing. *The Reading Teacher, 42*, 462–465.

Katz, L.G., and Chard, S.C. (1989). *Engaging children's minds: The project approach*. Norwood, NJ: Ablex.

Lapp, D., and Flood, J. (1997). Where's the phonics? Making a case (again) for integrated code instruction. *The Reading Teacher, 50*, 696–700.

Lapp, D., and Flood, J. (1998). Response to Patrick Groff. *The Reading Teacher, 52*, 142–143.

Limbrick, L. (1995). Literacy: Why the great debate? *Schools and Universities*, 8–10.

Mandler, J., and Johnson, N. (1977). Remembrance of things parsed: Story structure and recall. *Cognitive Psychology, 9*, 111–151.

Morrow, L.M., Tracey, D.H., Woo, D.G., and Pressley, M. (1999). Characteristics of exemplary first-grade literacy instruction. *The Reading Teacher, 52*, 462–476.

Moustafa, M. and Maldonado-Colon, E. (1999). Whole-to-part phonics instruction: Building on what children know to help them know more. *The Reading Teacher*, *52*, 448–458.

Ogle, D. (1986). K-W-L: A teaching model that develops active reading of expository text. *The Reading Teacher*, *39*, 564–570.

Read, C. (1975). *Children's categorization of speech sounds in English* (NCTE Research Report No. 17). Urbana, IL: National Council of Teachers of English.

Reutzel, D.R. (1999). On balanced reading. *The Reading Teacher*, *52*, 322–324.

Schulz, E. (1991). Whole language: A special report. *Teacher*, August, 30–34.

Silkebakken, G. (1996). Balanced reading: What is it? *The Oklahoma Reader*, Winter, 5–6.

Spiegel, D.L. (1995). A comparison of traditional remedial programmes and Reading Recovery: Guidelines for success for all programmes. *The Reading Teacher*, *49*, 86–99.

Stahl, S.A. (1992). Saying the 'p' word: Nine guidelines for exemplary phonics instruction. *The Reading Teacher*, *45*, 618–625.

Strickland, D.S. (1995). Reinventing our literacy programmes: Books, basics, balance. *The Reading Teacher*, *48*, 295–302.

Sulzby, E. (1991). Assessment of emergent literacy: Storybook reading. *The Reading Teacher*, *44*, 498–500.

Tierney, R.J., Carter, M.A., and Desai, L.E. (1991). *Portfolio assessment in the reading-writing classroom*. Norwood, MA: Christopher-Gordon.

Tompkins, G.E. (1990). *Teaching writing: Balancing process and product*. Columbus, OH: Merrill.

Tompkins, G.E. (1998). *Language arts: Content and teaching strategies*. Upper Saddle River, NJ: Prentice Hall.

Weaver, C. (1988). *Reading process and practice: From socio-psycholinguistics to whole language*. Portsmouth, NH: Heinemann.

Vacca, R.T., and Vacca, J.L. (1999). *Content area reading*. New York: Longman.

Children's book references

Martin, B. Jr (1989). *Chicka chicka boom boom*. New York: Simon & Schuster Books for Young Readers.

Seuss, Dr (1963). *Hop on pop*. New York: Random House.

Source

This is an edited version of an article previously published in *The Reading Teacher*, 53(3). 1999. Reproduced by permission of the International Reading Association.

Chapter 10

Reading Recovery and Pause, Prompt, Praise

Professional visions and current practices

Janice Wearmouth and Janet Soler

Introduction

In England and Wales as a result of the National Literacy Strategy (NLS) the emphasis has been on addressing standards of literacy through whole-class teaching. However, as we have argued (Wearmouth and Soler, 2001) this has left us with the tension between addressing the literacy standards of the whole group in the Literacy Hour, and addressing the needs of individual pupils who experience particular difficulties in literacy acquisition. Addressing the standards of the whole group through whole-class teaching assumes that all children can reach the same level. Yet there will always be pupils who will find it extremely difficult, or may not be able, to achieve a 'normal standard' in literacy. This particular group of children will usually need individual tuition to address their needs. The original Literacy Taskforce Report (1997) recognised this need to cater for individual differences in its proposal for a national literacy strategy and acknowledged that a significant number of children would need individual support and early intervention in addition to whole-class teaching. The only individual reading programme to be named in the preliminary Literacy Taskforce Report is Reading Recovery (RR) developed in New Zealand by Dame Professor Marie Clay:

> As our strategy is implemented (through the NLS) we see Reading Recovery playing the part it was designed to play in New Zealand, namely addressing the specific reading difficulties of those who, in spite of being taught well, fall behind. . . . This still leaves in the region of 5% of pupils. . . . It would be disastrous to write off this group by excluding them from the target. . . . Each of them needs an individual learning plan and we recommend that . . . plans are made to meet their literacy needs.
>
> (Literacy Taskforce, 1997, p. 14)

Since the implementation of the NLS, a number of strategies which involve pupils working in small groups have been put in place to support pupils who are failing to keep pace with peers, for example the early literacy intervention policy, summer schools and progress units. However, if the Literacy Taskforce

Report proposals are to be implemented in full, there is a need also to implement individual programmes to fulfil the requirements of pupils who experience a greater degree of difficulty in literacy acquisition. The fact that RR was the only named programme designed for use with individual pupils means that the likelihood is that this programme will be a prime candidate for consideration for addressing individual children's needs.

The model of reading that underpins Reading Recovery, however, has also led to the development of another individual reading programme in New Zealand which has developed a strong track record of success in schools (Glynn, 1995). This programme is Pause, Prompt, Praise (PPP), known in Maori as Tatari, Tautoko, Tauawhi, and is authored by Professors Stuart McNaughton and Ted Glynn. While PPP shares a common conceptualisation of the reading process with RR it has developed a different form of delivery, and has different resource implications and approaches to ownership and control. As argued in a previous paper (Openshaw *et al.*, 2002), issues of resources, ownership and control as well as efficacy of the model underpinning a particular programme are key elements in determining the successful uptake of a reading programme. The recent history of RR indicates that while it had proven efficacy and was initially supported by a national government it faced barriers to widespread adoption and continuity when these issues were not recognised and addressed.

Given the likely adoption of RR we need to be aware of its underpinning rationale and contexts for delivery in order ensure its successful uptake. This chapter will aim to provide a critical examination of these aspects of RR by comparing and contrasting it with PPP in its model of reading, form of delivery, resource implications and approach to ownership and control.

Aims and foci of Reading Recovery and Pause, Prompt, Praise

Reading Recovery is an intervention programme that attempts to prevent failure in learning to read by providing an intensive, highly structured programme of instruction to children who experience difficulty in learning to read after one year of formal schooling. This programme was developed by Marie Clay for New Zealand schools in 1976. The research programme consisted of six projects which took place between 1976 and 1981 (Clay, 1979; Clay, 1980; Clay, 1982; Clay, 1985; Clay, 1987). The Reading Recovery programme has been widely used both in New Zealand and internationally, and been intensively evaluated (Center *et al.*, 1995; Glynn *et al.*, 1992; Hiebert, 1994; Moore and Wade, 1998; OFSTED, 1993; Slavin and Madden, 1989; Sylva and Hurry, 1995).

Clay (1993a, p. 10) describes Reading Recovery (RR) as:

> A one-to-one tutoring programme which gives supplementary help to individual children after their first year at school if they are still low achievers in reading and writing relative to their agemates.

This approach is not intended as a 'remedial programme'. On the contrary, it is 'a prevention strategy' (Clay, 1993a) with two distinct goals both expressed in relation to norms of achievement in literacy:

> first, to accelerate the learning of the very weakest children to reach the average band of the class and to give them learning strategies so that they will be able to keep up
> second, to identify those who fail to achieve the level of the average group at an early age as needing long-term support.
>
> (Hobsbaum and Leon, 1999, p. 1)

The focus of RR is on problem-solving in the child:

> During their training, Reading Recovery teachers learn how to help children to problem-solve for themselves. . . . The stress on helping children to develop their phonological skills to hear and record the sounds in words as well as to ensure that they are deriving the meaning of a text reflects the combination of skills required to develop all aspects of literacy learning.
>
> (Hobsbaum and Leon, 1999, p. 3)

This focus on problem-solving operates through both reading and writing:

> We look upon reading and writing as helping one another. What you know in writing helps you in your reading and what you know in reading helps you in your writing and we work with both these activities in the half hour lesson.
>
> (Clay, 1995, p. 4)

The initial research work for Pause, Prompt, Praise (PPP) was carried out in South Auckland, New Zealand, in 1977, in home settings with a group of pupils and their parents. Subsequent research in Birmingham, England, led to the research monograph being published in the UK under the title *Pause, Prompt and Praise* (McNaughton *et al.*, 1987). Glynn (1995, p 34) describes *Pause, Prompt and Praise* as 'a set of behavioural tutoring procedures' whose aim is 'to provide additional support for older low-progress readers' without encouraging over-dependence on a more competent other. The focus of PPP is on changing the 'tutoring behaviours' of the tutor in order to: '. . . reinforce the child for using all cue sources available in a text, and to self-correct errors' (Glynn, 1985, p. 181). Glynn warns against 'remedial' strategies which: '. . . reinforce dependence on the teacher as a source of cues for correcting errors . . .' (1985, p. 181).

Tutors are taught to implement a simple but specific set of tutoring strategies: pausing to allow for self-correction, prompting to offer appropriate cues for unfamiliar words, and praising to reinforce desired behaviour. The efficacy of PPP has, like RR, been extensively evaluated (McNaughton, Glynn and Robinson, 1981; Glynn, 1995; Glynn and Glynn, 1986; Medcalf, 1989; Wheldall and Mettem, 1985; Scott and Ballard, 1983)

Development of RR and PPP

A comparison of the development of RR and PPP reveals the root of important differences in the manner in which they are currently implemented and in the ways in which these approaches have been modified over time. RR developed from Marie Clay's personal research into the literacy difficulties experienced by young children in schools, her response to requests from teachers that she should find a solution to children's failure to acquire literacy, and her desire to reduce overworked educational psychologists' waiting lists of pupils with difficulties in literacy development. Clay's observation of one hundred pupils' reading development in schools over the course of one year led to the development of a set of observation tasks based on this initial study. Her publication, 'An Observation Survey' (1993b), was designed to support teachers in looking at:

> whether they (children) know any letters at all, whether they are writing any words at all, what they do when they pick up a book, how they look through a book and re-tell a story. . . . They are very simple pre-school tasks in a way . . . they function like standardised tests in research analyses.
> (Clay, 1995, p. 3)

Clay (1993a, p. 11) states that, as a university academic responsible for training educational psychologists, she was approached by teachers using 'An Observation Survey', who asked her to research ways of working with children with literacy problems:

> About 1974, an accusation was directed at me by New Zealand teachers. Using my Observation Survey to monitor children's early progress, they watched some children becoming confused and failing to progress. Disturbed by what they saw and unable to think how to overcome the difficulties they were identifying, they held me responsible for their plight and recommended that I search for a solution.

Simultaneously, the educational psychologists whom she was training: '. . . had long waiting lists of children with about 60 per cent presenting them with literacy difficulty involvement' (Clay, 1995, p. 5).

Clay decided to investigate ways to reduce educational psychologists' waiting lists and simultaneously instigate professional development for teachers in the area of difficulties in literacy development. From her reconstruction of events it appears that, from the outset, she feels that she was viewed as a professional with expert knowledge in the field of difficulties in literacy development and, as such, with a moral responsibility to find ways of meeting the needs of children who experienced such difficulties.

Clay's response to the twin demands of waiting list reduction and teacher professional development was to research ways of teaching pupils through leading a development project which involved action research with practising teachers interested in literacy difficulties:

> I began a two-year research and development project in 1976. Six teachers with special interests in literacy issues formed a research team, and each week one taught a child behind a one-way screen while the rest of the team talked about what was occurring. They discussed the child's difficulties and how the teacher responded, relating this to their pooled knowledge of theory and practical experience.
>
> (Clay, 1993, p. 11)

The essential features of this research methodology are enshrined in the Reading Recovery training programme for teachers: an expert to lead regular teacher professional development sessions, teachers bringing their own experiences of individual children's reading difficulties into the training sessions, the use of the one-way screen so that the trained tutor and the group of teachers could observe and comment upon each other's teaching practices. RR has always focused, as it began, on the development of individual children's literacy acquisition through tuition by trained teachers working in a school.

In seeking to promote the coverage of the RR programme across New Zealand and also across the United States, Canada and the UK, Clay became aware of the political imperatives of 'proving' the efficacy and cost benefits of the programme:

> Before each of these changes one has to imagine an educative process in which the aims, delivery, research findings, benefits and costs of the programme were explored in many meetings of educators at every level of the profession, and articles on many aspects of the programme's features were published.
>
> (Clay, 1993, p. 12)

The requirements of a 'scientific' approach to evaluating the RR programme in different schools and national contexts demand that like is compared with like and thus constrain the development of the programme beyond its initial conceptualisation. Furthermore, the continued existence of RR as a national and international literacy programme is constantly under criticism from academics who disagree with the fundamental assumptions, for example the model of reading on which RR rests, and from resource providers seeking to reduce the costs of education. Consequently, there is the risk of 'dilution' of the programme in contexts where RR is operating in times of financial shortage. Clay is insistent, therefore, that there is strict adherence to the detail of the programme in order to maintain the programme's integrity and coherence. It is hardly surprising that many educators would conclude that there has been little development of the RR programme and that it remains almost as it was. This lack of focus on development but sharp focus on evaluation of every RR initiative across the world can be interpreted as both its strength and its weakness.

The PPP procedures were developed, initially, in South Auckland in 1977 when a group of university researchers undertook intensive observation and training of parents using tutoring procedures that had been specified in previous research with teacher and paraprofessional tutoring of oral reading. McNaughton, Glynn and Robinson (1981) set out their rationale for involving parents in overcoming the difficulties in reading experienced by older (10–12-year-old) children:

- research (Watson, 1979) suggested the existence of up to 7 per cent of older, lower-achieving children who had fallen increasingly behind, had developed inappropriate, inefficient reading strategies and needed special help to achieve the accelerated progress needed to catch up with peers. Insufficient trained teachers were available in schools to provide this help;
- older children experiencing difficulties in reading had limited opportunities to read appropriate, meaningful texts in schools. They tended to be given alternative tasks during lessons which depended on children's reading ability;
- class and remedial teachers tended to correct children's reading errors immediately rather than giving children chance to self-correct, offered little praise and varied considerably in their ability to prompt children to use meaning or visual information to guess unrecognised words;
- the texts attempted by children were often too difficult to read at either an independent or instructional level;
- there was 'a growing concern for parental involvement in the education of their children . . . parents, while still feeling and being held responsible for their children, are becoming more and more powerless to influence their own children's development. . . . The parents in our research certainly felt keenly the segregation of home and school. . . . We felt that parents, as well as being willing and able to help their low progress children, have a right to take part in their children's schooling' (McNaughton, Glynn and Robinson, 1981, p. 4);
- despite the apparent growing sense of powerlessness over children's education among parents there existed research to suggest that early educational initiatives that produced lasting effects were those where parents were trained to teach children who had fallen behind (Bronfenbrenner, 1974; Chilman, 1976; Donachy, 1979). It appeared that parents had the potential for assuming a direct teaching role with older, lower-achieving children.

A subsequent parallel study was conducted in Birmingham, England (McNaughton et al., 1987). One major lesson learned from research in the original South Auckland project (Glynn et al., 1979) and from the Birmingham study was that parents whom teachers had perceived as apathetic towards their children's school learning:

cared deeply about their children's reading difficulties at school, and were highly motivated to do something about it, to the extent of learning the Pause Prompt Praise procedures.

(Glynn, 1995, p. 34)

The focus of PPP on procedures has encouraged development and evaluation of this approach into a refinement of the procedures themselves and into a variety of cultural settings. In this approach, one variable can be changed at a time and its effect evaluated. For example, the 'prompt' procedure has the potential to incorporate consideration of recent research on phonemic awareness even though the predominant emphasis remains that of meaning in a text (Open University, 2002). The introduction of PPP into different settings has led to a greater awareness of the importance of cultural contexts for children's learning. For example, the 'Rotorua Home and School Literacy Project' (Glynn, Berryman and Glynn, 2000) was concerned with effective collaboration between schools and the communities they serve, with the shared aim of supporting the improvement of children's literacy achievement. This project was premised on respecting the family and community as primary learning environments for children in addition to that of the school:

While it is clear that home and school exercise joint influences on children's literacy, facilitating learning across the two contexts depends on home and school knowing and understanding what literacy values and reading and writing practices are operating in the other.

(Glynn, Berryman and Glynn, 2000, p. 9)

It was also premised on the view of the importance of recognising that different patterns of literacy in different communities 'meet particular purposes in particular contexts of use' (Glynn, Berryman and Glynn, 2000, p. 12) and, as such, carry particular cultural meanings for all community members. The corollary of this respect and recognition is that collaboration between home and school entails the sharing of understandings and actions that are reciprocal, not unidirectional from school to home:

the report signals that participation involves schools learning from families, as well as families learning from schools. Shared understandings of ways of teaching and learning, as well as sharing of goals and forms of literacy instruction are pivotal in successful family literacy programmes.

(Glynn, Berryman and Glynn, 2000, p. 8)

Furthermore, recent research into the use of PPP in a variety of settings, for example the Rotorua Home and School Literacy Project (see above), recognises the importance of achieving reciprocal understandings between home and school in order to pay due regard to the cultural context of children's literacy development.

Underlying model of reading

Understanding the model of reading on which RR and PPP are both based is important as it explains certain characteristics of the design of the RR and PPP approaches. Both RR and PPP appear to be premised on the whole-book/whole-language, psycholinguistic view of reading development. The design of strategies within both RR and PPP clearly relate psycholinguistic theory to practice. This perspective views reading as the active *construction* of meaning from text rather than a process dependent on the mastery of phonics and decoding of letter-sound relationships. This view of the reading process is influenced by psycholinguistics with its emphasis on how we make sense of our world through the use of language:

> as we read, our minds are actively busy making sense of print, just as they are always actively trying to make sense of the world. Our minds have a repertoire of strategies for sense-making. In reading, we can call these psycholinguistic because there's continuous interaction between thought and language. We start with the text, written language, and use the cues from the various language levels to construct our own parallel text and meaning. We draw on our sense-making strategies all the time we're reading, but some of the cycles draw on some strategies more than others. All of these strategies have their counterparts in making sense of what we hear (listening), and in making sense of the world.
>
> (Goodman, 1996, pp. 110–11)

This so-called 'psycholinguistic guessing game' (Goodman, 1967) sees the reader as having expectations of what a text might be about, and then testing these expectations and confirming or rejecting them as s/he proceeds:

> By calling reading a psycholinguistic guessing game, I wanted to empha-size the active role of the reader in making sense of written language as a new key element in our understanding of the reading process. I wanted people to take distance from the view that reading is the accurate, sequen-tial recognition of letters and words. I wanted them to understand that, in order to make sense (construct meaning), readers:
> - make continuous use of minimal information selected from a complex but incomplete and ambiguous text;
> - draw on their knowledge of language and the world;
> - use strategies of predicting and inferring where the text is going.
>
> (Goodman, 1996, p. 115)

This is the perspective which underlies the teaching methods that empha-sise 'top-down' skills and stress the use of semantic and syntactic cues such as those used in both RR and PPP:

> reading is a constructive process and . . . I want to undermine any tendency . . . to think of reading as the 'simple' act of recognizing letters and/or

words ... the sense you make of a text depends on the sense you bring to it ... much misunderstanding still exists about reading and written language in general. I believe that this confusion exists largely because people have started in the wrong place, with letters, letter-sound relationships and words. We must begin instead by looking at reading in the real world, at how readers and writers try to make sense with each other.

(Goodman, 1996, pp. 2–3)

Goodman summarises the key concepts in this approach:

- Reading is an active process in which readers use powerful strategies in their pursuit of meaning.
- Everything readers do is part of their attempt to make sense.
- Readers become highly efficient in using just enough of the available information to accomplish their purpose of making sense.
- What readers bring to any act of reading is as important for successful reading as anything they use from the published text.

(Goodman, 1996, p. 91)

In keeping with the view of reading as a guessing game, Goodman feels that those in the early stages of literacy development should be encouraged to decide for themselves whether they have read text correctly by continually monitoring for meaning. Only miscues that cause a loss of meaning need correction:

Readers who correct miscues that don't need to be corrected are inefficient: they distract themselves from the central task of making sense by their preoccupation with accuracy. Readers who persistently fail to correct when they need to do so are likely to be ineffective: they lose a lot of the meaning.

(Goodman, 1996, p. 114)

It is only when readers decide for themselves when they do or do not need to correct their reading that they are developing useful strategies for self-correction.

Clay's argues that, in learning to read, children learn strategies for predicting and working out unknown words, using contextual cues relating to meaning and syntax (grammar), grapho-phonic cues (relating to the visual and auditory patterns of words and their constituent letters) and self-monitoring. This view bears a close affinity to Goodman's psycholinguistic view of the reading process. Clay views children as becoming proficient readers by gaining better predictive skills and gradually managing increasingly more difficult texts. Those children who experience difficulty in reading acquisition need support from a teacher or tutor. Glynn (1985, p. 181) acknowledges Clay's model of reading as the basis of the PPP programme:

The (PPP) programme was based on a model of reading which stresses the importance of children extracting a sequence of cues from printed texts and relating these, one to another, so that they understand the precise message of the text (Clay, 1979). These cues include the context of the story, the structure and pattern of the language in the story, as well as the letter and sound cues available within individual words.

(Glynn, 1985, p. 181)

The corollary of this approach is that making mistakes (miscues) is an essential part of the process of learning to read. Goodman (1996) is highly critical of phonic instruction for children with difficulties in the area of literacy development:

For less sophisticated readers, the reading process is sometimes short-circuited by instruction. Instruction that strongly focuses on letter/sound matching or word identification can teach developing readers that the goal of reading is to decode print as sound, or to recognize a succession of words. Isolated phonics produces what some British folks have called 'barking at print.' Short-circuiting at the word level produces the monotone reading of a text as nothing more than a list of words. Only when the focus of the reader, at whatever level of proficiency, is on meaning is the whole process at work and short-circuiting minimized.

(Goodman, 1996, p. 115)

However, the authors of RR and PPP do not completely concur with this view in that both admit to the importance of grapho-phonic cues as an important source of information for the reader.

Adoption of the psycholinguistic perspective implies that it is crucially important in both the RR and the PPP approach that reading material is supplied to a child at an appropriate level of difficulty so the s/he meets some unfamiliar words but can make good predictions. It also implies the need to monitor children's reading very carefully and note miscues, hesitations and non-responses in order to gauge the development of appropriate predictive strategies and the rate of self-correction as an indicator of active agency in learning. Miscues can be analysed against contextual considerations of meaning and syntax, and against grapho-phonic requirements.

Model of the child-as-learner

Implicit in the view of reading as a 'psycholinguistic guessing game' is an awareness in both RR and PPP of the importance of the child's agency in his or her own learning in order to foster independence in problem-solving and self-correction of errors. Clay (1995, p. 4), for example, suggests that teachers should build on children's strengths in order to inculcate a sense of control in the child over his/her reading activities:

In the first two weeks of a child's programme . . . the teacher is not allowed to teach the child anything new but must devise activities which will use the child's strengths in old and new ways. By the end of the first two weeks the children should feel in control of what they are doing. It is not that they can choose what they do, the teacher chooses what they will do . . . but the child should always feel that they [sic] have a lot to bring to the reading or the writing activities and therefore in that sense they are in control.

The emphasis of PPP is always on metacognitive strategies, that is awareness of higher-level, self-regulatory strategies, to support the psycholinguistic guessing game of reading:

Proficient early readers learn a series of skills which help them to monitor and even to improve their own reading. These skills enable a reader to become both relatively independent within a particular level of difficulty and gain increasing independence at any difficulty level. Such skills include carefully checking what is read. . . . The gradual refinement of these self regulatory skills means a child shifts from being independent on external instructional support towards independence in monitoring and correcting errors.

(McNaughton, Glynn and Robinson, 1981, pp. 9–10)

Form of delivery

Principles of the tutoring programme

Clay (1993) feels that meeting the needs of pupils who experience difficulties in literacy development requires teaching programmes designed by teachers with a great deal of specialised knowledge about the reading process and an ability to analyse children's learning:

The Reading Recovery teacher must have an in-depth knowledge and a fine-grained analysis of things being learned. The . . . teacher must detect what is extremely difficult for a particular child – be it:
    Bringing meaning to the text,
    Or dealing with the language of the text,
    Or using the visual information in the print,
    Or making many competencies work together,
    Or knowing when it has gone well,
    Or initiating self-correction processes when it has not.

(Clay, 1993, p. 15)

The RR teacher is also expected to have a 'larger repertoire of solutions than a classroom teacher' (Clay, op. cit.) so that they can begin with the child's strengths, identify the barriers to his/her progress in reading and find

ways to overcome them. They are therefore seen by Clay as more knowledgeable than other classroom teachers without RR training. Thirty-minute
RR sessions are designed to be held every day for between twelve and twenty
weeks after which a child is 'discontinued' if s/he has reached the average level
of literacy for his/her class. If not, s/he is referred to specialist reading support
services for further individual attention.

PPP tutoring procedures, by contrast, were designed to be 'simple'
(McNaughton, Glynn and Robinson, 1981) so that 'ordinary' parents could
use them and, subsequently, other members of a local community and/or peers
more competent in reading than the learner. Albeit designed for simplicity,
the PPP tutoring procedures were designed to take account of

- the three components of proficient reading, as viewed from a whole-book;
  psycholinguistic approach;
- 'three basic learning principles' (McNaughton et al., op. cit., p. 10);
- the needs of ordinary parents.

The three components of proficient reading of which the procedures take
account are the use of both contextual (syntactic and semantic) and graphic
cues, discrimination of letters and words, and self-regulatory skills (McNaughton
et al., op. cit.).

PPP is a set of procedures based on behavioural principles. The three
learning principles are, firstly, 'setting events', that is general aspects of the
learning environment which can be altered to influence learning. The most
salient 'setting events' in the PPP approach are seen as the opportunity to read
meaningful texts, the difficulty level of texts read and the need for individualised instruction (McNaughton et al., op. cit., p. 11). The second learning
principle is that the consequences of children's behaviour influence their
moti-vation. Positive information, such as clear description of behaviour,
should therefore follow successful attempts at reading text. In the original
PPP study in South Auckland, parents were taught to use praise to encourage
progress in reading accuracy, efficiency, flexibility and attempts to self-correct
(McNaughton et al., op. cit., p. 12). The third principle is that the consequences of mistakes also influence learning. Seen in the context of PPP, this
principle implies attention to both the timing of feedback after mistakes and
also to the type of cues to solve unfamiliar words and text.

The authors of PPP recommend that the procedures are used at least three
times per week for twenty minutes. Texts are chosen on the basis of difficulty
level and also the child's interests. When the child makes a mistake, the tutor
is taught to pause in order to allow time for both the child to self-correct and
for the tutor to think about the nature of the mistake. Pauses should last for
up to five seconds or until the child has reached the end of the phrase or
sentence (Glynn, 1995). For a non-attempt the prompt is either to read on
or read again to encourage the child to think about meaning. If the mistake
is a word that does not make sense the tutor is trained to focus the child on
what the word means from either the context or the reader's own experience.

Where the word makes sense but is incorrect, the tutor uses a letter-sound prompt. The tutor praises all attempts, giving specific feedback on reading behaviour.

Contexts for reading instruction

The context for reading instruction through RR is clearly the school during the second year of formal schooling. Clay (1995, p. 1) expresses her view that the responsibility for children's literacy development lies with schools and the teachers within them:

> What went on before the child came to school was terribly important but the school still has a responsibility to get children into reading and writing whatever their previous experience has been. So if children have missed out on certain opportunities to learn about print or books before they come to school then we have to provide make-up experiences for those children when they first come to school . . . we really need a kind of safety net for some children once they get to school.

The RR programme operates after children have been at school for one year so that all children have had some access to formal reading instruction and so that not too big a gap has developed between those pupils who experience difficulties in literacy acquisition and peers:

> Remedial programmes that have been going for years in all the countries that we are working in . . . very rarely get them (children) back to the average level of their class. Their peers pull away from them all the time and while their own skills improve they still do not make it to the level of their average peers, whereas at this age level we seem to be able to do it and I think of it as a window of opportunity.
>
> (Clay, 1995, p. 6)

The context for reading instruction through the PPP procedures is, typically, the home. Glynn (1995) notes that, since children are already competent learners when they first enter formal schooling, there is clear evidence that the home has offered a powerful, structured, supportive and responsive learning environment for those children. There is therefore a strong argument for parents and teachers to

> share common learning objectives for the children with whom they interact, for example in the learning of oral language, reading and writing skills. . . . Facilitating learning in one context may depend on knowing what behaviours are being acquired and reinforced in the other. . . . Only by working together and freely sharing information data can parents and teachers enhance the generalization of skills learned at school to the home setting, and the reverse.
>
> (Glynn, 1995, pp. 33–4)

However, the principles of the PPP procedure do not demand exclusive use by parents in the home. The PPP procedures may be conducted at school, typically outside the mainstream classroom, by teachers, classroom assistants, community members and others, including peers who are more competent in reading, or at home by family members. What is crucial is the provision of 'frequent, individualised, interactive reading tutoring' (Colmar and Wheldall, 1992, p. 158) which ensures that:

- the child is provided with an appropriate level and type of text;
- the child's progress is carefully monitored with respect to the text using running records or simple miscue analysis;
- the teacher (or tutor) listens to the reading and gives appropriate feedback.

(Colmar and Wheldall, 1992, p. 159)

Professional development of reading tutors

Professional development for tutors is a consequence of both RR and PPP, the first by design and the second as an unintended consequence. Training of teachers in RR procedures takes place at fortnightly intervals over the course of one year using an apprenticeship approach. Training is organised predominantly through observation and discussion of each other's teaching practices and is led by experienced tutors who 'provide continuing support after the training year' (Hobsbaum and Leon, 1999, p. 1). Hobsbaum and Leon (op. cit., pp. 2–3) report three broad aspects of professional development that emerged from a (June, 1998) survey of RR-trained tutors:

- the acquisition of a profound understanding of the process of learning to read, especially compared with prior training, whether at Initial Teacher Training level or in various forms of INSET or Continuing Professional Development;
- the acquisition of skills to teach reading;
- the transfer of skills acquired during Reading Recovery training to other areas of practice, not necessarily in literacy but across the whole spectrum of class teacher or special needs teacher activity.

The training offered to PPP tutors is much shorter than that for RR. Nevertheless, particularly in recent research projects (Glynn, Berryman and Glynn, 2000), it shares some of the characteristics of RR in its clarity of purpose and focus, in its on-going support for tutors from experienced teachers and researchers and also in the increased sense of self-confidence and knowledge about the reading process reported by tutors. In its original conception in the South Auckland research project parents were trained in the PPP procedures and also to introduce each book or text to be used during the tutoring session 'by a variety of training methods, in both weekly training and weekly feedback sessions. All training sessions took place in the tutor's home' (McNaughton, Glynn and Robinson, 1981, p. 33). Parents were observed tutoring their children. In addition parents recorded their own tutoring for feedback from researchers. Furthermore, a booklet was published for parents *Remedial Reading at Home: Helping you to help your child* (Glynn, McNaughton, Robinson and Quinn, 1979) which contained advice on:

- arranging a time and place for reading at home;
- selecting suitable books for the child;
- helping the child become an independent learner;
- understanding mistakes in reading;
- using praise to help the child;
- helping the child to correct mistakes;
- checking on the child's reading progress;
- checking on tutoring skills.

More recently, PPP research projects have incorporated two preliminary workshop sessions. The first trains tutors to implement PPP procedures. The second prepares trainers to train new tutors and is attended by a member of the national PPP research team (Glynn, 1995).

Glynn, Berryman and Glynn (2000) note some unintended personal development that has resulted from tutors' participation in PPP projects. For example, reading gains have been reported for tutors as well as tutees (Medcalf and Glynn, 1987; Houghton and Glynn, 1993). Additionally, parent-tutors have progressed from the volunteer tutoring role to teacher training as a result of increased self-confidence and understanding of the reading process (Open University, 2002).

Ownership and control of Reading Recovery and Pause, Prompt, Praise

Clay constantly reiterates her view of reading as a 'complex' process. 'Reading and writing are complex processes, not simple ones' (Clay, 1995, p. 15). Given Clay's view of complexity, children in the RR programme must be taught by experts trained in reading development and in ways to meet children's difficulties through an apprenticeship approach. The apprenticeship approach to teacher professional development requires a high degree of organisation and structure, and a hierarchy of roles within the RR structure. Teachers in training receive their training at fortnightly intervals from tutors trained by trainers. Additionally, all evaluation data from across the world are returned to the National Reading Recovery Centre in Auckland, New Zealand, for processing:

> Reading Recovery has three tiers of organisation: the national level provides training and support for tutors and monitors all data from education authorities to ensure quality control. The local authority provides the tutor, the training centre and teacher training courses. The school supports the teachers who provide the programme. These three tiers are essential to maintain the integrity of the programme.
>
> (Hobsbaum and Leon, 1999, p. 5)

To the outside observer, quite clearly 'ownership' and control of the RR programme appears to rest with Reading Recovery training centres at national level, and, ultimately, the National Reading Recovery Centre in Auckland.

There is little room for parents to take an active role in the RR programme apart from carrying out tasks specified by the RR teacher such as re-reading texts sent home at the end of a RR session, and ensuring that their child goes to school regularly in order to attend RR:

> What happens in Reading Recovery is we do think that these children have had such a hard time learning that we don't want to confuse them any more but we arrange for parents to be involved in these ways. The school will usually inform the parents that they would like the child to go into the programme and ask those parents for their co-operation/consent. They will try to establish a kind of contract which says we need this child every day because the lessons must occur every day. . . . Then the story that the child writes each day for his writing lesson is written out on a card cut into pieces as a puzzle and that goes home for the child to do again with the parents. Also, some of the books that the child has already read to the teacher . . . might go home to be read to the parent. Parents are expected to enjoy that interchange rather than do any teaching.
>
> (Clay, 1995, p. 4)

In contrast, PPP is described by its proponents as a 'behavioural inter-actionist' theory of tutoring (Open University, 2002). By definition, therefore, successful tutoring depends on active engagement by both tutors and learners. In this sense PPP 'belongs' to, and is controlled by, both tutors and learners. Additionally, achieving the reciprocal understandings between school and home as outlined above requires careful consideration of the balance of power between home and school. This implies a greater level of control of the PPP initiative by parents and the local community, and may challenge the conventions of school hegemony over children's learning:

> To gain this understanding requires home and school collaboration . . . where teachers listen to and learn from the community. To achieve this, questions of power and control between school and home have to be addressed. Effective collaboration requires mutual acknowledgment of knowledge and expertise and of interdependence in problem solving.
>
> (Glynn, Berryman and Glynn, 2000, p. 11)

Summary

Reading Recovery (RR) is the only programme designed to raise the level of pupil achievement in the area of literacy development that was named in the Report of the English national Literacy Taskforce (1997). It has a number of characteristics in common with another New Zealand-based programme designed to address issues of problems in literacy acquisition, Pause, Prompt and Praise (PPP). They are:

- 'proven' to be effective in supporting the literacy development of pupils who experience difficulties, as evidenced in a multitude of evaluation studies;
- based on very similar perspectives on the process of reading: the whole-book/whole-language view akin to a psycholinguistic approach;
- targeted at the lowest-achieving pupil population;
- negotiated with, and carried out and evaluated through, the profession and/or local community;
- run on a one-to-one basis with individual children.

However, there are also significant differences between them. Some differences are obvious. For example, for Clay the reading process is a 'complex' one which some pupils have 'a hard time learning' (1995, p. 15). Teachers are often 'disturbed' by the problems faced by these children and 'unable to think how to overcome the difficulties'. Tutor training therefore must be long and rigorous. However, for McNaughton and Glynn, the difference between competent and poor readers lies in the efficiency with which they use appropriate cues in their reading. These cues can be taught systematically to children using 'simple' (McNaughton, Glynn and Robinson, 1981) cuing procedures which 'ordinary' (McNaughton et al., op. cit.) people can use. The consequence of these different views is variation in the length and rigour of the training programmes for tutors, in the professional status of tutors and in the cost of the infrastructure needed to maintain RR and PPP. Other differences in the visions of the respective authors of RR and PPP are less evident but are, nevertheless, very important to the implementation of the programmes. For example, different views of ownership and control have influenced the degree to which these programmes have had the potential to be modified and adapted to respond to the contexts in which they operate. RR remains largely the same as it was in its original conception. In contrast, recent projects using the PPP procedures have been able to adapt to take account of significant contextual features, particularly of the cultural background of the learner.

Conclusion

Successful implementation of any new initiative in education depends not only on 'proven' efficacy but also the structure and context within which it is delivered. Particularly pertinent are issues of resources, ownership and control. During the course of their development, the authors of *Reading Recovery* and of *Pause, Prompt and Praise* had different visions and different interpretations of the implications of the whole-book/whole-language approach for interventions seen as appropriate for pupils who experience difficulties in literacy development. As a result there are also significant differences in resource implications, ownership and control between the practices of RR and PPP which need to be recognised by anyone interested in implementing them in schools.

References

Bronfenbrenner, U. (1974) *Is Early Intervention Effective? A report on longitudinal evaluations of pre-school programs: Vol. 2*, Washington, DC: Department of Health, Education and Welfare, Office of Child Development.

Center, Y., Wheldall, K., Freeman, L., Outhred, L. and McNaught, M. (1995) 'An experimental evaluation of Reading Recovery', *Reading Recovery Quarterly*, 30, pp. 240–263.

Chilman, C.S. (1976) 'Programmes for disadvantaged parents: Some major trends and related research', in H. Leitenberg (ed.) *Handbook of Behavior Modification and Behavior Therapy*, Englewood Cliffs, NJ: Prentice Hall.

Clay, M.M. (1979) *Reading: The patterning of complex behaviour*, Auckland: Heinemann.

Clay, M.M. (1980) 'Reading Recovery: A follow-up study', *New Zealand Journal of Educational Studies*, 15(2), pp. 137–155.

Clay, M.M. (1982) *Observing Young Readers: Selected papers*, Exeter, NH; London; Auckland: Heinemann.

Clay, M.M. (1985) 'Engaging with the school system: A study of interactions', *New Zealand Journal of Educational Studies*, 20(1), pp. 20–38.

Clay, M.M. (1987) 'Implementing Reading Recovery: Systematic adaptations to an educational innovation', *New Zealand Journal of Educational Studies*, 22(1), pp. 35–58.

Clay, M.M. (1993a) 'Lifting the burden of illiteracy: Bringing a New Zealand solution to English schools', *British Review of New Zealand Studies*, 6, pp. 9–28.

Clay, M.M. (1993b) *An Observation Survey of Early Literacy Achievement*, London: Heinemann.

Clay, M.M. (1995) 'A radio interview with Marie Clay on the "Open Mind" programme', Dublin.

Colmar, S. and Wheldall, K. (1992) 'Three 'p's for the effective tutoring of low progress readers: Pause, Prompt and Praise', in A. Watson and A. Badenhop (eds) *Prevention of Reading Failure*, Sydney: Ashton Scholastic.

Donachy, W. (1979) 'Parent participation in pre-school education', in M.M. Clark and W.M. Cheyne (eds) *Studies in Pre-School Education*, London: Hodder and Stoughton.

Glynn, T. (1985) 'Remedial reading at home', in K. Topping and S. Wolfendale (eds) *Parental Involvement in Children's Reading*, London: Croom Helm.

Glynn, T. (1995) 'Pause, Prompt, Praise: Reading tutoring procedures for home and school partnership', in S. Wolfendale and K. Topping (eds) *Family Involvement in Literacy*, London: Cassell.

Glynn, T. and Glynn, V. (1986) 'Shared reading by Cambodian mothers and children learning English as a second language', *The Exceptional Child*, 33(3), pp. 159–172.

Glynn, T., McNaughton, S., Robinson, V. and Quinn, M. (1979) *Remedial Reading at Home: Helping you to help your child*, Wellington, NZ: New Zealand Council for Educational Research.

Glynn, T., Bethune, N., Crooks, T., Ballard, K. and Smith, J. (1992) 'Reading Recovery in contact: Implementation and outcome', *Educational Psychology*, 12 (314), pp. 249–261.

Glynn, T., Berryman, M. and Glynn, V. (2000) 'Reading and writing gains for Maori students in mainstream schools: Effective partnerships in the Roturua home and school literacy project', paper presented at the 18th World Congress on Reading, Auckland, New Zealand.

Goodman, K. (1967) 'Reading: A psycholinguistic guessing game', *Journal of the Reading Specialist*, 6(4), pp. 126–135.

Goodman, K. (1996) *On Reading*, Portsmouth, NJ: Heinemann.

Hiebert, E.H. (1994) 'Reading Recovery in the United States: What difference does it make to an age cohort?', *Educational Researcher*, 23, pp. 15–25.

Hobsbaum, A. and Leon, A. (1999) 'Catalyst for change: The impact of Reading Recovery in the United Kingdom', in *Viewpoint, No. 10*, April, London: University of London Institute of Education.

Houghton, S. and Glynn, T. (1993) 'Peer tutoring of below average secondary school readers with Pause, Prompt and Praise: Successive introduction of tutoring components', *Behaviour Change*, 10(2), pp. 75–85.

Literacy Taskforce/DfEE (1997) *A Reading Revolution: How can we teach every child to read well?* The Preliminary Report chaired by Michael Barber, London: Literacy Taskforce/DfEE.

McNaughton, S., Glynn, T. and Robinson, V. (1981) *Parents as Remedial Reading Tutors: Issues for home and school. Studies in Education No. 2*, Wellington: New Zealand Council for Educational Research.

McNaughton, S., Glynn, T. and Robinson, V. (1987) *Pause, Prompt and Praise: Effective remedial reading tutoring*, Birmingham: Positive Products.

Medcalf, J. (1989) 'Comparison of peer-tutored remedial reading using the Pause, Prompt and Praise procedures with an individualised tape-assisted reading programme', *Educational Psychology*, 9(3), pp. 253–262.

Medcalf, J. and Glynn, T. (1987) 'Assisting teachers to implement peer-tutored remedial reading using Pause, Prompt and Praise procedures', *Queensland Journal of Guidance and Counselling*, 1(1), pp. 11–23.

Moore, M. and Wade, B. (1998) 'Reading Recovery: Its effectiveness in the long term', *Support for Learning*, 13(3), pp. 123–128.

OFSTED (1993) *Reading Recovery in New Zealand: A report from the office of Her Majesty's Chief Inspector of Schools*, London: HMSO.

Openshaw, R., Soler, J., Wearmouth, J. and Paige-Smith, A. (2002) 'The sociopolitical context of the development of Reading Recovery in New Zealand and England', *The Curriculum Journal*, 13(1), pp. 53–69.

Open University (2002) 'Interview with Ted Glynn', *E801 Difficulties in Literacy Development*, Milton Keynes: Open University.

Scott, J. and Ballard, K. (1983) 'Training parents and teachers in remedial reading procedures for children with learning difficulties', *Educational Psychology*, 3(1), pp. 15–31.

Slavin, R.E. and Madden, N.A. (1989) 'Effective classroom programs for students at risk', in R.E. Slavin, N.L. Karweit and N.A. Madden (eds) *Effective Programs for Students at Risk* (pp. 23–51), Boston: Allyn and Bacon.

Sylva, K. and Hurry, J. (1995) 'Early intervention in children with reading difficulties: An evaluation of Reading Recovery and phonological training', *Literacy, Teaching and Learning*, 2(2), pp. 46–68.

Watson, J.E. (1979) 'Research in New Zealand in learning difficulties', paper presented at the Fifth Annual Conference of the Society for the Prevention of Early Learning Difficulties, University of Waikato, 1979.

Wearmouth, J. and Soler, J. (2001) 'How inclusive is the Literacy Hour?', *British Journal of Special Education*, 28(3), pp. 113–119.

Wheldall, K. and Mettem, P. (1985) 'Behavioural peer tutoring: Training 16-year-old tutors to employ the "Pause, Prompt and Praise" method with 12-year-old remedial readers', *Educational Psychology*, 5, pp. 27–44.

Source

This chapter was written especially for this volume.

Chapter 11

How inclusive is the Literacy Hour?

Janice Wearmouth and Janet Soler

Current curriculum contexts for inclusion and literacy difficulties

The national context within which the National Literacy Strategy has been introduced is one that attempts to reconcile principles of individuality, distinctiveness and diversity with inclusion and equal opportunities, and is therefore bound to be characterised by tensions and contradictions (Norwich, 1996). These tensions and contradictions permeate policy and practice throughout the whole education system in England. On the one hand there is a drive to raise standards of the learning of all pupils through whole-class and whole-group teaching, standardised forms of assessment (Broadfoot, 1996) and the encouragement of competition between schools through a focus on league tables of academic performance. On the other there is a statutory requirement to pay due regard to the principle of inclusion of pupils, and, within this, to address the identified learning needs of individuals who experience difficulties in learning. Ultimately, the dilemmas created in schools by what often appear to be somewhat fragmented and contradictory Government policies may be insoluble without a reconceptualisation of current policies. These dilemmas are particularly problematic for teachers in schools in England who are attempting to implement the requirements of two particular initiatives in the areas of literacy and special educational needs: the National Literacy Strategy and the statutory *General Statement on Inclusion* (GSI) in the current version of the National Curriculum for England and Wales (DfEE/QCA, 1999). A close investigation into the aims and objectives of both of these documents reveals these contradictions and exposes the difficulties for practitioners attempting to put the spirit of these policy documents into effect in the classroom.

Aims and objectives of the National Literacy Strategy (NLS)

Drawing upon the recommendations of the national Literacy Taskforce Report (February, 1997), a pilot literacy project and the subsequent National Literacy

Strategy (NLS) came into effect in August, 1997 (Beard, 1999). Associated with the NLS was a *Framework of Teaching Objectives* which spelt out the overall aims of the NLS and also gave guidance on the 'Literacy Hour' in which the teaching should take place.

In the NLS, literacy itself is ill-defined:

> Literacy unites the important skills of reading and writing. It involves speaking and listening which ... are an essential part of it. Good oral work enhances pupils' understanding of
>
> * language in oral and written forms;
> * the way language can be used to communicate.
>
> Good oral work is an important part of the process through which pupils read and compose texts.
>
> (Adapted from *The National Literacy Strategy*, DfEE, 1998)

This definition unites the skills of reading and writing and involves speaking and listening. As Corden (1999) points out, however, while speaking and listening are included in the aims of the NLS, they are not included in the Framework's planning of work for the Literacy Hour which offers no examples of what is meant by high quality oral work and no demonstration of what it means in practice.

The aims of the NLS, as outlined in the *Framework of Teaching Objectives*, are twofold:

* improvement of the quality of literacy teaching in the classroom;
* improvement of the management of literacy at whole-school level.

The NLS aims also make reference to the importance of literacy in communication. However, these aims are narrow and reflect a unitary definition of what constitutes literacy. They do not address the question of literacy as a broad social practice which has 'identifiable moral and ideological consequences' (Luke, 1995).

The ill-definition of what constitutes literacy and the narrowness of aims set up a prescriptive approach to teaching outlined in the formal *Framework for Teaching* of the Literacy Hour which sets out the pedagogical principles to which practitioners are expected to adhere in their teaching practice. Skidmore (1999), writing about the Literacy Hour, expresses concerns about the narrowness of this pedagogical approach:

> The monological view of pedagogy implicit in government policy receives ideological support from reportage which offers a purely technicist image of teaching as an activity akin to the skilled operation of a piece of machinery.
>
> (p. 13)

The Framework specifies that all classes should be taught literacy daily for one hour of continuous dedicated time. The work should include class 'shared' and group 'guided' reading and writing tasks and the teaching of phonics, spelling, vocabulary, handwriting and grammar, with approximately 60 per cent of the time in direct teaching and 40 per cent in independent working (DfEE, 1998). The pedagogical emphasis within the Literacy Hour, therefore, enforces whole-class teaching of skills and largely precludes practitioners' ability to develop a differentiated curriculum aimed at meeting the diversity of pupils' learning needs, family and social situations. While there is a need to teach literacy skills in a structured manner, there is also a need to address other aspects of literacy acquisition. Teachers, especially those concerned with difficulties in literacy development, need flexibility to create pedagogies and learning environments that respond to students' different literacy needs (Piotrowski and Reason, 2000).

The Literacy Taskforce Report that formed the basis for the NLS argued that, alongside whole-class teaching, there was a need to address individual differences. The Taskforce acknowledged that a significant number of children would need individual support and early intervention in the form of programmes such as Reading Recovery. Furthermore a small proportion of children would need more intensive programmes in addition to Reading Recovery:

> As our strategy is implemented (through the NLS) we see Reading Recovery playing the part it was designed to play in New Zealand, namely addressing the specific reading difficulties of those who, in spite of being taught well, fall behind. . . . This still leaves in the region of 5% of pupils. . . . It would be disastrous to write off this group by excluding them from the target. . . . Each of them needs an individual learning plan and we recommend that . . . plans are made to meet their literacy needs.
>
> (Literacy Taskforce, 1997, p. 14)

Thus while the Literacy Taskforce recognised the need for teaching for individual diversity and suggested ways of doing this, the Literacy Hour does not incorporate these recommendations. This has created subsequent problems in the implementation of the NLS. Dadds (1999), reporting on teachers' comments relating to the introduction of the Literacy Hour, noted concerns with the narrowness of the approach and inflexibility of the arrangements for meeting the learning needs of all pupils:

> Preset objectives determine an unresponsive, convergent teaching style dependent on single 'right' answers. Convergent teaching in the pursuit of predetermined objectives will have negative consequences for those children who experience difficulties.
>
> (p. 17)

The issues raised by the NLS's espousal of narrow aims and prescriptive teaching methods with an emphasis on whole-class and group approaches is particularly problematic for teachers addressing issues associated with inclusion as outlined by the GSI as discussed below.

'Inclusion' and 'special educational needs' in the General Statement on Inclusion

Policy makers have outlined the Government's definition of inclusion in the GSI. This document has resulted from national moves in England and Wales towards inclusion of all pupils in mainstream schools wherever possible. It attempts to construct a framework of educational provision for all pupils. This framework endeavours to take account of 'sameness' and, at the same time, pay due regard to 'difference' and 'diversity' among individuals (Norwich, 1996). The GSI aims to provide 'effective learning opportunities for all pupils' and sets out three 'key principles for inclusion':

- setting suitable learning challenges;
- responding to pupils' diverse learning needs;
- overcoming potential barriers to learning and assessment for individuals and groups of pupils.

In stressing teaching for diversity as opposed to one approach for all, these aims contradict the pedagogical framework of the Literacy Hour.

Within the GSI, reference to appropriate provision for pupils with special educational needs further contradicts the approach advocated by the Literacy Hour. In the GSI, in order to fulfil the terms of the 1996 Education Act in England and Wales, schools are urged to 'take action at all levels of curriculum planning' to meet the learning requirements of individual pupils' 'special educational needs'. Under the terms of this Act a child has special educational needs if he or she 'has a learning difficulty which calls for special educational provision to be made for him or her'. That is, a child only has 'special educational needs' when special provision is required to meet them. In law, the learning difficulty creates the need. The need is 'special' if the provision required to satisfy that need is 'special'. The emphasis on whole-class and whole-group teaching in the NLS precludes the individualised notion of 'need' supported by the definition of special educational needs in the 1996 Education Act. For those pupils whose special area of difficulty is literacy, it is extremely difficult to adhere to the principles of the Literacy Hour's whole-class and whole-group, non-individualised teaching while simultaneously fulfilling the terms of the 1996 Education Act and therefore the GSI.

The impact of national targets

Another problematic aspect of the Literacy Hour, for teachers attempting to implement the inclusive principles of the GSI, is the conceptualisation of national targets as a measure of the success of the NLS. The NLS is operating within the Government's programme of targets for success in every aspect of the education system in England and Wales. Evaluation of the original National Literacy Project and now the NLS was planned largely to assess norms of progress by the Office for Standards in Education (OFSTED). The first success criterion was identified as improving standards of literacy in relation to national expectations, norms and 'added value'. The Government has established a set of expectations for achievement in the area of literacy. By the year 2002, 80 per cent of 11-year-olds leaving primary school will be expected to reach the standards expected for their age in literacy.

This is problematic for principles of inclusion in the GSI because, although the NLS's aim of a high percentage of pupils achieving the designated level is laudable, these 'standards' refer to only a section of the pupil population. Twenty per cent is the proportion of the pupil population expected not to achieve the expected standard in literacy. Twenty per cent is also the proportion of pupils expected to 'have special educational needs' at some stage in their schooling (DES, 1978). There appears to be a worrying disregard for this group of pupils. Applying 'standards' to the majority does not explain how progress should be conceptualised for the remaining pupils. D'Arcy (1999) notes the pressure on teachers to teach to the test where the reputation of a school is judged on these test results. She gives the example, from the 1998 Tests of Reading and Writing, of pupils expected chiefly to 'retrieve information' from texts and to offer reasons for an occurrence, rather than to explain what the text means to them. She notes that the relevant marking schedules were written with preset answers which offer little scope for alternative or creative answers. From a different standpoint, Wedell (2000) also notes the stultifying influence of targets on meeting the diversity of pupils' needs. He comments that in some schools there is a strong emphasis on helping groups whose achievements lie just below one threshold to reach the next level, rather than putting the main effort into helping all children to achieve more.

As we have just seen, 'the centrally prescribed mechanism of the literacy hour is wedded to an apparatus of standardised testing and a set of arbitrary, quantified targets against which the performance of schools will be measured' (Skidmore, 1999, p. 13). Targets, together with the added pressure of competition and the need to attract literate pupils in order to achieve a high position on the academic league tables, may well function to squeeze pupils who experience difficulties in literacy development out of the mainstream system. It is difficult to see why schools, anxious to raise their overall standards, might wish to include less literate pupils who will never reach the national norm.

Pressure for a school to achieve well on the league tables may result in young people who experience literacy difficulties being given more work in those areas which are reported upon through standard attainment tasks in literacy and less work on other aspects of the curriculum. *The Times Educational Supplement* (Cassidy, 2000) reports the Department of Education and Employment's recommendation that all pupils 'struggling with literacy' spend an extra 90 minutes a week in English lessons at secondary level. This situation is clearly questionable in relation to both maintaining balance in the curriculum and stimulating young people's enthusiasm and interest.

The dilemma facing learning support teachers who attempt to meet the requirements of the GSI with regard to pupils who have literacy difficulties is whether to include them in the Literacy Hour in the name of equity, or to exclude them because the pedagogy is inappropriate for their learning needs. This dilemma is summed up in the elaborate 'disapplication' procedures in the 1988 Act and the injunctions not to use them in National Curriculum Council circulars (NCC, 1989) and elsewhere. The 'disapplication' procedures in the 1988 Act laid down particular circumstances through which children could be excused from aspects of the National Curriculum. On the one hand, the curriculum was palpably inappropriate for large numbers of children; on the other, special education professionals could not reject it without at the same time resegregating children with special educational needs (Dyson, 1997). As part of a national framework, the NLS applies to all children, including those with severe and complex learning difficulties, and therefore perpetuates this problem of prescribing a curriculum that is not designed to meet the needs of these children. Byers (1999) reports on the difficulties facing the teachers of pupils with severe and complex learning difficulties in conceptualising ways in which the Literacy Hour might be made relevant and accessible. The implications that this raises for a fundamental reconceptualisation of the literacy curriculum are supported by Dyson's (1997) analysis of the National Curriculum. He notes that most of the effort of professionals with regard to the National Curriculum, and now the Literacy Hour, was 'focused on the logistics of access and differentiation', rather than rethinking curriculum issues in a fundamental way. To fail to reconceptualise the Literacy Hour and make superficial changes may only serve to reinforce the status quo.

Contradictions in putting both policies into practice

An examination of the underpinning rationale of the NLS and the GSI in the first part of this chapter has clearly shown that there are contradictions between the two philosophies which underpin these documents. This conflict raises problems for practitioners attempting to put both documents into practice simultaneously. In the second part of this chapter we will show that early evaluation of the Literacy Hour indicates that this strategy is not addressing the needs of considerable numbers of children identified as having special needs in the areas of literacy development, overall cognitive learning difficulties, and behaviour. These contradictions in philosophies are compounded by inherent contradictions within each policy and by lack of resources to implement the demands made by both documents.

A number of studies have shown that children identified as having special educational needs are not benefiting from the Literacy Hour. In November 1998, OFSTED findings from the first cohort of pupils showed improved reading scores among all groups of pupils, but 'only modest improvement' in a 'stubborn minority of schools'. There was generally less progress among:

- boys compared with girls;
- pupils on free school meals;
- pupils identified as having 'special educational needs', especially where a learning support assistant was unavailable.

A survey by the Association of Teachers and Lecturers (ATL, 1999) showed that 80 per cent of those surveyed were very concerned about its effectiveness for pupils 'with special educational needs' and 75 per cent with the expectation of independent working for 20 minutes.

Further evaluation by the University of Newcastle (Smith, Hardman and Mroz, 1999) confirmed the slower progress of pupils on free school meals and those identified as having special educational needs. Interview data in this survey also suggested that pupils with special educational needs are, with a few exceptions, not benefiting from the National Literacy Strategy.

This exclusion of children with special educational needs can be explained in a number of ways. Firstly, as has been argued, there is a contradiction between the philosophies of the two documents which precludes both being put into practice at the same time. Arguably, it is not possible to emphasise whole-class and whole-group teaching simultaneously with teaching for diversity. Secondly, there is an inherent contradiction between the theoretical underpinning of the Literacy Hour in terms of children's learning, and its recommendations for teachers' practices. Corden (1999) notes that there is a constructivist theory of learning underpinning the literacy strategy. This theory emphasises the interactive process of teaching and learning and is particularly concerned with social discourse, collaborative learning and the joint construction of knowledge. The Framework highlights the importance of effective teacher intervention strategies such as:

- modelling: showing learners examples of work produced by experts;
- demonstrating: illustrating the procedures experts go through in producing work;
- scaffolding: supporting learners as they learn and practise procedures.

However, as Corden notes, the practices advocated in the Framework stand in opposition to its socially constructivist theoretical orientation because the Literacy Hour in practice limits the possibilities of facilitating 'creative conflict'. In social constructivist theory, the development of 'creative conflict' (Vygotsky, 1987; Bruner, 1985) relies upon the teacher creating a situation where the differences of opinion between individuals will give rise to new conceptual understandings. As the Framework does not articulate practices for speaking and listening in the planning of work for literacy, these are easily excluded from the implementation of the Literacy Hour. Dadds (1999) notes teachers' views that pressures of time and space will:

gloss over the struggles of some children to create their own meanings, especially in whole-class and whole-group sessions. Responsive teaching and exploratory talk are vital for the development of understanding.

(p. 17)

For children with cognitive difficulties in learning, the development of conceptual understanding through talk is particularly important. Because speaking and listening are excluded from the specifics of the Framework, these aspects may remain marginalised in a system dominated by target-setting directed by official documentation.

The requirement these documents place on practitioners to reconcile whole-class and whole-group teaching approaches with catering for diversity also has implications for resourcing. Teaching for diversity requires a recognition of the learning needs of individuals who experience particular difficulties. By definition, a pupil only has 'special' needs if s/he requires additional or alternative provision to address the difficulties s/he experiences. If no additional or alternative provision is made, then that pupil's difficulties will continue. *The National Literacy Strategy: A Framework for Teaching* (DfEE, 1998) contains little reference to pupils who experience difficulties in learning, apart from a suggestion that groups of pupils should be 'differentiated by ability' during the Literacy Hour, and that individuals should be 'well-trained' not to interrupt during the activities. Teachers are encouraged to use their professional judgement in approaching ways to teach pupils with special educational needs during the Literacy Hour, but not offered detailed guidance on what is considered an acceptable form of flexible arrangement. Later guidance from the DfEE on implementing the Framework for Teaching for pupils 'with special educational needs' shows official recognition of the inadequacy of this state of affairs. This guidance outlines a number of flexibilities in ways of approaching the Literacy Hour. Alternative approaches for pupils with complex difficulties in learning include, for example:

- different teaching strategies;
- work at different levels;
- variation in pace of presentation;
- access to alternative communications systems – signing, symbols, braille, electronic devices;
- use of 'parallel' groups for part of the Literacy Hour, with work linked to that of peers, so that pupils with similar prior attainment or learning objectives can be grouped across age bands during the group activities and independent work in the Hour.

Despite this official recognition of the demands that teaching for diversity places on teachers implementing the NLS, current guidance is contradictory and fails to support teachers to teach whole classes and groups and individuals within it. There is renewed emphasis on teaching to the level designed for the particular chronological age, as if pupils with difficulties should be expected to catch up with peers. In addition, although pupils may be grouped by ability for part of the Hour, the teacher is expected to bring the whole pupil group together in a final plenary session of review, reflection and consolidation of earlier work to 'share and celebrate achievement'. This implies that the principles of the GSI are secondary to the principles of the NLS. Whole-class teaching should prevail unless it can be demonstrated that an alternative is at least as good as NLS recommended practice. Since the success of a programme is clearly difficult to demonstrate in the case of pupils who experience difficulties in literacy and are therefore making little progress anyway, official guidelines are favouring the recommended practice of the NLS. As argued above, this contradicts the principles of the GSI and the terms of the 1996 Education Act in relation to pupils with special educational needs.

A further reason why the NLS does not address the difficulties experienced by children with special educational needs well is that of underfunding in some areas. The tensions and contradictions that permeate the philosophy within and without these documents put additional resource demands on teachers attempting to put both into practice. Implementing whole-class teaching and teaching for diversity requires a greater level of resourcing because the teacher cannot be doing both simultaneously and therefore requires additional support as well as more physical resources to cater for both strategies. There is evidence (see, for example, Piotrowski and Reason, 2000) that where classroom assistants are not available in the Literacy Hour pupils make less progress and there is a greater degree of disruptive behaviour. There is also evidence that the lack of adequate resourcing for whole-class teaching and teaching for diversity is resulting in teachers subsidising work in the Literacy Hour themselves. For example, the Association of Teachers and Lecturers Survey (ATL, 1999) showed that 50 per cent of the primary teachers surveyed supported the Literacy Hour from their own pockets because resources provided were felt to be inadequate to cover the diversity of needs. There was also a strong feeling among interviewees in the 1999 Newcastle University evaluation of the National Literacy Strategy (Smith, Hardman and Mroz, 1999) that pupils in socially deprived areas were making less progress as a result of lacking the necessary supporting resources. In addition, larger schools were perceived to be at a disadvantage because the amount of money given to all schools to support the introduction of the NLS was the same because it was assumed that all schools would be teaching the same thing for all pupils so that larger schools would not need additional materials to cover a broader diversity of a greater number of pupils.

Reconciling contradictions: teaching for all, teaching for diversity

As discussed earlier in the chapter, the NLS initially failed to take account of the English Literacy Taskforce Report's recommendations to implement early intervention strategies and individual learning plans for pupils failing to keep up with the progress of peers in literacy development. Since that time, early intervention strategies have been piloted for pupils working in groups under the direction of teaching assistants. However, the issue of differentiated teaching for individuals still remains. The recommendation to address individual pupils' difficulties in literacy development by implementing programmes such as Reading Recovery has not been taken up, for example.

There is a further problem in the way in which teachers' own expertise in addressing children's literacy development is regarded. The Taskforce assumed the need for external experts to train teachers to teach children to read. There is, therefore, a lack of recognition of the ways in which teachers in England may have developed specific pedagogical approaches to their children's literacy development:

> If all primary school pupils are to read well, then all primary teachers need to learn how to teach reading well. . . . Many primary teachers have not had systematic opportunities to update their skills. . . . This means that their teaching approach is often based upon a distant recollection of what they learnt when they trained and their experience since then. As we have seen this is an unacceptably haphazard state of affairs. Primary teachers have found themselves a target for criticism, particularly in relation to the teaching of reading over the past few years. . . . If teachers are to change, they need opportunities to learn the best approaches and incentives to adopt them.
>
> (Literacy Taskforce Preliminary Report, p. 9)

The NLS reinforces this construction of teachers as needing expert instruction in how to raise the standard of children's literacy in its provision of 'literacy consultants' employed from Local Education Authorities to demonstrate to teachers how to implement the Literacy Hour. This approach, like that of the Literacy Taskforce, is a technicist approach in that it emphasises specific techniques for delivering the Literacy Hour rather than awareness and understanding of children's literacy development (Stainthorp, 1999). Such a technicist approach fails to draw upon the professionally developed knowledge base derived from understandings developed by teachers working in the classroom.

While the Taskforce and the NLS assumed that teachers should be taught how to improve their practice by outside experts, there is evidence that there are many effective primary teachers in England who have developed their own expertise in pedagogical approaches to literacy development. Moreover they have developed ways of supporting pupils' literacy development which have the potential for reconciling the need to teach all pupils, while at the same time recognising the need to cater for diversity.

Examples of practices supporting literacy development for all children and meeting the needs of individuals were identified by the Exeter University Primary Improvement Project, a study of almost 1400 schools, 1994–7, funded by the Leverhulme Trust (Wragg, 1998a, 1998b). The Exeter researchers observed the teaching practices of 35 teachers rated by their own headteachers as successful teachers of literacy. Almost two-thirds of the 258 individual children in the study showed improvement beyond the mean over one year. There was a broad definition of 'improvement' which included positive changes in attitude and reading behaviour as well as raised test scores. Some teachers were identified as having the highest 'pupil-on-task' scores the research team had ever witnessed. Boys improved at the same rate as girls, but started from a lower base.

The Exeter University Primary Improvement Project, like the English National Literacy Taskforce, sought to identify the strategies used by effective teachers of literacy. However, unlike the Taskforce, the Exeter Project researched what effective UK-based teachers of literacy actually do, and therefore what other teachers in similar contexts might do, to raise the level of children's literacy. The project identified ten characteristics of a good teacher of literacy, few of which bear much relation to the narrow prescription of the pedagogy of the Literacy Hour. An inspection of these characteristics shows the extent of the difference between the pedagogical strengths in the literacy approaches of the teachers in the Exeter study and those advocated in the Literacy Hour:

- having a high level of personal enthusiasm for literature, often supplementing the school's resources with their own books;
- stressing the importance of literacy within a rich literacy environment while celebrating progress publicly and increasing children's confidence;
- teaching individualised programmes matched to pupils' ability and reading interests and providing systematic monitoring and assessment;
- organising regular and varied reading activities;
- encouraging pupils to develop independence and autonomy in attacking unfamiliar words, and backing pupils' judgement as authors;
- maintaining a high quality of classroom management skill and personal relationships with pupils;
- having high expectations of children whatever their circumstances.

During the lessons of the teachers seen as exemplary in the area of literacy development, there was a great variety of methods of teaching. However, none adopted the 15–15–20–10-minute recommended pattern of the Literacy Hour.

In order to implement the pedagogies identified as the hallmark of exemplary teaching of literacy in the Exeter research, there is a need to rethink continuing professional development for teachers. Implementation of pedagogies such as those outlined in the Exeter research requires a reconceptualisation of the concept of literacy and literacy development and the professionals' role within this development. As indicated by the Exeter research, effective literacy pedagogies demand the fostering of a greater awareness and understanding by teachers and classroom assistants of the process of children's literacy development. The current prescriptive framework does not support or enable such an awareness among and between practitioners, policy makers and those who implement educational policy.

Conclusion

There is an inherent contradiction between the philosophy behind the whole-class teaching of the Literacy Hour and the principles of the GSI. The emphasis on whole-class and whole-group teaching could no longer dominate teaching practice if the principles of teaching for diversity as advocated in the GSI were upheld. This contradiction has serious consequences for practitioners which have been explored in this chapter. Putting the GSI principles into practice and raising the standard of all children's literacy development demands a rethinking of the NLS at the level of policy as well as practice.

Reconciliation of the policy implications of the NLS and the GSI demands a major reconceptualisation of current literacy teaching policies and pedagogies. This reconceptualisation must foster a view of teaching as a learned profession where teachers make reflective judgements about their particular pupils and learning situations based upon a sound theoretical knowledge of literacy and literacy development and the practice of teaching literacy to children with difficulties in the area of literacy. The Exeter research discussed above reflects this view of teachers as learned, reflective professionals. This view is further exemplified by the creative way in which many teachers have grappled with the tensions between opposing expectations of the Literacy Hour and the GSI.

In England, the National Curriculum and, with it, the Literacy Strategy, have become increasingly centralised and driven by Government policy. In a centralised system, education policy has a direct impact on schools and teachers. This situation implies that policy makers need to be concerned with the overall coherence of the philosophy underlying policies. This coherence must be clear at the point of policy conceptualisation. In a key field such as the inclusion of pupils who experience difficulties in literacy development, coherence in policy making could be achieved, firstly, through dialogue between different groups working on policy initiatives in the areas of special educational needs, inclusion and literacy. It is possible to modify practice to accommodate conflicting policy ideals and principles. However, it would be far more effective and time-efficient to address these conflicts at the point of policy conceptualisation. Coherence could be achieved, secondly, through more active involvement of professional input to policy conceptualisation. In practical terms this means better liaison between policy makers and practitioners with powerful consultative mechanisms put into place to review the implications of policy implementation across policies. This needs to be built into every stage of policy development so that practitioners are given real power to influence policy formulation and contribute to change at the level of both policy and practice.

Chapter 12

Developmental dyslexia

Into the future

Roderick I. Nicolson

Important distinctions in learning disabilities

Different roles

It is apparent that the dyslexia community, broadly defined, includes a number of unlikely bedfellows. Researchers and practitioners; parents and teachers; teachers and educational psychologists; schools and local education authorities; local education authorities and governments – all have different priorities, and much of the time they are thrown into opposed roles. Furthermore, different groups of researchers often need to stress the distinctive nature of their own research, and this can disguise the important commonalities between them. It is important to perceive that this apparent oppositional rivalry reflects an attitude of mind rather than an immutable law. It derives from the normally correct assumption that funding is 'zero sum'. If one group gets more (whether it be one group of researchers, one set of children, or one lobbying group) then the zero sum assumption is that the rest get less.

However, imagine the situation in 2005, with the introduction of a system in which theoretical work led to the introduction of early screening tests that detected dyslexia at pre-school, and these in turn led to proactive and ongoing individualized support. This support would be based on applied research identifying dyslexia-friendly teaching methods, and would, where appropriate, involve specialists. This support would ensure that dyslexic children did not suffer reading failure and subsequent educational disadvantage. Similar scenarios can be foreseen for adult dyslexia, with fuller screening, expert subsequent assessment, especially for job-related goals, and much greater awareness of the requirements for 'dyslexia-friendly' working practices. These innovations would actually be 'win win', rather than 'zero sum', in that they would appeal to all participants – dyslexic individuals, dyslexia support specialists, schools, educational psychologists, funding bodies and governments.

A successful, effective and cost-effective policy will be a major step forward for all the participants in the wider dyslexia community. It is possible to justify the outlay of initial costs if the outcome is thoroughly beneficial, in terms of human resources, educational expenditure, national competitiveness, and scientific progress.

Different theories

One of the most important distinctions in scientific research is that between cause and description. Typically scientific research progresses by first getting a reasonably complete description of the facts, and then by inventing hypotheses considered to account for the facts, and then by evaluating the hypotheses against new data. It is hoped that by this means progress is made towards the true explanation. Hypotheses built on inadequate databases of facts suffer the danger of premature specificity.

The 'medical model' provides a reasonable starting point for investigations of abnormal states. Here the distinction is between cause, symptom and treatment. I normally use the analogy of malaria here, where all three accounts are clearly different.[1] Several diseases have similar-looking symptoms, but the treatments are quite different. It is therefore necessary to use further, more sensitive tests, administered by a trained specialist, to determine the true underlying cause, and thus the appropriate treatment. It is important to realize that, for practitioners, the primary task is treatment, for educational psychologists the primary task is identification of symptoms, and for theorists the primary task remains the discovery of the underlying cause(s). Despite these differences in primary motivations, a full understanding requires the investigation and integration of all three aspects.[2]

Turning to an alternative, complementary perspective from cognitive neuroscience theory, following Uta Frith (1997), it is important to distinguish between three 'levels' of theory: the biological, the cognitive and the behavioural level. The behavioural level is in terms of symptoms – poor reading and difficulty with rhymes for example. The cognitive level gives an explanation in terms of theoretical constructs from cognitive psychology – say reduced working memory, poor phonological processing, incomplete automatization, slow central processing, and so forth. The biological level attempts to identify the underlying brain mechanism – disorganization in cerebral cortex in the language areas, abnormal magnocellular pathways, abnormal cerebellum, and so forth. It is not that any one level of explanation is intrinsically 'better' than another. A complete explanation would involve all three. The cognitive level might at first sight appear to be an unnecessary one, both hypothetical and unobservable, but in much the same way as the cognitive construct of 'thirst' can be used to explain differing behaviours in differing circumstances it provides a valuable and economical explanation of a variety of behaviours and forms a crucial link between brain and behaviour.

What's in a name? Dyslexia versus specific learning difficulties versus learning disability versus reading disability

The advantage of the label 'dyslexia' is that it has no intrinsic meaning – it says nothing about the underlying cause, and is neutral as to whether the cause is visual, phonological, motor or some combination. The drawback (for educationalists) is that it has strong political and emotional connotations, that it suggests there is a single relatively uniform syndrome, and that dyslexia is somehow 'special'. From here it is but a short step to saying that dyslexic children need special treatment. While few would dispute this, many educationalists rightly stress the need for equally special treatment for non-dyslexic children with equally special educational needs (Siegel, 1989).

Furthermore, there was (and remains) considerable controversy over how distinct dyslexia may be as a syndrome. In the telling analogy of Andrew Ellis (Ellis, 1993), is dyslexia like obesity, with varying degrees and with arbitrary cutoff? If dyslexia is special somehow, is it then a collection of subtypes (Boder, 1973; Castles and Holmes, 1996) or do the majority actually show a common 'core' deficit (such as phonology)? Miles has termed this debate that between the 'splitters' and the 'lumpers'. Possibly in response to these problems in definition, UK educational psychologists preferred to use the term 'specific learning disabilities'.

Some time in the 1980s, influential US dyslexia researchers redesignated dyslexia as 'reading disability' rather than 'specific learning disability'. At first sight this seems entirely reasonable. After all, the specific problem is with reading. However, there is a deep consequence of the name change. The result is a change of emphasis from process to skill, from a 'specific learning' disability – that is a deficit in some (specific but not yet determined) form of the learning processes – to the skill of reading. Clearly if the problem is one of reading, then the solution must surely reside in a painstaking analysis of the reading process.

This is certainly a legitimate approach, but it is not the only approach. It has led to a schism between those who want to find the cause of dyslexia and those who want to find the cause of the reading problems. Given hindsight, it is clear that both approaches are needed for the 'grand vision' of dyslexia, as we discuss below.

Science, research and politics

When I first entered dyslexia research, I naively assumed that dyslexia research was science, science was search for the truth, and that nothing else really mattered. This is not so. Even in academia, scientific research is at least as much about academic politics as about science – as Medawar put it, science is the art of the soluble. If no one will fund the research, the scientific progress will not be made. Consequently, astute academics spend much time cultivating influential acquaintances and building their power base. Dyslexia research spans a particularly broad spectrum, including a range of 'pure science' theories, to a range of treatments and support that if successfully marketed might make their inventors millionaires, to overt lobbying of governments. Politics is the art of persuasion, and persuasion is most effective if a simple, coherent message is given. This is normally achieved by 'special pleading' – cherry picking the arguments in favour of one's position, and ignoring or denigrating inconvenient facts and alternative approaches. It is all too easy to apply the logic of politics (or, worse, marketing) to matters of science. Again, I empha-size that each has its place, and its specialists, but many dyslexia researchers have to wear several of these hats. Perhaps the way forward to maintain the credibility of the field is to introduce some system of 'kitemarking', or declar-ation of interests, allied to clear dissociations of function, so that lobbying, marketing and science are kept well apart.

The situation in 1990

In 1990 the most powerful theoretical framework for dyslexia research, both in the UK and internationally, was in terms of phonological deficit. In the UK the approach was inspired by seminal research by Bradley and Bryant, by Frith and by Snowling. In the US it reflected the results of a concerted effort by dyslexia researchers and educationalists to 'sing from the same hymn book', providing a coherent and unified vision that was instrumental in persuading US policymakers to provide substantial long-term funding via the NICHD Learning Disabilities programme – funding that is still continuing at around $20 million per year. The phonological message was a simple but powerful one: the core deficit for dyslexic children is with phonological processing, prob-ably attributable to brain abnormalities in the language areas. This deficit means that, at school age, they have greater difficulty hearing the individual sounds in spoken words, and this makes it more difficult for them to learn to read, because of poor awareness of phonological features such as rhyme, which are very important when building up the rules of grapheme (written letter) to phoneme (corresponding sound) translation rules. Clearly the key teaching requirement is to present more systematic and more thorough training in phonological awareness for children (especially those at risk of reading failure). The key research priorities were to investigate more fully the causes of the phonological difficulties. The key teaching priorities were to introduce better methods of assisting children to acquire phonological awareness. The key policy requirements were to support the phonological agenda by providing the necessary backing in terms of funds and statutes. . . .

Progress since 1990

. . . I shall consider progress from four perspectives: policy, theory, diagnosis, and support.

Policy

Policy is the area where dyslexia has made incontrovertible progress during the 1990s, a tribute to the dedication and adroitness of the Dyslexia Institute and the British Dyslexia Association. At the start of the decade, dyslexia was not recognized by the political and educational authorities, and many educational psychologists were openly and explicitly sceptical of the concept. In 1994, the

Education Act was passed, and the following Code of Practice for Children with Special Educational Needs made it the responsibility of the schools to identify and support children with special educational needs. Furthermore, a series of stages, interventions, and procedures was introduced that was designed to ensure that children received appropriate and effective support.

The Code provides a valuable summary of these early stages:

2.119 In summary, schools should adopt a staged response to children's special educational needs and:

- employ clear procedures to identify and register children whose academic, social or emotional development is giving cause for concern
- identify children's areas of weakness which require extra attention from their teachers or other members of staff
- develop, monitor, review and record, in consultation with parents and involving the child as far as possible, individual education plans designed to meet each child's identified needs.

Such plans should include written information about:

- individual programmes of work
- performance targets
- review dates, findings and decisions
- parental involvement in and support for the plans
- arrangements for the involvement of the child
- information on any external advice or support

- assess children's performance, identifying strengths as well as weaknesses, using appropriate measures so that the rate of progress resulting from special educational provision can be assessed
- call upon specialist advice from outside the school to inform the school's strategies to meet the child's special educational needs in particular, but not necessarily only, at stage 3.

Furthermore, the Code does consider dyslexia specifically under the heading of 'Specific learning difficulty (for example, dyslexia)' when considering criteria for making a Statutory Assessment (§3.60–3.63). A key requirement is that '. . . there is clear, recorded evidence of clumsiness, significant difficulties of sequencing or visual perception; deficiencies in working memory; or significant delays in language functioning' (§3.61iii).

In short, although the situation regarding dyslexia in UK schools remains far from ideal, exceptional progress has been made. It is fair to say that the situation for a dyslexic child in the UK is one of the most favourable in the world. The UK situation is considerably in advance of that in the US, where the devolution of power to the individual states appears to have hindered the introduction of a coherent policy, despite the best efforts of the US dyslexia community.

While the situation in the UK regarding adults is less advanced, there is reason to believe that the situation may soon be improved. The 1998 Adult Disability Act made it a requirement that most large firms introduce a systematic disability support system. Recently, the Moser Report (Moser, 2000) has highlighted the importance of adult literacy and numeracy skills and has led to the introduction of an ambitious programme of government support.

Theory

There have been major developments in several theoretical areas related to dyslexia. In particular, neuroscience, brain imaging, and genetics have made outstanding progress. This progress is reflected in several ways in dyslexia theory. ... Following Frith (1997) it is valuable to classify theories at the biological level, the cognitive level and the behavioural level. I shall additionally introduce the genetic level.

Genetic level

A range of new and intriguing findings have emerged, indicating that dyslexia is likely not to be caused by a single gene but through the interaction of multiple genes, with possibly different gene sets being involved with different phenotypes (behavioural systems). It is not clear what bearing these genes have directly on behaviour or even on the development of the brain. It is, for instance, possible that one gene might lead say to birth complications, and so it would have only an indirect effect upon the child's brain. Another gene might lead to sinus problems or 'glue ear' in infancy. The poor quality auditory input during the critical period for development of speech-related auditory cortex might lead to poorer quality auditory representations of speech, and thus phonological deficit – again an indirect effect. ... See Elman et al. (1997) for an incisive analysis of the links between genes and behaviour.

Biological level

New theories have been suggested, both in terms of magnocellular deficit (Stein) and cerebellar deficit (Fawcett and Nicolson). ... Both theories have a good deal in common, and both suggest that problems will be more widespread than just phonological deficit. A good deal more research is needed to establish the extent to which these theories account for dyslexia and, in particular, we need to establish the 'prevalence' of the different subtypes that might be expected under the different accounts.

Cognitive level

In addition to the automatization deficit and phonological deficit account, the major newcomer to the cognitive level accounts is the 'double deficit' hypothesis (Wolf and Bowers, 1999) that suggests that dyslexic children suffer not only from a deficit in phonological processing but also in central processing speed. . . . Rather than automatization per se, it now appears that there may be abnormalities in fundamental learning processes such as classical conditioning, habituation, response 'tuning' and error elimination. A particularly striking finding is [the] 'square root rule', that dyslexic people may take longer to acquire a skill in proportion to the square root of the time normally taken to acquire it. If a skill takes four practice sessions to master, it would take a dyslexic child eight sessions to reach the same standard. If it normally took 400 sessions, it would take the dyslexic child 8,000 sessions! If replicable, this finding would have striking implications for dyslexia support in that it mandates progression in terms of small, easily assimilated steps. This would not only provide theoretical support for existing good practice in dyslexia support but might also distinguish dyslexia support requirements from those for other poor readers. Clearly considerable further research is needed to investigate these hypotheses.

Behavioural level

We now have a wide range of skills on which groups of dyslexic children show significant impairment. These include sensory deficit (flicker, motion sensitivity, rapid auditory discrimination), motor (bead threading, balance), and cognitive (phonological, working memory, speed). The challenge is no longer to find skills where the dyslexic children perform poorly, but rather those where they perform at normal or above normal levels. These typically include non-verbal reasoning, vocabulary and problem solving. What is still not clear is whether there are different 'subtypes' of dyslexia, each corresponding to a different 'profile' of skills, and to what extent dyslexia is distinct from other learning disabilities. . . .

Literacy support

Much of the early work on reading support for dyslexic children was based on the timeless principles that literacy support needs to be individualized, systematic, explicit and structured, progressing a step at a time, and gradually building the skills needed (Gillingham and Stillman, 1960; Hickey, 1992; Miles, 1989). The difficulty with this approach is that it's hard to maintain motivation given such a gradual regime.

The major development in terms of literacy in the UK in the past decade was the introduction of the 'Literacy Strategy' in all infant and junior schools. The core feature of the strategy was the 'Literacy Hour', a dedicated hour every day devoted to literacy teaching, and with a systematic associated teaching methodology intended to make sure that all children progressed through the stages in reading in a predetermined sequence based on established good practice.

There is no doubt that introduction of the Literacy Strategy has had beneficial effects on overall literacy in UK schools. However, the sceptic might say that this is hardly surprising given that very much more time and resources are now being allocated to literacy. A dyslexia specialist might also enquire, with reason, whether there is evidence that the teaching methods used are in fact tuned to the teaching of dyslexic children.

In order to address these questions, it is necessary to consider evidence – controlled studies of the comparative effectiveness of different methods for teaching reading, especially for dyslexic children. Before evidence may be considered, however, it is necessary to devise a methodology for evaluating the evidence. In an ambitious series of controlled studies, US researchers have established high quality data on the effectiveness of a range of different interventions, recently published as (NICHD, 2000). . . . For my purposes here, . . . I provide a vignette from the third phase of our research programme, aimed at systematic screening–assessment–support.

Our main aim was to inform policy decisions on providing cost-effective support for dyslexic children, and we investigated two issues: first we needed to establish baseline data on how much improvement one might reasonably expect via a low cost standard intervention; and second we wished to establish whether such an approach was suitable for dyslexic children. From the viewpoint of policy, one needs to establish the cost-effectiveness of any intervention. It is clear that, if more resources are devoted to teaching reading, then that should lead to significant improvements in reading. The sharp policy question is: how can we best invest the resources so as to maximize the benefits per unit cost?

Rather to our surprise, despite decades of educational research, there appeared to be no accepted methodology for assessing cost-effectiveness. In particular, no extant research appeared to have noted the obvious point that the longer the intervention, the more effect it is likely to have.

In an initial study, we took children in infant and junior schools in Sheffield and Harrogate, identified those at risk of reading problems, and gave them reading-related support in groups of three for two 30-minute sessions per week for 10 weeks, and monitored how much they improved on standard tests of reading and spelling over that period. Naturally we also used matched control groups in matched schools who did not have an intervention, so that we could establish the relative improvement. The intervention used was the balanced 'step by step' approach to tailoring the reading support to the individual capabilities of each reader developed by Reason and Boote (1994).

Figure 12.1 provides an overview of the effects of the various interventions. The outcome measure displayed is the 'composite literacy score', which is the average of the standard scores for reading and spelling. A standard score is age-normed, with a mean of 100. The children under investigation were all struggling with reading, as indicated by their low scores of below 90 initially (worse for the junior school study than the infant school study). Two interventions were compared, Reason's 'traditional' (in the sense that it was not

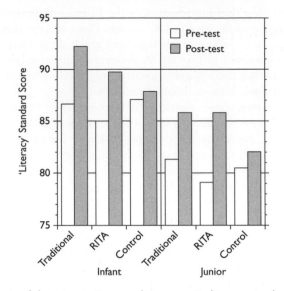

Figure 12.1 Effects of the interventions on the composite literacy standard scores

computer-assisted) intervention described above, and a computer-based inter-vention named RITA (Readers' Interactive Teaching Assistant) that I had developed myself and was designed to allow the teacher complete latitude in whether to use the computer, use traditional methods, or some combination thereof.

In all studies the intervention group made significantly more progress than the control group as measured by mean literacy standard scores. The overall effect sizes were 0.95 for the infant school and 0.67 for the junior school for the traditional interventions. Corresponding figures for RITA were 0.92 (infant) and 1.01 (junior). Effect sizes for the control groups were 0.23, both for infant and junior, demonstrating that the literacy strategy was having some beneficial effects.

The effect size alone indicates effectiveness (and if one subtracts the effect size for the control group, one gets the 'added value' of the intervention). An effect size in the region of 1.0 is considered 'large' statistically. The program-matic 'Reading Recovery' methods pioneered by Clay in New Zealand had added value effect size of between 0.70 and 1.30 (Nicolson, Fawcett, Moss, Nicolson and Reason, 1999). However, from the viewpoint of educational policy the key indicator is cost-effectiveness not just effectiveness. For cost-effectiveness one must divide the benefits (effect sizes) by the costs (teacher hours per child). The fact that our interventions took place in small groups for relatively short times (10 hours per group) means that both of our inter-ventions were very much more cost-effective than reading recovery.

Finally, we considered the results relating to dyslexia. Are there some chil-dren who do not benefit much from the traditional intervention? In fact in

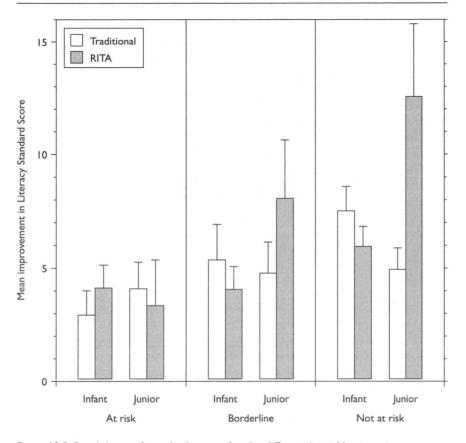

Figure 12.2 Breakdown of standard scores for the different 'at risk' categories

all studies there were children who did not improve much. Of these, almost all had 'at risk' scores on the DEST (infant) or DST (junior) tests. In the infant school traditional study, children at risk or borderline risk made very much less progress than the remainder (effect sizes 0.40, 0.35 and 0.96 respectively). For the junior school traditional study, at-risk children made very much less progress than the borderline or not at risk groups (0.35, 0.63 and 0.65 respectively). We had hoped that use of RITA would prove particularly helpful to the at-risk children, but this was not the case. It may be seen (Figure 12.2) that RITA was actually particularly beneficial in junior school for those poor readers who were not at risk, leading to an enormous mean improvement in standard score of around 12.5 points!

We concluded that the results confirm the importance and cost-effectiveness of early intervention in a child's initial school years – the 'stitch in time' approach. While cost-effective improvements in reading can be achieved at junior school, a significant proportion of junior children will fail to achieve lasting benefits from a relatively short intervention of this type.

I have spent too long on these illustrations since reading is not the primary focus of this chapter. ... [T]he comprehensive report of the US National Reading Panel and classics such as (Adams, 1990; Goswami and Bryant, 1990; Rayner and Pollatsek, 1989) provide excellent overviews. A broader account is given in Nicolson (1999).

The situation in 2000

In summary, outstanding progress has been made in the 1990s. Phonological deficit remains a central concept from the viewpoint of theory, diagnosis and early support. There is, however, an emerging consensus that a broader framework is needed for causal explanations and for diagnostic aids. In reviewing the 'state of the art', I will first note briefly the state of knowledge, and then consider in more detail the areas where knowledge is lacking, or there are unresolved difficulties.

Theory

Theoretically, at the cognitive level, hypotheses including slower speed of processing and abnormal fundamental learning processes have been added to phonological deficits. At the biological level, hypotheses including magnocellular deficit and cerebellar deficit have been proposed as alternatives to deficits in the cerebral language areas. Descriptions are now being introduced in terms of underlying genes, though the links to theories at biological, cognitive and behavioural levels are not yet established.

The new theoretical developments raise more questions than they answer. This is a strength rather than a weakness, reflecting the opening up of fruitful new research avenues. Limitations on knowledge are described below.

Lack of quantitative data on tasks 'across the board'

It is not enough to show that a group of dyslexic children differs significantly from controls on a particular skill. There will be significant impairments for most skills. What is needed is the profile of deficits (effect sizes), so that we can identify for which skills there are the most extreme deficits. A few small-scale studies have been completed, but it is not clear how representative these data are for the general dyslexia population.

Lack of quantitative data on prevalence and comorbidity

It is puzzling that despite a decade and more of intensive research, there are still few clear-cut data on whether individual dyslexic children and adults show one, two or more of the key indicators of phonological deficit, sensory deficit, speed deficit, and cerebellar deficit. What is needed is a large-scale study where all the children in a particular cohort are given standardized tests that cover the range of above skills, together with the different forms of learning, so as to assess the relative incidence and overlap ('comorbidity') of the possible different subtypes.

Lack of quantitative data on dyslexia and other learning disabilities

There are intriguing data that suggest there is unexpectedly high comorbidity between dyslexia and ADHD, dyslexic and specific language impairment, and dyslexia and dyspraxia. It is also likely that there would be comorbidity between dyslexia and generalized learning difficulty, if some measure other than IQ discrepancy could be established. Unfortunately, the underlying causes of these other developmental disorders are less well understood than those for dyslexia, but there is intriguing evidence of cerebellar abnormality in all of the specific disorders including ADHD (Berquin *et al.*, 1998; Mostofsky, Reiss, Lockhart and Denckla, 1998). Clearly there is considerable scope for studies comparing and contrasting different disorders, using the techniques outlined above.

Lack of complete, integrated accounts

Perhaps a key requirement is to develop the accounts at the biological, cognitive and behavioural levels, with the intention of providing not only explanations at the different levels, but also providing an account of how the various symptoms develop as a function of genes, brain and experience.

Lack of links with mainstream developmental cognitive neuroscience

There is a real danger that dyslexia research in the UK remains seen as something of an isolated backwater. It takes too long for concepts from mainstream science – development, cognition and neuroscience to become accepted in dyslexia research. An outstanding example of the benefits that can accrue from infusion of new scientific approaches derived from the Rodin Remediation Dyslexia Society, which organized a series of exceptional scientific conferences on themes related to dyslexia over the 1990s.

Screening and diagnosis

In terms of diagnosis, there are now good screening tests available that can be used by a teacher or adult specialist to identify quickly the profile of strengths and weaknesses of an individual. This information, when augmented with interview data, may be able to form the basis of an initial individual development plan. Furthermore, a good case can be made for screening for 'dyslexia' before a child reaches school, especially if appropriate support regimes can then be introduced so as to maximize the chances of the child learning reasonably normally at school.

Difficulties over discrepancy

Unfortunately, the situation regarding diagnosis (both formal diagnosis and support diagnosis) is unsatisfactory. Formal diagnosis depends on assessment both of reading and of IQ. There are longstanding and valid objections to the use of IQ as an indicator, but in the absence of positive indicators for dyslexia it is hard to see how a discrepancy definition can otherwise be maintained. There is a movement in the US and the UK to abandon the discrepancy criterion, but this appears to me to reflect confusion between theory, diagnosis and support. Failure to maintain discrepancy would prevent analysis of the key issues of whether dyslexia does have underlying cause(s) distinct from other developmental disorders, and whether a dyslexia-friendly support regime is in fact significantly different from a generalized special-needs-friendly support regime. The movement to abandon discrepancy should be resisted strenuously until these key issues have been resolved.

Lack of positive indices of dyslexia

In my view, the reliance on 'reading' as a primary determinant is misplaced. Reading is a learned skill. Despite their difficulties, dyslexic children do learn to read (fortunately). Nonetheless, they remain dyslexic. What is urgently needed is an index of dyslexia that is based on a more fundamental attribute than is reading. It seems likely that a range of indicators – speed of processing, fundamental learning processes, magnocellular system operation – will be needed. Current diagnoses are based on a 'snapshot' of performance at one time. As with the current Code of Practice, it is important to augment these tests with tests of response to learning opportunities.

Lack of clarity regarding diagnosis relative to other learning disabilities

A further key requirement is comparison of dyslexia with other learning disabilities. At present the diagnosis a child receives is too dependent upon the specialist to whom s/he is first referred. Early speech difficulties will lead to a diagnosis of specific language impairment. Early clumsiness may lead to a diagnosis of dyspraxia. A child with mild problems in speech and motor skill may be diagnosed as dyslexic or maybe attention deficit. Development of more fundamental diagnostic criteria should illuminate this vexed issue.

Difficulties regarding diagnosis in multilingual children

It is currently very difficult to know how to diagnose dyslexia in children whose first language is not English. Clearly some degree of reading impairment is likely. We would hope that identification of fundamental criteria should significantly alleviate this vexed issue.

Difficulties regarding diagnosis in non-English-speaking countries

It is important to stress that dyslexia is somewhat differently defined in countries where the language spoken has a more transparent (regular) orthography. In Spanish and German, for instance, the rules for pronouncing the written word are straightforward, with few exceptions. Consequently, most children are able to read, albeit slowly in some cases. One approach to the problem of diagnosis is to identify those children who read slowly as dyslexic (Wimmer, 1993). It is not clear whether this approach leads to the same classifications as would obtain if the children were English-speaking. Again, it seems likely that cross-linguistic research, finding commonalities between dyslexia in different languages, is likely to advance the search for fundamental positive indicators of dyslexia.

Support

There has been considerable progress in literacy and numeracy teaching. Nonetheless, there seems to be a lack of clear knowledge on a number of crucial issues.

Clarifying principles of dyslexia-friendly teaching

The central question is whether the techniques introduced are in fact dyslexia friendly. In my view, the 'one pace suits all' approach implicit in the UK literacy strategy is unlikely to be appropriate for dyslexic children. At the very least they will require considerable extra support. There is a clear need for carefully controlled evaluation studies aimed at identifying the cost effectiveness of different support methods for different groups of children with reading problems. Standard instructional theory established many years ago that, if one wants to teach a complex skill, it is necessary to perform a balancing act – to try to automatize the component subskills while also teaching the skill as a whole (Nicolson, 1998). This is pretty obvious in the case of a skill such as tennis – one needs to be able to practise the forehand as well as the backhand, and one needs to play a game in order to maintain interest. The consensus of studies in the past decade is that this is also true of reading. One needs to develop fluency and knowledge as well as phonological skills. It remains to be established whether the optimal dyslexia-friendly methods are the same as the optimal normal-reader-friendly methods or the optimal non-dyslexic-poor-reader-friendly methods. I doubt it.

Harnessing new technology

Computer-based opportunities (including voice recognition, multimedia and the Internet) have improved out of all recognition over the decade. One of the key support requirements is the issue of how to harness these opportunities to supporting dyslexic people. I believe that the computer provides the method to maintain enjoyment and fun while delivering the adaptive, carefully crafted and systematic schedules needed to develop automaticity. The challenge is to identify how best to use computer, human teacher and learner as a team.

How to exploit strengths as well as remedy weaknesses

It may be that dyslexic and non-dyslexic poor readers have a similar profile of weaknesses on reading. They certainly do not have the same strengths, and instructional science (and common sense) make it clear that good learning normally builds on strengths rather than weaknesses.

Policy

Finally, then, policy. In this area it would appear that successive UK governments have performed outstandingly, in terms of education Acts and adult disability discrimination Acts. It is unfortunate that UK research councils have failed to capitalize on this by dedicated funding for 'pure' dyslexia research.

What is the best dyslexia-friendly policy?

The thrust of the above review is that the UK government would be more than willing to introduce a popular, justifiable and cost-effective policy towards the identification and support of dyslexic individuals, and those with other special needs. The question, however, is, what should such a policy be? What would be the main objectives for theory, diagnosis and support? How would it be evaluated? It is surely time for the UK dyslexia research community to attempt to provide the answers – to design, propose and undertake a comprehensive and united research programme aimed at a complete and inclusive analysis of dyslexia theory, diagnosis and support. I outline below some considerations that may be relevant. My main aim, however, is to stimulate discussion of these issues, in the expectation that those with greater expertise in the specific areas will be able to improve significantly on the proposed framework.

Into the future

I start with 10 sober questions for dyslexia research, in the hope that researchers will attack these with relish, thereby significantly advancing the field. I move on to six 'injunctions' for dyslexia research, following the lead of Allen Newell. I then present a somewhat fanciful portrayal of the future, using the style of a third giant of my formative years, Isaac Asimov, in the hope that the artistic licence granted will illuminate the possible objectives for the next few years. I conclude with a plea for a concerted effort at a coherent, inclusive and integrated research programme into dyslexia theory, practice and policy.

Ten questions for dyslexia research

Q1. Is there a better way to teach reading, one that combines the important aspects of the systematic approaches known to help dyslexic children, but designed also to be intrinsically motivating, and natural?

Q2. How can we diagnose dyslexia as early as appropriate? In particular, how much can studies of development in infancy and in the pre-school period inform our understanding and identification? . . .

Q3. Are there different forms of dyslexia? Do some children have only phonological problems, others magnocellular plus phonological, others cerebellar etc.? How do differences relate to different genes?

Q4. If there are different forms, what are the implications for teaching and support?

Q5. How about 'alternative' methods of support? What credence should one attach to tinted lenses, travel sickness pills, dietary supplements, reflexology and other methods? For whom are they successful, and if so, why?

Q6. Does intelligence matter for diagnosis and/or support?

Q7. How about other learning disabilities/developmental disorders? What is the overlap with dyslexia, and how important is it?

Q8. How can we develop and introduce a systematic, cost-effective and valuable system for screening, assessment and support that is respected by all?

Q9. How can we integrate dyslexia research within mainstream developmental, cognitive and neuroscience research?

Q10. Can we really 'prevent' dyslexia? That is, can we develop a series of 'learning experiences' that 'scaffold' brain development on to an optimal track? For instance, is it possible to present speech sounds in such a sequence during infancy that the 'optimal' brain representation for speech sounds is ensured.

Injunctions for dyslexia research

Following Allen Newell, whose 1973 analysis of the way forward for cognitive psychology was formative for me, I offer five 'injunctions for dyslexia research'.

Injunction 1: Be open minded and inclusive

Too little is known about the mechanisms of brain development (normal or abnormal) to allow us the luxury of rejecting alternative support methods out of hand. Many will have a kernel of good sense that can be integrated into a fuller support system, or may provide a valuable perspective suggesting new research avenues.

Injunction 2: Gather quantitative evidence, using objective methods

As in other spheres, evidence-based research is the key requirement for progress. We need to evaluate the effectiveness of support methods using standardized criteria such as effect sizes and cost-effectiveness. Of course, if evidence suggests that a particular approach is not good, that approach should be discouraged, injunction 1 notwithstanding.

Injunction 3: Be inquisitorial, not adversarial

The adversarial (head to head) approach is largely discredited in psychological theory. Its overuse in psychological research derives more from politics than science. The inquisitorial (pursuit of truth) approach is the only way to hope to make cumulative progress.

Injunction 4: Groups are made of individuals

From Piaget's studies of his children to the sophisticated methods of cognitive neuropsychology, detailed case studies of individuals have presented fascinating insights into development, abnormal and normal cognitive processes. By contrast, traditional empirical psychology has studied differences between groups. When studying a heterogeneous syndrome such as dyslexia it is necessary to combine the techniques, studying both groups and individuals within groups.

Injunction 5: Respect differing roles and work together

Newell argued that, in order to make cumulative progress on a complex problem, it was necessary to integrate teamwork from diverse specialists. For dyslexia the teams should involve theoreticians (neuroscience, developmental, and cognitive), educationalists, and policy makers. Furthermore, people with first-hand experience of dyslexia may often have unique and distinctive insights that short laboratory tests may miss.

Injunction 6: Aim for a unified, complete approach

Newell made a convincing case that one needed to know where one was aiming for in order to get there (a theme going back to his classic work on means–ends analysis). He also took the view that it was better to think big, to aim for a complete explanation of a complex problem, than to mess around with a series of partial solutions. As with learning to read, one needs to perceive and play the whole game, rather than merely parts thereof. . . .

Conclusions

This has been a difficult chapter to write. It's probably a difficult chapter to read. In attempting to provide an overview from a range of perspectives, I lay myself open to the justified charge that I have gone beyond my sphere of expertise. That is so. I hope nonetheless that these outline analyses will prove a solid enough foundation for specialists to construct a more fully informed, more coherent, and better framework to guide research for the next ten years.

In conclusion, dyslexia research has made considerable progress. I think, though, we're at the start of a revolution in the learning disabilities field, where the different sciences and techniques of development, of neuroscience, of cognition and of education come together with the needs and opportunities of policy and government. The way forward is to be clear about what we need to achieve, and have a coherent strategy to move towards it. There is a need for consensus, for foresight, for an attitude of partnership, for inclusion. Balancing those characteristics, there is a need for objectivity, for comparative evaluation, for 'kitemarking', for better analysis and evaluation tools. Above all, we need to be able to respect and motivate the individual, as well as analysing the group.

The stage is set for undertaking ambitious, multi-disciplinary, multi-perspective projects aimed at redefining the field of dyslexia and learning difficulties as the field of learning abilities.

Notes

1   Perhaps, though, a more appropriate analogy is with allergy. The same allergy can lead to different symptoms in different people and the mechanisms by which allergies arise are poorly understood. Traditional medical science has had difficulties with allergies, and progress has been made primarily via the development of systematic procedures for narrowing down the potential causes.
2   A good example of the application of theory in diagnosis is the need for early diagnosis, before a child fails to learn to read. In order to diagnose dyslexia before reading failure, one needs to have a theoretical approach that indicates positive indicators in addition to reading.

References

Adams M.J. (1990) *Beginning to Read: Thinking and learning about print*. Cambridge MA: MIT Press.

Berquin P.C., Giedd J.N., Jacobsen L.K., Hamburger S.D., Krain A.L., Rapoport J.L., Castellanos F.X. (1998) Cerebellum in attention-deficit hyperactivity disorder: A morphometric MRI study. *Neurology* 50: 1087–93.

Boder E. (1973) Developmental dyslexia: A diagnostic approach based on three atypical spelling-reading patterns. *Developmental Medicine and Child Neurology* 15: 663–87.

Bryant P. (1985) The question of prevention. In M.J. Snowling (ed.) *Children's Written Language Difficulties*. Windsor: NFER Nelson, p. 42.

Castles A., Holmes V.M. (1996) Subtypes of developmental dyslexia and lexical acquisition. *Australian Journal of Psychology* 48: 130–5.

Ellis A.W. (1993) *Reading, Writing and Dyslexia: A cognitive analysis*. 2nd edn. Hove: Erlbaum.

Elman J.E., Bates E.A., Johnson M.H., Karmiloff-Smith A., Parisi D., Plunkett K. (1997) *Rethinking Innateness: A connectionist perspective on development.* Cambridge MA: MIT Press.

Frith U. (1986) A developmental framework for developmental dyslexia. *Annals of Dyslexia* 36.

Frith U. (1997) Brain, mind and behaviour in dyslexia. In C. Hulme, M. Snowling (eds) *Dyslexia: Biology, cognition and intervention.* London: Whurr.

Gillingham A., Stillman B. (1960) *Remedial Training for Children with Specific Difficulties in Reading, Writing and Penmanship.* Cambridge MA: Educators Publishing.

Goswami U., Bryant P. (1990) *Phonological Skills and Learning to Read.* Hillsdale NJ: Lawrence Erlbaum Associates.

Hickey K. (1992) *The Hickey Multisensory Language Course.* 2nd edn. J. Augur, S. Briggs (eds). London: Whurr.

Miles E. (1989) *The Bangor Dyslexia Teaching System.* London: Whurr.

Moser C. (2000) *Better Basic Skills: Improving adult literacy and numeracy.* London: Department for Education and Employment.

Mostofsky S.H., Reiss A.L., Lockhart P., Denckla M.B. (1998) Evaluation of cerebellar size in attention-deficit hyperactivity disorder. *Journal of Child Neurology* 13: 434–9.

NICHD (2000) Report of the National Reading Panel: Teaching children to read. Washington DC: National Institute for Child Health and Human Development.

Nicolson R.I. (1998) Learning and skill. In P. Scott, C. Spencer (eds) *Psychology: A contemporary introduction.* Oxford: Blackwell, pp. 294–343.

Nicolson R.I. (1999) Reading, skill and dyslexia. In D. Messer, S. Millar (eds) *Exploring Developmental Psychology.* London: Arnold.

Nicolson R.I., Fawcett A.J., Moss H., Nicolson M.K., Reason R. (1999) An early reading intervention study: Evaluation and implications. *British Journal of Educational Psychology* 69: 47–62.

Papert S. (1980) *Mindstorms: Children, computers and powerful ideas.* New York: Basic Books.

Rayner K., Pollatsek A. (1989) *The Psychology of Reading.* London: Prentice Hall.

Reason R., Boote R. (1994) *Helping Children with Reading and Spelling: A special needs manual.* Oxford: Routledge.

Siegel L.S. (1989) IQ is irrelevant to the definition of learning disabilities. *Journal of Learning Disabilities* 22: 469.

Wimmer H. (1993) Characteristics of developmental dyslexia in a regular writing system. *Applied Psycholinguistics* 14(1): 1–33.

Wolf M., Bowers P.G. (1999) The double deficit hypothesis for the developmental dyslexias. *Journal of Educational Psychology* 91: 415–38.

Source

This is an edited version of a chapter previously published in A. Fawcett (ed.) *Dyslexia: Theory and Good Practice.* 2001. Reproduced by permission of Whurr Publishers Ltd.

Part 4

Impact of social class, culture, ethnicity and gender

Chapter 13

Texts in context

Mapping out the gender differentiation of the reading curriculum

Gemma Moss

Introduction

Quantitative research shows a remarkably consistent pattern to boys' development as readers: they do less well than girls; they read less than girls; more boys than girls express a preference for non-fiction (Barrs, 1993; Millard, 1997). In some quarters, recent attention to these findings has led to calls for a greater emphasis on non-fiction in the primary reading curriculum, on the assumption that a change from narrative to non-fiction texts would better meet boys' existing interests. Such a move is represented as a turn away from a 'feminised' primary curriculum built round narrative, in which the main role models as readers are provided by a largely female staff, also to the detriment of boys. Recent revisions to the primary literacy curriculum in the United Kingdom through the government-sponsored initiative, the National Literacy Strategy, are, in certain respects, in line with this view, at least in the increased prominence given to non-fiction.

However, there are difficulties with this sort of analysis, which proposes that switching the kinds of texts taught will in itself transform the literacy curriculum. In the first place, such a view accepts boys' and girls' genre-preferences as given, and asks few questions about why such preferences arise. Only a cursory nod to adult role-modelling acts as much of an explanation. Rather, the argument seems to run that if boys prefer non-fiction, a more equitable curriculum would simply give them more of what they like, on the assumption that more of what they like will help them do better. (Nothing on whether such a change would lead girls to do worse.) Indeed, from this kind of perspective, there is little curiosity about what the salient differences between fiction and non-fiction texts might be for their readers, even though Margaret Meek has recently pointed out the difficulty of maintaining such an absolute distinction: 'I suspect that no one ... believes that the literary convention of dividing books into these two categories is either predictable or absolute. (Where do you put poetry?) ... So I begin by declaring that notions of fiction and non-fiction (the pleasurable and the serious) are neither useful nor helpful, tenable even, in contemporary children's learning' (Meek, 1996, p. 8).

On the contrary, in arguments about gender preferences, contrasts between fiction and non-fiction texts are assumed to be straightforward and painted at the level of content, often in the most stereotypic terms: narrative fiction stands for the (feminine) world of affect; non-fiction stands for a functional (and masculine) world of hard facts, devoid of emotions. Never mind that much of the non-fiction which sustains the adult market is actually structured as a prose argument, taking a stance and engaging the reader with that position, rather than reciting a list of indisputable truths. Or that the news is almost entirely sustained by narrative structures. Or that much of the non-fiction most popular with younger readers crucially revolves around visual, rather than verbal text, thereby primarily using the spatial resource of the page, rather than the linear resource of written language, to achieve its effect (Kress, 2000). Precisely because the content is taken at face value, and the contrasts between fiction and non-fiction perceived as well defined, there is little deliberation over the nature of the proposed changes, when balancing one kind of genre with another as part of the literacy curriculum. It is simply assumed that more non-fiction will (a) meet boys' interests better and (b) therefore enable them to achieve more.

By contrast, the *Fact and Fiction* project set out to look in much greater detail at what the current school literacy curriculum does with fact and fiction texts, in order to ascertain the extent to which this might contribute to boys' and girls' different development as readers. From the project perspective, what it means to read and to be a reader is socially constructed primarily in and through social interactions with others. In this respect, the project is part of a growing body of work that treats literacy as a social practice (Heath, 1983; Street, 1984; Barton, 1994). In the research design, contrasts between fact and fiction genres, and boys' and girls' preferences for them, were always explored in relation to: the social activity between participants which accompanies the reading of different texts; the social setting which gives it purpose; and how taken together these frame the way in which the reading gets done and, consequently, mediate the content of the text for the reader. It is at this level that the project looked for variation and, indeed, gender differentiation.

The research focus in the first instance was on the *literacy events* – those situated moments when reading is accomplished – which make up the school curriculum during the course of the day. Each literacy event was considered in relation to three dimensions: the *context* in which it took place; the *readers* who were involved and their relationship to the process; and the *texts* that were incorporated into the literacy event. Observation showed that, through their designation of the use of space, time and resources, teachers marked out and orchestrated different kinds of literacy events, with different consequences for reading. The project documented these processes, and also considered how pupils then appropriated and re-worked these distinctions, in order to explore if and how they might contribute to the gender differentiation of reading. The project did not confine itself to those moments that the teacher considered made up the official reading curriculum, but looked much more broadly at the full range of texts in use during the school day and the very different roles they played in the life of the class.

What soon emerged from the data was that different kinds of texts were routinely getting into different kinds of literacy events, which in turn established different expectations about what reading was for and how it should be conducted with attendant consequences for their readers. There were regularities in how this happened which ran across all four case study sites. Focusing in on these patterns led to the identification of three different ways of doing reading routinely invoked in the classrooms the project observed: procedural reading; reading for proficiency; and reading for choice. Each of these was underpinned by a distinct set of principles, which produced fundamentally different orientations to the business of reading. In each case there were different ground rules about who will read what, where, and how the business of reading will be conducted. These ground rules would be spelt out through the specific mobilisation of texts, readers and contexts, as the teacher orchestrated the particular curricular activity in which reading played a part.

Definitions

Procedural reading

Procedural reading steers much of the general work of the curriculum. This is reading to get things done, where, although reading takes place, it is regarded as incidental to some other kind of activity which holds the attention of teachers and pupils. It does not count as part of the official reading curriculum. Crucially, procedural reading is not seen as an end in itself, but rather leads to some other kind of output – the production of another spoken or written text. The individual child's performance will be judged against this second text.

Procedural texts are generally non-fiction, often non-narrative texts. Worksheets, textbooks, writing on the board as part of the lesson, letters home, are all prime examples. In procedural contexts, the texts are often embedded in teacher talk. Teachers read the text aloud first and may well explain what it means as they go along. This talk becomes the commentary, steering children to make sense of the text in particular ways. What the text means, what children are to do with it, is mediated through that talk. Later, as children work on their own or in groups using the text to steer that activity, they may call on help with their reading, either from peers or the teacher. Procedural reading becomes a group effort, in which individual competence is not a bar to working with the text.

Reading for proficiency

Reading for proficiency forms part of the official reading curriculum, where reading as an end in itself is the main focus. In proficiency encounters, how well the child reads, as judged by teachers or other adults, normally on the basis of hearing the child read aloud and alone is paramount. They are expected to accomplish this task unaided. If they require help, then that will impact on their perceived competence, and may also lead to them being told to choose another text that the teacher deems more appropriate. The judgements made are a matter of public record, and will be documented as such in home-reading books or on official school forms.

Proficiency texts are almost exclusively fiction and the emphasis is on matching the text to the child's level of proficiency. Consequently, the texts that are used for proficiency encounters between adults and children may or may not be the same as the texts which children choose to read for themselves at other times. Teachers largely dictate ground rules here. The books which children take to proficiency encounters in school are also the books which they take home and around which most active involvement with adults as part of the home–school reading curriculum is expected to take place. Children call these texts 'reading books'.

Reading for choice

This forms the other part of the official reading curriculum. In reading for choice slots (often run as quiet reading time, during the period of data collection), the range of texts available and the possibilities for enjoying reading are highlighted. In some respects, reading for choice operates as 'time out' from the disciplined working practices of the rest of the school curriculum. It is also where children get most freedom in relation to the kinds of texts they read and what they do with them: they may be able to share with a friend, read in a group, listen to story tapes or even use texts to play games. They are at least partially encouraged to direct this activity for themselves. The outcome of such activity is rarely turned into a matter of public discussion and, provided children keep to the general rules of classroom behaviour, teacher monitoring of what has gone on is light.

Reading for choice texts can encompass fiction and non-fiction; predominantly verbal or predominantly visual texts; ephemera such as newspapers and magazines, as well as children's own writing. Whatever the particular criteria employed, in reading for choice slots the widest selection of texts are made available to choose from. Whilst schools vary enormously in terms of the range they put on offer, the project data consistently showed children making use of a greater variety of texts during this time, encompassing both fiction and non-fiction, as well as exercising greatest freedom over what they then did with them.

Standing back from the curriculum: contexts for reading

At the broad brush level the distinctions made here hold fast across all of the case study sites, although the relative weightings given to one way of reading rather than another vary. Nevertheless, the categories are sufficiently robust to make allocating particular literacy events to one rather than another relatively straightforward. They do not quite account for everything: for instance, one of the schools had a religious affiliation, which meant that prayers and religious observance formed a key part of the daily routine. These literacy events took on a different character because reading the texts in these contexts involved saying the words aloud and together, often drawing on memory, rather than any written document immediately to hand. The oral text thus created took precedence over the written form from which it stemmed. In some respects, this practice seemed to spill over into other parts of the curriculum. Oral texts created in this way had a prominence in the daily routine of the classroom not found elsewhere. Even so, the tripartite split identified above still held good in relation to the bulk of curricular activity.

Bringing together a range of literacy events under the same heading allows for detailed comparisons to be made between individual instances, stemming from the same site and across sites. For instance, literacy events designed to deliver reading for choice can be constructed in very different ways. The same curriculum slot, performing the same function, yet in a different setting and mobilising different resources, turns out differently.

Reading for choice: the pupil way

Every case study site included quiet reading time as part of its weekly activities. In School 4, quiet reading time happened alongside morning and afternoon registration, and was interrupted by routine administrative tasks, such as taking the register and notices. Reading could be substituted by finishing off homework or other classroom writing. This meant the majority of the children could well be doing other things besides reading. The books available for use during this time – the class library – were by and large not the books children could actually borrow to take home. With the exception of about five titles, they were all fiction, mostly chapter books. (In this school non-fiction texts were kept in a central reference library for use in topic work.) The most popular books in use during this slot were the few picture books in the stock. These had the advantage of being easy to read in one sitting. Some of the boys had smuggled in favourite non-fiction books from the school reference library, which they kept in their trays and could therefore hold over to the next session. Otherwise books were expected to be returned to the class library when the time was up. In fact, most of the class library books went unread: the length of the texts didn't fit the length of the time available to read them in. Many children sat with their reading books in front of them. These were largely from reading schemes. Provided they were quiet, not much actual reading needed to go on.

In School 1, quiet reading had its own slot on the curriculum, alternating with paired reading, group reading and the class reader. The class library contained a wide range of texts of different lengths and requiring different kinds of attention: fiction, non-fiction, pupil-made, a newspaper. It occupied a different space, separate from the main classroom and away from the teacher's gaze. Pupils could congregate on the comfy chairs and soft cushions, or lounge on the floor, as they gathered to change books or stayed to read. The official injunction was to read silently, but quiet talk was tolerated and friends would often look at books together. Books with a strong visual element – picture books, puzzle books, some kinds of non-fiction – were often used in this way. Sometimes the class would be asked to talk about their reading at the end of the session, but more often they would pack away and then return to the business of the curriculum proper by congregating on the mat in front of the teacher. The children could make use of this same space and resources whenever they had finished work earlier than others in the class. When a sufficiently large number of children were making use of the facilities, the teacher would draw the curricular activity to a close and bring all the children together again to start the next lesson sequence.

Commentary

Both schools have a curriculum slot nominated as quiet reading in which notions of range and choice play a part. Yet the overall effect is different. Notionally speaking, children are free to choose what to read for themselves in both sites. During this slot they are also much freer to move around the class than they would be at other times, ostensibly because of the need to change books. They can also choose much more freely where they sit, and whether to read alone or with others. In these respects, quiet reading time has the character of self-directed activity. This, in itself, sets it apart from much of the rest of the curriculum. Once quiet reading time is over the teacher will take back control of the agenda again, allotting tasks, directing the pace, orchestrating the round of activities. Through these contrasts in both sites it is possible to view quiet reading time as time for play, rather than time for work. Yet in School 4, in part because of the mismatch between the resources and the context for their use, in part because reading competes with other activities, rather than being the sole focus, reading remains low profile. The occasion doesn't function to strongly underline what reading is, or to build a collective sense of its possibilities. By contrast in School 1 'range' and 'choice' are more than just rhetorical flourishes, they are materially underpinned. At the same time, the kind of devolution to the level of individual responsibilities seen here is part of a range of teacher strategies used elsewhere on the curriculum within this site. It is part and parcel of how teachers manage the classroom. In this instance, with the resources to back it up, the specific responsibility individuals have for reading becomes much more highly visible and well defined.

Reading for choice: the teacher way

An example from School 2 shows a different means of implementing reading for choice. Here, choice of texts was largely managed by the teacher. Range was her expectation of what the class would cover at her direction, rather than what they would choose between for themselves. At first, during quiet reading time children would be allotted a turn with a particular genre – from distinct collections of information books; poetry; plays; topic books and (story) tapes – and told to choose from the basket where that collection was kept. Later they were restricted to their current reading books – the ones they would take to proficiency encounters. In this classroom, choice then became the range of texts the teacher taught during English curriculum time. Below are extracts from field notes taken whilst the class were doing joke books as part of English:

> T: This morning we are going to be looking at jokes. In your reading groups you are going to be looking at these [photocopies] and a couple of books from the book box. You can swap them around. Think about which one is the funniest.

> T: I've gone round . . . most people have found their favourite joke . . . you were reading them beautifully. . . . Just bring your favourite joke, sheet or book, and we'll read some of them on the carpet.

Here, the activity of reading is dominated by the teacher's stated purposes and the point she is leading them to: the written outcome from the reading – a class joke book. Yet, along the way, the teacher continues to frame individual activities in terms of pupil choice. Pupils have to choose their favourite joke, even if that means no more than choosing between so many jokes on a photocopied page, where none are really more interesting than the others. They read a range of texts in order to select from the many. In contrast to the quiet reading times outlined above, this occasion remains strictly teacher controlled. Yet there is an oscillation between teacher talk that frames the activity as monitored work, and teacher talk that frames the children's activity as self-motivated fun.

In part, what this occasion points to is the potential hybridity of different literacy events. Different elements within them can pull different ways. In this instance teacher judgement on how well individual readers are doing is never far away. 'You were reading them beautifully', edges the encounter towards a proficiency frame; whilst the end point of the activity – a class joke book – evokes the routines of classroom work and a procedural frame. Yet the request is to find and pool individual favourites, to stake a claim for oneself through the choices one has exercised, whilst the texts themselves suggest fun, not work, as the agenda. Placing this incident in the category Reading for Choice, highlights a number of key contrasts which run through the data as a whole: the extent to which teachers visibly manage the reading curriculum from the centre or, sometimes by sleight of hand, devolve that management to the periphery; the extent to which reading is cast as work or play (see also Solsken, 1993); the extent to which reading is conducted as a collective or individual activity; the extent to which reading itself is backgrounded or foregrounded;

and the different subjectivities which are formed as a result. The key analytic task has been not so much to arbitrate between the combinations of different elements within particular literacy events, as to map out how they interact.

Reviewing the data as a whole, it is possible to observe the oscillations/ tension between different elements within a single literacy event, and the ways in which they seem to sometimes pull in different directions. Sometimes the tensions are greater than at others. On the whole literacy events which revolve around reading for proficiency show most homogeneity across the different sites, and their boundaries are most clearly defined. Literacy events, which revolve around reading for choice, show maximum variation, within sites as well as between them, and in the extent to which they permeate other areas of the curriculum. (The project data includes instances from one site where the ground rules for reading for choice seemed to underpin reading topic books in history.) In an attempt to examine these variations more thoroughly, the project established an analytic matrix to guide closer scrutiny of individual literacy events, and to build up a more complex picture of activity in any one site. This involved returning to those literacy events which had been identified as representing a procedural, proficiency or choice axis, and then reviewing in more detail the relationship between texts, readers and contexts within key events.

From the project perspective, texts, readers and contexts are the semiotic resources, which are drawn on in particular literacy events. Each has its own semiotic potential, or semiotic affordances and resistances, to use Kress's terms, which can be drawn on (Kress, 1998). The semiotic potential encoded in the resources of text, reader or context, may or may not be fully realised, and this in part depends on how the various resources interrelate, the extent to which they reinforce each other or pull in different directions. To give an example, all of the classrooms documented by the project included a 'soft area', however vestigial, often close to the class library or book corner, usually carpeted and containing at least one comfy chair, maybe fabric drapes. This setting was most strongly associated with reading for choice. Often, this area would only become available to children during quiet reading time, when they would be allowed to lounge on beanbags, recline on a comfy chair or simply spread out on the carpet. The setting encouraged pupils, as it were, to take time out from the rigours of proper lessons where they had to sit up straight and pay attention, adopting a quite different bodily posture. The material and physical resources of the setting, through their invocation of the comforts of a well-furnished front room, reinforce notions of reading as (domestic) leisure, even if practically speaking they can only do so in a token way: there are never enough chairs for everyone to have one. However, their potential to do this may not be fully realised: imagine the same setting used for a one on one proficiency encounter, with the child in the comfy chair sitting up straight and reading aloud to the teacher, whilst the teacher assesses the child's performance. Within a given literacy event, temporary alliances between elements happen through the mobilisation of resources this time round. All the different

Table 13.1 The fact and fiction matrix

	Procedural (School 4, Year 4)	Procedural (School 1, Year 5)
Context		
Curriculum slot	History topic: Ancient Greece	History topic: Ancient Greece
Location	Seated at the tables	Freedom to move around the classroom
Activity, official/ unofficial	With the textbook page open, children listen as the teacher reads from the text, then pauses to explain and add to the passage before going on	Using the topic books in class to compile the information about the Greek Gods, for writing up as a Fact File. Get the best books quick before they go and find the good bits
Framing	'Today we're going to find out about Alexander the Great'	'Some of you know lots about this already, more than I do. Find out as much as you can'
Readers		
Formation	The teacher is the main reader; the children listen together, whilst sharing one book between two	The pupils are the main readers, working in friendship groups, mainly single sex
Access	Equal access to the same text	Unequal access to a range of texts some of which the children themselves have brought in
Subject identity	Children as novices	Children as experts
Text		
Textual characteristics	Historical narrative; double spread; verbal text, with sub-headings and some images	Various, most non-fiction, with relatively high ratio of image to verbal text, using double spread
Material object	Paperback, stapled folio	Most hardback, bound folio
Use category	Textbook	Topic books
Location/source	Teacher's desk	Display table, pupils' trays and topic shelf

	Proficiency (School 1, Year 3)	Choice (School 1, Year 3)	Choice (School 2, Year 3)
Context			
Curriculum slot	Science/reading to helper	Finishing work	English
Location	Two chairs at a table in the quiet reading area	Bean bags and comfy chairs in the 'soft' area by the class library	Tables
Activity, official/ unofficial	Child opens her reading book and reads aloud whilst the adult helper corrects any mistakes. The child stops when asked	Finding a book to read/ browsing and chatting with friends whilst choosing books from the kinder box	Finding a passage to read out loud/browsing and chatting
Framing	'Can I have your home reading book to just write in it, darling? Well done, E. Next? Um, N'	'If you've finished your work, you can go to the kinder box'	'The reason I've asked you to do this is that we're going to put our favourite jokes into a book'
Readers			
Formation	Parent helper and child	Children who have finished their work	Whole class, sharing text with partners on their tables, mixed-sex
Access	Regulated access to texts. The child must bring their home reading record book. If the reading book is too hard they may be asked to change it	Unequal access	Unequal access to the selection of texts given to each group by the teacher. (More girls than boys ended up with the photocopied texts.)
Subject identity	Child as novice, subject to scrutiny	Subject identity regulated by peers, not teacher	Positioned by the teacher in between being good pupils and working well, and having fun
Text			
Textual characteristics	Picture book, narrative fiction + handwritten record	Wide range: fiction, non-picture books	Joke books
Material object	Large quarto hardback + school exercise book	Non-fiction, mostly hard-back, large quartos; fiction mostly small format paperbacks	Some photocopies of double spreads; some paperbacks including stapled folios
Use category	Reading book + reading record book	Class library	Year 5's class library
Location/source	Kinder box via book bag + book bag	The kinder box	Basket, labelled Joke Books

elements within a given literacy event can fall the same way, reinforcing each other, or they can begin to pull in different directions. Part of the aim of the project was to begin to explore these dimensions. That meant looking much more carefully at the semiotic potential of the resources in use and what happened as they stacked up, as it were, in a particular literacy event. The sample analysis of key literacy events provided in the matrix below gives an idea of the scope of the analytic endeavour.

The ways in which text, context and readers are configured, separately, and then in combination, is laid out in sequence within the matrix (Table 13.1). The vertical columns represent individual literacy events, documented in the project field notes, here grouped under the headings of procedural, proficiency, choice; and stemming from different school sites, as indicated at the bottom of the chart. The rows deal in turn with context, readers and text. The sub-categories represent different aspects of texts, contexts and readers that seemed to have an impact on how reading was realised within a given event.

Gender differentiation and the reading curriculum

The initial impetus for this enquiry, outlined above, was to examine how fiction and non-fiction texts are embedded in the school literacy curriculum, as part of a broader investigation examining the social construction of gender-differentiated genre preferences. One unexpected finding from the project data was the strength of the proficiency framing round reading in school, and the extent to which this permeates children's use of fiction texts. Whilst reading for choice remains a strong frame at the rhetorical level, both in teacher talk about their practice and, indeed, as part of official documentation on the curriculum, it was harder to find it fully operationalised on the ground.

Many of the texts in use in school underline the link between reading and proficiency. They do so as material objects, through their use of typeface and layout, and through the ways in which they combine verbal text and pictures. This is particularly true of fiction texts. Children's publishers differentiate and segment fiction texts according to proficiency levels, using agreed standards: the bigger the type face, the larger the spaces between the lines of type, the higher the proportion of picture to text, the easier the book will be to read. Libraries and bookshops sort and store their fiction collections by similar criteria: picture books, read-alones, junior fiction, will be housed on different shelves. Together they construct a reading ladder and, by implication, the reader's place on it. Children, like grown-ups, can recognise an 'easy' book from a 'hard' book because of the way it looks. The fiction books they choose to read thus also spell out their place on the proficiency ladder to others. The fact that in many classrooms weaker readers are often restricted to reading scheme books which spell out these distinctions even more clearly serves only to underline the point.

By contrast, very few non-fiction texts surface in proficiency encounters. The rare exceptions in the project data stem mainly from reading schemes.

Indeed, in some classrooms non-fiction texts were only officially made available in the context of task-driven, procedural reading. Yet non-fiction texts remained popular choices, particularly amongst weak boy readers, during times when they could choose what to read for themselves. Even in classrooms where non-fiction was hard to come by and no official provision was made, they would still surface during quiet reading time.

Closer examination of the non-fiction texts weaker boy readers preferred revealed a highly motivated selection of texts with a number of shared features. First, they were highly visual. Page layouts were constructed on a double spread, with the visuals leading the verbal text, rather than vice versa. What verbal text there was often amounted to no more than an individual heading and accompanying paragraph, related to the image, but relatively free-standing of the rest of the verbal text on the page. Paragraphs could therefore be read in any sequence, with the visuals steering the selection individual readers make. Secondly, unlike the bulk of fiction texts, the most popular non-fiction texts eschewed carefully graded point size of typeface as a way of signalling the level of proficiency of their intended readership. Instead, the range of typefaces used varied according to the prominence given to the verbal text on the page: large typefaces for headings; smaller for sub-headings; smallest for the individual paragraphs which accompanied the visual images. The bulk of the verbal text on the page would be in a point size most normally associated in fiction with adult readers. This immediately set these texts apart from much of the rest of the book stock the school provided and, indeed, caused some concern amongst many of the teachers in whose classrooms these materials circulated as they weren't sure how far the verbal text matched the reading proficiency of the children in the class, let alone the readers who seemed to make a beeline for them. Finally, such texts were almost always large, bound hardbacks. Again, in distinct contrast to the predominantly paperback, small-size fiction texts or the stapled, soft-backed reading scheme books. Non-fiction texts as material objects and in terms of their internal characteristics – layout, visual style – signal 'adults' as their intended readership. At the same time, they give weaker readers plenty to do, precisely because it is possible to steer round them using visual images alone, only browsing the headings and short paragraphs. For the weakest readers, the pictures act as prompts for them to announce what they already know. They can spend time on them without having to spend time on the verbal text at all.

Approaching the genre preferences children make through the range of social contexts for reading which frame texts in school suggests a new way of understanding their choices. In the project data, weaker girl readers were happy to go along with teacher judgements about their proficiency as readers, many of the weaker boy readers were not. During quiet reading time, weaker girl readers often chose to spend time on fiction texts which were well within or even below, their competence, turning this kind of reading into a collaborative exercise in which they helped each other through the pages. Weaker boy readers often did everything they could to avoid spending time on text, thus disguising their status as readers from their peers. Low proficiency rankings seemed to conflict more with their sense of self-esteem. Weaker boy readers were in flight from negative proficiency judgements in ways in which girls were not. Non-fiction texts give them somewhere to go. Indeed, precisely because of the role of visual rather than verbal text, they provide one of the few arenas where more and less able boys can meet on a level, as it were. Weaker boys can muster their expertise in response to such a text, without having to stumble through the print to identify what is going on. This is an advantage in relation to boys' status politics. It works less well in terms of making progress with their reading. One net result of the strategies they employ is that they spend less time on verbal text. The kind of visual competencies some of the weaker boy readers showed in steering their way round non-fiction texts have their place. But alone, they are not enough.

Making a difference

The *Fact and Fiction* project data were collected prior to the introduction of the National Literacy Hour to British schools. The Hour now provides a means of structuring delivery of the English curriculum in a highly focused way, as part of wider government sponsored initiative, the National Literacy Strategy. What are the implications of the project's findings in this new context for children's development as readers and writers?

The National Literacy Hour offers the potential for re-working some of the key literacy events the project documented. Indeed, part of its explicit mission is to make more manageable teachers' preoccupation with listening to individual children read, which the project saw happening as reading for proficiency slots. The National Literacy Hour addresses this aim by shifting the focus for teachers listening to readers from the individual to the group. In each hour, 20 minutes of teacher time is dedicated to working with one of five groups in the class. This becomes the new context for teachers to listen to, assess and support readers' development. Some National Literacy Coordinators advocate choral reading during this time, with children reading along out loud together, whilst the teacher selectively tunes in to the relative performance of different readers. Some of the training videos show the more familiar pattern of each child in the group taking it in turns to read one page before handing on to the next reader. The way in which individual teachers handle this slot and the kinds of material they use, all have a bearing on how the occasion will turn out. Lynda Graham's work with teachers in Croydon provides some intriguing examples of how sharing of texts read aloud can become the focus of a kind of staged group performance, in which the emphasis is on picking up the rhythms of the printed language, rather than assessing individual competence (see Graham, 1999). Graham sees this as inducting children into acquiring what Myra Barrs calls the tune on the page (Barrs, 1993). Interestingly, in the contest of the *Fact and Fiction* project material, this kind of event also provides a more collective setting for reading aloud in which the voice of the group supports the voice of the individual, and potentially leads to less conflict over self-esteem for weaker readers.

One consequence of the introduction of the Literacy Hour, with its stress on guided teacher input in the context of whole-class or small-group work, is that silent reading as an activity is no longer getting the priority it did as part of the official reading curriculum. Some schools, to accommodate the hour, have dropped the silent reading curriculum slot from their menu of class activities altogether. Others struggle to justify its space on the curriculum. As the examples quoted in this chapter above show, silent reading in itself is not always an unqualified good. What does matter is the extent to which it is used to actively encourage children to develop a sense of themselves as committed readers. If, in abandoning silent reading on the curriculum, the aim of encouraging children to range more widely as readers goes too, then something will indeed have been lost. Once again, it remains to be seen how the opportunities the National Literacy Hour provides are used. There is a danger that the Hour will lead to death by extract and surfeit of worksheets. Seen by some as the main tools for managing the transition from whole-class to small-group activities, and fulfilling the prescriptions for content outlined in the National Literacy Strategy Framework document, they run the risk of turning all reading into school work. The Hour will have reinvented the comprehension box, where children trudge through texts which have no merit except that they support the questions which can be asked of them.

There are other ways of using the Hour, most importantly to build and sustain a reading culture which can encompass but also substantially expand the range of interests in the class. Evidence collected on the *Fact and Fiction* project and supported by work elsewhere suggests that fewer boys than girls see themselves as committed readers, able and willing to purposefully steer their reading across a range of texts (Millard, 1997; Moss, 1999). One reason for this difference is that, whilst girls often sustain each other's interests in reading, in the contexts of girls' friendships, for many boys reading remains an individual and private affair. The *Fact and Fiction* project data shows the importance of teachers actively intervening to promote the widest range of reading to the full audience in class in ways that take children beyond existing gender-differentiated preferences. Those teachers who knew the stock best, who appreciated the widest range of texts and what their potential was, who sought to expand the reading horizons of all the pupils in their class, and who in some instances deliberately targeted reluctant readers, had the greatest impact (Moss, 1999). The project's findings share a number of similarities with Lynda Graham's work which in turn outlines a number of practical approaches which can help achieve these aims, and can be used within the Hour (Graham, 1999). What the *Fact and Fiction* project data reminds us is that supporting reading is always more than providing children with the resources; it is also about closely observing the relationship between text, context and reader and the ways in which they work together to establish what reading is, for whom.

Acknowledgements

The ESRC-funded project, R000236470, called 'Fact and Fiction: The gendering of reading in the 7–9 age group' was staffed by Dr Gemma Moss and Dena Attar, Centre for Language in Education, University of Southampton. Data was collected prior to the introduction of the National Literacy Strategy to schools in England.

References

Barrs, M. (1993) Introduction: reading the difference, in M. Barrs and S. Pidgeon (eds) *Reading the Difference*. London: CLPE.

Barton, D. (1994) *Literacy: an introduction to the ecology of writing*. Oxford: Blackwell.

Graham, L. (1999) Changing Practice through Reflection: the KS2 Reading Project, Croydon, *Reading*, 33, pp. 106–113.

Heath, S.B. (1983) *Ways with Words: language, life and work in communities and classrooms*. Cambridge: Cambridge University Press.

Kress, G. (1998) *Modes of Representation and Local Epistemologies: the presentation of science in education*. London: Institute of Education.

Kress, G. (2000) Knowledge, Identity and Pedagogy, *Linguistics and Education*, 11 (1), pp. 7–30.

Meek, M. (1996) *Information and Book Learning*. Stroud: Thimble Press.

Millard, E. (1997) *Differently Literate: boys, girls and the schooling of literacy*. London: Falmer Press.

Moss, G. (1999) *The Fact and Fiction Research Project: interim findings*. Southampton: Centre for Language and Education, University of Southampton.

Solsken, J. (1993) *Literacy, Gender and Work in Families and at School*. Norwood: Ablex.

Street, B. (1984) *Literacy in Theory and Practice*. Cambridge: Cambridge University Press.

Source

This is an edited version of an article previously published in *Pedagogy, Culture and Society: Journal of Educational Discussion and Debate*, 7 (3). 1999. Reproduced by permission of Triangle Journals Ltd.

Chapter 14

The literacy acquisition of Black and Asian EAL[1] learners

Anti-racist assessment and intervention challenges

Theresa Reed

Learning from the Lawrence Inquiry: the need to establish anti-racist practice to avoid institutional racism

In Britain, all academic and professional development must now be guided by the 'Macpherson (Lawrence) Report' (Macpherson, 1999) as well as by new amendments to the 1976 Race Relations Act (which emphasise the 'enforcible duties of public bodies and institutions to positively pursue and achieve Race Equality outcomes'). This means that the rights and entitlements of Black and Asian ethnic groups must be protected at all costs, that there can be no justification for woolly thinking that might lead to gaps in services/inappropriate provision and that complacent/exaggerated views can no longer be excused or tolerated. The essence of anti-racist practice is the acceptance by professionals that they are duty-bound to be vigilant at all times in case their behaviour, even momentary lapses, should impinge on those groups that are most vulnerable to discriminatory actions. It demands, then, that constant checks be made, following closely the definitions in the Macpherson (Lawrence) Report, to ensure that professionals' responses conform precisely to the requirements set down in the text:

- 'Racism' in general terms consists of conduct or words or practices which advantage or disadvantage people because of their colour, culture or ethnic origin. In its more subtle form it is as damaging as in its overt form (Macpherson, 1999: 6.4).
- 'Institutional racism' consists of the collective failure of an organisation to provide an appropriate and professional service to people because of their colour, culture or ethnic origin. It can be seen or detected in processes, attitudes and behaviour which amount to discrimination through unwitting prejudice, ignorance, thoughtlessness, and racist stereotyping which disadvantage minority ethnic people (Macpherson, 1999: 6.4).

[1] 'English-as-Additional-Language' (EAL).

The onus is now on professionals (including researchers) to examine the nature of their practices as well as to be accountable at the process level, so that the risks of inadequate/inappropriate actions which may disadvantage or damage the long-term interests of Black and Asian groups are not overlooked or excused on grounds of professional expediency, unavoidable 'ignorance' or mere 'thoughtlessness'. Hence it is vital for professionals to question the process involved as well as to examine closely the areas of 'ignorance' and 'thoughtlessness' for themselves, to save being challenged. Institutional racism is maintained when powerful professionals seek to defend/influence ways of doing things that suit white agendas, in spite of the cost/risks to which minority groups are subjected. Thus professionals have to bear in mind that proposals they are keen to put forward, such as seeking to link dyslexia with multilingualism, may not turn out to be the universal panacea they are assumed to be. In fact, it may be naive ('ignorant') to believe that monocultural views apply equally in a multicultural context, and it would be 'thoughtless' of professionals if the risks associated with the simple wish of extending the monolingual definition and assessment rationale developed for dyslexia to a multilingual context have not been carefully weighed up before the first step is undertaken, since the concern was originally defined in relation to 'white monolingual English-speakers' whose literacy skills in their first language (L1) were judged not to be commensurate with other areas of functioning.

The context of racism

The history of racism should have warned us that it is ill-advised to force western practices (i.e. often developed purely with the white person's needs in mind) onto Black and Asian groups when their interests have not featured in the thinking or development process at the outset. Therefore time must be given to take stock, instead of railroading questionable notions (e.g. it is a good thing to donate white monolingual ideas to Black and Asian multilingual groups), which can be fraught with danger if these ideas are driven through with enthusiasm, but without initial clarification of the nature of diverse needs or a questioning of the legitimacy of putting the Black and Asian multilingual groups on the spot for the sake of having a 'white agenda' more widely endorsed.

Ironically, even if there is a genuine wish to share a good thing with the Black and Asian groups, there is often a serious long-term cost attached, which may well outweigh limited, short-term benefits. If white professionals are not even aware (in their 'ignorance') of the need or have failed (through their 'thoughtlessness') to assess the risks (e.g. those attached to 'labelling') to which Black and Asian groups are vulnerable (i.e. the risk that pejorative views/negative stereotypes are likely to be reinforced, even in cases where 'labels' bring positive benefits for the majority group), then the interests of Black and Asian groups are ill-served through 'labels' becoming exploited to affirm existing prejudices and raise anxiety/fear. Thus, in an uncanny way, what suits the white majority tends to make things much worse for Black and Asian groups.

The fact is that the 'ignorance' and 'thoughtlessness' displayed by western psychologists (e.g. in extending the application of psychometric tests before considering the question of their validity for Black and Asian groups) have cost the latter dearly. If the same blunders of misassessment and misplacement continue (as documented in Coard, 1971; Fish, 1985; Carter and Coussins, 1986; Tomlinson, 1989; CRE, 1996), then 'ignorance' has been allowed to prevail, as psychometric testing is being carried out regardless of its consequences (CRE, 1996). Professionals are clearly 'thoughtless' if they choose to gloss over the inherent cultural–linguistic bias that invalidates the use of such tools/discriminatory data (Usmani, 1999).

It is equally problematic if organisations/professionals seek to push through a white agenda in blind faith (even if the belief is that the 'dyslexia' label can, for instance, ensure a share of the benefits for minority-language groups, hence offering a way out of the fundamental inequity in resourcing), since they are thereby ignoring the real risk of misassessment, especially at a time when the distinction between EAL needs and special needs continues to confuse many professionals, and the momentum that could drive development of valid assessment practice (that takes cultural, linguistic and religious contexts properly into account) is perpetually sapped by energies being diverted to a white agenda.

The marginalising process

It is always risky to extend favoured white models across all cultural–linguistic groups unless there is strong evidence of fit and proven benefit. The process should involve appropriate, specific research development and curb white presumptions, until valid conclusions can be drawn and all sides are well satisfied with the balance of the ongoing debate. It is vital that such a process should never be shortened or neglected, otherwise it is indicative of a double standard (i.e. matters to do with Black and Asian interests can be disregarded as being straightforward, and can therefore be considered at the general level).

The reality is far more complex whenever Black and Asian interests have to be taken into account, so that a great deal more should be done to create collaborative partnerships with Black and Asian bilingual professionals/communities in such endeavours. This means issues must not surface in a way that takes them by surprise (by being based on white concerns and brought up by the white group). It also means they must feel at ease, when airing issues, to consider and formulate their own views properly. Thus the due process of consultation would entail respecting the reservations and different wishes of Black and Asian communities, including their need to explore the pros and cons without time restrictions or pressure, and to have the confidence to adopt whatever stance or perspective they feel to be right, without the risk of being ridiculed, ostracised or becoming enticed/resigned to going along with the flow of majority wishes.

In order to participate properly, the Black and Asian groups must have access to sound evidence data, which are best drawn from independent, quality research. Research validity is more likely to be safeguarded when it is conducted by professionals who have appropriate cultural–linguistic expertise and can offer different ways of viewing difficulties encountered by Black and Asian groups so that their complex needs, together with any disadvantages, constraints and barriers they face, are properly understood and addressed in a holistic manner. Otherwise, there is a 'thoughtless' tendency on the part of professionals to overgeneralise: e.g. they may quote as evidence of dyslexia research that has been designed for a different purpose/population sample; they may bring under the umbrella of dyslexia, as if this were the underlying reason, all learners who under-perform: (a) 'monolingual English-speakers' who struggle with literacy skills of their first language (L1); (b) 'foreign-language (L2) learners' who fall behind in L2-class, though their L1 may be faring well; and (c) 'Black and Asian EAL-learners' perceived as struggling insofar as the pace/standard is set by L1-English peers, their situation being made worse by the unnecessary barrier of a 'subtractive' learning environment. Since such indiscriminate classification is bound to mislead and confuse the people, it will be useful at this point to clarify the situational difference between the three groups: Baker (1996: 66) defines an 'additive' bilingual situation (i.e. groups 'a' and 'b') as one 'where the addition of a second language and culture is unlikely to replace or displace the first language and culture (Lambert, 1974)', and a 'subtractive' bilingual situation (i.e. group 'c') as one where 'the learning of a majority second language may undermine a person's minority first language and culture'.

Anti-racist assessment for Black and Asian bilingual pupils: the validity of process and interpretation

Professional expectations and assessment criteria based on unfounded assumptions are racist in effect if they damage or disadvantage Black and Asian bilingual pupils' educational opportunities and career prospects, or if they favour white monolingual pupils as a result. The danger is obvious if the presumptions about the rate of acquisition of EAL and associated literacy proficiency are that these pupils should quickly catch up with first-language (L1) English speakers. Such a premise is unsupported by the evidence: the process took eight years (Hakuta and D'Andrea, 1992) among a group of Mexican-Americans, and Cummins (1984) estimated that it would take at least five to seven years before EAL-Canadian children could cope with cognitively demanding tasks in a context-reduced environment (English classroom). Thomas and Collier (1997) further confirm, through their large-scale longitudinal bilingual study, that it takes pupils starting with no English at least seven to ten years to reach average level in English reading, if they are educated in a 'subtractive' context, though progress can be accelerated (four to seven years) if they are taught in an 'additive' bilingual setting.

While dyslexia may offer a way of assessing children who encounter specific difficulties, it offers too restricted a view for bilingual learners whose learning experience is dependent on many contexts (family, institution and society) as well as interacting effects (e.g. physical/psychological problems, socio-economic/refugee status, degree of acculturisation). A narrow assessment approach risks condoning the 'thoughtless' dismissal of a whole range of crucial factors that need to be understood as well as encouraging 'ignorance' by viewing Black and Asian EAL pupils as having learning difficulties on account of attainment gaps. Quality teaching, that is teaching which promotes 'additive' bilingual development, ensures appropriate language/literacy scaffolds and effective aids. It adopts an 'assessment-through-teaching' approach in all curricular areas and facilitates interaction in two-way bilingual exchanges. A conducive learning environment is one that is free from racism, motivated by engineering success through a 'cooperative learning' culture and through taking community mentors as role-models. Such environments have not been provided well enough or for long enough to raise achievement. Therefore the primary task should be to address these problems immediately, since they are the root cause of low achievement, as opposed to resorting to labelling.

Equally the emotional dimension must also be considered. Ellis (1997) cites studies (Horwitz, 1987; Wenden, 1987) which have examined how 'individual learner differences' (e.g. learners' beliefs about their own language learning) affect second-language acquisition and found evidence that such feelings may facilitate or inhibit learning. He also reports studies which showed some students feeling fearful and anxious at having to learn or compete in L2: for instance, Horwitz and Young (1991) highlighted the issue of 'language anxiety'; Ellis (1989) himself found some learners were frightened by teachers' questions, feeling stupid and helpless in class; Oxford (1992) listed alienation as one source of anxiety, akin to 'culture shock'. Ellis and Rathbone's (1987) finding that learners were unable to focus on the learning task when troubled by emotional stress, was supported by MacIntyre and Gardner's (1991) studies review, substantiating the claim that anxiety not only has negative effects on performance in the second language but also bears a high correlation to achievement. Even though many of these studies are based on white learners acquiring foreign languages, it is easy to imagine Black and Asian bilingual pupils suffering a similar situation-specific anxiety when functioning in a monolingual 'subtractive' environment, especially in a predominately white school-setting. Thus the issue of comparing Black and Asian EAL performance with that of L1-English speakers is not as straightforward and as fair as we sometimes tend to presume.

The accountability involved in assessment

Although assessment is usually justified on the grounds that professionals require information for decision making, the process of gathering the necessary data and how judgements are made should be subjected to tighter scrutiny than at present, if institutional racism is to be challenged effectively. As long as the risks of 'process-bias' and 'misjudgement' continue to go unchecked (statistical data reviewed in Reed, 1999: 94), then professionals must be held to account. However, racist practices will be perpetuated if professional training remains inadequate, with the result that there will be little leadership or direction for stringent anti-racist assessment. If the will to examine professional practice stops short of anti-discriminatory considerations, this will in effect risk marginalising racial equality issues because of an imprecise focus. Priority action is to engage expertise and independent mechanisms for objective process-monitoring. This should always involve Black and Asian bilingual professionals who have the relevant skills and are given the legitimacy to lead on practice, in order to end the kind of 'inappropriate' assessment which uses labels simplistically whilst ignoring crucial bilingual/cultural contexts. If there exists confusion/disagreement over the label's definition, then it should not be used for Black and Asian bilingual learners, who are particularly vulnerable to 'false-positive' judgement errors, the effects of confused assessment being much more damaging in their particular case. Similarly, labels which endorse unrealistic expectations are dangerous (easily fostering the view that 'learning disability' can be judged by the attainment gap in EAL-related skills): that alone would cause irreparable damage to the life chances of such pupils. When professionals continue to accept this state of affairs or the risk of misjudgement as an inevitable 'margin of error', institutional racism then occurs.

The validity of the assessment, judged in terms of 'best outcomes', without being compromised by 'false-positive' errors or questionable assumptions

The only way to avoid the risk of confused and restrictive assessment practices and their racist effects is to develop a comprehensive contextual assessment framework, by thoroughly exploring 'enriched cultural' and 'language-transfer' strengths and constraints imposed by the socio-cultural context in education/experience of racism. The quality data will help professionals to see that the 'thoughtless' pursuit of simplistic answers and convenient short-cuts, while useful for meeting report deadlines, is too superficial to constitute a meaningful exercise. The improved outcomes will also open the eyes of professionals to the inappropriateness of generalising white models/paradigms and the inadequacy of white tools for Black and Asian EAL-assessment, raise their awareness of the importance of valid psychological research into Black and Asian bilingual needs and, hopefully, allow them to clarify for themselves the misconceptions they have as monolingual 'majority' professionals.

'Comprehensive contextual assessment' encourages professionals to make careful checks so that the information used is verifiable/can be validated. Misinterpretation is further minimised if assessment is done over time and fully involves the family (an involvement which need not be constrained by the 'language/communication barrier', if bilingual professionals are available). However, the demands placed on the professionals are clear: they must have sufficient competence to appreciate the interplay between complex linguistic/ cultural/racist contexts and academic achievement. It is also essential to bear in mind that institutionalised racist practice will prevail as long as white views and white thinking are allowed to dominate; misinterpretation and negative expectations will also persist. But as long as changes in professional practice are made on an ad hoc basis, led by perpetual swings between professional 'complacency'/'anxiety', 'ignorance'/'thoughtlessness', then misinterpretation and negative expectations will persist.

More valid assessment practices will result in improved outcomes, bringing satisfaction to Black and Asian professionals and bilingual pupils alike. Institutional racism is divisive and disenfranchises partnerships, maintaining barriers which severely restrict Black and Asian families' access to information, communication and entitlement to quality services. Furthermore, these families are left in no position to protest or complain, either being kept ignorant of the cost/risks they might bear if their participation in the decision-making process is ineffectual or being forced to rely on 'helpful advocates' to take up issues on their behalf.

Intervention framework: learning from bilingual research

Access to valid, large-scale, longitudinal bilingual data reduces the risk of misleading or misdirecting professional practice. One such study (Thomas and Collier, 1997) is worthy of attention because its findings dispel many unhelpful myths and misassumptions about bilingual development, and rightly put the focus on 'institutional practice' and 'programme deficiencies'. Their recommendations could form a basis for 'best practice' when considering EAL-intervention because they are based on the 'best achievement' quality bilingual educational programmes can effect. The message is this: if raised achievement has not been realised, then professionals must focus on the provision of bilingual input first (apart from tangible physical problems). Indeed, this line of thinking is substantiated by the central message in the most recent DfEE guidance. Removing the Barriers (DfEE, 2000) advises professionals to adopt a 'positive approach to expectations', aided by 'ethnic monitoring' of academic attainment/level of EAL (which dispenses with the need to rely on 'standardised test' data/labels): 'Look at the results in terms of shortcomings in provision rather than as problems with the pupils themselves' (DfEE, 2000: 26).

Professor Tim Brighouse (Chief Education Officer for Birmingham) also emphasised the need for 'positive attitudes' and to 'avoid deficiency models' in the same DfEE Conference (Birmingham, February 2000), reflecting the sentiments expressed by one primary head teacher, quoted in the conference document (DfEE, 2000):

I think we've moved on. We don't talk so much about faults lying with the child. We are looking much more closely at our teaching.

(DfEE, 2000: 26)

The key to efficient intervention is to nurture bilingual development. This calls for a thorough understanding of the 'second language acquisition' process (Ellis, 1997). Monolingual professionals have to accept the fact that proficient EAL acquisition is bound to take time (in terms of years), that it cannot be rushed merely on the basis of needs generated by curricular demands or consideration of 'attainment league-tables'. In fact, monolingual professionals have also to realise that their own anxieties could form the basis of institutional racism: the risk is that Black and Asian EAL learners might be judged unfairly when subjected to the common but erroneous expectation that nursery–reception phase is quite adequate for EAL preparation, and that it is evidence of failure if they struggle with L2-literacy from then on, when white yardsticks (e.g. based on L1-language/literacy skills norms) form the basis for judging learning progress (particularly damning when applied to the 'Infant base-line'). The fact that these same pupils may excel in home-language/L1 literacy and numeracy is rarely perceived as a noteworthy achievement, neither does such success help to dispel the suspicion of 'learning difficulties'/an associated 'condition', or to tilt the balance if 'negative-expectations' hold sway.

The 'proof of the pudding' for effective intervention is when 'institutional racism' can be dismantled in a way that will bring real opportunities to all bilingual learners, which is first and foremost the realisation of a 'bilingual–biliterate' curriculum. To provide anything less is a poor substitute which will limit opportunities and undermine the chance of success. The fundamental message that comes out of Thomas and Collier's research adds weight to the familiar wisdom from the study of 'bilingualism', which is that Black and Asian bilingual pupils (even those born here) will be best served if they can use their dominant language (i.e. home-language), because this will enable them to operate at their highest cognitive level, thus allowing them to exploit their life-experience and cultural learning in a dynamic way. Conversely, being made to use a less familiar language-medium (EAL) is bound to be restrictive, needlessly disadvantaging them during the primary years, especially when they are required to deal with complex, cognitively challenging tasks that are set in a culturally alien context.

Being wise and joining forces to make a difference

Unequal educational outcomes have arisen as a result of totally neglecting to promote a bilingual and biliterate heritage. Professionals would do well to heed the wisdom gained in the field of bilingual research: 'children learning to read in their home language . . . are not just developing home language skills. They are also developing higher-order cognitive and linguistic skills that will help with the future development of reading in the majority language as well as with general intellectual development' (Baker, 1996: 155). Many monolingual countries invest a great deal in order to develop into 'bilingual' nations, and countries that are fortunate enough to possess language diversity in their population have wisely nurtured 'bilingualism' in an 'additive' manner, 'bilingual' classes no longer being provided by subsidising a 'voluntary community effort' or being viewed as 'additional luxuries'. They have thus been receptive to the overwhelming evidence that 'integrated-bilingual' provision offers a 'first-class' education for every pupil.

Not surprisingly, many governments maintain first-language teaching for their nationals abroad (including British English schools) as a priority, and some minority languages are successfully revived through political negotiations (e.g. French in Canada, Spanish in the US, Welsh in Britain). The cost of 'thoughtless' action (e.g. employing monolingual support with bilingual-funding, and failing to exploit 'home-language'/associated literacy in the academic curriculum) is to court failure, a failure which not only depresses Black and Asian bilingual achievement but also reduces our country's global prospects. Thus professionals must join forces to press for more appropriate resources to match the distinctive needs of Black and Asian language minority groups (rather than sweeping them onto a majority agenda), and they can indeed make a difference by pooling energy/influence to improve the state of Black and Asian bilingual education (Thomas and Collier, 1997: 77–79); by addressing the wider context of developing the 'home-language' through academic work which would aid EAL acquisition, by fostering interactive discovery-learning and peer-tutoring, in an 'anti-racist, additive-bilingual' socio-cultural context that all effective schools can offer. Professionals have to accept that an anti-racist perspective demands a clear vision that focuses exclusively on the interests of the Black and Asian communities, which cannot sit with other self-serving agendas.

References

Baker, C. (1996) *Foundations of Bilingual Education and Bilingualism*, 2nd edn. Clevedon: Multilingual Matters.

Carter, T. and Coussins, J. (1986) *Shattering Illusions: West Indians in British Politics*. London: Lawrence and Wishart.

Coard, B. (1971) *How the West Indian Child is Made Educationally Sub-normal in the British School System*. London: New Beacon Books (reprinted by Karia Press, 1991).

Commission for Racial Equality (1992) *Set to Fail? Setting and Banding in Secondary Schools*. London: CRE publications.

Commission for Racial Equality (1996) *Special Educational Needs Assessment in Strathclyde: Report of a Formal Investigation*. London: CRE publications.

Commission for Racial Equality (2000) *Learning for All: Standards for Racial Equality in Schools – for Schools in England and Wales*. London: CRE publications.

Cummins, J. (1984) *Bilingualism and Special Education: Issues in Assessment and Pedagogy*. Clevedon: Multilingual Matters.

DfEE (2000) *Removing the Barriers: Raising Achievement Levels for Minority Ethnic Pupils*. London: DfEE publications.

Ellis, R. (1989) 'Classroom learning rules and their effect on second language acquisition: a study of two learners', *System* 17, 249–262.

Ellis, R. (1997) *The Study of Second Language Acquisition*, 5th impression [first published in 1994]. Oxford: Oxford University Press.

Ellis, R. and Rathbone, M. (1987) *The Acquisition of German in a Classroom Context*. Mimeograph. London: Ealing College of Higher Education.

Fish, J. (1985) *Educational Opportunities for All? The Report of the Committee Reviewing Provision to meet Special Educational Needs*. London: ILEA publications.

Horwitz, E. (1987) 'Surveying student beliefs about language learning', in Wenden, A. and Rubin, J. (eds) *Learning Strategies in Language Learning*. Englewood Cliffs, NJ: Prentice Hall.

Horwitz, E. and Young, D. (1991) *Language Learning Anxiety: From Theory and Research to Classroom Implications*. Englewood Cliffs, NJ: Prentice Hall.

MacIntyre, P. and Gardner, R. (1991) 'Methods and results in the study of foreign language anxiety: a review of the literature', *Language Learning* 41, 25–57.

Macpherson, W. (1999) *The Stephen Lawrence Inquiry Report*. London: HMSO.

Oxford, R. (1992) 'Who are our students?: a synthesis of foreign and second language research on individual differences with implications for instructional practice', *TESL Canada Journal* 9, 30–49.

Race Relations Act (1976) Halsbury's Statutes (4th edition, volume 7). (1999 reissue). *Civil Rights and Liberties* (pp. 115–192). London: Butterworths.

Race Relations Act (1976) With Amendments (2000 reissue).

Reed, T. (1999) 'The millennium objective: give our minority communities a good deal by eliminating white yardsticks and institutional racism', *Educational and Child Psychology* 16(3), 89–100.

Thomas, W. and Collier, V. (1997) *School Effectiveness for Language Minority Students*. Washington, DC: National Clearinghouse for Bilingual Education.

Tomlinson, S. (1989) 'Asian pupils and special issues', *British Journal of Special Education*, 6(3), 119–122.

Usmani, K. (1999) 'The influence of racism and cultural bias in the assessment of bilingual children', *Educational and Child Psychology* 16(3), 44–54.

Wenden, A. (1987) 'How to be a successful learner: insights and prescriptions from L2 learners', in Wenden, A. and Rubin, J. (eds) *Learner Strategies in Language Learning*. Englewood Cliffs, NJ: Prentice Hall.

Source

This is an edited version of a chapter previously published in L. Peer and G. Reid (eds) *Multilingualism, Literacy and Dyslexia: A Challenge for Educators*. 2000. Reproduced by permission of David Fulton Publishers.

Chapter 15

Bilingualism and literacies in primary school

Implications for professional development

Deirdre Martin

Introduction

This chapter looks at some of the issues involved in developing literacies in bilingual learners in primary school in England. The chapter considers key issues which impinge on literacy development in pupils aged 5 to 11 years from linguistic minority and bilingual backgrounds in England. These issues are discussed through the central challenges facing continuing professional development (CPD) of teachers of pupils developing English as an Additional Language (EAL). Firstly, there is the challenge of the widely-held 'deficit' hypothesis, where being or becoming bilingual is perceived as a problem and a disadvantage to learning, and language and literacy development. This is linked to linguistic racism, epitomised in views demanding language assimilation and expressed in terms of 'If you live in England then you should speak English'. Secondly, there is the challenge of widening teachers' knowledge base, appreciating different frameworks for thinking about literacies, particularly that of the National Literacy Strategy, and understanding the relationships between spoken and written forms of language. Finally, there is the challenge of the implications for teaching linguistic minority pupils by developing a range of principles, pedagogies and resources for teaching and developing literacies, not only in the classroom but also for working with parents from linguistic minority communities to build on the literacy practices developing at home.

This discussion is relevant and timely in England because of the reconceptualisation of specialist language support for bilingual learners.

There are increasing moves to collocate EAL needs with literacy needs and special educational needs, exemplified in changes of funding and in expressions of alarm by specialist language teachers (TES, 1998). It is important that professional development of teachers of literacy to linguistic minority learners, whether specialist language support teachers or mainstream teachers, addresses the challenges in an informed and critically evaluative manner.

Perceiving bilingualism as a problem

The 'deficit' hypothesis has a negative perception of becoming and being bilingual, in several ways. It proposes that learners who speak little English, and are emergent bilinguals, from linguistic minority backgrounds, bring little or nothing to classroom learning about literacy. These learners are perceived as substantially disadvantaged not only linguistically but also in terms of appropriate and relevant experiences, and school and classroom are perceived as having to provide them. Further, the 'deficit' hypothesis may also extend to include the language and literacy environment of the home, where parents are perceived as being 'illiterate' and not providing or not being able to provide literacy experiences for their children.

The 'deficit' hypothesis has some support in the wider, fiscal policies discourse. In England, the Swann Report (DES, 1985) set the scene for the language of instruction in schools. English is the medium of instruction and home languages can be used only as a learning support in the process of language transition to English. Home languages can and sometimes are used in nurseries, early years and classrooms of some schools. These languages are usually not used for learning the subject curriculum but rather in support and complementary curriculum areas. In this respect, English is awarded higher *cultural and linguistic capital* (Bourdieu, 1986) than community languages. Knowing and learning through English brings higher rewards than through other languages. In fact, following the Swann Report the education system in England does not officially recognise the currency of other languages for learning.

The case is different though in Wales and parts of Scotland where the indigenous languages of Welsh and Gaelic are used in bilingual curricula for teaching and learning. There is much recorded success of bilingual education in these parts of the country, showing that being bilingual and learning through two languages can bring cognitive advantages to the learners; for example, higher metalinguistic skills, higher level thinking skills and better social skills than monolingual peers (e.g. Campbell and Sais, 1995; MacNeil, 1994; Cummins and Swain, 1986; Cummins, 1984).

Furthermore, the other linguistic minority languages are attributed low status as languages, being perceived as less prestigious than European languages, although it is possible to take GCSE examinations in some community languages. Interestingly, the cognitive advantages of being bilingual are not attributed in the English education system to being bilingual in community languages. The education system works towards learning in English only as soon as possible in learners' careers and the community language is not included in general learning. It is a *subtractive* situation for emerging bilinguals.

Attributing values to different languages and discriminating between them is linguistic racism (also called 'linguicism', Skutnabb-Kangas, 1988). It may be expressed in demands for linguistic minority pupils and their families to speak English and may prompt misguided 'advice' to linguistic minority parents to speak only English to their children. Linguistic racism is often not recognised. The *Reform of the Race Relations Act 1976* (CRE, 1998) does not include linguistic racism in its discussion. However, such views would profoundly influence the approach and practices of teachers towards linguistic minority pupils. Consequently, it is important that the 'deficit' hypothesis and linguistic racism are explicitly addressed in initial teacher education as well as in CPD, particularly around language and literacy teaching.

Most teachers in England are likely to teach one or more bilingual pupils, where 'bilingual' means that these children live in communities which use two or more languages and they are expected to interact in both in their daily lives. Between 7 and 8 per cent of the pupil population in England are lingu istic minority pupils, which is likely to increase to about 20 per cent in the next decade with increasing population movements from mainland Europe. Moreover, linguistic minority learners are not homogeneous, and, speaking approximately 200 languages, they bring many home languages to the class-room, with a variety of heritages and home experiences. Despite the prevalent 'deficit' hypothesis, most minority families share similar high expectations of educational achievement for their children (e.g. Ledoux *et al.*, 1997). The challenge is: how can teachers use this diversity to the advantage of children's learning? Good teachers will want to draw on the fundamental principle of teaching and learning which is to build on learners' knowledge in order to progress.

Two frameworks for understanding literacy

In a workshop which the author conducted recently, practitioners were asked to consider what they think literacy is. Here are some of their ideas:

processing	accessing your culture
understanding codes	enjoyment
writing skills	communicating ideas
auditory memory	visual communication
encoding/decoding skills	letters, lists
genre and style	religion, prayers, songs, hymns

They fall into two groups loosely coinciding with the two main theoretical frameworks for thinking about literacy. That is, one approach is through the technical skills of literacy and the other is through the social practices of literacy.

Psycholinguistic approach/technical skills

The 'technical skills' framework sees literacy as the development and achieve-ment of literacy skills, such as letter-sound correspondence, phonological awareness, knowledge of words, sentences and paragraphs as well as punctua-tion. It also includes the notion of meaning through reading and writing, such as story, genre and style. It encompasses all the teachable/learnable skills to do with reading and writing. It is also called the psycholinguistic approach to literacy. Skills can be tested and learners can achieve different levels of accomplishment. Implicit in this framework is the understanding that, once these skills have been achieved, they can be applied successfully to different situations involving reading and writing. Literacy skills can be learnt without a cultural context.

Social practices

The idea that literacy can develop without a social context is rejected by educationists such as Freire (1972) and Street (1995). They and others argue that literacy is a vehicle for culture, a social practice, and 'a tool . . . used to interact with, describe and construct their . . . environments' (Luke and Kale, 1997, p. 15). It is what we read and write *about* that is important, and makes literacy meaningful. Consequently, situations and communities, that is, places and people, create their own meanings, purposes and practices for reading and writing; for example, business, entertainment, religion, heritage, value and belief systems. Hence, this approach often refers to *literacies* rather than literacy. Literacies contribute to forming personal and community identity. There is also a further important distinction not made by the technical skills approach. There are literacy practices and literacy 'events' (Street, 1995), where events are the regular happenings in the use of literacy, such as reading stories, singing hymns, signing documents, writing letters.

For the purpose of developing literacy, these two approaches are complementary rather than exclusive. Learners need to develop the technical skills of literacy, as well as to understand the notion of literacies, in terms of meanings and social and cultural practices and events. This is particularly the case for linguistic minority pupils who often have experiences of multilingual literacies, that is, literacies across their languages. The challenge is to develop a new pedagogy from these two approaches for developing literacies with primary bilingual learners.

In school the overarching practice and purpose of literacy is to develop and achieve levels of technical skill which allow learners to access the reading and writing needed for curriculum learning. There are also other literacy practices within the school, exemplified by events such as reading for the social organisation of school, e.g. rules, rewards and punishments, sport fixtures, drama rehearsals and lunch menus. While in the community, there are other literacy practices, such as reading/writing for safety (fire escape instructions, medicine and food labels), for information (the A–Z map, TV programme schedules), for memory support (shopping lists), for greeting (cards and letters), for enjoyment (newspapers, comics). These practices demand different *types*, rather than levels, of literacy skills.

The national concern which has grown over primary school children's measured achievement in literacy skills has drawn the response from the government to establish a National Literacy Strategy. Within which framework does the National Literacy Strategy (NLS) lie? The National Literacy Framework offers the following definition:

> Within the aims and purposes of the National Literacy Project, literacy is defined simply as 'the ability to read and write'. Literacy is treated as a unitary process with two complementary aspects, reading and writing.
> (DfEE, 1997, p. 45)

Thus, it locates itself within the psycholinguistic, technical skills approach to literacy development. Its recommendations for best practice include analysis of the language demands of the curriculum, attending to links between spoken and written language, and reading and writing for meaning (DfEE, 1997, pp. 34–5). Examples of this practice are documented in the literature (e.g. Verma et al., 1995) and in the Literacy Hour document itself (DfEE, 1998). The NLS does not concern itself with the social purposes of literacy whether they are for the community inside school or outside. The remainder of the chapter explores the implications of this for teachers working with literacy with emerging bilingual learners.

Implications for bilingual learners

Good, effective teaching and learning draws on the knowledge and experiences that learners bring with them to the classroom. This section looks at the theoretical frameworks of learning which support developing literacies. Issues are explored concerning literacy development in bilingual learners, such as the relationship between spoken literacy, interdependence and interference in language development, and the social experiences of literacy, and books in particular, that bilingual learners bring to school.

Spoken language and literacy

There is debate about the relationship between spoken and written language (Street, 1995). Spoken language is sometimes referred to as 'orality' as opposed to 'oracy' which has come to be associated with notions of Standard English in the national curriculum and earlier (see Peate, 1995 for discussion). The debate focuses on issues such as the form of spoken and written language, natural vs taught development and social vs developmental relationship.

For some, there is a clear divide between spoken language and written language, where literacy is always a written, orthographic form, and spoken language is not. This perception allows no link between story telling, singing and clapping rhymes and their written forms. Furthermore, this perception would exclude other visual representations such as maps, photographs, time tables and signs from literacy. Such a relationship between spoken language and literacy is mutually exclusive and defines literacy too narrowly. Teachers working with bilingual learners need to explore broader, more open relationships between orality and literacy, since many primary school bilingual learners have story telling and songs at home with their parents and families (Blackledge, 1998).

However, some cultures may also perceive the relationship between spoken language and literacy as one of formality, where the orthographic form is the more formal and correct (Martin et al., 1998). In Martin et al.'s study it was difficult to persuade the Panjabi assessor to write as she spoke, because she perceived the social practices and purposes of written and spoken forms as being different and not interchangeable. This finding has implications for how teachers approach working with bilingual colleagues and multilingual literacies in school.

Another perspective of the relationship between spoken language and literacy is between natural skills and taught skills. That is, most people develop effortlessly and without teaching, skills in speaking and expressing themselves verbally, which we all need to be taught literacy as a separate set of skills. Teachers' roles are concerned with teaching literacy skills. However, teachers of bilingual learners need to be aware that these learners may be being exposed to multilingual literacies through peers, parents and community language teachers.

In research studies the development link between spoken language and literacy is well established. In the psycholinguistic framework one aspect of the relationship is explored through phonological awareness, such as rhyming and alliteration skills, and the meaning of words and sentences. Speaking, reading, spelling and writing depend on a shared set of cognitive representations and processing mechanisms of language forms (Stackhouse and Wells, 1997). It is seen as a developmental relationship where expertise in language skills is a predictor of literacy skills (e.g. Bryant and Bradley, 1983). In a social practices approach there is a similarly close relationship between spoken language and literacy, although, in contrast to the psycholinguistic approach, it is not necessarily developmental. The relationship is based on shared purposes, and spoken language and literacy are linked by communicative need and appropriateness. Spoken language and literacy have a complementary relationship.

The implications for teachers of linguistically diverse classes are that they offer learners the opportunity to explore and develop their spoken language and literacy through both psycholinguistic and social purposes approaches.

Interference, interdependence and independence

In bilingual studies, it is acknowledged that the relationship between developing languages and literacies is one of interdependence. That is, the development of one language/literacy helps the development of subsequent languages and literacies (Cummins and Swain, 1986). However, there may be a reluctance to accept this based on an older idea of 'interference' (Lado, 1957). This is an interpretation of bilingualism which argues that, where two languages are developing and functioning together, one language, the first usually, 'interferes' with the development of the other, shown by grammatical, phonological and lexical confusions. In psycholinguistic studies of early years bilingual learners, either in the first years of school or as recent arrivals, 'interference' between written forms is explained as 'transfer'. For example, Durgunoglu *et al.* (1993) show that Spanish/English speakers will read a visually ambiguous word in the non-target language. Elsewhere, in another study, 10-year-old English/Greek speakers who had recently arrived in Greek schools sometimes identified Greek letters with English speech sounds, showing that they transferred between languages (Bekos, 1997).

Regardless of 'transfer' occurring, Edwards (1998) shows in many examples of classroom practice with multilingual literacies, that bilingual learners are enriched by developing two literacies. They draw on their skills and knowledge across literacies to progress their learning through contrast and similarity. For example, decontextualised knowledge of print on a page allows children to generalise about features of print, such as words, punctuation, paragraphs. On the other hand, understanding the notion of story facilitates them to look for literal and non-literal meaning, although the cultural, contextual interpretation may be difficult.

An hypothesis about 'independent' literacy development across both languages also finds support. Research investigating phonological awareness skills in Panjabi/English bilingual children aged 6–7 years shows that they are developing phonological representations independently in both languages (Martin, 1997; Stuart-Smith and Martin, 1997). The differences in performance across the two languages seem to be influenced by at least two factors, phonological characteristics and teaching. The children respond to the inherent characteristics in processing the two phonologies; for example, English has more initial and final clusters of sounds, e.g. *spr-*, *-mp*, than does Panjabi, which seems to be more difficult to process. There was evidence that the children did significantly better in English on alliteration and rhyming tasks which seems attributable to English teaching approaches to literacy.

Experience of literacies through books

Many children have literacy experience with books before coming to school and continue to have literacy experience with books outside and beyond school. Primary school bilingual children encounter books and written materials in the home, church, temple and mosque, community language classes and in the library. Books serve different purposes. By examining three examples which show respect, cultural distance and enjoyment obtained from books, we can get some insight into the experiences of books which young learners, particularly those from linguistic minority communities, bring to school.

For many linguistic minority communities in England religion plays a central role in their community and home life. Holy books are treated respectfully and some may not be touched by human hand. Followers of religions such as

Sikhism, believe that their holy book is the living word of God. Gregory (1996) recounts an experience with a Moslem colleague, making her aware of the respect for the Koran by Moslems.

A recent research study explored bilingual children's perceptions and feelings about developing literacy skills in school in English and in Panjabi (Martin and Stuart-Smith, 1998). The children, aged 6–7 years and with only 2 or 3 years of formal English literacy teaching, were considerably more positive about developing English literacy skills. More striking was that they voiced many negative feelings about developing Panjabi literacy skills which were related in most cases to the 'difficulty' of doing it, as well as to the poor quality books and stories which were 'boring' and unrelated to their lives because they were about India. Yet they all showed very positive feelings about reading religious books with the teacher in the Gurdwara, and reading books and telling stories at home with their families. These findings suggest that the context for developing literacy skills is important, where the context is people, books, location and purpose. When literacy serves the purpose of enjoyment and endorsing cultural and community identity then children are happy developing English literacy and Panjabi literacy.

The third example is from Ferdman (1990) where, at one point, he describes himself as an 11-year-old and his delight in returning home from school to read his books in Hebrew. He knows that reading in Hebrew is his world which he does not have to share with school. The feelings expressed by Ferdman, of enjoyment, enrichment of identity and development of personal empowerment, are likely to be shared by many bilingual learners who are developing multilingual literacies.

These examples reflect that many bilingual children may have experiences with literacies and books before they come to school and while they attend school, which never impinge on the school. Importantly, young bilingual learners may initially experience some tension within their familiar experiences with books and their new experiences in school. The implications for teachers concern finding out about the nature and role of multilingual literacy experiences which bilingual children bring to school and maintain beyond school. It may be important for teachers to explore any tensions which might emerge to influence motivation. Teachers also need to consider how they can build on these experiences positively and to develop materials and practices in order to build on multilingual literacy experiences effectively to develop literacy in English.

Building on knowledge and experience

One of the serious challenges facing teachers in England who teach in classrooms with linguistically diverse learners is the lack of documented examples of practice which seek to embrace and develop bilingual learners' strengths. Thus, it is too easy to work from a 'deficit' hypothesis, as set out at the beginning of this chapter.

In the early years of formal literacy teaching it is important to use the knowledge of both/all of the languages and literacies of bilingual learners. This does not mean that teachers must teach the range of languages and literacies of the learners. The issue here is to support the development of English literacy through knowledge about languages and literacies which the bilingual learners already have. While some difficulties may be encountered, there is a great deal that can be learnt from offering these opportunities to bilingual learners.

The importance of developing other practices and pedagogies is based not only on notions of cultural tolerance but also on sound pedagogic principles which will enable bilingual learners to have equal opportunities to achieve more of their potential. Approaching literacies from pupils' experiences takes a Vygotskian perspective. That is, we identify the level of knowledge where the learner is functioning and introduce new learning within the learner's Zone of Proximal Development (ZPD) (Vygotsky, 1962). Through negotiation and 'scaffolding' familiar multilingual experiences, new learning about English literacy is introduced, through both psycholinguistic and social practice approaches. This is illustrated in some examples of practice in the literature and by other examples from teachers' work.

Examples of multilingual classroom practice

One teacher recounts how monolingual English teachers in his primary school provided bilingual learners with opportunities to bring to the classroom the languages and stories of their cultures. Pakistani, Bangladeshi and Malaysian children told stories in their home languages (Blackledge, 1994). The discussion generated in the classroom educates all the learners, monolinguals and bilinguals, because it focuses on knowledge of language and raises metalinguistic awareness (being able to talk about language) of languages and literacies.

Another example is given in the work of Charmain Kenner (1997). She describes how nursery and reception classes create 'literacy corners' where the multilingual literacies of many of the bilingual learners are displayed in forms of handwriting, letters, books, signs, with interesting materials for children to become involved, and experiment, with the range of literacies. Parents are involved with the development of the literacy corners and some are also involved in curriculum literacy events such as letter writing, story telling and reading in different literacies.

A further example is taken from the practice of a teacher working in a reception class with 4–5-year-olds. In order to find out the range of languages and literacies among her young learners, she asked them to tell her about their home languages. She found some were knowledgeable and accurate in talking about their home languages. Those who were not were helped by the opportunity to talk about their home languages and became more aware and knowledgeable, for example knowing the name of their home language. She went on to explore the learners' other languages and literacies by suggesting they bring a book from home, written in their community literacy. While this started during the school's book week, it was easy to develop into a regular weekly class event. The potential for discussion was substantial, for example, around story telling, discussing orthographies, pictures and drawings, and the purpose of the book. There was much potential to involve parents as well.

The fourth example is also from the practice of a teacher working in a primary school. During drama lessons with a class of 10-year-olds she encouraged the pupils to develop a play which would involve several of their languages. The children developed a story which moved easily between the languages to allow monolingual English listeners also to follow the plot. The children wrote the script of the different languages using English orthography. There were instances where the parents became indirectly involved. For example, at home the parents would give advice when their children asked them about the appropriateness of a word or phrase in their home language. Another example of parental involvement was the high attendance from the parents of the bilingual learners in the class, when the play was performed.

The important point to note about these examples of practice is that they are able to embrace multilingual literacies across a range of languages and literacies. Hence discussions about knowledge of language and raising meta-linguistic awareness are natural and rich because of their appropriateness. Furthermore, in these discussions the status and values of minority languages and literacies are recognised and foregrounded. The cultural and linguistic capital of the children's and parents' experiences are highlighted and brought into perspective alongside English. The bilingual learners do not feel that they need to keep their other literacies hidden. Talking about them and sharing them does not diminish the development of literacy in English.

There is an increasing number of these kinds of examples, often disseminated among teachers in local education authorities (LEAs) by their own staff. They now need to be drawn together and theorised to form a principled pedagogy, based on socio-cultural theories of learning, for multilingual literacies' teaching.

Working with parents

The NLS included recommendations about 'home–school collaboration' in supporting literacy development of their children (DfEE, 1997, pp. 32–33). However, there is little accommodation for linguistic minority families. Given that many bilingual children have multilingual literacies at home, and schools expect parental support for school literacy, this section explores home–school liaison with linguistic minority families. It also notes the role of schools, literacies and bilingual learners in wider society.

There is a concern among teachers about the difficulty they experience in involving linguistic minority parents in school events, particularly beyond the early years. From the examples above of multilingual literacies class practice, literacy events and practices in school which recognise the cultural and linguistic capital of the languages and literacies of bilingual learners are likely to gain support both directly and indirectly from linguistic minority parents.

Studies of parents show that 'middle-class' parents are likely to liaise more with schools and have more informed relationships than parents from lower socioeconomic groups (Lareau, 1987). Linguistic minority families also have little contact with schools, particularly at secondary level (Ledoux, with Deckers and Koopman, 1997). This can lead teachers once again towards a 'deficit' model for interpreting parental motivation and to have negative perceptions of liaising with linguistic minority parents and families. Certain views may be expressed about the parents such as: 'They don't speak English; they don't want to speak English; they aren't literate in any language; they aren't interested in their children's schooling'.

The implication of these findings is that schools which have learners from minority communities need to consider modifying their mechanisms of liaison with linguistic minority parents. They need to review their attitudes towards linguistic minority parents and to develop a range of flexible, parent-centred approaches for literacy support. There are documented examples of alternative approaches to home–school collaboration through linguistic minority family literacy projects which work with parents, exploring parental and family literacy practices (Delgado-Gaitan, 1990; Allexsaht-Snider, 1994). These projects perceive literacy as a social process and they achieve a great deal beyond supporting children to achieve levels of literacy, such as improved communication within the family, and a less inhibited attitude to school by the parents.

Hargreaves (1994) argues that organisational change comes through recognition of 'expertise and process'. Thus, if schools are to effectively liaise with linguistic minority parents and families they must recognise the *expertise* that many minority parents have in languages and literacies other than English and develop a *process* which empowers them to support their children's learning. Parents' evenings and open days which lack well-advertised multilingual/interpreter support, and are held only in the school and at times of the day which are difficult for shift workers, are unlikely to be supported by linguistic minority parents. On the other hand, structures and processes which show flexibility and sensitivity, such as recruiting trained bilingual personnel, electing minority parent representatives on governing bodies and developing curriculum approaches which recognise and include home literacies, are likely to gain more support from linguistic minority families (Delgado-Gaitan, 1990).

However, it is well-documented (e.g. Cummins, 1997; Corson, 1993) that schools reflect and reproduce the power relations of wider society. The inequalities of power and status which operate in society outside the school influence interactions in the classroom between teachers, learners, and peers, and between teachers and parents (Allexsaht-Snider, 1994; Lareau, 1987). The

NLS is developing in this social and education situation. The role of continuing professional development of teachers, particularly specialist EAL teachers, is crucial in understanding how to support the development of literacy/ies in bilingual learners.

Professional development

At the beginning of the chapter three challenges were identified for teachers of literacy to bilingual learners in primary school. Most professional development helps teachers to understand and respond to the first two challenges; to debunk the 'deficit' hypothesis about developing two languages and to show that developing multilingual literacies is enriching for all learners. Professional development courses on teaching literacy encourage teachers to develop a wider knowledge base, by becoming more knowledgeable about language and literacy development in emerging bilingual learners. Most teachers' courses link growth in content knowledge with practice, through developing and enhancing skills, strategies and through collaborative practice by EAL teachers and mainstream teachers. They encourage teachers to become reflective practitioners. In this way most professional development courses for the NLS aim to respond to the challenges facing teachers of bilingual learners.

Unfortunately, the third challenge of evaluating critically the dominant framework of the NLS often remains unaddressed. This is not surprising since it would mean challenging not only ministerial authority about the curriculum, but more importantly, the wider societal discourse about the pedagogy of developing literacies and their appropriateness for bilingual learners. To address this third challenge, professional development needs to raise teachers' awareness of the power structures which support dominant discourses about literacy, education and linguistic minority learners. Professional development needs to offer teachers ways of questioning these discourses and to reorganise their knowledge about literacy and bilingualism in order to develop practices which are more inclusive of learners' knowledge of language and literacies. In addition, professional development needs to be continuous and to support teachers in documenting changes of practice which are driven by their own reorganised conceptual frameworks so that a body of evidence becomes available. With such a body of evidence, power structures implicit in current policies for developing literacy in young bilingual learners can be challenged, and alternative, more advantageous approaches be set out.

Conclusion

This chapter has argued that the NLS has adopted a psycholinguistic/technical skills approach to literacy development, defining literacy as a unitary process concerned with reading and writing. It does not take account of the importance of the social practices and purposes of reading and writing, nor of the influence that they have on developing literacies. The implication for bilingual learners is that the NLS excludes the other literacy experiences which they may encounter through the multilingual literacy practices of their families and community. Further, contrary to teaching and learning principles, the NLS does not encourage teachers to build on and develop bilingual children's knowledge of literacies in the widest sense. In the face of the serious challenge to teachers developing literacy with bilingual learners, which is the lack of documented practice developing multilingual pedagogies, the chapter has offered examples of practice which embrace bilingual learners' multilingual literacies and it has pointed out the need to theorise these examples into a pedagogy for developing multilingual literacies in primary school learners. Finally, the chapter shows that the NLS offers teachers no guidance for working specifically with linguistic minority families. Yet research confirms that this group of families are among the most alienated from the schooling process and that schools are aware of this. The chapter argues that the home–school situation reflects a power relationship which operates in wider society. Teachers, and in particular EAL teachers, through professional development and their own personal agency, will need to develop and document practices building on the strengths of bilingual learners in order to offer real alternatives to current policies and practices.

References

Allexsaht-Snider, M. (1994) The social process of a family literacy project with bilingual familes, in: A. Blackledge (ed.) *Teaching Bilingual Children*, pp. 71–81 (Stoke, Trentham Books).

Bekos, I. (1997) Phonological awareness and the process of learning to read in Greek-English bilingual children, unpublished Ph.D. thesis, University of Birmingham, UK.

Blackledge, A. (1994) 'We can't tell our stories in English': language, story and culture in the primary school, in: A. Blackledge (ed.) *Teaching Bilingual Children*, pp. 43–59 (Stoke, Trentham Books).

Blackledge, A. (1998) A study of school-focused home literacy practices in Bangladeshi families in Birmingham, unpublished Ph.D. thesis, University of Birmingham, UK.

Bourdieu, P. (1986) The forms of capital, from J.E. Richardson (ed.) *Handbook of Theory of Research for the Sociology of Education*, Greenwood Press, pp. 241–258, in: A.H. Halsey, H. Lauder, P. Brown and A. Stuart Wells (eds) (1997) *Education: culture, economy, society*, pp. 46–58 (Oxford, Oxford University Press).

Bryant, P. and Bradley, L. (1983) Categorising sounds and learning to read: a causal connection, *Nature*, 301, pp. 419–421.

Campbell, R. and Sais, E. (1995) Accelerated metalinguistic (phonological) awareness in bilingual children, *British Journal of Developmental Psychology*, 13, pp. 61–68.

Commission for Racial Equality (CRE) (1998) *Reform of the Race Relations Act 1976* (London, CRE).

Corson, D. (1993) *Language, Minority Education and Gender* (Clevedon, Multilingual Matters).

Cummins, J. (1984) *Issues in Assessment of Bilingual Children* (Clevedon, Multilingual Matters).

Cummins, J. (1997) Cultural and linguistic diversity in education: a mainstream issue?, *Educational Review*, 49(2), pp. 105–114.

Cummins, J. and Swain, M. (1986) *Bilingualism in Education* (New York, Longman).

Delgado-Gaitan, C. (1990) *Literacy for Empowerment* (London, Falmer Press).

Department for Education and Employment (DfEE) (1997) *The Implementation of the National Literacy Strategy* (London, HMSO).

Department for Education and Employment (DfEE) (1998) *The National Literacy Strategy* (London, HMSO).

Department of Education and Science (DES) (1985) *Education for All: The Swann Report* (London, HMSO).

Durgunoglu, A.Y., Nagy, W.E. and Hancin-Bhatt, B.J. (1993) Cross-language transfer of phonological awareness, *Journal of Educational Psychology*, 85, 3, pp. 453–465.

Edwards, V. (1998) *The Power of Babel: teaching and learning in multilingual classrooms* (Stoke, Trentham Books).

Ferdman, B.M. (1990) Literacy and cultural identity, *Harvard Educational Review*, 60, pp. 181–204.

Freire, P. (1972) *Pedagogy of the Oppressed* (London, Sheed and Ward).

Gregory, E. (1996) *Making Sense of a New World: learning to read in a second language* (London, Paul Chapman).

Hargreaves, A. (1994) Restructuring restructuring: postmodernity and the prospects for educational change, from *Journal of Education Policy*, 9, pp. 47–65, in: A.H. Halsey, H. Lauder, P. Brown and A. Stuart Wells (eds) (1997) *Education: culture, economy, society*, pp. 338–353 (Oxford, Oxford University Press).

Kenner, C. (1997) A child writes from her everyday world: using home texts to develop biliteracy at school, in: E. Gregory (ed.) *One Child, Many Worlds*, pp. 75–86, (London, David Fulton).

Lado, R. (1957) *Linguistics Across Cultures* (Ann Arbor, Mich., University of Michigan Press).

Lareau, A. (1987) Social-class differences in family-school relationships: the importance of cultural capital, *Sociology of Education*, 60, pp. 73–85.

Ledoux, G. with Deckers, P. and Koopman, P. (1997) The meaning of 'social class' for Rukish, Moroccan and Dutch 'social climbers', in: G. Heyting, J. Koppen, D. Lenzen and F. Thiel (eds) *Educational Studies in Europe* (Oxford, Berghahan Books).

Luke, A. and Kale, J. (1997) Learning through difference: cultural practices in early childhood language socialisation, in: E. Gregory (1997) *Making Sense of a New World: learning to read in a second language* (London, Paul Chapman).

MacNeil, M.M. (1994) Immersion programmes employed in Gaelic-medium units in Scotland, *Journal of Multilingual and Multicultural Development*, 15([fr2/3]), pp. 245–252.

Martin, D. (1997) *ESRC End of Award Report: phonological processing and literacy skills in bilingual/biliterate children*. Obtainable from the author.

Martin, D. and Stuart-Smith, J. (1998) Exploring bilingual children's perceptions of being bilingual and biliterate: implications for educational provision, *British Journal of Sociology of Education*, 19(2), pp. 237–254.

Martin, D., Stuart-Smith, J. and Dhesi, K.K. (1998) Insiders and outsiders: translating in a bilingual research project, in: S. Hunston (ed.) *Language At Work*, pp. 109–122 (Clevedon, Multilingual Matters in association with the British Association for Applied Linguistics).

Peate, M.R. (1995) Oracy issues in ESL teaching, in: M. Verma, K. Corrigan and S. Firth (eds) *Working with Bilingual Children*, pp. 154–163 (Clevedon, Multilingual Matters).

Skutnabb-Kangas, T. (1988) Multilingualism and the education of minority children, in: T. Skutnabb-Kangas and J. Cummins (eds) *Minority Education: from shame to struggle*, pp. 9–44 (Clevedon, Multilingual Matters).

Stackhouse, J. and Wells, B. (1997) *Children's Speech and Literacy Difficulties: a psycholinguistic framework* (London, Whurr Publishers).

Street, B. (1995) *Social Literacies: critical approaches to literacy in development, ethnography and education* (London, Longman).

Stuart-Smith, J. and Martin, D. (1997) Investigating literacy and pre-literacy skills in Panjabi/English schoolchildren, *Educational Review*, 49(2), pp. 181–197.

Times Educational Supplement (TES) (1998) 'Don't asset strip Section 11', letter by Alsop, Bismal, Harding, McKen, Tyskerud and Wall, 23 October, p.18.

Verma, M., Corrigan, K. and Firth, S. (eds) (1995) *Working with Bilingual Children* (Clevedon, Multilingual Matters).

Vygotsky, L. (1962) *Thought and Language* (Cambridge, Mass., MIT Press).

Source

This is an edited version of an article previously published in *Educational Review*, 51(1). 1999. Reproduced by permission of Taylor & Francis Ltd.

Chapter 16

Psychosocial factors in the aetiology and course of specific learning disabilities

Thomas G. O'Connor and Robert C. Pianta

Our understanding of the aetiology and course of learning disabilities and of how to assess, diagnose, and treat them has progressed greatly in recent years (Maughan and Yule, 1994). In this chapter on aetiological factors we focus on several sets of key findings regarding the environmental influences associated with such disabilities in general, with special reference to *specific* learning disabilities. In addition we draw attention to the difficulties of interpreting research findings and suggest directions forward for further studies.

Four major themes are addressed. First, we review what is known about the epidemiology of specific learning disorders and highlight the variations in prevalence rates across ethnic, geographic, and demographic settings. The variability in prevalences of specific learning disorders and of general cognitive impairment across socio-economic status is consistent with the notion that the aetiology of learning problems may be linked to psychosocial factors, and raises many questions about which environmental influences might be important and by which mechanisms they exert their influence.

Second, using the model of research on the environmental influences – broadly defined – on intellectual development (e.g. Detterman, 1996), we identify some of the lessons and challenges for research into links between psychosocial influences and learning disorders, whether specific or global. There are numerous parallels between research on general intellectual functioning and research on learning disorders: in both cases there is a need to integrate genetic and psychosocial factors, to assess any correlations with and between psychosocial risk factors, and to address the extent to which specific learning disorders are aetiologically distinct from individual differences in cognitive skills within the normal range.

Third, we examine how environmental influences may indirectly contribute to the development and course of learning disabilities in children through their influence on co-occurring behavioural and emotional disorders. It has been known for some time that the population of children with learning problems has an elevated prevalence rate of psychopathology; recent findings suggest that environmental factors may be most aetiologically salient through their influence on the likelihood of a child's developing behavioural problems.

Finally, we examine what clues interventions provide regarding the environmental aetiology of specific learning disorders. To be sure, interventions may alleviate learning problems through mechanisms unrelated to those that caused the disorder. Nonetheless, research into intervention may provide clues to the psychosocial correlates of learning disorders and to the most effective primary prevention strategies. Throughout this chapter we pay close attention to the distinction between broadly defined and specific learning disabilities. The distinction is important in a chapter covering a range of topics, as not all research distinguishes between the two, and, to complicate matters further, much more is known about some specific learning disorders than others.

The role of epidemiological findings in identifying psychosocial risk factors

Epidemiological studies are critical to an understanding of a disorder in at least two ways. First, epidemiological data provide an estimate of the prevalence, which makes it possible to estimate the need to address the problem and the cost of doing so. Second, and more central to this chapter, by revealing the social correlates of a disorder as well as trends over time and across regions, epidemiological data can provide clues to the underlying causes of the disorder (Rutter and Smith, 1995). Although there are important limitations to inferring causal mechanisms from epidemiological data (Taubes, 1995), gathering such data is nevertheless a critical first step in understanding a disorder. In this section we briefly examine three risk indicators – socio-economic differences, sociocultural differences, and sex differences – that epidemiological research has shown to be associated with learning problems. A fourth finding, regarding the overlap of learning and behavioural problems, is considered in the penultimate section.

In the study of specific learning disorders, several issues regarding epidemiological findings should be noted. There is a clear consensus that individuals with learning disorders form a heterogeneous group, even when children with a specific type of learning disorder (e.g. reading disability) are examined (Rourke, 1983). Thus, underlying each prevalence rate and variation in base prevalence rates is a complex mix of individuals who vary with respect to, among other dimensions, co-occurring learning problems, co-occurring behavioural problems, genetic risk, response to interventions, age-based changes in the profile of difficulties, and putative underlying cognitive and processing difficulties. In addition, studies vary in how they define learning problems. Some studies have assessed distinct subtypes of learning disorder, most notably the distinction between specific reading disorder and general reading backwardness (see Maughan and Yule, 1994), whereas other studies have not made such a distinction. Also, certain problems of definition plague research on learning difficulties from country to country, and even from region to region within the same country (Hallahan and Kauffman, 1991; Chapman, 1992). Moreover – as further evidence of the definitional problems in the field – even experts have difficulty in differentiating individuals with learning disorder from low-achieving individuals (Shinn et al., 1986; Algozzine and Ysseldyke, 1988).

Furthermore, large-scale studies of learning problems cannot include the detailed assessments that are the hallmark of small-scale and clinical studies. Consequently, large-scale studies cannot identify specific deficit profiles and thus cannot assess heterogeneity in much detail. Large-scale studies also cannot examine processes such as qualities of parent–child interactions, which have been implicated in the development of learning problems (Pianta and McCoy, 1997).

Thus there are several reasons to expect variability in estimated prevalences of specific learning disorders. To the extent that such variability reflects methodological rather than substantive influences, it will inevitably obscure some of the clues to causation that epidemiological data could otherwise provide.

There have been several epidemiological studies of general learning problems, but few of specific learning disorders, and it is quite rare for studies to assess each learning disorder independently (e.g. each of those listed in DSM IV (American Psychiatric Association, 1994) or ICD–10 (World Health Organization, 1993)). Consequently, little is known about geographic and demographic variations in rates of these specific disorders. Thus we limit our discussion of what connections there may be between variation in prevalences of learning problems and psychosocial aetiology to reading problems. It remains to be seen whether the lessons learned from research on reading problems provide a more general model of research on specific learning disabilities.

Some of the initial and now best-known epidemiological data on reading disorders were derived from an epidemiological study of 10-year-olds on the Isle of Wight in the UK (Rutter et al., 1970). The finding that approximately 4 per cent of the children were affected has been replicated in other normal-risk studies, and most estimates range from 4 to 10 per cent. Cross-cultural prevalences of learning problems are relatively consistent with this range (e.g. Silva et al., 1985).

The base prevalence of specific learning problems in very deprived (e.g. developing) countries has not been reported and may not be obtainable given the need for established schools and validated and culturally sensitive assessment measures. Accordingly, little can be concluded at present regarding the variation between cultural economic deprivation and relative prevalences of diagnosed learning problems across cultures. Nonetheless there has been an increase in the number of studies examining the cognitive and social development of children in very poor countries. Among the important findings that have emerged is that nutrition, physical health, and the extent to which basic needs are met are clearly linked both to general cognitive development and to specific learning abilities (Wachs et al., 1993; Gorman and Pollitt, 1996). Thus, although it may not be possible to ascertain the prevalences of specific learning problems in diverse cultures, it is fairly clear that risk exposure varies significantly across cultures.

Socioeconomic status

The link between socioeconomic well-being and the prevalences of specific learning problems can be explored by examining the variation in prevalences across socioeconomic status and demographic groups *within* a culture. Studies of low-income and urban populations have reported prevalences of learning problems much higher than 4 to 10 per cent – often double or triple in magnitude (Eisenberg 1966; Berger *et al.*, 1975). These findings provide some of the most compelling evidence for risk factors relating to social class, but leave unanswered the question of which psychosocial factors associated with socioeconomic conditions might be most important, and by what mechanisms these factors operate.

The mechanisms underlying the link between the level of socioeconomic disadvantage and the prevalence of learning problems need to be examined in the context of the many risks correlated with economic adversity. That is, low socioeconomic status indexes a wide range of causally more proximal influences. Among those factors associated with low socioeconomic status *and* with cognitive development are birth complications, very low birth weight, poor prenatal nutrition, and exposure to environmental toxins such as lead (Sameroff *et al.*, 1987; Fergusson *et al.*, 1993; Wachs *et al.*, 1993). In low socioeconomic groups, there are not only elevated medical 'environmental' risks but also elevated risks relating to environmental stimulation at home and at school.

Sociocultural factors

It is very difficult to isolate the 'effects' of one risk factor from another. Although it is certainly possible to examine statistically the independent effects of correlated risk factors (see Fergusson *et al.*, 1992), such an approach may have little meaning outside a research context; that is, they may have little ecological validity. Similar difficulties arise in understanding the significance of the variation in prevalences of learning problems and poor school performance across ethnic groups *within* cultures, because minority status is correlated with many of the risk factors already mentioned. When environmental and medical risks are accounted for, sociocultural and ethnic differences in prevalences of learning problems are eliminated or substantially reduced (Fergusson *et al.*, 1991; see also Brooks-Gunn *et al.*, 1996). The difficulties that correlated risk factors create for understanding *how* psychosocial factors influence the aetiology and course of (specific) learning disabilities are examined in more detail in the next section.

Sex

The disproportionate numbers of boys diagnosed with learning disorders is a replicated epidemiological finding that might have implications for psychosocial aetiology. The difference between the base prevalences of learning problems is not disputed: most studies find that boys are anywhere between two and five times more likely than girls to receive a diagnosis of reading disorder. This finding parallels the reported sex differences in verbal ability within the normal range in children and adults (Hyde and Linn, 1988).

Some authors have suggested that the sex ratio of diagnosed learning problems in boys to those in girls may be inflated because of referral biases that stem from associated disruptive behaviour. That is, boys may be more likely to be identified as having learning disabilities not because of the disability per se but rather because of the higher prevalences of the associated behavioural problems (notably, poor conduct and hyperactivy/inattention) that prompt the referral. Some support for this hypothesis is found in the report by Sanson and colleagues (1996), who used different cut-off scores for boys and girls to define the presence or absence of behavioural problems comorbid with learning problems in order to identify a group of boys and girls large enough for statistical analyses. Another piece of evidence supporting the hypothesis of a referral bias in children is that in adults the prevalences of specific learning disorders in the two sexes are roughly equal (see Maughan and Yule, 1994).

However, assuming that boys do outnumber girls in the actual prevalence of learning problems, it is not clear what psychosocial implications this imbalance may have for understanding the aetiology of learning disorders. Both psychosocial and genetic or other biological explanations have been proposed to explain the sex difference within the normal and clinical range. Boys may be more vulnerable to learning disorders, but it is not clear whether sex is a 'main effect' or modifies key environmental risks (Morisset et al., 1995). We address this question in the next section.

At the very least these findings highlight the severe limitations of relying on clinic samples and the continuing need to include psychiatric and specific and global learning disorders in epidemiological research on children and adults. The usefulness of future epidemiological research in identifying direction for detailed experimental and clinical investigations in this field will depend on how far it goes beyond assessing risk indicators such as social class and economic resources, and cultural and sex differences, to assess the risk factors associated with these indicators, and the putative processes by which these factors operate.

Assessing psychosocial influences on learning disorders

Much is known about the ontogeny of specific language skills and disorders, how they can be assessed, the presumed underlying cognitive structures, and the rate of development (Bradley and Bryant, 1979; Bishop, 1992; Goswami, 1994; Wagner et al., 1994). Fewer studies focus on the social context associated with learning difficulties and the development of related learning skills or on the relation between individual differences in specific learning abilities and psychosocial experiences. Before discussing some recent and key findings, we examine the current debates and controversies regarding the mechanisms by which psychosocial influences operate – that is, how they increase the risk of learning disorders and how they shape the developmental paths of the affected individuals. We then examine three issues that are central to interpreting the available findings, in particular those from research in developmental psychology: the aetiological distinction between individual differences within the normal range and severe or clinical disorders, the need to integrate environmental and genetic models of development and disorder, and the power of longitudinal follow-up studies for sorting out risk processes.

Models of psychosocial influence

If the role of psychosocial risks in learning disorders is to be understood, the mechanisms by which these risks may operate must be explained. Research relating psychosocial influences to individual differences in learning abilities has adopted one of two general models. The most straightforward model assumes 'direct effects', whereby psychosocial influences have a direct impact on the emergence and course of learning skills and disabilities. For example, lack of support for learning and reading in the family, which may especially characterize families with low socioeconomic status, has been linked to a long-term trajectory of academic failure (Walker et al., 1994). This finding, which has been replicated in many studies, underlies the 'cultural/familial' model of mental retardation. The assumption underlying these studies is that the cause of the delay is the child's poor social environment. Factors other than those directly involved with socieconomic status have also been cited as playing a direct role in the development of learning problems or, as is more often assessed, academic failure, including stressful life events, family type, and behavioural problems. An issue that often goes unrecognised in these studies is that a model that assumes direct effects is compelling only if the mechanism of action (rather than just the risk factor) is also specified. Unfortunately, research has tended to focus more on identifying risks than on specifying the mechanisms.

In the other model, psychosocial factors are assumed to act indirectly. Risks such as those associated with lower socioeconomic status may exacerbate existing biological and medical risks but not lead to learning problems in the absence of other risks. Evidence is accumulating that this process may hold for babies with low birthweight, as low-birthweight babies who show poor cognitive and academic adjustment in childhood are disproportionately from families with low socioeconomic status. Similarly, studies are increasingly adopting a model positing cumulative effects (Sameroff et al., 1987), in which the accumulation of risk factors, rather than a particular factor or combination of factors, is linked to learning difficulties. In these studies, the risk processes are assumed to be multiplicative, not additive (e.g. Pungello et al., 1996).

Understanding the mechanisms by which psychosocial factors operate is critical to understanding their role in learning disorders. General models proposed by, for example, Bronfenbrenner (1986), and many others, assume a bi-directional, multiplicative, and hierarchical arrangement of psychosocial influences in normal and abnormal development, and the conceptual advantages of such inclusive models are widely acknowledged. There is, however, considerable confusion about how such models can be reified and empirically tested. Although attempts have been made to operationalize some of the implications of these models in the context of cognitive development (Super and Harkness, 1986; Pianta and O'Connor, 1996), progress in the field of learning disabilities lags behind, especially in integrating research on genetic and psychosocial risks. Despite the absence of an accepted general and empirical model for understanding psychosocial influences on learning development (and development generally), it is clear that a 'main effects' model has fallen out of favour. Researchers are playing closer attention to the factors that moderate and mediate the connection between specific risk factors and learning skills, and it is this research into the covariation among risk factors that has made the most important contributions to our understanding of learning disorders and individual differences in learning abilities.

A critical theme in recent discussions of the nature of psychosocial influences is the question of whether there are correlations between social factors and cognitive development. Similarly, medical and psychosocial risks for learning disorders are correlated with one another, such that birth complications and poor prenatal care and a poor learning environment in the home and school are all more common among families with low socioeconomic status. Recent findings in research on the psychosocial factors associated with intellectual development further underscore the correlated nature of genetic and psychosocial influences, as those environmental factors associated with academic success and intellectual development are more common among intellectually more able parents (Pianta and O'Connor, 1996). These findings underscore the complexity of documenting the specific ways in which psychosocial factors operate and simultaneously emphasize the need for a multidisciplinary perspective in research designs.

Natural experiments are often very helpful in distinguishing the correlated social and biological influences in the development of specific learning abilities – and perhaps disorders. A recent study by Morrison et al. (1995) provides a good example. The authors made use of the fact that whether a child is enrolled in first grade or in kindergarten depends on an arbitrary cut-off date – the child's fifth birthday. By comparing children who were just old enough to enter first grade with those who were not, those authors could compare the development of cognitive skills as a function of maturation and of the more 'academic' environment of first grade. After the first year, the children who had attended first grade had much better memory skills than those who had attended kindergarten, but this gap disappeared after the second group of children had attended first grade for a year. The design also allowed the authors to conclude that advances in phonological skills that are critical for reading (such as segmentation of sounds) are related to exposure to formal reading instruction in first grade rather than to maturational changes (Morrison *et al.*, 1995).

Categories and dimensions

Many studies report psychosocial correlates of learning problems, but few report whether these risks are associated with learning disorders, that is, what percentage of the children in the sample have diagnosed problems, as distinct from, for example, underachievement. Of course many intervention studies focus on policy implications of psychosocial interventions, and these reports make explicit an estimate of the number of children whose learning problems may have been prevented (Campbell and Ramey, 1994; Seitz and Apfel, 1994). However, the majority of studies examining psychosocial factors associated with learning abilities and school success adopt a dimensional view of learning abilities and pay little attention to learning disorders as distinct from comparatively lower ability. Consequently it is difficult to interpret findings that link qualities of maternal interaction, extent of reading and of exposure to academic materials in the home, quality of school (and day-care) environments, exposure to school, the extent to which numeracy is practised, and many other factors (e.g. see Morisset *et al.*, 1995), to the aetiology of learning disorders. Virtually all of the studies that have examined the above factors have examined them in relation to individual differences in learning abilities and not in relation to the presence or absence of disorder. An important general lesson from psychiatric research is that the aetiology of the extremes (i.e. of a disorder) is often not different from the aetiology of individual differences, though there may be exceptions. Using research on intelligence as an example, it is clear that the aetiology of extreme mental retardation is qualitatively different from the aetiology of mild mental retardation and of individual differences within the normal range.

The need to integrate psychosocial and genetic influences

Research into the aetiology of learning disabilities has been changed dramatically by recent findings regarding the important role of genetic influences (Lewitter *et al.*, 1980). Much of quantitative genetic and molecular genetic research on learning disorders has focused specifically on reading disorders. The degree of genetic influence found has differed, but most studies now suggest that in reading disorders approximately one-third of the variance in individual differences can be attributed to genetic factors (Stevenson, 1991). While questions remain about the nature of genetic influences and the mechanisms by which they act (Bishop *et al.*, 1995), it is clear that future studies on the aetiology of specific learning disorders must take into account the role of genetic and familial factors.

What are the implications of these findings for psychosocial studies of specific learning disorders? As several authors have pointed out (Plomin, 1994), behavioural genetic studies provide some of the most critical support for environmental influences in development and pathology, by examining the role of environmental factors while controlling for genetic influences. This is certainly true in the context of specific learning disorders: if genetic influences account for one-third of the variance in individual differences in learning disorders, then non-genetic factors account for the remainder. There are, of course, many pitfalls in estimating the relative contributions of genetic and non-genetic factors on the basis of analyses that partition the relative influences in quantitative models, but it is significant that behavioural genetic analyses ascribe an important role to psychosocial and other non-genetic influences.

At the very least these findings highlight the need to incorporate both genetic and environmental hypotheses in research designs. To date, relatively few studies hypothesizing that parent–child interactions and related proximal processes explain individual differences in children's learning abilities have included controls to take parental cognitive abilities into account (Pianta and O'Connor, 1996). Pianta and McCoy (1997) found, for example, that the quality of child–mother interaction was predictive for learning problems even after maternal education had been taken into account. Similarly, in a different sample of children Pianta and Egeland (forthcoming) found that changes in children's intellectual abilities in the early school years were significantly associated with the quality of parent–child interactions even after the effects of maternal cognitive ability had been taken into account. This approach needs to be extended to research on children with specific learning disabilities.

The genetic evidence also suggests that these findings on the variation in prevalences of learning disorders across social class do not unambiguously suggest psychosocial risks. Adults with learning disorders are reported to be more likely to drop out of school and less likely to obtain educational qualifications than their peers without learning (and especially reading) disorders. Consequently it is hardly surprising that these adults have lower wages and lower-skill occupations as adults (Maughan, 1995). Thus the finding that children and adolescents in low social classes have relatively high prevalences of learning problems may be partly influenced by a higher prevalence of learning problems in their parents – that is, the risk rises from genetic factors rather than from social class per se. Similarly, the finding that children from lower social classes experience a less positive reading environment (for example are read to less often, or have fewer books available) may be a function of the disinterest and difficulty their parents have in reading. In this way a correlation exists between environmental risk and genetic risk, and social class is accordingly an ambiguous variable from the perspective of aetiology.

An additional lesson learned from recent studies is that genetic influences may act not on the phenotype per se but rather on the central component processes underlying the disorder. Thus the genetic influence on reading disorders appears to operate through phonological processing (rather than through orthographic coding; Stevenson, 1991). There is a need to take a similar approach in linking psychosocial influences to learning disorders. The implication is that social class and related factors (including, for example, birth complications, nutrition, school quality) may influence reading abilities via their connection with phonological processing or other related skills rather than directly. Although few studies have examined the association between psychosocial factors and phonological processing, available data do not support a link (MacLean et al., 1987). Differences in phonological processing between able and poor readers and between disadvantaged and advantaged children appear only after the children have started school and have been exposed to formal reading instruction (Goswami, 1994; cf. Morrison et al., 1995). These null findings may help to narrow the focus in further research on specific psychosocial influences and specific components of learning disorders.

Follow-up studies

Follow-up studies are reviewed in more detail in the next section. Suffice it to note here that longitudinal research has significantly shaped the emerging models of psychosocial influence in learning disabilities. For example, research findings indicate that the negative long-term effects of learning problems appear to bear most heavily on lower socioeconomic groups; the eventual educational and occupational attainment of better-off individuals appear unaffected, or at least less affected (O'Connor and Spreen, 1988; Maughan, 1995). As already noted, the many factors indexed by social class may play a central role in the developmental course of learning problems, but here again the available studies do not allow firm conclusions. This matter is revisited in the last section, on intervention.

The role of social factors in learning disorders: links with behavioural problems

Research from more than two decades has identified behavioural problems, usually defined as inattentiveness, overactivity, and problems of conduct, as a frequent correlate of learning problems in children. For example, Sanson et al. (1996) reported that 36 per cent of children with behavioural problems have reading problems, and 69 per cent of children with reading problems have behavioural problems. The mechanisms underlying this association are unclear. The disorders may share a common biological or genetic cause, or the overlap may be entirely psychosocially mediated. Many researchers have used longitudinal designs to test the temporal association between learning problems and behavioural problems (Rutter and Yule, 1970; Sanson et al., 1996). The findings offer clear evidence that behavioural problems, especially inattention and conduct problems, lead to later reading problems and underachievement (Horn and Packard, 1985), and evidence also suggests that reading problems exacerbate behaviour problems (McGee et al., 1986). Thus the effects are reciprocal.

Several studies have examined whether comorbid reading and behaviour problems are aetiologically different from problems solely of reading or of behaviour. In a longitudinal cohort investigation spanning nearly 8 years and including a range of temperamental problems, behavioural problems, and social class variables, Sanson and colleagues (1996) found that, among children as young as 3 to 4 years of age who later were found to have a reading disorder, those who turned out to have co-occurring behavioural problems could be distinguished from those without behavioural problems; in contrast there was a striking absence of distinguishing characteristics of children who later had reading problems only and those who later had no reading or behavioural problems. Those findings are consistent with other reports (cf. Pennington et al., 1993) suggesting that single disorders have a different causal pathway from comorbid disorders. Equally importantly, the overlap of learning and behavioural problems at such an early age suggests that, at least for a subset of children with co-occurring learning and behavioural problems, feelings of frustration and failure in school cannot explain comorbidity. However, very few studies, including that of Sanson et al. (1996), have examined the differential patterns of social and demographic risk associated with single and comorbid groups of children.

In a subset of studies focusing on the link between learning and behavioural problems, the problem of inattention and overactivity has been distinguished from problems of conduct. The evidence from these studies suggests that antisocial behaviour or conduct problems arise primarily through their association with inattention and overactivity rather than through a direct link with reading problems (Frick et al., 1991; Maughan et al., 1996). These findings underscore the need to study the patterns of comorbidity among the behavioural problems as well as in relation to learning problems, and to anticipate the problems that will arise if the subtle but critical distinctions among the disruptive behaviour disorders are ignored.

Finally, age-based change in the patterns of learning and behavioural disorders may offer important insights into aetiology. In particular, long-term follow-up studies suggest that learning problems per se are stable and continue into adulthood, but that the patterns of co-occurring behavioural and emotional problems may be limited to adolescence (Maughan et al., 1996). Implications of the above findings for aetiology and intervention are examined in the next section.

Lessons from interventions and follow-up studies

In this final section some lessons for understanding the aetiology of learning disorders are drawn from intervention and follow-up studies. An important distinction is that between aetiology and course. Factors that maintain or shape the course of a disorder may be very different from those that initiate the disorder. To date, much more is known about the psychosocial influences on the course of learning problems than on their aetiology.

The research findings on the influence of social class on the aetiology and course of learning problems are relatively consistent. Children from the middle and upper classes are not only less likely to be diagnosed with learning problems, but also more likely to have a positive prognosis in terms of educational and occupational attainment if they do have a learning problem. Rawson's (1968) follow-up of children with learning problems in childhood suggested that the adjustment in young adulthood was relatively favourable in terms of college attendance and occupational status. However, the vast majority of the children were from very privileged backgrounds and had relatively high intelligence. Thus it is not clear what can be concluded from these findings except that social class may carry significant protective effects. It is also not clear what processes associated with higher socioeconomic status afford the protection; some of the more likely explanations would be access to remedial care, prevention of the development of co-occurring behavioural and emotional problems, and promotion of academic attainment outside the range of the particular learning disability. Alongside these findings it is important to note that an increasing number of intervention studies report that interventions based at home, school, or day care centre have beneficial effects only, or at least mainly, for children considered to be at risk (for socioeconomic or related reasons) and not for children in normal or low-risk categories (e.g. Caughy et al., 1994).

As noted above, several early-intervention studies that included a day-care-based or school-based component appeared to prevent the development of learning problems, and some family-based intervention approaches showed that the decrease in learning and school-related problems applied not only to the targeted children but also to their siblings born after the intervention had ended (Seitz and Apfel, 1994). Unfortunately, few specific conclusions regarding the mechanisms of influence of social factors on learning problems can be drawn from the extant intervention and prevention studies because they vary widely in their treatment focus, with some being very clearly focused on learning and school-related success (Campbell and Ramey, 1994) and others being focused on more general family social and economic needs and paying more attention to social and emotional than to cognitive development (Seitz and Apfel, 1994). Specifying the mechanisms of treatment is the next step for intervention research. Intervention studies are also positioned to assess both direct and, perhaps more importantly, indirect mechanisms of influence. For example, interventions originally designed to treat learning difficulties may reduce their severity across time or prevent their emergence by treating behavioural problems, promoting sensitive parent–child interactions, increasing family support, or other processes.

An additional caveat is required in interpreting the intervention research. Many intervention studies do not define the type of learning problems, so it remains to be seen whether they are concerned more with underachievement than with specific learning problems in reading, mathematics, and other areas. Nonetheless, extant studies provide ample evidence of a link between

individual differences in experiences at home and school, and learning competence and learning difficulties.

Case studies in learning disabilities and psychosocial factors

The case of U (all initials have been changed)

U is a 9-year-old boy who attends an elementary school in the suburban USA.
He is the oldest of three children of highly educated parents. His appearance
is somewhat odd, though not remarkable for any specific features or patterns.
He is healthy and growing normally and his size is above the 50th centile
for his age.

From the time he started school U appeared somewhat socially odd. He was
highly verbal; most of his interactions were (and still are) with adults. In
kindergarten he was identified as a precocious reader, yet his focus was mostly
on 'scary' books. His quantitative and spatial skills were weak and his handwriting and gross motor skills were poor. Specifically, he had difficulty with
early mathematic concepts and skills and required considerable help to perform
skills the other children in the kindergarten mastered more easily. His fine
motor coordination was poor (his handwriting was illegible) and so was his
gross motor coordination (he was clumsy). Although he played soccer on a
local team of children his age and was mildly interested in the game, he rarely
participated on the field. When he attempted to charge the ball and kick, he
would usually miss. Socially, U was an outsider. He appeared to not know the
'rules of engagement' with peers, even in fairly structured situations in which
there was an adult present to mediate his peer interactions. In less structured
situations he stayed apart from the group and the vast majority of his interactions were with adults. Despite these concerns, no referrals were made for
special education or other concerns for U throughout his first four years of
school (kindergarten to grade 3), although he did receive some tutoring with
a volunteer in maths. U was not bothered by children, who mostly ignored
him. Adults viewed him as somewhat odd.

When U was in the second grade (age 7 years) his parents, concerned about
his poor mathematics, asked for an assessment by the school's special-education
teacher. He scored in the 'mildly retarded' range on an IQ test. His performance on an achievement test was high in reading and language and was low
for age, but not for IQ, in mathematics. The parents were quite upset at the
IQ score, believing it did not adequately reflect his verbal abilities. At that
time the team did not identify a need for him to have special-education
services. In the fourth grade U became increasingly withdrawn and appeared
stressed and generally depressed. He often cried himself to sleep. His parents
grew increasingly distressed. In interactions with his peers, U rarely if ever
sought out age-mates and instead interacted only (and rarely) with younger
children. Interactions were almost exclusively with adults and were repetitive,

focusing on the same idea over several instances on interaction, and increasingly were narrowed and rigid. He clearly had little or no age-appropriate interaction or social skills. In the classroom he was quiet and isolated, but worked hard.

The parents consulted an independent psychologist (outside the school) for an evaluation, which indicated that U's scores were widely scattered. His verbal scores were at the 98th centile while nonverbal reasoning, spatial processing, and attention were in the 10th to 15th centile range. At that time U was viewed as having a severe learning disability. An independent consultant worked with the school, which now provided tutoring for U. At the end of the fourth grade, U's parents enrolled him in a summer programme at a private school for learning-disabled children. The director of that programme noted that U had one of the most serious learning disabilities she had seen; she also emphasized his social problems.

The case illustrates several issues raised in the discussion of the research. First, it illustrates how thorny diagnostic issues make epidemiological and other types of research difficult in practice. U's learning disability is neither clearly specific (for example to quantitative or spatial skills) nor clearly global (for example he has above-average verbal ability). Moreover, although there is clearly evidence of a learning disability it is also clear that U has impairments in a range of other cognitive areas, notably social cognition and the ability to process social information. Impairments in these areas are often not assessed directly, but they may nonetheless be a source of considerable disability and distress. In fact U shows some mild signs of pervasive developmental disorder. Second, the case highlights the complex ways in which learning and behavioural problems coexist. It is difficult to know for sure, but it seems most likely that U's behavioural and emotional problems were secondary to his learning difficulties and problems of social cognition. It also seems that his learning problems led to emotional difficulties and frustrations and had ever-increasing social impact on his standing in the class and his self-esteem. The case also illustrates how development modifies the relations among behavioural and learning problems. U's apparent lack of interest in interacting with others initially may have led to classification of his difficulties and of the range of abilities affected, thus delaying intervention that might have prevented further problems. Third, the case illustrates the difficulties of matching intervention to the types of U's needs. Although tutoring and other academic interventions may help, it is clear that U also needs an intervention for his social problems, which are presumed to derive from difficulties of social cognitive processing. School programmes for these types of complex problems are essentially non-existent.

The case of B

An underachiever who has no apparent emotional or social problems, B was given special education from grade 2 (he is now in grade 6, age 11 years). An amiable, social boy with friends throughout the school, he performs at an average level on cognitive tests. His performance indicates little scatter, but his verbal IQ is somewhat lower than his nonverbal IQ. B's achievement is significantly lower, at the 25th centile.

Although his early school performance was generally positive, by the second grade (age 7) – when academic expectations rise – B had a hard time keeping up with his classmates. His achievement plummeted that year after the death of his parents in a car accident. B was adopted by an aunt and uncle. Late in the school year he was referred for special education because of his very poor academic 'behaviour' in school. The test scores, noted above, indicated that he performed in the normal range in cognitive abilities but had lowered achievement. No behavioural problems were reported by the school, which in general made no attempt to understand his emotional development and concerns regarding his parents' deaths. He was identified as having a learning disability and received resource-room help (20 hours per week). The label 'learning disability' was applied because of the discrepancy between achievement and IQ.

B flourished in the resource environment for 2 years. He worked very hard and formed a close attachment to teachers in that environment (with whom he remained for 3 years of middle school). By the end of the sixth grade (age 11 years) he was achieving at near-grade-level expectations.

The case of B raises a number of additional issues. First, as with the case of U, there are inevitable diagnostic issues. In practice the school primarily saw B as having a 'learning disability'; little effort was put into understanding the nature of the problem (i.e. which skills were affected) or what the possible causes were (i.e. the role of the traumatic loss). Thus the label 'learning disability' was what the school was interested in. Second, regarding the intervention, was B 'cured' of his learning disability, or had his problem been misdiagnosed (specifically on the basis of discrepancies between IQ and achievement)? Children may underachieve for many reasons, only some of which pertain to issues concerning learning disabilities. How sensitive and specific is the IQ–achievement discrepancy commonly applied in schools? This diagnostic practice has received relatively little close empirical scrutiny. Third, what aspect of the intervention may have had the greatest impact on B's 'recovery': his increased contact with a teacher, his relationship with a teacher, or some other aspect? How might an intervention be specifically designed for B given the school's resources and expertise? Fourth, in this case it seems likely that the learning disability was secondary to the emotional trauma of his parents' death. Nonetheless it is striking that the school recorded no behavioural or emotional problems in B; therefore from the perspective of traditional research methods he would probably not be seen as having a learning disability secondary to behavioural or emotional problems.

These cases highlight the complex ways in which (a) questions raised in research programmes may seem unrealistically clear-cut in contrast to the complex realities of school systems, (b) precise diagnosis sometimes plays a remarkably minor role in the intervention applied by schools, and (c) behavioural and emotional problems may lead to, exacerbate, or result from learning disabilities. The cases also illustrate that the relation between learning disabilities and behavioural and emotional problems changes as the child develops.

Conclusion

In his chapter we reviewed some of the current debates and findings regarding the psychosocial influences on the aetiology and course of specific learning problems. Epidemiological data suggest an important role of social and cultural influences on the aetiology of learning disorders, and intervention and follow-up studies are equally convincing that social factors play a critical role in the course of these individuals. In the absence of research focused on risk mechanisms, no firm conclusions can yet be drawn about specific factors or the manner in which they operate. Directions for further clinical and epidemiological research are highlighted with a particular emphasis on the types of challenges clinical and developmental research must address.

References

Algozzine B., Ysseldyke J.E. (1988) Questioning discrepancies: Retaking the first step 20 years later. *Learning Disabilities Quarterly* 11: 307–18.

American Psychiatric Association (1994) *Diagnostic and Statistical Manual of Mental Disorders*. 4th ed. (DSM IV). Washington, DC: American Psychiatric Association.

Berger M., Yule W., Rutter M. (1975) Attainment and adjustment in two geographic areas – II. The prevalence of specific reading retardation. *British Journal of Psychiatry* 126: 510–9.

Bishop D. (1992) The underlying nature of specific language impairment. *Journal of Child Psychology and Psychiatry* 33: 3–67.

Bishop, D., North T., Donlan C. (1995) Genetic basis of specific language impairment: Evidence from a twin study. *Developmental Medicine and Child Neurology* 37: 56–71.

Bradley, L., Bryant, P.E. (1979) The independence of reading and spelling in backward and normal readers. *Developmental Medicine and Child Neurology* 21: 504–14.

Bronfenbrenner U. (1986) Ecology of the family as a context for human development. *Developmental Psychology* 22: 723–42.

Brooks-Gunn J., Klebanov P.K., Duncan, G.J. (1996) Ethnic differences in children's intelligence test scores: Role of economic deprivation, home environment and maternal characteristics. *Child Development* 67: 396–408.

Campbell F.A., Ramey C.T. (1994) Effects of an early intervention on intellectual and academic achievement: A follow-up study of children from low-income families. *Child Development* 65: 684–98.

Caughy M.O'B., DiPietro J.A., Strobino D.M. (1994) Day-care participation as a protective factor in the cognitive development of low-income children. *Child Development* 65: 457–471.

Chapman J.W. (1992) Learning disabilities in New Zealand: Why Kiwis and kids with learning disorders can't fly. *Journal of Learning Disorders* 25: 362–70.

Detterman D. (1996) *Current Topics in Human Intelligence. Volume 5, The Environ-ment.* Norwood, NJ: Ablex.

Eisenberg L. (1966) Reading retardation: I. Psychiatric and sociologic aspects. *Pediatrics* 37: 352–65.

Fergusson D.M., Lloyd M., Horwood L.J. (1991) Family ethnicity, social background and scholastic achievement: An eleven year longitudinal study. *New Zealand Journal of Educational Studies* 26: 49–63.

Fergusson D.M., Horwood L.J., Lynskey M.T. (1992) Family change, parental discord and early offending. *Journal of Child Psychology and Psychiatry* 33: 1059–75.

Fergusson D.M., Horwood L.J., Lynskey M.T. (1993) Early dentine lead levels and subsequent cognitive and behavioural development. *Journal of Child Psychology and Psychiatry* 34: 215–27.

Frick, P.J., Schmidt M.H., Lahey B.B., *et al.* (1991) Academic underachievement and the disruptive behaviour disorders. *Journal of Consulting and Clinical Psychology* 59: 289–94.

Gorman K.S., Pollitt E. (1996) Does schooling buffer the effects of early risk? *Child Development* 67: 314–26.

Goswami, U. (1994) Development of reading and spelling skills. In: Rutter M., Hay D. (eds) *Development Through Life: A handbook for clinicians.* Oxford: Blackwell Scientific, pp. 284–302.

Hallahan D.P., Kauffman J.M. (1991) *Exceptional Children.* 5th ed. Englewood Cliffs, NJ: Prentice Hall.

Horn W.F., Packard T. (1985) Early identification of learning problems: A meta-analysis. *Journal of Educational Psychology* 77: 597–607.

Hyde J.S., Linn M.C. (1988) Gender differences in verbal ability: A meta-analysis. *Psychological Bulletin* 104: 53–69.

Lewitter F.I., DeFries J.C., Elston R.C. (1980) Genetic models of reading disability. *Behaviour Genetics* 10: 9–30.

MacLean M., Bryant P.E., Bradley L. (1987) Rhymes, nursery rhymes and reading in early childhood. *Merrill-Palmer Quarterly* 33: 255–82.

Maughan B. (1995) Annotation: Long-term outcomes of developmental reading problems. *Journal of Child Psychology and Psychiatry* 36: 357–71.

Maughan B., Yule M. (1994) Reading and other learning disabilities. In: Rutter M., Taylor E., Hersov L. (eds) *Child and Adolescent Psychiatry.* 3rd edn. Oxford: Blackwell Scientific, pp. 647–65.

Maughan B., Pickles A., Hagell A., *et al.* (1996) Reading problems and antisocial behaviour: Developmental trends in comorbidity. *Journal of Child Psychology and Psychiatry* 37: 405–18.

McGee R., Williams S., Share D.L., *et al.* (1986) The relationships between specific learning retardation, general reading backwardness and behavioural problems in a large sample of Dunedin boys. *Journal of Child Psychology and Psychiatry* 27: 597–610.

Morisset C.E., Barnard K.E., Booth C.L. (1995) Toddlers' language development: Sex differences within social risk. *Developmental Psychology* 31: 851–65.

Morrison F.J., Smith L., Dow-Ehrensberger M. (1995) Education and cognitive development: A natural experiment. *Developmental Psychology* 31: 789–99.

O'Connor S., Spreen O. (1988) The relationship between parents' socioeconomic status and education level and adult occupational and educational achieve-ment of children with learning disabilities. *Journal of Learning Disabilities* 21: 148–53.

Pennington B.F., Groisser D., Welsh M.C. (1993) Contrasting cognitive deficits in attention deficit hyperactivity disorder versus reading disability. *Developmental Psychology* 29: 511–23.

Pianta R.C., Egeland B. (Forthcoming) Predictors of instability of children's mental test performance at 24, 48, and 96 months. *Intelligence*.

Pianta R.C., McCoy S. (1997) The first day of school: the predictive validity of early school screening. *Journal of Applied Developmental Psychology*, 18: 1–22.

Pianta R.C., O'Connor T.G. (1996) Developmental challenges to the study of specific environmental effects: An argument for niche-level influences. In: Detterman D. (ed.) *Current Topics in Human Intelligence. Volume 5, The Environment*. Norwood, NJ: Ablex, pp. 45–58.

Plomin R. (1994) *Genes and Experience: The Interplay between nature and nurture*. Thousand Oaks, CA: Sage.

Pungello E.P., Kupersmidt J.B., Burchinal M.R., Patterson C.J. (1996) Environmental risk factors and children's achievement from middle childhood to early adolescence. *Development Psychology* 32: 755–67.

Rawson M. (1968) *Developmental Language Disability: Adult accomplishments of dyslexic boys*. Baltimore: Johns Hopkins University Press.

Rourke B.P. (1983) Outstanding issues in research on learning disabilities. In: Rutter M. (ed.) *Developmental Neuropsychiatry*. New York: Guilford, pp. 564–76.

Rutter M., Smith D.J. (eds) (1995) *Psychosocial Disorders in Young People: Time trends and their causes*. Chichester: Wiley.

Rutter M., Yule W. (1970) Reading retardation and antisocial behaviour – the nature of the association. In: Rutter M., Tizard J., Whitmore K., (eds) *Education, Health and Behaviour*. London: Longmans, pp. 240–55.

Rutter M., Tizard J., Whitmore K. (1970) *Education, Health and Behaviour*. London: Longmans.

Sameroff A.J., Seifer R., Barocas R., et al. (1987) Intelligence quotient scores of 4-year-old children: Social environment risk factors. *Pediatrics* 79: 343–50.

Sanson A., Prior M., Smart D. (1996) Reading disabilities with and without behaviour problems at 7–8 years: Prediction from longitudinal data from infancy to 6 years. *Journal of Child Psychology and Psychiatry* 37: 529–41.

Seitz V., Apfel N.H. (1994) Parent-focused intervention: Diffusion effects on siblings. *Child Development* 65: 677–83.

Shinn M.R., Ysseldyke J.E., Deno S.L., Tindal G.A. (1986) A comparison of differences between students labelled learning disabled and low achieving on measures of classroom performance. *Journal of Learning Disabilities* 9: 545–52.

Silva P.A., McGee R., Williams S. (1985) Some characteristics of 9-year-old boys with general reading backwardness or specific reading retardation. *Journal of Child Psychology and Psychiatry* 26: 407–21.

Stevenson J. (1991) Which aspects of processing text mediate genetic effects? *Reading and Writing: An Interdisciplinary Journal* 3: 249–69.

Super C.M., Harkness S. (1986) The developmental niche: A conceptualisation at the interface of child and culture. *International Journal of Behavioral Development* 9: 545–69.

Taubes G. (1995) Epidemiology faces its limits. *Science* 269: 164–9.

Wachs T.D., Moussa W., Bishry Z., et al. (1993) Relation between nutrition and cognitive performance. *Intelligence* 17: 151–72.

Wagner R.K., Torgesen J.K., Rashotte C.A. (1994) Development of reading-related phonological processing abilities: New evidence of bi-directional causality from a latent variable longitudinal study. *Developmental Psychology* 30: 73–87.

Walker D., Greenwood C., Hart B., Carta J. (1994) Prediction of school outcomes based on early language production and socioeconomic factors. *Child Development* 65: 606–21.

World Health Organization (1993) *The ICD-10 Classification of Mental and Behavioural Disorders: Diagnostic criteria for research.* Geneva: World Health Organization.

Source

This is an edited version of a chapter previously published in K. Whitmore, H. Hart and G. Willems (eds) *A Neurodevelopmental Approach to Specific Learning Disorders.* 2001. Reproduced by permission of Mac Keith Press.

Part 5

How can political, social and cultural factors impact upon individual difficulties with literacy?

Chapter 17

Myths of illiteracy

Childhood memories of reading in London's East End

Eve Gregory

Introduction

> I realised that books speak of books; it is as if they spoke among themselves.
> It [the library] was the place of a long murmuring, an imperceptible dialogue
> between one parchment and another, a living thing, a receptacle of powers
> not to be ruled by human mind, a treasure of secrets . . . surviving the death
> of those who had produced them.
>
> (Eco, 1980: 286)

In late twentieth century Britain, a paradigm of early literacy prevails within
which the home *story-reading* experience, taking place between parent and
child, is seen as an essential prerequisite for later school success. During the
1970s, responsibility for children's early educational success shifted noticeably
from the school to the parents and the family environment. Official education reports during the 1970s and 1980s stressed the 'vitally important role'
(DES, 1975: 5.1) played by parents in preparing a young child for school. As
regards literacy, reports left little doubt as to the precise material and form
necessary for these early reading experiences: 'the best way to prepare the very
young child for reading is to hold him on your lap and read aloud to him
stories he likes, over and over again. . . . We believe that a priority need is
. . . to help parents recognise the value of sharing the experience of books with
their children' (DES, 1975: 7.2).

The official view that 'Babies need books', and that it is the duty of parents
to provide these, has changed little in later decades; during the 1980s, the
directive states clearly that 'parents should read books with their children from
their earliest days, read aloud to them and talk about the stories they have
enjoyed together' (DES, 1988: 2.3). Very recently, we read that parents of the
very youngest children should support learning through 'reading and sharing
books' (SCAA, 1996: 7). This interest in one particular language activity has
meant that children are now considered 'disadvantaged' if they lack a knowledge of language in one context: that of written narrative.

This view of what differentiates 'good' from 'poor' parenting has gained
momentum throughout the 1980s and 1990s. It was enhanced by results from

a ten-year longitudinal study of 128 children's literacy performance at ages 7 and 11 (Wells, 1985, 1987); this work claimed that, of all the factors in pre-school literacy investigated, only listening to written stories at home had a strong correlation with early school literacy success. This finding alone would have been uncontentious; schools were teaching reading using precisely the texts that such children would be familiar with from home. However, the reports went further to claim that the absence of story-reading in lower social-class homes meant that children continued a cycle of disadvantage and failure. Such children, the findings claimed, 'urgently need the experience of books and being read to' (Wells, 1987: 146).

Where does this leave children whose families either cannot or do not participate in this activity? Must unfamiliarity with one particular literacy prac-tice mean that a child is 'disadvantaged' as a reader in school? A number of studies claim this to be the case (Heath, 1982; Wells, 1985; Segel, 1994). Consequently, little attention has been paid to families who do not share these ways of life. In the present chapter, I examine a contrasting paradigm of home literacy, and I argue against the view that disadvantage leads to school diffi-culty. I investigate early reading in the lives of different generations living in Spitalfields, East London – who, in the terms of Bourdieu (1977), did not share the cultural capital of story-reading possessed by some children upon entering school. In other words, they were not trained in a set of knowledges, prac-tices, and dispositions: of looking like a reader, being familiar with the materials of school, citing from appropriate texts, etc. (Carrington and Luke, 1997), as did some of their 'school-oriented' peers who lived in more favoured areas. However, unlike studies that point to difficulties experienced by chil-dren in calling upon 'unofficial' literacy knowledge in school (Heath, 1983; Michaels, 1986), the present study gives a voice to readers across languages, cultures, and generations, in two schools, who used their home knowledge to become 'successful' readers in the eyes of society.

In this chapter I outline key features of a paradigm of successful early literacy that is distinct from that upheld in official reports and the educational press. The theoretical framework informing this research synthesises perspectives from the 'New Literacy Studies', cultural psychology, and cultural anthro-pology. The New Literacy Studies support an ideological model of literacy which signals explicitly that literacy practices are aspects not only of culture but also of power structures (Street, 1995; Baynham, 1995). Viewed in this way, school-sanctioned literacy – or 'Literacy', as referred to by Street (1995: 14) – is just one of a multiplicity of literacies which take place in people's lives, in different domains, for a variety of purposes and in different languages. Within this model, children and adults draw upon a number of 'mediators of literacy'; such a mediator is defined as 'a person who makes his or her skills available to others, on a formal or informal basis, for them to accomplish specific literacy purposes' (Baynham, 1995: 39). They may be teachers at out-of-school community language classes, clubs, drama activities, etc.; or they may be 'guiding lights' – mediators of literacy who are especially inspiring as mentors or role models, such as grandparents (Padmore, 1994) or siblings (Gregory, 1998).

Cultural psychology offers a 'cultural mediational model of reading' (Cole, 1996: 273) which stresses that

> successful adult efforts depend crucially upon their organising a 'cultural medium for reading' which . . . must use artefacts (most notably, but not only, the text), must be proleptic, and it must organise social relations to coordinate the child with the to-be-acquired system of mediation in an effective way.

This model recognises as vital the actual roles that significant 'experts' play in giving 'guided participation' (Rogoff, 1990) or 'scaffolding' (Bruner, 1986) to the learning of the novice. This concept is exemplified by the work of Wagner (1994), whose comparative study on children in Morocco shows how those engaged in formal learning of the Qur'an revealed different skills and strategies from those whose literacy learning took place only within the official school.

Nevertheless, an important argument of this chapter is that young people are not trapped within any single practice of early childhood literacy. The families in all phases of this study reveal a complex heterogeneity of traditions whereby reading practices from different domains are blended, resulting in a form of reinterpretation which is both new and dynamic. Duranti and Ochs (1996) refer to this type of blending as *syncretic literacy*, which merges not simply linguistic codes or texts, but different *activities*. Their example is the activity of doing homework by Samoan Americans, and they provide a fine-tuned analysis of the way in which Samoan and American traditions, languages, teaching and child-rearing strategies are blended. In the present study, I argue that *contrasting* home and school strategies and practices may provide children with a enlarged treasure trove, upon which they can draw in the official English school.

The setting

> 'What will save East London?' asked one of our University visitors of his master. 'The destruction of West London' was the answer and, insofar as he meant the abolition of the space which divides rich and poor, the answer was right. Not until the habits of the rich are changed and they are again content to breathe the same air and walk the same streets as the poor will East London be saved.
>
> (Speech of Canon Barnett, founder of Toynbee Hall, the Universities' settlement in Spitalfields, at St. John's, Oxford, 17 November 1883)

The participants in this study spent their childhood in the neighbourhood of Spitalfields in the East London Borough of Tower Hamlets.[1] Separated firmly from the traditions and conformity of the City of London, by Aldgate and Bishopsgate to the west and north, this square mile has always been known for its contrasts of poverty and wealth. From the twelfth century, it was a refuge for dissidents and the home of nonconformity; a stone's throw from the City, onlookers could view the pillories that held Baptists, Quakers, and others seeking 'liberty' from the required oaths. During the century following the edict of Nantes (1685), which outlawed French Protestants from their country, at least seven French churches were built. By 1750, the area had a fabric-like patchwork reflecting its population; the minority of wealthy French silk merchants built fine Georgian houses, yet these were few between the narrow, timber-framed tenements of the poor artisans. Records tell us that, in the mid-eighteenth century, the parish scavengers could speak only French (Sheppard, 1975). Just over a century later, the language and culture had changed, but not the poverty. Between 1750 and 1901, the population almost doubled to 24,246, of whom 18,000 were of foreign birth. These inhabitants, largely Eastern European Jews speaking Yiddish and other Eastern European languages, worked their way out of abject slums; they often progressed from working for others in the tailoring trade to managing their own shop, stall, or small business. By the 1960s, all but a handful had disappeared to live in the wealthier, more suburban areas of north and northeast London.

In the last two decades of the twentieth century, the area of Spitalfields has undergone rapid and dramatic change which polarises yet further the contrasts of poverty and wealth. Money from the City is spilling over to the east. The earnings of a growing number of City workers, especially in the financial sector, have exploded, resulting in a mushrooming of wine-bars and restaurants, which overflow during lunch breaks and after-work gatherings. Along-side these, previously neglected old Victorian warehouses, schools, and even the former Jewish soup kitchen are suddenly being renovated, their exterior façades restored to their original beauty, and their interiors converted into luxury pied-à-terre apartments for the business world. Significantly, the new population has little real commitment to the area. At weekends the area empties out and appears abandoned. Most City workers return to their country homes; the restaurants, wine-bars, and pubs remain closed, leaving champagne bottles alongside other rubbish piled up in the picturesque Victorian alleys.

At these times, Spitalfields' 'invisible' yet majority community comes to light – a community worlds apart from the City and its wealth. This community lives largely tucked away in side streets, in local authority accommodation. Some families survive in impossibly cramped conditions with seven or more children in a small Victorian apartment, and only an internal courtyard in which the children can play. The centre of the community is the new housing development built on the site of Jack the Ripper's first murder. Families living in these houses are the luckier ones; spacious accommodation is built around a tree-lined and paved courtyard, with a Community Centre where Qur'anic and Bengali classes take place.

This community consists of the new British whose origins lie in Sylhet, a region in northeastern Bangladesh; their mother-tongue is Sylheti, a local variety of Bengali. Although there had been a tradition since the 1920s of men from Sylhet working on British merchant vessels and jumping ship, larger numbers arrived only during the 1960s and 1970s. They came principally to escape poverty and landlessness; and their initial aim was to acquire a job, save money, and return home (Adams, 1987). At the end of the twentieth century, Spitalfields houses a Bangladeshi British population of approximately 36,000, of whom 95 per cent are from Sylhet.[2] The old Jewish synagogue has become a mosque; shops and restaurants are Bangladeshi owned. Only occasional street names like 'Adler Street' and one remaining 24-hour 'Biegelbake' (a bread and bagel shop) reveal the area's earlier history.

Although Bangladeshi British are often regarded as a homogeneous cultural group, different generations, or even individuals of the same generation, may be worlds apart. One section of the Bangladeshi British community,[3] though sometimes more than twenty years in Britain, remains isolated from the local networks of English speakers, and from public institutions in Britain where the dominant culture is reproduced. Young women who have been educated in rural Bangladesh, and who speak very little English, have often joined much older husbands in London during the last ten years. Life for this group generally revolves around the family, the mosque, neighbours, and shops – many of which sell a variety of books and newspapers in Bengali. Many families prefer to watch videos in Hindi, rather than English television, with the result that some of their young children understand more Hindi than English upon school entry.

However, a new generation of Bangladeshi British men and women, now in their twenties, have been born and educated in Britain. Living and learning in Britain has led to remarkable changes, particularly for many Bangladeshi British girls. In contrast with their peers who come from Bangladesh as young brides to older men, many young Bangladeshi British women are independent, strong – and in spite of economic difficulties, have been successful in the British school system. Whether or not the women follow tradition and marry Bangladeshi or Bangladeshi British husbands, they are knowledgeable about the British educational system, and they are anxious for their children to succeed. At school parents' meetings, therefore, we now find professional Bangladeshi British women, alongside those who have received their schooling in rural Sylhet and entered Britain only at the time of their marriage.

The study

The findings presented below are drawn from a larger study which has been taking place over six years.[4] The study examines the home, school, and community reading practices of past and present generations of teachers and pupils in two Spitalfields schools. The part of the study presented below coincides with the introduction, by the New Labour Government in Britain, of measures to increase parental responsibility in their children's learning through 'home–school contracts' which will attempt to instil school practices in the home.[5] In many schools of this area, there is already a move to encourage children to attend school homework clubs, instead of community language classes. This part of the Spitalfields study, therefore, aims to examine the reading histories and memories of two groups of ex-pupils who have succeeded in school while *not* working within the official school paradigm of what counts as a successful reader.[6]

The data for this part of the study comprise in-depth interviews lasting one and a half to two hours, following a phenomenographic approach (Francis, 1993). According to this approach, subjects speak freely on the topics proposed by the interviewer, as well as suggesting their own. The subjects in this phase of the research have been asked to talk about their memories of going to school in the area, of home language and literacy traditions, of learning to read at school and at home, of the role played by their family and other mediators of literacy, of 'guiding lights' in their literary development, and of their current reading habits. Each interview has been transcribed in full and analysed by highlighting common categories.

Participants in the study

The two groups of participants in this part of the Spitalfields study are: (a) young professional Bangladeshi British women in their twenties, born and educated in Britain, and (b) Jewish or non-Jewish or indigenous English men and women over 40. All the subjects are alumni of two adjacent schools which have long been establishments of learning. One school, just within the boundary of the City, was founded by a philanthropic alderman and has been educating children for nearly three centuries (see Williams, 1997). It is a Church of England school which currently has approximately 70 per cent Bangladeshi children on roll. The other, a Victorian Board school, was one hundred years old at the turn of the century. Until the 1950s, many of its pupils were Jewish, and it catered by having a Jewish kitchen. Now all its children speak English as an additional language; 98 per cent are Bangladeshi British and Sylheti speakers, and its kitchen has become *halal*. Although both schools now have only Primary-aged children (3–11), both formerly provided education to age 14 – the statutory leaving age until 1945, when the older participants in this study were at school.

The older generation

Unlike some rural communities in the US (see especially Heath, 1983), this is an area of considerable change; many ex-pupils have departed from the immediate neighbourhood, from London, and even from Britain. Thus ex-pupils above the age of 40 are not easy to trace. Help in finding nine older ex-pupils was provided by local organisations, by word-of-mouth in the schools, and by the Springboard Educational Trust for Jewish history in London. The only criterion for selection of the subjects was that they all had lived in the area as children, and had attended one of the two schools for a number of years. Therefore it cannot be claimed that the group is generally representative of older ex-pupils of the schools.

All still live within 100 miles of the schools. Abby, Norma, and Gloria are Jewish, and are active in their community. Abby, the eldest, aged 82, still lives just next to the school in her small apartment on the Flower and Dean estate. Her walls are lined with books on every possible topic, and she claims that she has read them all. Abby is well-known to the school in her role as ex-governor.[7] She started as a pupil at one of the schools in 1920 at the age of three, and continued there until she was eleven, when she went to the Jewish Free School until she was fourteen. She now represents the elderly on the Health and Community Care Council; she is also in the Pensioners' Action Group and the Joint Planning Group for people with disabilities in the area. Norma, aged 68, has moved to a wealthy area in north London, where she lives in a large detached house with a magnificent, established garden. As a child, she lived with her younger brother and sister in two rooms, adjacent to the same school as Abby. Her parents ran a market stall. Norma remembers, 'they worked very, very hard from morning to evening. They fed us and clothed us, but they didn't teach us anything. I learned to read in school.' She also recalls telling her teachers: 'My daddy says, "One day, we're going to live in a nice house in Hendon."' Although she had no idea at the time where Hendon was, this is where she now lives, sixty years later. Gloria, nine years her junior, also attended the school. Her family was poorer than Norma's, as her father worked as a presser: 'He wasn't, I think, a top presser, and there was only the one income.' Gloria also now lives in a favoured suburb, close to Norma. Both are active as workers for the Jewish Board of Deputies and in other charitable activities.

Ronald, Linda, and Anthony are second-generation Irish, whose parents were so poor that Raymond, the eldest, remembers feeling lucky to have an orange as a Christmas present. Raymond attended one of the schools, Linda and Anthony the other. Christine's parents came from Wiltshire to London to find work; Richard and Eileen's parents came from just five miles down the road further east. Both fathers joined the large army of 'housekeepers' who 'cared for' the City office blocks.[8] Their mothers took on small jobs, making tea or cleaning the offices.

It is interesting to note that, although the participants have had very different lives and fortunes, many of the group have continued into higher education. Older participants all emphasised the struggle involved in this. Richard was assisted by the links between his football club and Oxford University to gain an exhibition there in the 1950s; Anthony and his sister Linda (also siblings of Ronald) managed to study only after a lengthy break from school. During this time, Anthony went 'from rags to riches' through a number of varied jobs, while Linda stayed at home bringing up a family. It is

Table 17.1 Data on participants

Name	Age	Education	Profession	Lives in area
Abby	82	14	horticulturalist	yes
Norma	68	15	charitable work	no
Richard	63	higher	lecturer	no
Gloria	58	15	charitable work	no
Ronald	52	15	unemployed	yes
Christine	51	higher	podiatrist	no
Eileen	50	higher	lecturer	no
Linda	44	higher	teacher	no
Anthony	40	higher	teacher/actor	no
Annia	29	16	social work	yes
Afia	27	16	housewife	yes
Rumi	26	16	class assistant	yes
Halima	23	higher	charitable trust	no

* higher = degree or higher degree

noticeable that, of the older generation (40+), only two of the nine – Ronald and Abby – are still living in the area. All but one entered teaching or the 'caring professions' (see Table 17.1). Only Ronald, who had experienced considerable difficulties in school learning, which he put down to constant ear infections and lengthy hospitalisation, is currently unemployed.

The older generation share an ambivalent view of the area in which they grew up. All remember that their parents aspired to leave the poverty associated with the area. In spite of this, all except Raymond (the only person who still lives in the area) have happy memories of both their teachers and schools. Significantly, perhaps, Raymond assigns his unhappiness to being seen as 'stupid' by his teachers – a consequence of his deafness, which was undetected for a number of years.

The younger generation

The four younger subjects (Annia, Afia, Rumi, and Halima) are Bangladeshi British women in their twenties. They were selected to represent the new generation of Bangladeshi British women whose parents came to Britain either before they were born, or when they were of preschool age. Three of the four have young children who attend one of the schools. Halima attended this school for a short time herself – as did her brother and sister, who now also have young children at the school. All the other women grew up and attended neighbouring schools in the area.

These women's views on language, literacy, and child-rearing practices are important, in that they will form part of the knowledge brought by their children into school. In many respects, the group is very different from women educated in Bangladesh who are often just a few years their senior. The young women are fluent English and Sylheti speakers, ambitious for themselves and for their children. Yet all the group stress the importance of bilingualism and biculturalism for their children. All their children attend Mosque and Bengali classes. Insofar as most see the future of their families as being outside Spitalfields, they parellel the Jewish families living in the area half a century earlier. However, the two groups differ in at least three important aspects. First, while the older generation of Jewish subjects saw themselves as 'English', and praised their school for giving them knowledge of the English literature and culture – knowledge which in no way threatened their 'Jewishness' – these young women stress their view of themselves as 'Bangladeshi British'. Second, the older Jewish generation grew up in an age where most people managed to obtain some form of work; Norma's stall-holding parents were typical of many who 'made good'. But all the younger women speak of wanting to leave the area for fear that their children will take on bad habits, become drug-takers, fall into crime, fail to pass exams, and risk unemployment. Third, the older generation mentioned only a low level of racism against Jews, and all remembered going out freely after dark; but the younger women have the fear of attack at the forefront of their minds. They ensure that their children do not venture out alone to their community classes.

Findings

The purposes of reading

The dominant home story-reading practice equates 'fun' with 'serious work' (i.e., serious learning can be fun); but participants in this study differentiated strictly between the two. Exams and tests figure importantly in all the subjects' lives. After studying for their degrees late in life, Linda and Anthony want to return to complete a master's degree, because learning is 'addictive':

Linda: I don't really enjoy reading, but I do enjoy studying. I read to study, really . . .
Interviewer: Why do you want to keep on studying, do you think?
Linda: So as not to be a fraud.

Linda voices the paradox, existing generally in the group, that 'studying' is more important, and indeed more enjoyable, than 'reading for fun'. For all the participants, school learning is serious; it must be earned, not simply given. The purpose of learning to read and of reading is principally for 'learning' or 'self-improvement'; the notion of 'having to prove oneself' is strong among older and younger subjects alike.

    Learning to read in school has not come easy to many. All the younger women had experienced some apprehension and difficulty when learning to read in English in school. In spite of having later gained a master's degree at a prestigious London university, Halima (age 23) still remains aware of this:

I always used to feel limited with my English language 'cos I felt I never had enough words to play with. In the third year we went to Bangladesh for 14 months and I became even more obsessed with my lack of vocabulary . . . and then I worked out that if you read a lot of books it improves your learning anyway and it did. I think I spent one summer trying to get my reading. . . . At that age [nine] I hadn't really worked it out that by reading you develop in so many ways, your critical abilities, your faculties, your spelling, your learning. You know, I didn't consciously work it out in my head, but subconsciously I worked it out. 'Oh, it's getting easier, what you have to do . . .'

All the younger Bangladeshi British women want to return to study when their children are more independent.

Of the older group, Christine (51), Ronald (52), and Gloria (58) vividly remember having difficulties with learning to read. Christine says:

I missed out on learning to read. I could have had a bit of dyslexia . . . my daughter's dyslexic [though she has now studied at university]. So it runs in the family. I couldn't tell a 'b' from a 'd'. I can't tell my left from my right, lots of strange things. . . . But words I've learned later on in my professional life, long chemical words, no problem. But what I learned pre-ten year old, I just can't cope with. And I don't worry. That's the lovely thing. It doesn't worry me . . .

Christine went on to study podiatry, is proud of having just completed History 'A' level, and says she is 'always studying for something'.

Gloria experienced similar problems:

I can't spell very well. . . . At the age of six, I had a very severe bout of jaundice and I was in hospital for six months . . . at no time did a teacher come to teach us. You know, I was just left there. And therefore, whether that was the reason, or whether I was just a slow learner, I didn't start reading properly until I was about nine or ten . . .

Both Ronald and Abby also lost months of schooling, owing to hospitalisation for ear trouble, and experienced set-backs in their reading. All three went on to become fluent and avid readers, yet none takes the privilege of reading and learning for granted.

At 82, Abby sums up the seriousness of reading throughout her long life:

I used my reading for learning. I went to evening classes, then I had to pass exams for gardening. I did those when I was in the land army for a year, for the Royal Horticultural Society, then I did the second class exam, written and practical, then the first class which is the equivalent of Kew . . . now I'm on the Community Health Council for the elderly group. I'm also on the Pensioners' Action group and the joint planning group for people with disabilities.

Reading may also be occasional pure escapism into an unreal world, strictly differentiated from 'reading as a serious matter'. All the participants in the study spoke of Enid Blyton's *Sunny Stories*, even *Little Black Sambo*; individual titles like *Angela of Brazil* stuck in Norma's mind. Eileen loved the Rudyard Kipling stories. Both generations lived for the weekly comics, and devoured those for children as well as their mothers' *Woman's Own*. Both Norma (68) and Anthony (40) stress that reading enabled them to escape the grim reality of their everyday poverty:

> Reading takes you to a faraway place. Like the first book I ever read. . . . I was eight years old and the first book I ever read cover to cover was *The Waving Bamboos*, which was about pandas in China. Fabulous book. And I was in China. You know, before I knew where I was, I was wafted off to China. There was these pandas roaming around the place and it was fuel for the imagination. You know, before I knew where I was, I was literally in China . . .

Mediators and access points for literacy in children's lives

In contrast with the current emphasis on the responsibility of the parent as story-provider and reader, childhood initiation into literacy is seen by the participants in this study as a collaborative group activity, whereby the cultural knowledge of generations is passed on through a whole variety of mediators and methods. This in no way denies the vitally important part played by parents in fostering children's literacy development. However, the nature of the role is very different from that of story-reader in a dyadic relationship with one child. It is also very different between the older and younger generations of parents.

For the older generation (40+), parental participation in their children's reading took two forms: (a) passing down literacy-related knowledge in the widest sense; and (b) enabling access for the child to learn from other mediators of literacy, through encouragement and provision of opportunity. The passing down of literacy-related practices highlights the variety of skills that do not involve traditional story-reading or the presence of 'good' literature. Anthony and Linda's mother told stories. She had been born in a work-house (a dreaded prison-like institution for the homeless and destitute in nineteenth-century Britain), and her tales were imprinted in their minds. As Linda says:

> When the electric used to go out 'cos you didn't have two shillings for the meter, she used to tell you stories and we enjoyed that. . . . She [her mother] was born in the work-house. It was a real story . . . I've been meaning to write it down for 30 years. I remember it all . . .

Other parents passed on a variety of skills; from the age of five, Richard and Eileen learned to read music at the same time as nursery-rhyme texts. Christine remembers that, although her parents were too busy to read, she watched her grandmother – who could listen to the radio, read a thick book, and knit a complicated pattern all at the same time. Her father also practised sums on scraps of paper with her. Gloria (a second generation immigrant whose family came from Poland) relates how she and her mother regularly escaped from the gloom of the East End, where her father worked as a presser, to the glamour of the West End of London:

> My mother had ideas above her station. She liked to take me to Lyons Corner House [famous restaurant and coffee house in the West End] and she taught me how to use a serviette and general table manners and not talking with food in your mouth and not eating with your mouth open. . . . She would take me to matinees at the theatre and show me how to behave . . .

However, the main role of parents was to provide access for the child to both mediators and access points to culture, as well as to literacy outside the home. Three major access points proved significant in the families' lives, and are outlined briefly below: Toynbee Hall (Universities' Settlement), which figured prominently in the lives of all the 40+ group; religious or community classes, which were and are significant for both Jewish and Bangladeshi British participants; and the library, which has been of importance for everyone.

The magic of Toynbee Hall

The older generation all spoke of the 'magic' of one very special access point for language, culture, and literacy in Spitalfields: Toynbee Hall (Universities' Settlement). This was founded in 1884, financed by Colleges of Oxford and Cambridge to be a society formed of members of all classes, creeds, and opinions, with the aim of trying to pass on to East London the best gifts of the age. A replica inside and out of a traditional College, it had 15 rooms for residents from the universities, a lecture hall, seminar rooms, reception rooms, etc. It would be impossible to list the scope of activities taking place here, or portray the importance it held in the lives of those over 40. Anthony sums it up:

> I went to drama club there. It was brilliant. . . . It was the beginning . . . 'cos I went into entertainment. One of our teachers is a famous producer now. . . . I did my first play when I was ten and a half. It was called 'The Italian straw hat'. It's a very old Italian play. I'd only been there six months and I was saying, 'I can do that. No problem . . .'. And Toynbee is a world in itself. To me, it was escapism, somewhere I could go to and get away from my real life which was horrible. . . . Toynbee Hall has always been

the place. And that's never changed. Asian, Jewish, Catholics . . . Toynbee Hall has never, ever changed. Yes, Toynbee Hall was a brilliant experience for me . . .

Anthony went on to become an actor, as did others attending these inspirational classes. Abby, Norma, and Gloria remember lectures, English and dance classes, and Brownies meetings. Richard was entered for piano exams there, and still has piano classes. The poorest children of the area sat alongside dignitaries invited to speak. Tea-time lectures in the hall featured Lenin, who predicted a bloody uprising of the colonies against Britain, as well as Marconi, who demonstrated the first wireless in 1896. Unfortunately, by the end of the twentieth century, very few classes remained, and none of the young Bangladeshi British women mention any significance of Toynbee in their lives.

Religious classes: learning for the life hereafter

Perhaps the most significant access point for childhood literacy, in the outside-school lives of both young Bangladeshi British women and older Jewish participants, were the community and religious classes. For the former group, this meant up to twelve hours per week at Bengali and/or Qur'anic classes; the Jewish participants, as girls, were only required to attend Hebrew classes on Saturday. Nevertheless, they were steeped in the knowledge and traditions brought home by their brothers, who attended such classes for an amount of time similar to that of the younger Bangladeshi British group. The role of religious classes in the literacy development of children has generally received little attention; but some studies have been undertaken (Zinsser, 1986; Gregory, 1994) that detail ways in which children learn to read different scripts, using a variety of methods, as well as procedural rules of how to behave in formal classrooms. The importance of both Qur'anic and Bengali classes has remained undiminished in the lives of young Bangladeshi British women: Afia's daughter started Qur'anic classes for a short time at age three, and will return when she is five; Rumi and Annia's children – at five, six, and seven – attend both classes. Both older Jewish and younger Bangladeshi British participants stress the importance of religious classes in giving them 'a sense of belonging'. Thus the teaching of reading was and remains a collaborative activity provided by different mediators, parents, and teachers in community classes, for different purposes. This is true even when parents appear to be capable of providing tuition themselves.

The library

Finally, all participants emphasise the place of the local library as a vital access point for literacy and culture in their early lives. The library held particular importance for older Jewish participants whose parents had been recent immigrants. Norma speaks for other families that share her background:

> I remember going to the library on my own. It used to be pitch black
> . . . my mother didn't have any time to devote to me . . . although they
> were ambitious for me, they didn't have time to teach me anything . . .
> but my mother did send me to elocution classes . . .

Undoubtedly, the importance of the library was partly due to the dominance
of the Whitechapel Library which opened in 1893, with 20,734 books, and
with a Reading Room with the prime aim of being 'a friend to the people of
Whitechapel' (as stated by Canon Barnett in the formal opening speech). The
library played a vital role as an access point for literacy, since it enabled children to take hold of their own learning – to syncretise knowledge and
experiences from home, school, and community classes through interpreting
the borrowed book. In Halima's words:

> I think in my third year I started taking books home. I discovered books
> if you like. Prior to that, it was something I just did because the teacher
> told you to . . .

Toynbee Hall and the library show the importance of community resources as
access points for literacy in these children's lives. These resources opened
doors to literacies far beyond the reach of their parents – literacies which
became part of their own cultural capital, to be passed on to their children in
later life.

Syncretism of home, school, and community literacy practices

The existing paradigm of 'parental story-reading' not only assumes homogeneity of a reading practice with a single mediator of literacy; also, importantly, it implies a common knowledge shared between home and school,
whereby the child needs only to transfer knowledge and skills from one domain
to the other. Previous published work related to the research in this chapter
has also revealed the dynamic and innovative nature of teaching by older
Bangladeshi siblings, using a complex syncretism of Qur'anic and school
literacy practices (Gregory, 1998). Both studies show how contrasting home
and community strategies and practices may provide children with an enlarged
treasure trove on which they can draw in the English school. This argument
was put forward by older Jewish participants, who commented that their
knowledge of grammar and phonics from their Hebrew classes may well have
given them a head start over their English-speaking peers.

A different syncretism takes place as participants worked, or currently work,
with their own children – blending aspects of their own experiences with what
they interpret 'school reading' to demand. Both the younger and older generations who have had children contrast their own participation in their
children's reading with that of their parents. In Linda's words:

Whereas our Dad would say, 'Go to the library and make sure you do it', we would say, 'Let's see what it is and do it together.'

Linda and Anthony explain how they both taught their two-year-old infants to spell their names through singing them together; Linda's own daughter is repeating this with her own young child. This family talks of quizzes and games (Hangman, Scrabble, etc.) and poring over atlases, encyclopedias, and gardening books, as well as sharing newspapers and magazines. Their child-hood memories of reading in English at home span Enid Blyton, Ladybird (fairy stories), and Peter and Jane (a reading scheme).

The younger generation of Bangladeshi British women all work hard to teach their young children – blending what they themselves remember of reading in school (Ladybird fairy stories, the Peter and Jane reading scheme) with their home and community childhood reading experiences. Annia gives formal written comprehension and spelling exercises to her five- and six-year-olds; Afia also tests spelling, and has taught her three-year-old many nursery rhymes from tapes. As a classroom assistant, Rumi has access to school-based activities, and she incorporates play into a still formal teaching routine. Thus we see that a complex syncretism, both within and between reading practices, affords children a different kind of knowledge than that often expected by their teachers in school.

Conclusion

... there's nowhere in London that I love more than Spitalfields. Its trans-formation mirrors my own. I love some of the ways that it's changing. I love its vibrancy, the energy within it ... (Halima)

The evidence presented in this research reveals patterns of success by gener-ations of readers across languages and cultures in two school communities – readers who all insist upon the importance of their 'invisible' or 'unofficial' home and community literacy practices in contributing to their school reading success. Thus the evidence both supports and extends theories of literacy as a social and cultural practice. The evidence from this study questions the monolithic view of poverty that relates it to disadvantage in education, and particularly in literacy. Many subjects were proud of the area in which they grew up, equating it with dynamism, contrast, and change. It is precisely these features which are intrinsic to the alternative paradigm of early reading success that is suggested in this chapter – a paradigm based upon skill in mastering a variety of contrasting literacy activities, interacting with a range of literacy mediators and an ability to syncretise home, community, and school practices.

This work contributes to the growing number of studies in the US, Australia, and Britain on home and community literacies in the lives of urban families, and the ways that these contrast with the literacy which is counted as valid in school (Heath, 1983; Moll *et al.*, 1992; Freebody *et al.*, 1995; Bhatt and

Martin-Jones, 1996; Barton and Hamilton, 1998). All the above studies show the wealth of literacy practices in low-income families. However, the Spital-fields study is unique in tracing this wealth back across generations attending the same schools, and in showing how contrasting practices can, themselves, provide children with additional resources for use both in and outside school. Studies which link generations of pupils, attending the same schools in economically disadvantaged areas, are particularly important, since they can identify patterns of success by people whose families do not provide 'officially' recognised literacy support. Interestingly, the older (40+) generation felt that parental help in reading was not demanded by schools when they were young, but the younger group were aware of difference and exclusion. Paradoxically, this feeling of exclusion is most clearly voiced by Halima, academically the most successful of the younger group:

> I read Enid Blyton and The Famous Five. Prior to my 'A' levels I read a little bit. I tried to get acquainted with some of the classics but I got bored straight away. . . . I didn't read *Winnie-the-Pooh* or *The Jungle Book* or anything like that. You know, if I speak to a lot of my white friends, they were really into *Winnie-the-Pooh*. It was an integral part of their bed-time stories. You know, the concept of a bed-time story didn't exist in my family.
>   Interviewer: Would you have Bengali stories read to you?
>   Halima: No. It depends on the dynamics of your family unit. Some families do, some don't. It's got nothing to do with the nationality of a family. And I didn't have any *Winnie-the-Pooh* stories or their Bengali equivalent. So Enid Blyton I read . . .

Intergenerational studies are also important, since they reveal the wide range of mediators and access points for literacy in children's lives, and the ways that these may change over time. A number of recent studies emphasise the need to show that literacies are embedded in activities that are carried out for purposes other than direct reading instruction (Anderson and Stokes, 1984; Duranti and Ochs, 1996; Kale and Luke, 1997). While affirming this view, the research reported here suggests that parents play a vital role in providing opportunities for children to participate in activities with which they them-selves are unfamiliar. These opportunities (religious classes, drama, music lessons, Brownies, etc.) are the stepping stones to becoming literate in the wider world. Preliminary data suggest that access points to literacy available to older participants, as well as to younger Bangladeshi British women and their children, may already be undergoing replacement by TV, videos, and computers in the lives of their monolingual peers. Further research will be necessary to examine what effect these different mediators may have.

Finally, research across generations can trace the transformation and change in people's lives, their literacy development, the cultural and literacy practices in which they participate at different times, and the contrast of their involvement in children's reading versus that of their parents. As shown in Linda and Anthony's alphabet singing, in Annia's structured exercises, and in Afia's rhymes, their teaching syncretises childhood experiences of reading from home, community, and school with current ideas on what children need to know, rather than simply rejecting old learning. The result is something new, personal, and dynamic, and shows how success in reading and learning can step outside any single 'official' paradigm. Halima's slip of the tongue inadvertently says it all:

> and the only other book [besides Enid Blyton stories] that made an impact on me during my formative years was the Malcolm X autobiography. . . . I think that these writings make an impact on you because they address you as a political individual. You know, I'd read my *Withering Heights* and all the classics and the archetypal nineteenth-century English novels, but they were something separate to my own development . . .

Notes

1   Tower Hamlets has recently been criticised in official documents for its low standards of literacy both for children at ages 7 and 11 (Mortimore and Goldstein, 1996) and for adults (Basic Skills Unit, 1998).

2   The number 36,000 represents between 60.7 per cent (Decennial Census 1991) and 95 per cent (City Challenge) of the population of the community (information cited in Kershen, 1997). It should also be noted that there is undoubtedly a considerable number of illegal immigrants, as well as legal immigrants who were unwilling to declare themselves on the Census because of the Poll Tax then in operation (Kershen, 1997).

3   This is unanimously how the young generation interviewed describe themselves.

4   The findings below are drawn from a large bank of data, collected over six years, on home, school, and community reading practices among past and present generations of teachers and pupils in the two schools. The question investigated is: How have young children in Spitalfields, throughout the century, set about learning to read in their homes, schools, and community? The scope of the question is wide, and separate phases of the research have addressed different issues – attempting to piece together a complex jigsaw of the role of reading in the lives of families whose learning practices, in many cases, do not fit those required by 'official' school demands. Phases 1 and 2 of the research (1992–6) examined the literacy histories and current reading practices in seven Bangladeshi British and six monolingual English families whose five-year-old children attended the two neighbouring schools. The question investigated was: What is the nature of reading practices taking place in the children's lives, and how far do children transfer reading strategies from home to school and vice versa? (Gregory, 1994, 1998; Gregory and Williams, 1998). The mothers of all Bangladeshi British children in these earlier phases of the work had been educated in Bangladesh, as is still mostly the case for parents living in this area. This chapter draws principally upon data collected during Phase 3 of the research (1997–8); it investigates the reading histories and early reading memories of two groups: (a) past generations of pupils who have attended the schools who are now over 40 years of age; and (b) young professional Bangladeshi British mothers in their twenties, who themselves attended neighbouring schools and whose own children are now pupils of one of the two schools.

5   These were compulsory for all schools from September 1999.
6   A combination of methods from ethnography (participant observation, inter-
     views, life-histories, etc.) and ethnomethodology (conversation analysis) have
     been used during different phases of the work (Gregory and Williams, 1998).
     Members of the research team have all been teachers, and are very familiar with
     both the area and the schools. The family of the Bangladeshi British researcher
     had previously lived in the area; the principal researcher had been a pupil at
     one of the schools, and is Chair of Governors of the second school. This has
     given our work ecological validity (Cole, 1996) as well as facilitating access to
     families and permitting the collection of emic definitions of 'reading'. Data have
     been analysed using the method of multi-layering (Bloome and Theodorou,
     1987). This approach has enabled us to examine the social context within which
     individual functioning is embedded through in-depth ethnographic analyses (the
     outer layers) as well as individual teaching strategies, and the role of the child
     in negotiating interactions through conversation analysis (the inner layers); see
     Gregory, 1998.
7   Each school in Britain has a Governing body comprising parents and teachers,
     as well as political and commercial interests.
8   Although 'caretaker' might appear more appropriate, this group preferred the
     name 'housekeeper'. These were generally gifted men who could repair boilers
     and lifts, generally maintain buildings, and do accounts for cleaners' wages. They
     usually had no formal qualifications.

References

Adams, Caroline. 1987. *Across seven seas and thirteen rivers: Life stories of pioneer Sylheti settlers in Britain*. London: THAP.
Anderson, Alonzo and Stokes, Shelley. 1984. Social and institutional influences on the development and practice of literacy. In Hillel Goelman *et al.* (eds), *Awakening to literacy*, 24–37. Portsmouth, NH: Heinemann.
Barton, David and Hamilton, Mary. 1998. *Local literacies: Reading and writing in one community*. London: Routledge.
Basic Skills Unit. 1998. *A survey of adult basic skills in the United Kingdom*. London: Adult Literacy & Basic Skills.
Baynham, Mike. 1995. *Literacy practices: Investigating literacy in social contexts*. London: Longman.
Bhatt, Arvind and Martin-Jones, Marilyn. 1996. *Literacies at work in a multilingual city*. Economic and Social Research Council, Report R 22 1534.
Bloome, David and Theodorou, Erine. 1987. Analysing teacher–student and student–student discourse. In Judith Green and Judith O. Harker (eds) *Multiple analysis of classroom discourse processes*, 217–49. Norwood, NJ: Ablex.
Bourdieu, Pierre. 1977. *Outline of a theory of practice*. Cambridge: University Press.
Bruner, Jerome. 1986. *Actual minds, possible worlds*. Cambridge, MA: Harvard University Press.
Carrington, Vicki and Luke, Allan. 1997. Literacy and Bourdieu's sociological the-ory: A reframing. *Language and Education: An International Journal* 11(2): 96–112.
Cole, Michael. 1996. *Cultural psychology: A once and future discipline*. Cambridge, MA: Harvard University Press.
Cook-Gumperz, Jenny. (ed.) 1986. *The social construction of literacy*. Cambridge: University Press.
DES. 1975. *The Bullock report: A language for life*. London: HMSO.

DES. 1988. *The Cox Committee report: English for ages 5–11*. London: HMSO.

Duranti, Alessandro and Ochs, Elinor. 1996. Syncretic literacy in a Samoan American family. In Lauren B. Resnick *et al.* (eds), *Discourse, tools and reasoning*, 169–202. Berlin: Springer.

Eco, Umberto. 1980. *The name of the rose*. London: Picador.

Francis, Hazel. 1993. Advancing phenomenography: Questions of method. *Nordisk Pedagogik* 2: 68–75.

Freebody, Peter, Ludwig, Christine and Gunn, Stephanie. 1995. *Everyday literacy practices in and out of schools in low socio-economic urban communities*. Brisbane, Australia: Faculty of Education, Griffith University, and Dept. of Education, Queensland.

Gregory, Eve. 1994. Cultural assumptions and early years' pedagogy: The effect of the home culture on minority children's interpretation of reading in school. *Language, Culture and Curriculum* 7(2): 114–25.

Gregory, Eve. (ed.) 1997. *One child, many worlds: Early learning in multicultural communities*. New York: Teachers' College Press.

Gregory, Eve. 1998. Siblings as mediators of literacy in linguistic minority communities. *Language and Education: An International Journal* 11(1): 33–55.

Gregory, Eve and Williams, Ann. 1998. Family literacy history and children's learning strategies at home and at school: Perspectives from ethnography and ethno-methodology. In Geoffrey Walford and Alexander Massey (eds), *Children learning: Ethnographic explorations*, 194–46. Stamford, CT: JAI Press.

Heath, Shirley Brice. 1982. What no bed-time story means: Narrative skills at home and at school. *Language and Society* 11: 49–76.

Heath, Shirley Brice. 1983. *Ways with words: Language and life in communities and classrooms*. Cambridge: University Press.

Kale, Joan and Luke, Allan. 1997. Learning through difference: Cultural differences in early language socialisation. In Gregory (ed.), 11–29.

Kershen, Anne J. (ed.) 1997. *London: The promised land? The migrant experience in a capital city*. Aldershot, UK: Avebury.

Michaels, Sarah. 1986. *Narrative presentations: An oral preparation for literacy with first graders*. In Cook-Gumperz (ed.), 94–116.

Moll, Luis C., Amanti, Cathy, Neff, Deborah and Gonzalez, Norma. 1992. Funds of knowledge for teaching: Using a qualitative approach to connect homes and classrooms. *Theory into Practice* 31: 133–41.

Mortimore, Peter and Goldstein, Harvey. 1996. *The teaching of reading in 45 Inner London primary schools*. London: Institute of Education, University of London.

Padmore, Sarah. 1994. Guiding lights. In Mary Hamilton *et al.* (eds), *Worlds of literacy*, 143–56. Clevedon, UK: Multilingual Matters.

Rogoff, Barbara. 1990. *Apprenticeship in thinking: Cognitive development in social contexts*. Oxford: University Press.

SCAA. 1996. *Looking at children's learning: Desirable outcomes for children's learning on entering compulsory education*. London: School Curriculum and Assessment Authority.

Segel, Elizabeth. 1994. 'I got to get him started out right': Promoting literacy by beginning with books. In David K. Dickenson (ed.), *Bridges to literacy: Children, families and schools*, 66–79. Oxford: Blackwell.

Sheppard, Francis H.W. (ed.) 1975. *Survey of London*, vol. XXVII. London: Athlone.

Street, Brian. 1995. *Social literacies: Critical approaches to literacy in development, ethnography and education*. London: Longman.

Wagner, Daniel. 1994. *Literacy, culture and development: Becoming literate in Morocco.* Cambridge: University Press.

Wells, Gordon. 1985. Pre-school literacy related activities and success in school. In David R. Olson et al. (eds), *Literacy, language and learning,* 229–55. Cambridge: University Press.

Wells, Gordon. 1987. *The meaning makers.* Cambridge: University Press.

Williams, Ann. 1997. Investigating literacy in London: Three generations of readers in an East End family. In Eve Gregory (ed.), 89–106.

Zinsser, Caroline. 1986. For the Bible tells me so: Teaching children in a fundamentalist church. In Bambi Schieffelin and Perry Gilmore (eds), *The acquisition of literacy: Ethnographic perspectives,* 55–74. Norwood, NJ: Ablex.

Source

This is an edited version of an article previously published in *Written Language and Literacy,* 2(1). 1999. Reproduced by permission of John Benjamins Publishing Company.

Chapter 18

New times! Old ways?

Colin Lankshear and Michele Knobel

Background

During recent years governments otherwise concerned with trimming public sector spending have often trumpeted 'funding packages' dedicated to improving 'literacy competence' among school-age and adult populations. Whenever such packages are announced, our own immediate response has increasingly been to wonder 'what does this package *really* mean so far as promoting a more literate and educated public is concerned?'

One of the authors recalls that during his final year of high school, in the context of a lesson on political reform in Britain, the history teacher made a link between three events and a political pronouncement. The events were the 1867 Reform Act (which extended the vote to some 1 million artisans living in the towns), the 1870 Education Act (which established a universal system of elementary schools for working-class children), and the 1884 Reform Act (which extended the vote to many 'unskilled' workers). The political pronouncement in question derived from Robert Lowe (Viscount Sherbrook), a champion of what became the 1870 Education Act. As interpreted by the history teacher, Lowe/Sherbrook was overtly advocating that a link be institutionalised between compulsory education, social control and economic interests. In other words: now that they are being given the vote, 'We must educate our masters.' The history teacher was, of course, far from alone in this interpretation. It has been almost a standard position among Marxist historians of British working-class education, notably Brian Simon (1960).

Lowe's views repay closer attention. In his letters and other written works, Lowe argued that, since they were the majority of the voting population, working-class males would have the numerical potential to become:

> masters of the situation [with the power] to subvert the existing order of things, and to transfer power from the hands of property and intelligence, and so to place it in the hands of men whose whole life is necessarily occupied in the daily struggle for existence. ... I believe it will be absolutely necessary to compel our future masters to learn their letters.
>
> (Martin, 1893: 262; Simon, 1960: 354)

At the same time, the higher classes would need 'superior education and superior cultivation', in order to 'know the things the working men know, only know them infinitely better in their principles and in their details'. By this means the higher classes could 'conquer back by means of a wider and more enlightened cultivation some of the influence which they have lost by political change' (Lowe, 1867: 8–10; Simon, 1960: 356).

Given the benefits of such historically informed hindsight, it makes good sense to begin from the assumption that compulsory mass schooling probably has a lot less to do with *educating* and *making literate* (in any truly expansive sense of these terms) than it has to do with producing other outcomes: outcomes which we should strive to make clear, and for which we should call governments, education officials, and teacher educators to account. We should train ourselves to recognise evidence for this assumption when we see it – which is often.

We will proceed from this assumption here and try to turn some everyday assumptions upside down. Our aim is to expose some anomalies and contradictions, and to assess some high profile trends apparent within literacy education at present against criteria that do not (in our view) figure sufficiently in public and political debate around education.

Two questions: Wayne O'Neil (1970)

In a powerful short polemic, 'Properly literate', Wayne O'Neil prompts us to rethink some 'common sense' assumptions about (il)literacy and disadvantage.

Who's disadvantaged?

O'Neil says:

> I have known but two illiterate adult Americans. . . . One was an ancient, a Mr Cole, North Carolina potter of a line of North Carolina–Staffordshire, English potters as far back as memory reaches. He runs a prospering pottery shop on Route 1 just outside Sanford, NC. He finishes a firing every two weeks, everything gone long before the next firing is out of the kiln. People come in and order pots of all sizes and shapes and he has them write their orders in a fat, black book. Too bad. He can't read. They never get their pots. So they learn to buy what he has or leave a picture behind and then get back before someone else buys it.
>   He does well.
>
> (O'Neil, 1970: 261)

Who's literate?

According to O'Neil:

> In the tangled, demanding revolution that is America, if you're illiterate you have no control or at most you have only narrowly limited control. If you can only read and remain illiterate, you're worse off: you have no control.
>
> Make a distinction: Being able to read means that you can follow words across a page, getting generally what's superficially there. Being literate means you can bring your knowledge and your experience to bear on what passes before you. Let us call the latter proper literacy; the former improper. You don't need to be able to read to be properly literate. Only in America and such like.
>
> (ibid.: 261–2)

O'Neil believes children arrive at school properly literate relative to their experience, even though many (if not most) do not yet read and write. In teaching them to read and write, however, schools undermine and undo that proper literacy. The ways of school instruction displace bringing knowledge and experience to bear on what passes before one. In its place they impose the following of mere words – whose words?, which words? – across printed surfaces. O'Neil rejects this 'usurper literacy', calling it *improper*. This, however, is precisely what Robert Lowe wanted from mass schooling; an 'antidote' to the highly effective political organisation and agitation working people had engaged in throughout the nineteenth century. The organised political practices of the working classes were, indeed, grounded firmly in 'bringing knowledge and experience to bear on what passed before them' – every day.

There are good reasons for believing that, collectively, we are doing a pretty good job in education of keeping faith with the Viscount. Peter Freebody's (1992) account of what counts as being a successful reader, given the everyday demands of our cultural milieu, provides a good starting point for our argument.

Four roles as a literacy learner

Freebody argues that to become a successful reader an individual must 'develop and sustain the resources to play four related roles: code breaker, text-participant, text-user, and text-analyst' (1992: 48).

1. Code breaker: This is a matter of cracking alphabetic code/script – understanding the relationship between the twenty-six alphabetic written symbols and the forty-four sounds in English, and being able to move between sound and script in reading/decoding and writing/encoding.
2. Text-participant: This involves being able to handle the meaning and structure of texts, by bringing to the text itself the additional knowledge

required for making meaning from that text – for example, knowledge of the topic, the kind of situation involved, the genre of the text, etc. Mere ability to decode is not sufficient for making meaning from a text: we can read plenty where we cannot understand, or that we understand differently from other successful decoders. Much depends on what we bring to the text with us. When we are faced with texts that we cannot bring much to, or where we cannot bring what others (who are deemed to comprehend better than we do) bring, we are disadvantaged by, or in relation to, that text and other readers.

3.   Text-user: Successful reading requires ability to operate effectively and appropriately in text-mediated social activities. According to Freebody (1992: 53), being a successful text-user 'entails developing and maintaining resources for participating in "what this text is for, here and now"'. Reading, then, is a matter of matching texts to contexts, and knowing *how*, *what* and *why* to read and write within given contexts. It is what we sometimes refer to as getting the register or, perhaps, the genre 'right'. To foreshadow a theme we will return to later, Freebody comments that these resources 'are transmitted and developed in our society largely in instructional contexts, some of which may bear comparatively little relevance to the ways in which texts need to be used in out-of-school contexts' (ibid.).

4.   Text-analyst: The reader as competent text-analyst is consciously aware that 'language and idea systems' are 'brought into play' whenever a text is constructed and, furthermore, that these systems are what 'make the text operate' and, thereby, make the reader, 'usually covertly, into its [i.e., the text's] operator' (ibid.: 56). Readers, in other words, become complicit in the work that texts do. This makes it very important to be aware of the need to interrogate texts, and to know how to interrogate them – since otherwise we may unwittingly participate in producing or maintaining effects we would not knowingly choose to. As basic examples of text interrogation, Freebody suggests asking 'What are the beliefs about the topic of a person who could utter this text?', and, 'What kind of person could unproblematically and acceptingly understand such a text?' This can be pushed further, by asking what kind of world – as lived contexts and sites which shape human identities and ways of being – do such and such texts sanction, promote, bolster and implicate us in making and maintaining?

Freebody concludes by insisting that these four roles not be seen as some kind of a sequence – developmental or otherwise. Rather, they are jointly necessary conditions for being a successful reader. Hence, they are necessary components of being a reader at each and every phase of our development and practice as readers. Whatever students' ages or developmental points, their reading programmes must promote and deal with each role in systematic and explicit ways (ibid.: 58).

Occupational hazards

From an account of guidelines to intervention strategies for reading and writing (Department of Education, Queensland, 1995a) we derive what we call two easy steps to improper literacy:

Two easy steps to improper literacy: tread carefully

Step 1

According to the guidelines:

> Our current beliefs about language learning lead us to understand that language is learned through using it, through talking about it and through seeing it in action in real contexts for real purposes.
>
> This is especially important for children who are experiencing some difficulties. They need to be able to experience language in real-life or lifelike contexts. . . .
>
> Without meaningful and relevant contexts the less successful learners are trapped into reading, writing and speaking texts that are not natural and not related to the texts with which they are already familiar because of their life's experiences.
>
> (Department of Education, Queensland, 1995a: 7)

Step 2

From the same guidelines, a few pages later:

> Question: What provision is made for ongoing one-to-one support for children's reading?
> Answer: The two recommended programmes are: Support-a-Reader and Reading Recovery.
>
> (ibid: 8)

Recovering what?

Let us take Reading Recovery as an example of a literacy intervention which is currently popular – and funded – in various parts of Britain, North America, Australia and New Zealand. Reading Recovery is a resource intensive intervention, enacted during the second year of schooling. It draws on the lowest performing 15–20 per cent of students in terms of reading achievement, and gives them up to six months – typically, twelve to twenty weeks – of individual instruction for a short period on a regular basis. The instruction is delivered by a Reading Recovery tutor, specially trained under the trademarked Reading Recovery regime, using Reading Recovery theory, resources and trainers. It is presented as an early detection/warning and prevention strategy.

Its approach to diagnosis is based on a series of tasks and tests whereby student performance is documented as running records which observe the following dimensions – and which, thereby, define what reading is so far as the programme is concerned.

1. *Accuracy* – this is determined by keeping a running record of everything the child says or does as they read a book chosen by the RR teacher.
2. *Self-correction* – running records are kept by the RR teacher of self-correction by the child.
3. *Letter identification* – based on letters of the alphabet (randomly ordered and upper and lower case).
4. *Canberra word test* – correct responses to fifteen graded and often-used words are recorded.
5. *Concepts about print* – concepts that are tested include direction, text position, purposes of illustrations and visual patterns.
6. *Writing vocabulary* – the RR teacher records correctly spelled words from the 'bank' of words a child thinks s/he knows.
7. *Burt word reading test* – scores are calculated against an increasing order of difficulty.
8. *Dictation test* – provided by the RR teacher.

(cf. Trethowan et al., 1996)

Each one-to-one tutorial session comprises a number of tasks, including reading familiar and unfamiliar texts from a set of carefully graded readers. The focus of these sessions is on enabling the students to comprehend 'messages' in the text (Department of Education, Queensland, 1996: 5), and running records of the relationship between what the text says and what the child reads are maintained by the tutor as the child is reading. One or two teaching points are selected from the running records as teaching foci for the tutorial session.

What happens when we look – as altogether too few commentators do – at Reading Recovery, and similar approaches, against the kind of model of successful reading proposed by Freebody? (It is worth keeping O'Neil's ideas in mind here as well.) What are children being apprenticed to in the name of literacy when they enter such programmes?

We suggest that they are being apprenticed to reading as the mechanics of code breaking, pure and simple. The Reading Recovery programme undoubtedly helps with code breaking but, other things being equal, we should not expect it to help with much else. Wherein lies a real danger. If taken seriously as any kind of panacea it is likely to divert attention from other areas of literacy education where, for many, learning is often less than the ideal dictates: notably, text-use and text-analysis. Interestingly, Marie Clay (1992) says that most graduates of Reading Recovery can return to classrooms and perform at average levels. From one perspective this is undoubtedly an achievement. From another, however, it may pose serious questions about what constitutes average performance – especially in relation to realistic notions of successful reading of the kind Freebody proffers, where the roles in question go far beyond code breaking.

On its own, approaches like Reading Recovery can make only a strictly limited contribution to resourcing these other roles, because they effectively reduce reading (these days referred to by their proponents as 'literacy') to the mechanics of breaking code. Larger aspects of participating in the text, let alone using and analysing texts, are simply not factored into the programme design. Whatever else 'recovering learners' get in the way of these wider elements of successful reading is left to the contingencies of their particular classroom teachers, their school programmes, and their wider life experiences (cf. Tancock, 1997). What is supposed to be an exemplary literacy intervention effectively bypasses three of our four necessary conditions for being a successful reader. Approaches like Reading Recovery appear to operate on the assumption: 'We will take care of code breaking. It's up to others to look after the rest.' This, however, fragments reading. It sends messages to learners that reading is code breaking. After all, if it were not, why would they be getting this special reading assistance on an individual basis? It would indeed be surprising if this message did not work against learners developing the richer conceptions and practices that literacy teachers are supposed to be enabling.

If we want learners to understand and practise reading in its fullness and richness, then that fullness and richness have to be there from the start, and in concert with each other as integral facets of any act of reading – as Freebody (1992: 58) notes. In this context we should recognise that it is, precisely, similar 'logics' of reductionism, compartmentalising and fragmentation (of literacy) that turn up at other points within schooling as, for example, 'keyboarding', masquerading as 'technological literacy', and in such ways reduce the use of electronic technologies to mere 'add ons' – rather than as an integrated part of three-dimensional social practices in which text production, distribution and exchange are organically embedded.

We find it interesting that the challenges and critiques we have seen addressed to Reading Recovery over the years by 'reading experts', and responded to by RR gurus, rarely come within a mile of having anything to do with analysing and using texts, or even *participating* in text, in Freebody's sense (cf. Clay, 1992). This is disturbing. The debate remains effectively at the level of whether and to what extent measured gains in code breaking can be attributed to the distinctiveness of Reading Recovery as a method, or whether some other method would do the job better (cf. Shanahan and Barr, 1995; Hiebert, 1996). This kind of debate simply reinforces the reduction of reading – let alone *literacy* – to code breaking. A fair analogy would be to say that learning to become a good driver is a matter simply of learning how to operate the vehicle's controls, and that the key issue is whether these operational skills are best acquired from Driving School A, Driving School B, or from a simulator.

Literacy validation

Further concerns arise when we turn to assessment and validation guidelines and practices such as those currently unfolding in a range of modern public education systems. In Queensland, for example, a Year 2 Diagnostic Net is being developed to catch and recover children 'who are experiencing difficulties in literacy and numeracy' (Department of Education, Queensland, 1995b: 1). Validation is one of four processes which collectively make up the Diagnostic Net. Teachers are to observe and map the progress of children in their classes using designated criteria. In validation, they verify (or disconfirm) these observations and maps using specially designed assessment tasks, and identify learners who need support. The other processes are providing literacy and numeracy learning support for the children identified as needing it, and reporting to parents.

Not surprisingly, we find further worrying traces of afflicted notions of literacy in such practices of validation. While the points sketched below warrant much deeper and more exacting investigation than can be provided here, we believe literacy educators and curriculum and policy developers should pay such matters very close attention. Readers are encouraged to make their own local adjustments to the examples which follow.

The four texts identified for use as validation instruments in Queensland in 1996 were themselves highly problematic (Department of Education, Queensland, 1995b). They were: *My Grandma*, by Sarah Keane; *Mrs Goose's Baby*, by Charlotte Voake; *Fancy That*, by Pamela Allen; and *Some Snakes*, by Kathleen Murdoch and Stephen Ray. (Equivalent texts were chosen for 1997: cf. *The Elephant Tree*, by Penny Dale; *Walk Through the Jungle*, by Julie Lacome; *Ants*, by Ron Thomas and Jan Stutchbury). The problem is not so much with the books in and of themselves, but rather that they represent a very narrow range of texts and text types, reflect an unacceptably narrow range of textual purposes (effectively reducing young learners as language users to the status of consumers of stories), and, for many children in the target range, are highly unlikely to comprise authentic texts. An obvious point of comparison so far as promoting and assessing competence around authentic language purposes are concerned can be found, for instance, in the work of teachers described by Shirley Heath in *Ways with Words* (1983). Progressive and useful assessment purposes would be far better served by employing richer and more 'authentic' texts. This, of course, is to say nothing of wider concerns about the particular discourse of assessing (testing) inherent in the validation exercise described here. In fact, the very *criteria* for text selection – readability, literary quality and the extent to which they satisfy social justice criteria – are problematic in this particular case. The social justice criterion, while a very important principle in its own right, is undermined by the texts chosen. Readability and literary quality can be seen to be inadequate in terms of acceptable notions of what counts as successful reading.

The notion of *contextualising* involved in the teaching and validation process appears to be at odds with promoting serious text participation (cf. Freebody,

1992). The point about text participation is that meaning will be made more effectively where readers bring lived forms of experience and knowledge to bear on a text. The suggestions provided for contextualisation activities around the texts build on problematic constructions of children as readers. Once again, if we take, for example, the activities suggested for working with *Mrs Goose's Baby*, and compare these with the modes of contextualisation enacted by Heath's exemplar teachers, the point becomes quite clear (cf. Department of Education, Queensland, 1995b: 41–3; Heath, 1983).

The text-user resourcing potential of such texts is limited inherently and in terms of range. How, exactly, might learners be enhanced as text-*users* within the parameters of these texts and the construction of reading as social practice they invite?

Much the same point holds for resourcing the role of text-*analyst* – although the problem here has less to do with the choice of texts than with the fact that the validation process seemingly has no concern whatsoever for this role.

As it happens, the kind of assessment in question is perfectly coherent and appropriate given what is envisaged as subsequent *support*. In terms of the ideas and values integral to a defensible concept of successful reading, however, the nature of that support, and its underlying 'philosophy', is highly problematic.

Tape recorders as tools for literacy

The sorts of issues we have been trying to get at so far can be neatly illustrated by reference to two very different approaches to using tape recorders in literacy enhancement activities. One approach is outlined in *Intervention Strategies: Reading and Writing* (Department of Education, Queensland, 1995a). Here the tape recorder is used in conjunction with written texts as an aid to helping readers identify words and follow the text – i.e., break the code – and, perhaps, to get better access to the meaning of a text they might otherwise find difficult to make meaningful. The procedure is augmented by use of oral cloze exercises, where the person making the tape leaves a generous pause so that the learner can fill in the gap.

A very different approach is evident in the rich examples provided by Heath (1983; see also Heath and Mangiola, 1991). Heath describes tape recorders being used by teachers and learners to tape real-life transactions, conversations, and participation in other literacy events – such as constructing narratives and other generic forms. These are then exchanged – at times among different year levels and different schools (from different kinds of community) – and used as opportunities for making differences in kind and quality among various texts explicit; for editing purposes; for accessing different cultures; and for expanding the range of text types over which learners gain mastery. In one example, Heath (1983: 297–8) reports how a previously low achieving African-American child learned to produce written stories which obeyed the conventions of mainstream print narratives through a process of 'augmenting' tape-recorded oral texts, thereby accessing modes of school discourse which are more highly rewarded than those she had available to her via her 'primary discourse' (Gee et al., 1996). Over a two-year period this child moved from being a very low performer to acting as editor of collaborative text productions. In other cases, teachers who transcribed their students' recorded oral stories found some children rejecting these oral versions upon seeing them in print, and developing new sensitivities to the kinds of accounts other classmates liked to read (and why). In such cases we find rich and real approximations to the kinds of outcomes Freebody sees as integral to successful reading. We also find learners attaining the kinds of 'higher order literacy' outcomes espoused in a range of education reform statements: outcomes which are put at risk by emergent narrow and one-dimensional regimes of assessment and validation. Not surprisingly, reports of teachers teaching to the validation tests from Year 1 began to surface in Queensland shortly after literacy validation was announced. This is a perfectly understandable and predictable response on the part of 'accountable teachers'. It is, however, bad news for successful reading.

How do we get out of such messes? One way is by paying less homage to psychology-based approaches to reading, and directing greater attention instead to what James Gee calls 'a sociocultural approach to literacies'.

A sociocultural approach to literacies[1]

When we take a sociocultural approach to literacy we turn our attention from the mind and, ultimately, the school, and enter instead the *world*, including the adult world of work. From a sociocultural approach, the focus of learning and education is not *children*, nor *schools*, but, rather, *human lives* as *trajectories* through multiple *social practices* in various social institutions. If learning is to be efficacious, then what a child or adult does *now* as a 'learner' must be connected in meaningful and motivating ways with 'mature' ('insider') versions of related social practices.

The focus of education should be on *social practices* and their connections across various social and cultural sites and institutions. Learners should be viewed as life-long *trajectories* through these sites and institutions, as *stories* with multiple twists and turns. What we say about their beginnings should be shaped by what we intend to say about their middles and ends, and vice-versa. As *their* stories are rapidly and radically changing, we need to change *our* stories about skills, learning, and knowledge. Our focus, as well, should be on multiple learning sites and their rich and complex interconnections.

If learning is not to be a senseless activity (which, regrettably it sometimes is), it is always about entry into and participation in a Discourse.[2] Unfortunately, a focus on children and schooling tends to obscure the role of social practices and Discourses. Some Discourses, like law, have a separate domain for (initial) initiation into the Discourse (namely, law school). Others, including many Discourses connected to workplaces, do not engage in such a separation to any such extent. In these cases, much learning and initiation into the Discourse occurs 'on the job'. In both cases, however, the connection between learning and participation in the 'mature' Discourse (law or work) is relatively clear. The same is true of family, community and public sphere-based Discourses.

School-based Discourses are quite anomalous in this respect. Schools don't merely separate learning from participation in 'mature' Discourses: they actually render the connections entirely mysterious (as we will see in some cases provided below). Schools and classrooms most certainly create Discourses, that is, they create social practices that integrate people, deeds, values, beliefs, words, tools, objects and places. They create, as well, social positions (identities) for kinds of students and teachers. However, the discourse of the school or classroom is primarily a Discourse devoted to learning – but, learning for *what*? Is it learning for participation in the school or classroom Discourse itself, or learning for Discourses outside school? Which Discourses outside of school? And what sort of relationship to these outside Discourses should (or do) school and classroom Discourses contract?

These are complex questions and issues. The separation between school-based Discourses and 'outside' Discourses may be a good thing, or it may not be. It all depends on how we answer such questions as 'What is the point (goal, purpose, vision) of school-based Discourses?' 'What is the point (goal, purpose, vision) of this or that specific school-based Discourse (e.g., elementary school reading or secondary school English)?' What we *can* say, without much doubt, is that turning school Discourses of literacy into so many intervention programmes that undermine apprenticeship to 'mature' versions of social practices does no one much good in the long run. Neither does turning literacy into distinctively *school* Discourses. For evidence of this, let us turn, finally, to some real-life cases from local research.

Right now we are at an important literacy conjuncture. New literacy practices are emerging around new technologies which are making ever deeper incursions into everyday social practices, spanning the range from leisure to work, via communications, business, trade, etc. These changes have major implications for literacy learning, forcing us to consider what is involved in being a text-participant, text-user, and text-analyst in 'new times'. The cases which follow are intended to provide some insights into how different learners and teachers are negotiating the present conjuncture. They are based on fieldwork done in Queensland school, home and community settings (cf. Knobel, 1997), and have been further described in other publications (see Knobel, 1996; Lankshear and Knobel, 1996a, 1996b, 1997).

A case in point

Jacques (thirteen years) was a Year 7 student in a large state primary school. His teacher described him as experiencing much difficulty with literacy at school. He belongs to a self-employed single-income family. Jacques' father runs an earth-moving business, while his mother administers the home and is heavily involved in volunteer church work. The family lives in a predominantly white executive neighbourhood.

There was no computer in Jacques' classroom. His teacher lamented 'poor decision-making' (prior to the time she began working at the school) which established a computer lab stocked with little-known machines for which no up-to-date software was available, and which broke down regularly, requiring costly and time-consuming repairs. She had given up trying to use them. All but three of her thirty students had computer access at home, and she occasionally set word-processing tasks for homework.

Jacques loathed school, and was patiently 'doing time' until he could leave in Year 10 and work with his father. He found the world of adult work far more compelling than school. He insisted he was 'not a pen man', and could not see any point in going to school. During class, Jacques would engineer elaborate strategies and ruses for evading school work, particularly where there was any writing involved. Indeed, his teacher bemoaned his treatment of the Writers' Centre, in the corner of the classroom, where Jacques had recently spent two hours stapling together a miniature blank leaf book on which he subsequently wrote a narrative comprising two or three words per page – effectively 'sending up' the process writing approach adopted in this classroom.

There was a computer at home, which was mainly used by Jacques' father for keeping records and accounts. Jacques, too, used it for business purposes. With some editorial help from his mother and brother, he designed and published a flier advertising 'JP's Mowing Service'. The flier, complete with a carefully produced graphic, was exemplary in its business-like language and practices: 'efficient reliable service', 'all edging done', and 'for free quote phone . . .'. It was printed, photocopied and dropped in neighbourhood letterboxes, and Jacques had soon established a thriving mowing business over the summer holidays.

This 'snapshot' juxtaposes Jacques' home literacy practice against his classroom practice. At home he integrates a computer into a discourse to which he has been apprenticed and with which he feel an affinity. This is a business discourse, which was certainly marginal to the point of being invisible in class during the period of data collection, yet which is a powerful discourse so far as adult life is concerned. The technology-mediated literacy which Jacques engaged at home, despite the fact that he finds typing laborious, is likewise a potentially powerful literacy, assuming an enterprise (sub)culture. This contrasts markedly with his response to school literacy practices where, if computers were employed, he would likely reject them in the same way that he rejected the technologies (pen and paper) of conventional print.

On being advantaged in acquiring and learning new literacies

Alex is five years old. He began school recently. He reads and writes conventional texts, but much of his text production is computer mediated. Alex has his own web site, *Koala Trouble*, which he produces with the assistance of his father, Scott. Alex creates the images for stories featuring Max, a young koala bear. Several Max stories have now been published on the site, with more in process. All employ a simple hypertext format, with instructions (typically in the form of clues or questions) about where to click to move to the next page. Alex produces the drawings by hand as a story sequence in the manner of a story board and, with help from Scott, scans them into a PC and colours them using a paintbox program, 'Animator Pro'. The page includes a feedback link enlisting active involvement of other children from around the world. Their collaboration takes two main forms. Many send e-mail messages to Alex's page responding to the stories. Others (also) 'host' Max on his new 'round the world trip' – by sending back to Alex and Scott pictures, stories and ideas about Max visiting and having adventures in their part of the world, to be added to the page.

The idea behind this site is to promote cooperative activity by children who are stimulated by material designed and drawn by their peers (beginning with Alex): a global classroom as seen through the eyes of children, based on information delivered by children for children in a format they can relate to. Alex is described by Scott as 'a mean Net surfer' who finds most of the material on the Net 'boring' – hence the *Koala Trouble* web, 'a page for kids (of all ages)'. Alex's page registered more than 60,000 'hits' – national and international – during January and February 1996. Among the accolades for *Koala Trouble* are included an 'awesome page' rating from *Kid on the Net* author, Brendan Kehoe, a 'must see' rating from *Yahoo!*, and a 'wonderful' from *Berit's Best Children Sites*. Alex replies personally to all his e-mail, often by typing 'Alex', leaving the message to Scott, and hitting the Send button. With so many messages to reply to, there is a risk – which Scott is keen to avoid – of Alex becoming bored with and alienated from the medium. At five, there are other things to do!

Scott completed Year 12 at age fifteen, but never went on to tertiary education. He began a computer-based marketing industry in his tool shed in 1990, and by 1994 had formed four companies involved in all areas of multimedia (touch screen kiosks to floppy-disk-based presentations). His clients have included some major national, international, and multinational companies in areas as diverse as air transportation, banking and newspapers, as well as government departments. After doing a computer-based presentation of his 'vision for the electronic community of the future' to a city council in Queensland, Scott was contracted to set up that city's electronic network. At the end of his contract, Scott established Global Web Builders (GWB), a company which builds commercial webs for clients. GWB's home page is called *The Definitive Lifestyle Guide to Australian Webs* (DLG), and is found at http://www.gwb.com.au/gwb/guide.html. It attracts an enormous amount of global traffic and is today the Australian gateway on the Internet, registering more than 360,000 national and international hits in the week 5–12 February 1996.

The DLG concept is now being franchised globally through a multinational company called GLOBE (Global Online Business Enterprises) International. GLOBE International have sites in New Zealand and are in the process of signing up GLOBE Asia with 9 Asian countries participating. *Koala Trouble* is a specific niche market on the DLG – (i.e., families and kids): one of a number of niche market content-based webs generating traffic for the DLG.

Scott laments the fact that at school 'they play silly games on computers', adding 'that's fine for a start', but maximum use of the Internet 'within a controlled project-based environment must be part of the very early curriculum' if children's education for life in the information age is not to be stunted. According to Scott, Alex's *Koala Trouble* page is much more than just a web: 'it's a major educational "lifestyle" opportunity for Alex', comprising the hub of an electronic community of Internet users who receive monthly e-mail newsletters on what's up at *Koala Trouble*, and who reciprocate with e-mail correspondence – much of it from school classes in the US.

The company was approached by the Australian Koala Foundation (AKF) and the two have collaborated to produce a line of T-Shirts which carry Alex's pictures of Max as well as the Alex's Scribbles URL. Sale of the T-Shirts provides funds for the AKF, and Alex's Scribbles receives a share of the profits. 'With our e-mail list we have a ready market and credibility through the AKF. Alex at five has a business. I registered Alex's Scribbles last week. I (on Alex's behalf) have entered into preliminary arrangements on a profit share of the Koala Trouble T-Shirt' (Scott in e-mail interview 29 February 1996). Looking beyond schooling toward Alex's education for his later years, Scott emphasises the relevance of the discursive logic which is integral to their joint activity: namely, 'global contacts, global perspective, product line, business based on his (i.e., Alex's) work, and new opportunities as he embraces the technology' (e-mail interview, 29 February 1996). The joint venture was launched publicly on 19 April 1996. Alex performed his part well.

Whatever we may think of such social practices and the literacies they 'house', there is no question that what Alex is acquiring and learning at the age of five has everything to do with be(com)ing 'connected' in meaningful, motivating and motivated ways with mature versions of related authentic social practices. What is at issue here is more the principle(s) evinced by the case than the specific nature and detail of the social practice itself. The point is that if we are to promote equal or better literacy learning in the times that lie ahead as we have managed in the present and the recent past, we will need to come to terms with what constitutes successful *reading* in these times, and observe the importance of establishing meaningful and motivating links between what learners learn now and what they will encounter as 'the real thing'. These two cases provide the basis for a perspective on this claim.

Critical social literacy as a millennium literacy

There are some ironies here. First, if we accept that education is about preparing people for the society they will enter, what we are currently doing in the way of literacy education may work just fine – as it has since the time of Robert Lowe. We can continue to develop and even enhance the capacity of people to break codes, participate in text-mediated social practices, and use the normal range of texts – and take our chances on the shrinking range of pathways to viable and dignified futures, and all that goes with it: from escalating views among youth that there is no future; escalating rates of youth suicide; and escalating enactments of desperation. If nothing else, that may create jobs in property-guarding and personal security and the like. Schools can continue to generate established patterns of 'success' and 'failure', and to legitimate these through school Discourses and forms of assessment that deliver up league tables of 'good' schools and 'bad' schools, and that continue to generate interventions that focus on enhanced code breaking performances that are effectively roads to nowhere – or nowhere much. Equally, we can place our faith in high-tech classrooms that permit similar outcomes to be achieved with still larger class sizes – albeit with more alienating work conditions and lower remuneration rates for teachers, together with continuing experience of being blamed for the alleged consequences of a failing school system.

Alternatively, we can embrace a second irony: namely, that the literacies we need for the new millennium contain elements that have been practised and refined for thousands of years – as well as containing elements that are distinctively new. The call to interrogate texts critically in search of the good life is, in the Western tradition, at least as old as Socrates; and in other traditions as old if not older again. The call to create and engage texts which search for ways of actualising humanity on just and reciprocal bases is absolutely fundamental and binding to the 'post-everything' age. What we need to do as literacy educators is to reinvent textual practices that enable us to bring our knowledge and experience to bear on what passes before us, filtered through an ideal of lives of dignity and fulfilment for all, and grounded in a conviction that a world in which this ideal is possible remains open to people prepared to collaborate in building it. This is much more than a matter of being able to 'follow words across a page [or a screen], getting generally what's superficially there' – although for some time to come it will probably *include* the capacity to decode and encode print.

We do well to remember this when we look at multimillion dollar budget breaks for literacy. And we do well to remember also that much of what we need to consider is *already* available to us. It is, for example, available in concepts like C. Wright Mills' notion of 'sociological imagination' (Mills, 1959), when suitably reworked to take account of recent developments in social, ethical and epistemological theories advanced in response to distinctive conditions of lived experience in new times. It is also, we venture, available in a sociocultural approach to literacy which insists that language and literacy must always be understood in their social, cultural and political contexts. One of these contexts is the globally interconnected space of the new global economy, with its new competition and its new work order, *and in all its ramifications.* For

> language – indeed, our very humanity – is in danger of losing meaning if we do not carefully reflect on this context and its attempts to make us into 'new kinds' of people . . . e.g., people who are 'smart' because they [produce and] buy the highest 'quality' [with the greatest efficiency, accountability, and cost effectiveness], but do not care about – or even see – the legacies of their greed writ large on the world.
>
> (Gee, Hull and Lankshear, 1996: 150–1)

Endword

In the end, we have more to recover than our *reading*, although we have *that* to recover as well: albeit in a much more generous and expansive sense than many of our current practices admit – including some of those most in favour among politicians and administrators at present.

Notes

1   This section draws directly on Gee, Hull and Lankshear, 1996: 4, 6, 15–16.
2   In what follows we observe James Paul Gee's distinction between 'Discourse' and 'discourse'. For Gee, a Discourse is a 'socially accepted association among ways of using language, other symbolic expressions, and artefacts, of thinking, feeling, believing, valuing and acting that can be used to identify us as a member of a socially meaningful group' (Gee, 1991: 131). Gee uses 'discourse' to refer to the 'language bits' in Discourses: that is, connected stretches of language that make sense within some Discourse community or other (e.g., a report within a research Discourse), an essay within a scholastic Discourse.

References

Balson, A. and Balson, S. (1996) *Alex's Scribbles – Koala Trouble*, http://www.scribbles.com.au

Balson, S./Global Web Builders (1996) *Definitive Lifestyle Guide to Australian Webs*, http://www.gwb.com.au/gwb/guide.html

Clay, M. (1992) 'Reading Recovery: the wider implications of an educational innovation'. In A. Watson and A. Badenhop (eds) *Prevention of Reading Failure*. Sydney: Ashton Scholastic, 22–47.

Department of Education, Queensland (1995a) *Intervention Strategies: Reading and Writing*. Brisbane: Department of Education.

Department of Education, Queensland (1995b) *Literacy Validation*. Brisbane: Department of Education.

Department of Education, Queensland (1996) *Reading Recovery Queensland: Information Package for Schools 1996*. Brisbane: Department of Education (mimeo).

Drucker, P. (1993) *Post-Capitalist Society*. New York: Harper Books.

Freebody, P. (1992) 'A socio-cultural approach: resourcing four roles as a literacy learner'. In A. Watson and A. Badenhop (eds) *Prevention of Reading Failure*. Sydney: Ashton Scholastic, 48–60.

Gee, J.P. (1991) 'What is literacy?' In C. Mitchell and K. Weiler (eds) *Rewriting Literacy*. New York: Bergin and Garvey, 1–11.

Gee, J.P. (1992) *Social Linguistics and Literacies: Ideology in Discourses*, second edition. London: Taylor and Francis.

Gee, J.P., Hull, G. and Lankshear, C. (1996) *The New Work Order: Behind the Language of the New Capitalism*. Sydney and Boulder CO.: Allen and Unwin and Westview Press.

Heath, S.B. (1983) *Ways with Words: Language, Life and Work in Communities and Classrooms*. Cambridge: Cambridge University Press.

Heath, S.B. and Mangiola, L. (1991) *Children of Promise: Literate Activity in Linguistically and Culturally Diverse Classrooms*. Washington, DC: National Education Association of the United States.

Hiebert, M. (1996) 'Revisiting the question: what difference does Reading Recovery make to an age cohort?' in *Educational Researcher* 25 (7): 26–8.

Jones, C. (1996) 'Big boosts for literacy and health programs'. *The Australian*, May 16, p. 5.

Knobel, M. (1996) 'Language and social purposes in adolescents' everyday lives'. *Australian Journal of Language and Literacy* 19 (2): 120–8.

Knobel, M. (1997) 'Language and social practices in the everyday lives of four adolescents.' Unpublished Ph.D. thesis. Brisbane: Faculty of Education, QUT.

Lankshear, C. and Knobel, M. (1996a) *Different Worlds*, http://www.fed.qut.edu.au/crn/index.html

Lankshear, C. and Knobel, M. (1996b) 'Different worlds: technology-mediated classroom learning and students' social practices with new technologies in home and community settings'. Symposium presentation to American Educational Research Association Annual Conference, April. New York: AERA.

Lankshear, C. and Knobel, M. (1997) 'Different worlds: new technologies in school, home and community' in C. Lankshear, *Changing Literacies*. Buckinghamshire: Open University Press.

Lowe, R. (1867) 'Primary and classical education'. Cited in Simon, 1960.

Martin, A. Patchett (1893) *Life and Letters of the Right Honourable Robert Lowe Viscount Sherbrook*. Vol II. Cited in Simon, 1960.

Mills, C. Wright (1959) *The Sociological Imagination*. New York: Oxford University Press.

O'Neil, W. (1970) 'Properly literate'. *Harvard Educational Review* 40 (2): 260–3.

Reich, R. (1992) *The Work of Nations*. New York: Vintage Books.

Shanahan, T. and Barr, R. (1995) 'Reading Recovery: an independent evaluation of the effect of an early instructional intervention for at-risk learners'. *Reading Research Quarterly* 50 (4): 958–96.

Simon, B. (1960) *Studies in the History of Education 1780–1870*. London: Lawrence and Wishart.

Tancock, S. (1997) 'Catie: a case study of one first grader's reading status'. *Reading Research and Instruction* 36 (2): 89–110.

Trethowan, V., Harvey, D. and Fraser, C. (1996) 'Reading Recovery: Comparison between its efficacy and normal classroom instruction'. *Australian Journal of Language and Literacy* 19 (1): 29–36.

Source

This is an edited version of a chapter previously published in F. Christie and R. Misson *Literacy and Schooling*. 1998. Reproduced by permission of Taylor & Francis Ltd.

Part 6

Ethical and social justice issues

Chapter 19

Justice, literacy, and impediments to learning literacy

Joseph A. Diorio

Introduction

People use different languages, and even within single language communities there are significant differences among users in the level and range of linguistic activities. Human societies commonly deal differently – for better or worse – with persons depending on which languages they use, how they speak, whether they can read and write, and what kinds of written materials they can understand and produce. One's abilities to meet socially varying standards for language use affect one's life chances throughout the world. The definition of linguistic standards, and the teaching of language use, thus raise issues of social justice.

Anyone whose access to language is restricted or whose ability to use it is impaired will be hugely bereft of opportunities for meaningful living. Language and literacy are complex and multi-faceted phenomena, and literacy cannot be considered in isolation from oral speech. While the focus of this chapter is on literacy, our discussion will encompass ways in which language in general is socially orchestrated, rewarded and constrained. After considering the role of language generally in the pursuit of justice, we briefly will examine three types of situations in which issues of justice bear on the learning of literacy: multilingual contexts in which some people must learn to read and write in a language other than their first language; unilingual contexts in which some people have special difficulties acquiring literacy; and situations in which some people are thought to have difficulty in acquiring literacy skills because of internal neurological defects.

Language, instrumentalism, and the public good

Spoken and written language functions in at least two interrelated ways in our lives. First, language is an instrument through which we express ourselves, act on the world, and pursue our objectives. Second, language acts upon us to shape our consciousness, construct our identities, and situate us within the world. Language is the primary means through which we make sense of the world to ourselves, by enabling us to share in the ways other people have made sense of it before and around us. Language has a constructive impact on the world we live in but, because we are part of that world, we make ourselves in the process of constructing our environment. Collectively through language we interpret the world and ourselves for each other, thereby generating an overlapping consensus which constitutes our shared, socially produced consciousness. This consciousness includes conceptions of the kinds of beings we are and the ways we should behave. Because languages differ, however, and because individuals are differently positioned within particular language communities, people's sense of themselves and their world varies.

According to linguist M. A. K. Halliday:

> in the development of the child as a social being, language has the central role. Language is the main channel through which the patterns of living are transmitted to him, through which he learns to act as a member of a 'society' – in and through the various social groups, the family, the neighbourhood, and so on – and to adopt its 'culture', its modes of thought and action, its beliefs and its values.
>
> (1978, p. 9)

Language thus plays both an instrumental and a constitutive role in our lives; we use it, but it also helps to make us what we are, and it thereby constitutes an intersubjective component in our personal identity (see Sandel, 1982, esp. p. 62).

In *A Theory of Justice*, John Rawls introduced the notion of 'primary goods'. These are:

> things which it is supposed a rational man wants whatever else he wants. Regardless of what an individual's rational plans are in detail, it is assumed that there are various things which he would prefer more of rather than less. With more of these goods men can generally be assured of greater success in carrying out their intentions and in advancing their ends whatever these ends may be.
>
> (1971, p. 92)

Primary goods are generically useful instruments for pursuing the variable life plans of different people. It makes sense to want as much of primary goods as possible because they help us to get more of whatever else it is we want given our particular plans of life. Language clearly is such a good. Language provides:

> access to all the independently valuable ends that ... [it] is used for: forming relationships, playing games, learning a craft, carrying on a profession, keeping up with the news or the gossip, buying groceries or shares on the stock market, formulating rules for social conduct.
>
> (Reaume, 2000, p. 248)

Because of the constitutive role of language in individual lives, however, the plans that people pursue with it and the things they use it for are not determined by individuals in isolation. Through language, the formulation of plans of life and the identification of the objectives of language use are at least partly collective processes. This potentially generates conflict between individual and collective language purposes.

In many societies today social debates over language focus on the problems of teaching and learning literacy, to the extent that learning to read and write are identified as major purposes of elementary schooling:

> of all the things that children have to learn when they get to school reading and writing are the most basic, the most central and the most essential. Practically everything else that they do will be permeated by these two skills. Hardly a lesson can be understood, hardly a project finished unless the children can read the books in front of them and write about what they have done. They must read and write or their time at school will be largely wasted.
>
> (Bryant and Bradley, 1985, p. 1)

There is widespread international concern at present that a lot of elementary school time is in fact being wasted, and that children are not acquiring adequate reading and writing skills. This concern is sparked less by fears that children leaving school with inadequate literacy skills will be limited in their abilities to implement life plans for themselves, and more by worries that these children might impact negatively on economic productivity:

> In the popular discourse, the bottom line for concern about illiteracy . . . is economic. . . . Again and again we hear worker illiteracy being linked directly to big economic losses: due to poor reading and writing skills, workers make costly mistakes, they don't work efficiently, they produce inferior products, and, apparently, they stay at home a lot. A related economic argument is that since many [illiterate] people cannot qualify for jobs, North America is also losing the buying power of a significant segment of the population.
>
> (Hull, 1997, pp. 8–9)

Views such as these have been criticised on the grounds that the literacy standards set by employers can be irrelevant to the skills actually needed for work; that assessments for 'illiteracy' mask practices which exclude workers on grounds of class, ethnicity and gender; and that persons lacking certain literacy skills often can function socially and economically without them (Street, 1995, pp. 18–19, 124–27). The claim that individual deficits in literacy threaten collective productivity highlights two important points; first, that the instrumental value of language accrues socially as well as individually, and second, that defining purposes for the collective use of language is a political issue rather than a matter of objective fact. Collective definitions of the objectives of language use achieve acceptance through the exercise of social power, and thus privilege certain forms of life to the potential disadvantage of specific individuals or groups.

Literacy is a socially variable concept, rather than a natural phenomenon which provides a universal, all-or-nothing standard of achievement. The content and methods of teaching literacy cannot be 'read of' directly from the natural world and the common qualities of language. It has been said, for example, that in the United States in the late eighteenth century, literacy meant the ability to read and to write one's name, whereas in that country today:

> advanced readers must be able to use literacy for creative and critical thinking and for problem solving ... [and to] apply strategies to text in order to construct meanings from different perspectives and understand how their meanings differ from those of others.
>
> (Braunger and Lewis, 1997, p. 2)

This form of literacy, supposedly required of 'knowledge workers' in the twenty-first century, differs from that of people who learned to read by adopting a respectful and accepting stance towards religious texts or authoritative scholarly works. It always must be asked which conception(s) of literacy predominate in a society, and which social interests may be served by that dominance. By enforcing conceptions of literacy through instructional programmes, schools reflect the power relations that help to define the routes to social success. (Cummins, 2000, p. 97; Rassool, 1999, p. 184ff).

As a socially variable concept, literacy is inherently contestable. The socially variable quality of literacy often is overlooked, however, and debates about the curriculum and pedagogy of literacy teaching in schools commonly turn on appeals to what are taken to be the objective needs of society – usually for economic productivity – and for objective literacy skills (See Street, 1995, p. 126). Collective literacy needs commonly are thought of as discoverable in some objective and neutral space untainted by the distorting perspectives of competing social interests. Literacy skills thus are to be understood, taught and used in a common, natural and neutral fashion by all for the good of all (Hull, 1997, p. 17). As Simon has noted, however, 'skills are always defined with reference to some socially defined version of what constitutes competence' (1983, p. 243, quoted in Hull, 1997, p. 18; see also Street, 1995, pp. 124–5; Cummins, 2000, pp. 93–8). These socially defined versions emerge, not out of a landscape of perfect equality, but from a hierarchy of power relations. Would-be universal definitions of curriculum content and pedagogical practice – in literacy as in other fields – are not neutral with respect to the hierarchial social positions. A concern for justice requires unravelling these social links and examining the ways in which definitions and instructional methods in literacy differentially advance or retard the life chances of various groups and individuals.

The social purposes of language and literacy are politically problematic, but it is clear that the effects of language and literacy skills do 'spill over' beyond individual lives into the public domain. Consider the following statement from *The New York Times*:

> millions of Americans are locked out of good jobs, community participation and the democratic process because they lack adequate reading and writing skills.
>
> (Quoted in Hull, 1997, p. 5)

Exclusion from work, community and politics is bad not just for the people to whom it happens, but arguably for everyone else as well. Overall standards of living are decreased, the quality of community life is diminished, and the democratic process is impaired – i.e., the public good is damaged. The implicit solution to the problem is to ensure that everyone has reading and writing skills adequate to get them good jobs (though it is not clear what would happen to any not-so-good-jobs when adequate skills are universalised, nor whether good jobs will materialise as fast as people acquire these skills).

What are these 'adequate' skills? Because literacy is socially dependent, someone has to decide which skills are relevant to getting the good jobs (to say nothing of identifying which jobs these are). People who have jobs to distribute will have a vested interest at least in influencing this decision. By appealing to the public interest, employers may gain a disproportionate control over the definition of the literacy skills needed by workers and hence taught in schools, supposedly for the good of us all.

Insofar as they can exert influence in the debate over language teaching in society, employers and others thus are in a position to shape the language abilities of other people. Since language has both an instrumental and a constitutive role in human life, this shaping influences not just what other people can do with language, but also what kinds of people they will be. In one respect this is not surprising, since as a social phenomenon language shapes us all. But in another way it is problematic, because it means that people with social power can exert greater degrees of influence in shaping the lives of others.

The notion of the public good is problematic because, like literacy, there is no objective fact of the matter. The public good is not a natural phenomenon to be discovered. It is not something which stands outside of individual understandings and sectarian interests, and against which these understandings and interests can be measured. Rather, every attempt to define it is implicated in these varying conceptions and interests. The public good is inherently socially contestable.

The public effects of language make it a prize in social contests over power. As a primary good, language is used by individuals as an instrument in their pursuit of life plans. But the public effects of language mean that it also can be captured as an instrument in the pursuit of sectarian interests. Individuals use language to pursue their own ends, but the language they use is not plucked from a natural void. The first language we learn as young children has variable status in different social contexts. The language and literacy skills we are taught in school is the product of implicit social assumptions and explicit decisions which reflect the views about language held by people who are able to determine educational policy and practice. To the extent that these policies and practices reflect the interests of sectarian social groups, they will determine the kinds of language learning children undergo in schools, which in turn will influence the kinds of lives these children are able to live.

Multi-lingualism and intrinsic language value

In most societies advanced reading and writing skills will not get one a good job if these skills are not in the dominant – or at least a significant – language in one's locality. Literacy in Hindi is unlikely to gain one a good job in New Zealand unless coupled with similar skills in English. A monolingual Hindi user in Christchurch will be immensely restricted in her ability to use language instrumentally in achieving her life aims. Many people around the world face this kind of restricting situation, as a result either of voluntary migration or of violent upheaval in their home territories. These people are seriously impaired relative to the people who speak the prevailing language around them. Do societies containing linguistic minorities have any responsibility to rectify the unequal opportunities faced by these people?

Rawls distinguished between natural and social primary goods:

> assume that the chief primary goods at the disposal of society are rights and liberties, powers and opportunities, income and wealth. . . . These are the social primary goods. Other primary goods such as health and vigor, intelligence and imagination, are natural goods; although their possession is influenced by the basic structure [of society], they are not so directly under its control.
>
> (1971, p. 62)

While the ability to learn and use *any* language in part is a natural primary good, the acquisition and use of *specific* languages for the most part is a social good. Literacy skills in specific languages largely are at the disposition of society to distribute. How should society deal with people who do not use the language of the majority?

Waldron writes that:

> the inhabitants of any country have a duty to . . . come to terms with one another, and set up, maintain, and operate the legal frameworks that are necessary to secure peace, resolve conflicts, do justice, avoid great harms, and provide some basis for improving the conditions of life. I shall call this the duty of civic participation . . . [this duty] means . . . participating in a way that pays proper attention to the interests, wishes, and opinions of all

the inhabitants of the country. (Correlative to this aspect of civic responsibility is a fundamental right of each of the inhabitants that his interests, wishes, and opinions be properly attended to.)

(2000, pp. 155–6)

What does this right entail with respect to persons who do not know the majority language of the country? It is in the interests of the Hindi user in Christchurch to be able to use language to pursue her objectives in life, and she has a right that the people around her attend properly to this interest. But how are they to do this? Before answering this, we must consider another claim, different from but compatible with Waldron's statement, which demands that we offer adequate recognition to the cultural identities of all persons (see Taylor, 1994). A person's first language readily can be seen to be a constituent of their cultural identity:

culture has been recognized as important because it is the context within which other important individual choices are made ... planning one's own life is not valuable merely because it promotes some further valuable end, but rather it is good in itself ... [it] is intrinsically good. So far, this argument could be interpreted to attribute intrinsic value to culture as well, because it treats the cultural context of choice as a logical condition of the making of life choices ... if individuals are entitled to the protection of their ability to choose a life plan, the context that makes choice possible must deserve protection. To the extent that language is an aspect of culture, this sort of argument can be applied more narrowly to provide an account of the grounds for protecting language.

(Reaume, 2000, pp. 246–7)

Individuals have a right to use language in formulating and pursuing life plans, because language is inherent in, and intrinsically valuable to, such projects. But, as Reaume goes on to argue, this intrinsic value does not attach logically to any *particular* language. Thus our Hindi user in Christchurch – call her Usha – has a right to speak, read and write, but not necessarily to be socially supported in doing so in Hindi. This is because her use of Hindi as a specific language has instrumental, but not intrinsic, value as a tool in her life (Reaume, 2000, p. 247). While she needs *some* language to pursue her life plans, it is not obviously the case that these plans could be pursued *only* through the use of Hindi.

To pursue life effectively, Usha will have little choice but to learn English, and the English-using society around her will have at least two good reasons for assisting her in doing so. The first reason is that Usha's own fundamental right that society pay proper attention to her interests requires it to assist her to communicate with the people around her in pursuing her objectives. This may include providing her with free English classes in a culturally supportive environment. As Carens has noted:

because the ability to navigate in civil society and to take advantage of educational, economic and social opportunities is so dependent on linguistic competence, a commitment to equal opportunity entails an obligation to ensure that all members of society are able to function effectively in the common language.

(2000, p. 79)

The second reason for assisting Usha to learn English is that the effects of her doing so will reach outside her pursuit of her own life interests and impact on the quality of common life. Again, according to Carens:

there is also a public interest at stake here . . . under modern social conditions a shared, standardized medium of communication is an essential public good.

(2000, p. 79)

In the pursuit of both individual and collective interests, language as such is necessary, but not any given language. Particular languages have only instrumental value in the pursuit of extra-linguistic objectives. This does not exhaust the value of language in human life, however, for as Reaume argues:

most people value their language not only instrumentally, as a tool, but also intrinsically, as a cultural inheritance and as a marker of identity as a participant in the way of life it represents. Their language is a repository of the traditions and cultural accomplishments of their community as well as being a kind of cultural accomplishment itself. It is the vehicle through which a community creates a way of life for itself and is intrinsically bound up with that way of life. Participation in these kinds of communal forms of human creativity is an intrinsic part of the value of human life. The particular form it takes for a particular group of people takes on intrinsic value for them because it is their creation. For the group as a whole, its language is a collective accomplishment. An individual member's use of the language is at once a participation in this accomplishment and an expression of belonging to the community that has produced it.

(2000, p. 251)

Reaume – along with Carens – is concerned primarily with the linguistic situation in Canada, where two substantial foundational language communities co-exist alongside numerous smaller aboriginal and more recent language arrivals. All of these languages are equally intrinsically valuable to the people who use them. In Reaume's account, intrinsic value lends support to the protection of any language wherever it is found, with one important rejoinder – size counts. Reaume and Carens both are concerned with when it is appropriate to designate a language an 'official language', meaning that users of that language are guaranteed the right to carry out their public business in it, and that government services will be provided in it. While discussion of this issue is beyond the scope of this chapter, we need to refer to one aspect of it. Reaume states that, while every language is intrinsically valuable to its users, that value does not generate equal rights to use that language in official contexts, including education:

> because the use of a language in its fullest sense is a group practice and not a wholly individual endeavour, the right to official-language status depends upon there being a viable community of speakers of a particular language. If one interprets the official-language rights as going beyond the freedom to the use of one's language in private and the purely negative right to speak it is public contexts; if language rights require that certain institutions be able to operate in certain languages, size is important. A community must be of a certain size before it is feasible to provide the appropriate services by delivering them within the community itself.
>
> (2000, pp. 266–7)

Just when a community becomes big enough for this feasibility to apply cannot be addressed here. We must accept, however, that in many instances minority language groups cannot expect to have official services provided in their own language. Thus Usha cannot claim the right to send her children to publicly supported schools in which Hindi is the language of instruction and in which literacy skills in that language are taught. This is despite the fact that her children – assuming that their own first language is Hindi – will be disadvantaged relative to local children by virtue of having to acquire literacy skills in a language which is not their first. How can we claim to respect the intrinsic value of Usha's language, when at the same time we acknowledge that our practices disadvantage her children in acquiring the literacy skills which will help them to pursue their own life plans effectively?

At issue here is the question of what it means positively to recognise the intrinsic value of a language to the people who use it, even when we cannot use it or provide services in it ourselves. The fact that any group of people happen to use the majority language in a given place has no moral value. As Rawls' could have argued, whether we are born into, or move into, a majority language community, or whether we find ourselves in a linguistic minority, is morally arbitrary, and our pursuit of justice should work against, rather than build on, such natural and social contingencies (Rawls, 1971, p. 15). None of us merits membership in a majority language community, and all of us risk – though the level of risk varies with where we live – being uprooted into minority status.

I believe that we can recognise the intrinsic value of different languages to different people, and acknowledge and respect the ways that languages define and express their communal identities and accomplishments, while at the same time facilitating their participation in the prevailing language(s) of our society.

We need to do this, however, in ways which enhance rather than denigrate the sense of identity and self-worth of minority language users. This will require critical openness on the part of the majority – and in particular those who design and control the curriculum and pedagogical practices of majority-language literacy – to the possible ways in which teaching majority language may be demeaning to, or counter-productive for, successful learning on the part of minority language users.

Impediments to literacy

Many factors which impede literacy acquisition have their roots in institutionalised failures to recognise the intrinsic value of the prior language abilities of learners. This problem is exemplified in cases where children must learn literacy in a language (L2) other than the one they speak. Such children face an additional burden:

> children who receive literacy instruction in an L2 are faced with a dual task: Besides the characteristics of written language, they will have to learn an unfamiliar language, partly referring to an unfamiliar cultural background.
>
> (Verhoeven and Durgunoglu, 1998, xiii)

This extra burden is reflected in the gap between the literacy achievements of mainstream students and of those from 'diverse' backgrounds, including different first languages (Au, 2000, p. 835). Some of the reasons for lower achievements by L2 literacy learners are fairly obvious, such as the lack of symmetry between the language spoken at home and that read at school. For example, oral vocabulary has been linked to the development of word recognition skills in reading. If a child has an especially limited spoken vocabulary – which is likely if the child is learning to read a language she has not spoken at home – her reading progress is likely to be slowed (Snow and Tabors, 1993, p. 9).

Even very young children do not come to school devoid of language. Pedagogical writing over the past several decades has recognised that the knowledge and understandings which children bring with themselves to school are not just errors to be replaced or hollows to be filled in with the correct content of the curriculum. Rather, they are often irreducibly different approaches to the world which teachers ought to work with and build upon in leading children to an open-ended dialogue with each other and the curriculum. Recent writing also has challenged the view that the content of curriculum knowledge is extra-cultural, objective and neutral, and has argued that curriculum knowledge must be recognised as arising from specific cultural, gendered, class-based and other positions within society.

This conception of curriculum knowledge is compatible with viewing literacy as socially variable. Many – perhaps most – children coming into school, including those with a different first language, will have had some contact with the use of literacy even if they cannot read or write themselves. The attitudes towards and values associated with written materials and those who can read and explain them might be quite different in the homes and cultures of some children than those that prevail in linguistically majoritarian public schools. When they are present, and unless they are recognised and dealt with positively, these differences can compound the difficulties faced by L2 literacy learners. Not only must these children learn to read and write in a language other than the one they speak, but they must do so under a conception of literacy and a set of language values which may be alien to that with which they are familiar.

These differences are missed when teachers assume that literacy is a universal constant across all languages. When this happens, the literacy standards of the language of the school are taken as objective criteria against which the attitudes and performances of students are to be measured. In this kind of teaching, the prior language understandings of the pupils are assumed to be irrelevant or erroneous – unless they are congruent with those of the language of the school. Pupils are drawn to reject their prior language knowledge and linguistic values and to adopt those of the language they are being taught (Cummins, 2000, pp. 255–6).

When the prior language of pupils is dismissed unless congruent with that of the school, the intrinsic value of that language to pupils and their families is denied. It has been argued that successful language teaching, like teaching in every subject, accepts and builds upon the language and culture of pupils' homes (Au, 2000, pp. 837–8). According to Cummins:

> students' identities are affirmed and academic achievement promoted when teachers express respect for the language and cultural knowledge that students bring to the classroom . . . all aspects of children's cultural and linguistic experience in their homes should form the foundation upon which literacy instruction in school builds.
>
> (2000, pp. 34, 75)

The situation of children who are learning to read in a second language indicates that children come to school with language and, most often, with implicit orientations towards literacy, both of which can differ from the language of instruction and literacy values of the school. Once we accept that literacy is socially dependent, we must reject the idea that the role of the school is to impose objective literacy standards without regard for the language skills and orientations which learners bring with them. Both justice and effective pedagogy require respecting and building on the prior language knowledge of children.

The impediments faced by second language literacy learners are not unique to these children. Similar obstacles confront many children who are learning to read and write in their own first language. Language usage and values vary not just across different languages, but within single language communities as well. People from different socio-economic backgrounds may all use the same language, but they often do so in different ways. English-speaking children entering an English language school may appear linguistically homogeneous, but this appearance can be deceptive. A working-class English-speaking child in an English language school can face obstacles that are similar in kind, though not necessarily in degree, to those faced by a Spanish-speaking child entering the same school. Gerald Coles, for example, has noted that:

> studies on literacy learning of children from different classes and linguistic cultures have concluded that there are differences in the types, meaning, and function of respective literacy activities but not any of them is better or worse than any other. These studies say that the literacy activities of middle-class children differ from those of lower-class children only when literacy is equated, for example, with storybook reading or with numbers of books read and available. Lower-class families engage in their own considerable literacy activities.
>
> (1998, p. 151)

If different families from different class or other backgrounds use and value the same language differently, and if we are prepared to respect the differing language approaches of people who use different languages, then since language is of intrinsic value to all individuals we need to respect the differing approaches to language of people using the same language. Our responsibility to respect people's language as intrinsically valuable does not arise only when we are dealing with people who use different languages. And if respecting language involves respecting it in the classroom and building on children's own language in literacy instruction, then this holds also for children who speak nominally the same language but come from different class or other backgrounds which influence linguistic usage and values.

The ways literacy instruction is presented in our schools is not necessarily any more neutral with respect to class-based differences than it is with respect to overt language differences. The content and processes of literacy teaching are more likely to match the language approaches and values found in middle-class homes, thereby disadvantaging some children. For example:

> American working-class, teenage girls participating in discussions of serious topics share turns with one another, the audience audibly echoing or even anticipating the speaker's points, whereas middle-class girls tend to take long and uninterrupted turns producing, in effect, brief oral editorials. . . . It is equally challenging to participate effectively in discourse forms where the responsibility is shared with the audience and in those where it rests almost exclusively on the speaker; practice with the latter,

however, transfers more effectively to the kinds of writing American children are expected to do in school.

(Snow and Tabors, 1993, p. 13)

Speaking, reading and writing are bodily performances which can be impeded by physical disabilities of various kinds. Visual impairments make reading difficult, hearing impairments impede speech. In mild cases these impairments can be rectified relatively easily – hearing aids and corrective lenses often are sufficient – and the right of each person to have their interests properly attended to, in a context of mutual respect and equal opportunity, entails the social guarantee of the availability of such corrective devices when needed (vision and hearing may be natural primary goods, but glasses and amplifying devices are socially disposable).[1]

Many children – estimates range as high as more than 20 per cent – experience serious difficulties in reading, including children who are learning to read in their own first language (Coles, 1998, p. 120). Since reading involves using the physical apparatus of the body and the brain, it is not unreasonable to think that the problems experienced by at least some of these children might be the result of neurological malfunction. Attempts to identify such malfunctions, however, are fraught with conceptual difficulties and at present are highly contentious.

The concept of reading disabilities locates the source of reading difficulties internally within individual children rather than externally in institutional and social practices:

the term *reading disabilities* is reserved for reading problems that are attributable to some factor intrinsic to the reader. Examples of intrinsic factors include deficient phonological processing skill, comprehension deficit, and peculiar cognitive learning styles.

(Aaron and Malatesha Joshi, 1992, p. 87)

Numerous research studies have been conducted attempting to identify areas of cerebral malfunction in persons who have reading difficulties. Most of this research has been driven conceptually by a particular theorisation of the reading process, namely, that learning to read involves the mastering of a series of discrete skills, including the ability to recognise the component sounds in words and to map these sounds onto written symbols. This theorisation itself is contested, and those who advocate it have been accused, among other things, of mistaking a particular culturally-derived conception of reading for the whole of reading itself (see Coles, 1998; Coles, 2000; also Bryant and Bradley, 1985). While it has been lauded in many places as the solution to reading difficulties, the skill-based or phonics approach to teaching reading also may inhibit literacy acquisition on the part of children whose linguistic background is not congruent with it.

Various techniques have been used to compare brain functioning while reading between good and poor readers, and differences in blood flow and activation levels have been found in different parts of the brain between these two groups (Shaywitz, *et al.*, 2000). But it is impossible to conclude from these studies that the brains of weak readers are inherently different, much less deficient, relative to those of good readers. Because of the interactive relationship between reading activities and levels of brain functions, it is impossible to tell whether differences in brain functions cause reading difficulties, or if experiences with reading generate different patterns of functioning within the brain. Thus the search for neurological reading disabilities so far is a 'red herring' in attempts to explain differential success in achieving literacy on the part of children.

We know that many children have difficulty reading. We have argued that individuals, by way of their right to have their interests properly attended to by society, are entitled to access to language and literacy on instrumental grounds, and to have their own language respected for its intrinsic value to themselves. We have acknowledged that many children will have to acquire literacy in a language which is different, in whole or in part, than that which they speak. The extra burdens faced by these children must be balanced, and their difficulties eased, by according them respect for the language they bring with them, both because this accords them respect as persons in their own right, and because it facilitates the pedagogy of literacy instruction.

Even if these requirements were to be met fully in our schools, learning difficulties in the acquisition of literacy no doubt still would arise, and it is tempting to blame these on learning disabilities internal to individual children. So far research has not uncontentiously identified neurological literacy disabilities in any but the most severe of cases. When children function effectively in non-literacy contexts, but experience difficulties in reading and writing, our responsibility to attend properly to their interests requires us to look primarily for social structural and institutional causes for their problems, and to seek pedagogical solutions for them. While some of these difficulties may be caused by disabilities intrinsic to individual children, this is a judgement which at present is not available to us if we take seriously our responsibilities to others in the pursuit of justice.

Note

1   Here we must be cautious not to slip into a singular mentality of 'serving justice through the compensation of deficits' because, as Howe notes, '"disadvantaged" groups might very well *not want* compensation because of the cost it exacts from them in terms of their identity' (1996, p. 56). Debates over the proper approach to the education of deaf students provide an example of the dangers of this mentality. The point is that while some impediments to learning, such as nearsightedness, can be thought of relatively straightforwardly as 'deficits' which can and should easily be rectified, others, like coming to school with a divergent language background, constitute differences to be respected rather than

deficiencies to be corrected. Distinguishing the two types of impediments can be problematic.

References

Aaron, P. G., & Malatesha Joshi, R. 1992. *Reading Problems Consultation and Remediation*. New York and London: Guilford Press.

Au, K. H. 2000. A multicultural perspective on policies for improving literacy achievement: equity and excellence. In M. L. Kamil, P. B. Mosenthal, P. D. Pearson and R. Barr (eds), *Handbook of Reading Research Volume III* (pp. 835–51). Mahwah, NJ and London: Lawrence Erlbaum.

Braunger, J., & Lewis, J. 1997. *Building a Knowledge Base in Reading*. Portland, OR: Northwest Regional Educational Laboratory.

Bryant, P., & Bradley, L. 1985. *Children's Reading Problems*. Oxford and Cambridge, MA: Blackwell.

Carens, J. H. 2000. *Culture, Citizenship, and Community*. Oxford: Oxford University Press.

Coles, G. 1998. *Reading Lessons*. New York: Hill and Wang.

Coles, G. 2000. *Misreading Reading*. Portsmouth, NH: Heinemann.

Cummins, J. 2000. *Language, Power and Pedagogy*. Clevedon: Multilingual Matters.

Halliday, M. A. K. 1978. *Language as Social Semiotic*. London: Arnold.

Howe, K. R., 1996. Educational ethics, social justice and children with disabilities. In C. Christensen and F. Rizvi (eds), *Disability and the Dilemmas of Education and Justice* (pp. 46–62). Buckingham and Philadelphia: Open University Press.

Hull, G. 1997. Hearing other voices: a critical assessment of popular views on literacy and work. In G. Hull (ed.) *Changing Work, Changing Workers* (pp. 3–39). Albany: State University of New York Press.

Rassool, N. 1999. *Literacy for Sustainable Development in the Age of Information*. Clevedon: Multilingual Matters.

Rawls, J. 1971. *A Theory of Justice*. Cambridge, MA: Belknap Press.

Reaume, D. G. 2000. Official-language rights: intrinsic value and the protection of difference. In W. Kymlicka and W. Norman (eds), *Citizenship in Diverse Societies* (pp. 245–72). Oxford: Oxford University Press.

Sandel, M. J. 1982. *Liberalism and the Limits of Justice*. Cambridge: Cambridge University Press.

Shaywitz, B. A., Pugh, K. R., Jenner, A. R., Fulbright, R. K., Fletcher. J. M., Gore, J. C., & Shaywitz, S. E. 2000. The neurobiology of reading and reading disability (dyslexia). In M. L. Kamil, P. B. Mosenthal, P. D. Pearson and R. Barr (eds), *Handbook of Reading Research Volume III* (pp. 229–49). Mahwah, NJ and London: Lawrence Erlbaum.

Simon, R. I. 1983. But who will let you do it? Counter-hegemonic possibilities for work education. *Journal of Education*, 165, 235–55.

Snow, C. E., & Tabors, P. O. 1993. Language skills that relate to literacy development. In B. Spodek and O. N. Saracho (eds), *Language and Literacy in Early Childhood Education* (pp. 1–20). New York and London: Teachers College Press.

Street, B. 1995. *Social Literacies*. London and New York: Longman.

Taylor, C. 1994. The politics of recognition. In A. Gutmann (ed.), *Multiculturalism* (pp. 25–73). Princeton: Princeton University Press.

Verhoeven, L., & Durgunoglu, A. Y. 1998. Perspectives on literacy development in multilingual contexts. In A. Y. Durgunoglu and L. Verhoeven (eds), *Literacy Development in a Multilingual Context* (pp. ix–xviii). Mahwah, NJ and London: Lawrence Erlbaum.

Waldron, J. 2000. Cultural identity and civic responsibility. In W. Kymlicka and W. Norman (eds), *Citizenship in Diverse Societies* (pp. 155–74). Oxford: Oxford University Press.

Source

This chapter was written especially for this volume.

Chapter 20

Reforming special education

Beyond 'inclusion'

Michael M. Gerber

Often outside the awareness of its practitioners, special education contains elements that make it subversive to universal public education systems. Special education's focus and priorities challenge schools to produce a radical form of social justice: equality of educational opportunity for students who are sometimes characterized by extreme individual differences. Attempting to accommodate these differences raises questions as well about the meaning of equality, the meaning of opportunity, and indeed the relationship between schooling and education. Much of the American understanding and equality of educational opportunity begins with assumptions of normal – i.e. typical or modal – ability and learning potential. School policies and structures have evolved following more or less implicit expectations that children develop and learn 'normally' (i.e. in a tolerably similar manner).

However, it is a simple fact that some children, for a variety of reasons, are handicapped as learners by a complex interaction of individual characteristics and circumstances, on the one hand, and constraints imposed by social structures or material scarcities, on the other. Their observed trajectory of development and learning is atypical, sometimes profoundly so. Mass public schooling was not designed and has not evolved with these children in mind. Therefore, the very concept of a 'special' education can be and has been subversive to the extent that accommodation of extreme individual differences tends to undermine those structures within schools that have evolved to satisfy both expectations of tolerable similarity among children as well as the several social and political purposes of schools.

As I will attempt to show in this chapter, the current reform movement in special education – 'inclusion' – is merely a variation on a theme. I will argue that the stridency of reformers bent on inclusion inadvertently nurtures and legitimizes attempts by school administrators and policy-makers to regain control over an enterprise that for a hundred years has threatened the traditional structure, economy and culture of American public schooling.

Contradiction and conflict

It is not well understood that the conflict between mass public education and 'special' education is fundamental. It has always existed and, during eras of school reform, it frequently has made special education a source of deep discontent, a focus of controversy and a target of criticism. The public tends to view special education as a loose collection of unusual practices used by specially prepared teachers to instruct and manage an exotic, homogeneous population. In fact, special education in the twentieth century is better understood as a school enterprise, as an organizational strategy schools have adopted to accommodate sometimes extreme differences in children. That is, schools create, organize and allocate resources to satisfy instructional demands presented by the challenging behaviours of students with disabilities. Historically, special educational programming emerges as the unavoidable consequence of the immutable fact of human differences in conflict with the ambition to build systems of universal mass education. As a result, special education has proved to be a troubling and troublesome offspring to public school officials, chronically demanding extraordinary effort, contingent resources, and most of all, constant institutional transformation to achieve a radical form of social justice.

In many ways, special education's explicit concern for individual differences has been the source of its moral strength, but also its fatal political weakness. Even in societies professing democratic ideals, individuals are valued more at the high rather than low end of ability, achievement and performance distributions. The history of civil liberties flows from contemplation of social justice for competent more than for incompetent individuals. Historically, the latter individuals have been extended protection more often than opportunity following a common-sense expectation that equal social privileges and opportunities will fail to yield equal successes. Even when, in the first years of this century, special day classes seemed progressive and innovative, the subtle, unrelenting pressure exerted by special education advocacy for individual children was in contradiction to the mass educational system that school managers were attempting to build.

The heart of this contradiction lies in the distinction between access and opportunity. Mere access to the physical environment of schools or classrooms within schools confers no specific or necessarily appropriate opportunity to learn. Children who are very difficult to teach may provoke contingent and individual responses from teachers, but these responses do not necessarily constitute an 'opportunity'. Allowing such children into the schools in the early part of this century was an early form of inclusion that was popularly conceived as new educational opportunity for children with disabilities. But it wasn't until very difficult students received a planful response that was reasonably calculated to promote satisfactory progress in the curriculum that a real educational opportunity existed. It is, therefore, unfortunate that contemporary reformers who urge 'inclusion' have emphasized place over instructional substance and confused 'participation' with real opportunity (Kauffman, 1993; Gerber, 1995).

Criticism and reform

Despite its origins as a form of inclusion, special education is described today by reformers as a segregating, insulated, self-protecting, racially biased philosophy and array of practices, a product of an outdated modernism and misguided scientific positivism, or merely as an ineffective, overblown solution to easily solvable school problems (Dunn, 1968; Heller *et al.*, 1982; Tomlinson, 1982; Madden and Slavin, 1983; Will, 1986; Cole, 1990; Skrtic, 1991). Hardly ten years after the passage of a national special education mandate, its most uncompromising critics had weighed its worth and found it absolutely wanting, absolutely beyond redemption in its current forms (Stainback and Stainback, 1984; Gartner and Lipsky, 1987; Wang *et al.*, 1988). The remarkable policies of inclusion that led in this century from special day classes to mandated public school education for *all* disabled children in the 'least restrictive environment', policies that once were lauded as dramatic signs of a profound social 'revolution', now seem to have lost both the public's confidence and support amid a sea of change in political attitudes about abnormal development, achievement and behaviour.

The current reform movement is complex, containing strands of various interests that converge only on the perceived need to change special education. Administrators and policy-makers, for example, using the rhetoric of inclusion have advocated for integration of funding, more than for integration of students, and deregulation more than improvement of programmes (National Association of State Boards of Education, 1992; 'Governors seek authority to merge IDEA, other money', 1995). Policy rhetoric and philosophical debate aside, administrators and other public officials recognize a 'bottom line' – attempting to organize instructional resources to suit the learning differences among children is very costly (Chaikind *et al.*, 1993; Bacdayan, 1994). These critics are focused on managing schools more efficiently and effectively, so their expressed concern for improving special education must be evaluated in that light.

A quite different set of critics who strongly identify themselves with needs and rights of disabled people, advocate a new more radical policy of 'inclusion' in place of existing forms of special education (Catlett and Osher, 1994; Fuchs and Fuchs, 1994). They aggressively demand and define educational opportunity for all disabled students in terms of its location in regular, age-appropriate classrooms. These critics believe and intend that, under great moral and political pressure, schools, curriculum and instruction will remould themselves to accommodate individual learning needs of students with disabilities and, therefore, produce a fuller and more genuine equality of educational opportunity.

Advocates for special education resist these radical proposals as misguided zealotry and believe that the philosophy and legal framework created by legislation ultimately is a more powerful and reliable vehicle of change (Gerber, 1989). Advocates for gradual, research-based improvement in implementing present policies believe that the political stress created by more radical reformers will be expropriated easily by school administrators and policy-makers who seek mainly to gain greater local control and discretion over educational programmes for students with disabilities. These 'gradualists' believe that school administrators are supportive of changes in special education only because, as currently constituted, it evades local control and limits degrees of managerial freedom to such an extent that traditional forms of schooling are threatened (Kauffman *et al.*, 1988; Gerber, 1989, 1994; Kauffman and Hallahan, 1995).

If the 'gradualists' are correct, it will be ironic if it is those who have most thwarted current policy by their bureaucratic resistance who ultimately benefit from the intense criticism and political agitation of radical inclusionists. In fact, radical inclusionists and policy gradualists *both* seek improvement for students with disabilities although they have engaged in fractious, often harsh debate over who best speaks for the interests of children with disabilities (Fuchs and Fuchs, 1994; Kauffman and Hallahan, 1995). An objective analysis reveals that *both* positions and the courses of action they might recommend have an important underlying commonality. Followed to their logical conclusion, both represent the continuation of the same implicit threat to public schooling that was posed by the establishment of special day classes almost a hundred years ago.

Special education became a formal part of public schooling in the United States during the closing years of the nineteenth century while a system of mass public education was still emerging. The story of its origins reveals why over the ensuing years and especially today it so seriously threatens the *status quo* of public schooling. Beneath the progressivist – some might say, modernist – language of the story, however, is the hard material fact that extant knowledge and technology of instruction, organized for 'schooling' as it has been over most of this century, is incapable of providing either meaningfully equal or equally meaningful educational opportunity for all students. It is in reaction to this fact and its long-term implications that special education is singled out and vilified by current reformers.

Past is prologue

In response to rapid industrialization, urban growth and massive immigration, the institution of public schooling at the beginning of the twentieth century served several different public purposes. One set of purposes wished to secure and improve a democratic society by improving its citizenry and controlling those disintegrative and anarchistic forces thought to be latent in unsocialized – uneducated – people. Another set of purposes sought a general grading and upgrading of the labour force as one component in the production equation to support better expanding capitalist industry and interests.

At an accelerating rate, a subtle political consensus developed following the American Civil War. Different purposes and interests coalesced in support of universal, publically financed compulsory schooling. By 1900, fewer than half of the states had compulsory attendance laws, and those that did varied in the vigour of their enforcement. But public education was far more easily legislated than accomplished. Organizing and operating schools for so many children at the scale contemplated faced substantial practical barriers especially in fast-growing urban centres. Children appeared in classrooms who, for reasons of ability, background or motivation, caused teachers significant difficulties. Any first-order approximation to the kind of school system intended required management and control, not only of numerous but also highly diverse children. As early as 1894, for example, a researcher, Will S. Monroe, revealed that teachers perceived 2 per cent of their students as 'imbeciles' or 'idiots', and almost 9 per cent as 'mentally dull'. Monroe and others knew that children who were extremely low functioning would eventually find their way into state institutions. But he crystallized the core problem of universal compulsory education by pondering if schools were or could be the proper place for so many 'mentally dull' students who were so 'below the general average' (cited in Trent, 1994: 147).

At the turn of the century, teaching consisted of oral presentation and recitation of subject-matter and an array of drill and practice for acquiring basic academic skills. Teachers expected and sought to command student behaviours conducive to large-group instruction in classrooms. Professional teaching, still in its infancy, was wholly unprepared for students who differed in so many obstructive ways. Teachers were not trained or encouraged to develop repertoires of adaptive methods or techniques suitable, let alone optimal, for addressing significant individual differences in learners.

In conventional wisdom, learning was a product of crudely understood interaction of opportunity, provided by schooling, and ability and character, sufficient amounts of which were assumed to exist in a 'typical' student. There was as yet no psychology of child development or useful educational psychology. Neither the intelligence-testing nor 'child study' movements had begun. In practice, school personnel made little formal distinction between students who were unwilling or unable to learn the curriculum teachers presented to them. Rather, they and the public at large believed that merely being at school provided students with an opportunity to learn. If they succeeded, then they had obviously used this opportunity to good advantage. If they did not succeed, then just as obviously they had squandered their opportunity and must accept responsibility for doing so.

The first reform

In the first years of the century, however, a new progressivist philosophy gained a foothold in urban affairs and spread easily to urban schools particularly. According to Ravitch (1974), new ideas contributed to a vision of a 'new education' that undermined traditional thinking 'that school was a place to learn reading, writing, and arithmetic, and that students who failed had only themselves to blame' (p. 167). Progressivists urged schools as agents of the community to assume and accept more responsibility for the success of students' learning. Ultimately, the public's perception of the source of educational success or failure shifted away from students to what schools were thought to provide – how instruction was organized, the curriculum offered, the quality of teachers, and the nature of teaching itself. In this view, schools did not merely manufacture education by a set of technical production processes. Rather, schools, through the kind of educational opportunities offered, were vanguards of societal redemption and renewal.

It was natural, therefore, that someone would view educating children with learning and behavioural problems as similar to public health nursing or social work. One of the most prominent leaders of a new movement to establish special day classes for these children in schools was Elizabeth Farrell, a teacher in New York City. Farrell gained the active support of social activists associated with Lillian Wald's nearby settlement house and from other progressive figures, including New York City's Superintendent of Schools, William Maxwell (Sarason and Doris, 1979; Hendrick and MacMillan, 1989). As Farrell herself describes it, the idea for special day classes

> was not the result of any theory. It grew out of conditions in a neighborhood which furnished many and serious problems in truancy and discipline. The first class was made up of the odds and ends of a large school. There were over-age children, so-called naughty children, and the dull and stupid children. . . . They had varied interests but the school, as they found it, had little or nothing for them.
>
> (cited in Sarason and Doris, 1979: 297)

Thus, while the still-emerging concept of 'public school' emphasized universal exposure to a common curriculum in age-graded classes, early special education advocacy by teachers like Farrell promoted *differentiated* treatment and curriculum in *ungraded* classes for students considered wayward, mentally deficient or simply difficult to teach (Hoffman, 1975). Despite what appear to be obvious contradictions in trying to incorporate special classes, teachers and curriculum within the otherwise rigid framework of public schooling, the idea caught fire. By 1913, there were special day classes and special schools in 108 cities. Ten years later, this number had increased by 55 per cent with over 33,000 students in special education programmes (Trent, 1994: 147). Clearly, not every teacher or administrator shared Farrell's and Maxwell's enthusiasm for special class programmes for retarded students within the contexts of graded public schools. Indeed, it isn't clear that Farrell and Maxwell had precisely the same motives or vision. It seems, rather, that the concept of special day classes was embraced widely because it satisfied different needs for different constituencies.

When Farrell, encouraged by local support, finally presented her ideas to members of the Board of Education, she was praised as a 'genius whose vision was essentially practical' (Lillian Wald, cited in Sarason and Doris, 1979: 299).

That phrase – a vision that was essentially practical – is a succinct expression of the unusual consensus achieved by the new 'special' education. To administrators, special day classes appeared to meet two important goals, attendance *and* containment, while also providing an orderly professional context for addressing significant management difficulties. However, although administrators won control and containment of a segment of the school population who were difficult to teach and manage, they failed to see how porous and troubling the boundaries between general practices and the new special education actually would prove to be. On the other hand, advocates for special day classes won a kind of autonomy within the school from which they hoped to organize more appropriate, more meaningful curriculum and instruction for students with disabilities, but failed to see how potentially threatening they would become to the deepest interests of those who built and supported public schooling.

Almost immediately, these different purposes began to conflict, surfacing as debate over how special day classes were to be administered, to what extent their curriculum would vary from normal curriculum, methods of identification and classification, and the nature of professional preparation and certification. Most school districts established separate supervisorial authorities and administrative channels to manage those specially designated teachers assigned to special day classes. It was separation, to be sure, but separation by mutual consent (Sarason and Doris, 1979: 360). If special educators pushed the boundaries of their autonomy, general educators worked as aggressively to circumscribe, contain and limit the overall impact of special education on the general structure and operation of schools. Thus, the bifurcation of the public school system into two mutually contradicting, asymmetrically empowered strands – one for 'special' and one for 'normal' students – arose not from the insistent advocacy of any particular group, so much as from a tacit agreement about the practical conditions and possibilities of public schools. It was – it is – an unworkable arrangement as long as schools maintain their traditional structure, economy and culture.

In remembering Farrell's vision as it was shared with members of the Henry Street Settlement House, Lillian Wald in 1935 understood more accurately than most the implications of what was being proposed by the young teacher. It was *not* simply about optimal development of every individual's potential. Rather,

> Miss Farrell's originality lay in applying the idea to the education of the atypical in the public schools. She was optimistic enough to believe that the largest and most complex school system in the country – perhaps in the world – with its hundreds of thousands of children, its rigid curriculum, its mass methods, could be modified to meet the needs of the atypical – often the least lovely and potentially the most troublesome of its pupils.
>
> (Wald, cited in Sarason and Doris, 1979: 298)

Education, income and social justice

Without some reference to material well-being, the concept of social justice is ultimately a philosophical abstraction. Differences and variations in status or power or specific rights are important because they ultimately contribute to greater equality or inequality of material well-being. After 1900, greater social equality and material well-being, as indexed by distribution of income, was presumptively related to access to and equality of educational opportunity. In these terms, social justice does not require strict equality of income, but it does demand that some basic level of material and psychological well-being (i.e. income) should not be withheld from individuals by society for arbitrary or capricious reasons. There is historical confusion and room for debate, however, over what constitutes 'arbitrary' or 'capricious' justifications for social inequality.

In capitalist societies, apologists explain observed inequalities of income distribution as a product of supply and demand for qualities of labour as they are differentiated and allocated blindly by competitive market mechanisms. Beneath this explanation is a broad-based and tenacious conventional wisdom that lifespan social achievements of individuals reflect unfettered expressions of innate differences in ability in competition with one another. For some, this belief provides a satisfying explanation for income and social class disparities because natural abilities do not seem arbitrary or capricious. The concept that education obtained in schools frees natural ability for fair competition also establishes an explicit strategy for social advancement and, therefore, the value of an *equal* educational opportunity.

Much of the social value of publicly supported education in this century begins with an abiding faith in the transformative or modifying effects of learning as a process leading to expression of natural abilities. In American society, at least, there was no expectation that schools would produce absolute equality. Despite educational opportunity, income disparities certainly would still exist because individuals differ in natural ability. Following from this logic, public schools were embraced as an instrument of social justice for individuals in the marketplace and in society at large. For example, in a recent call for educational opportunity for African-Americans, John Hope Franklin has written: 'Economic and social progress in the United States has long been rooted in access to quality education. What worked so well for millions of immigrants must at last be made to work for black Americans' (Committee on Policy for Racial Justice, 1989: ix). His statement succinctly captures how strong still is the popular expectation that American public education has the ability as well as the purpose to transform American social and economic life and promote social justice.

In the 1960s, when this belief was applied to the problem of substantial domestic poverty through a series of unprecedented education policies, it seemed logical that public schools could be recruited to redress income disparities simply by offering compensatory educational opportunities for those who were unfairly disadvantaged. The expected result was not the elimination of poverty so much as a correction of *disproportional* poverty among some social groups. Thus, the equality of opportunity sought was equality of opportunity to *compete* without restrictions other than those imposed by differences in ability. The core belief was unchanged that ability differences, once freed from unacceptable social suppression and enhanced by educational opportunity, were still the legitimate determinants of income disparities.

Limitations and disability

Individuals with disabilities occupy an ambiguous and sometimes paradoxical space in this scheme of things. In particular, there is only a tenuous relationship between access to schooling and economic well-being. As a group of learners, individuals with disabilities are heterogeneous. Despite confusion in individual identification, as a group they are neither like immigrants nor racial minorities. Also unlike these latter groups, we make no assumption that their social identification distorts or disguises an underlying average ability. Instead, we presume that they will face serious and chronic barriers to achievement over their lifespan and generally will not compete successfully with non-disabled individuals for employment.

To be sure, there is considerable debate over whether these perceived limitations are a product of innate characteristics or the result of arbitrary social assignment or some interaction of both. Teachers recognize children with disabilities less by diagnostic signs and more because they are relatively difficult to teach and less likely to benefit from typical instructional arrangements. On the other hand, inclusionists stridently argue that teachers either underestimate their achievement potential if professional training is improved, instructional environments modified and adequate support provided. Whichever view one holds, it is difficult to dispute the fact of 'disabled' students' lower achievement compared to that of non-disabled peers. There is also little dispute that available remedies will cost more on a *per capita* basis than the public typically expends for students not considered disabled. And therein lies the source of the durable concern special education of any kind raises for school managers.

When the public perceives disabilities as unalterable barriers to achievement and, thus, future employment, it is unwilling to invest scarce resources in what seem to be futile educational opportunities. On the other hand, especially during times of economic prosperity, the public also rejects the social devaluation and economic disadvantage that follows from little or no educational opportunity for individuals with disabilities. These two views ultimately are not reconcilable within the current economic and organizational framework of public schooling. The special day class curriculum was designed with alternative, not simply lower, achievement and employment expectations. Contemporary special education is more complex, allowing for remedial and compensatory academic programmes for some, alternative curricula for others. Nevertheless, whatever special education the public has supported inevitably reveals a critical paradox in nominally 'universal' schooling. It really cannot accommodate the full range of human differences without substantial cost and structural change.

Paradox revealed

To achieve its ambitious scale of universality, public schooling largely ignores individual differences that contribute to variable instructional outcomes. Special education throughout its almost one-hundred-year history has been concerned *mostly* with individual differences and how they might be accommodated by institutional transformations. The intrinsic nature of this paradox is revealed best by asking whether the claim that public schools work for *all* children, without exception, is supported by an extant evidence? More specifically, is equality of educational opportunity really offered to each and every American child, again without exception? What, indeed, does it mean to provide equality of educational opportunity for children with disabilities if these children will always be at a competitive disadvantage compared to their more normally achieving peers?

Under most existing instructional arrangements, exposure to precisely the same instruction designed for more normally achieving peers condemns children with disabilities to achievement below their potential and at great disadvantage for developing socially valued levels of independence and productivity. This, in essence, defines disability and is axiomatic in any construction of a 'special' education. Equal physical access to school and strict equality of instructional resources therein are precisely the conditions that created special education in the first place. The subversive quality of special education arises from the organizational disruption and fiscal burden imposed on schools when they legitimize attempts to provide individually variable levels of access and instructional resources.

Early special day class programmes revealed this paradox because, in an attempt to gain control over the consequences of enrolling diverse, often difficult students, school officials legitizised the internal organization of special effort that was fundamentally antagonistic to the organization of the school as a whole. Special class teachers required *additional* resources but also used these resources *differently* to create instructional arrangements meant to obtain *different*, not just lower, achievement outcomes from those expected for students in the general programme. Although now criticized by inclusionists and others, is it instructive to consider how special education seeks to establish equality of opportunity? That is, in what sense can a *different* instructional programme aimed at *different* goals with *different* resources be considered equal? Clearly, any such description of equality must accept not only that children may consume different resources to reach similar goals, but also that they may consume different resources to reach *different*, equally valid goals.

In past decades, policy-makers have overemphasized the amount of school resources, or inputs, for calculating equality while ignoring whether similar resources provide an equally substantive educational opportunity for students who differ. For students with disabilities, substantive opportunity is not necessarily provided either by access or by social participation in universally accessible programmes, but is provided when and if an individually tailored educational programme exists that is reasonably calculated to promote at least satisfactory levels of development and achievement. If such opportunity is provided to each child, then educational opportunity is equally meaningful. The public school establishment, focused on equal access to equal resources, constrained by fiscal limitations and conflicting political demands, has recognized from the beginning both the resource and organizational implications of special education's more radical formulation of equality and, therefore, has resisted it at every turn.

Public schools may have *attempted*, at varying times and to varying degrees, to give access to *all* children, but truly universal public education remains really more of an ideal than a reality. Despite early advocacy for special day class programmes, public schools in the United States have always acted to deny or restrict access – sometimes absolutely, sometimes contingently – for some students. As a matter of law, *all* American children were not guaranteed equal access to public education until 1975 and the passage of the Education of All Handicapped Children's Act (popularly known as Public Law 94–142, or simply PL 94–142 and revised and reauthorized in 1990 as Individuals with Disabilities Education Act, or IDEA). Even so, schools still require students to demonstrate desirable general standards of conduct to *remain* in normal public school programmes. Students with severe behaviour problems, particularly those whose behaviour is considered dangerous or otherwise criminal, tend to be segregated and eventually expelled from public schools.

The hot dispute currently raging over suspension and expulsion policies in the United States illustrates how special education disturbs school administrators and their sense of control over schools. Court decisions like *Honig v. Doe* underscore how strongly anti-exclusionist contemporary special education policy is in its philosophy and current regulatory scheme (Bartlett, 1989; 'House IDEA draft would lift discipline barrier', 1995). Once identified, students are explicitly entitled to appropriate educational interventions that cannot be limited or interrupted by unilateral decisions by school administrators. School authorities perceive this policy as serious interference with their ability to suspend or expel unilaterally any student who is disruptive, aggressive or violent regardless of whether such behaviour is related to disability. Special education policy, on the other hand, permits no exclusion and, in any case, intends an active search for educational rather than administrative solutions to undesirable behaviour.

More important than loss of discretion over misbehaviour, schools balk at the open-ended and contingent commitment of resources that special education demands. In other recent litigation, *Timothy W. v. Rochester*, school officials sought relief from what they perceived to be a burdensome and inappropriate expenditure of scarce resources for a completely unresponsive profoundly retarded child. An appeals court, overturning a lower court's ruling in favour of the schools, indicated that federal law mandating special education required no test of educability as a precondition for the provision of special education and related services (Whitted, 1991). Simply stated, children do not have to prove they can learn before schools must commit themselves to an exploratory effort to teach them.

This principle, central in special education history and policy, contradicts the traditional assumption around which traditional school organization has evolved, namely, that learning opportunities are provided and children may or may not take advantage of these opportunities. Either way, whether students are successful or not, the school's obligation ends with provision of whatever instructional arrangements it chooses to designate as an opportunity. Special education policy, on the other hand, imposes on schools an obligation to seek actively and continually means to instruct all students without exclusion. Society cannot presuppose or legislate individual outcomes, so what is required by such a mandate is effort itself. That is, special education law in the United States commits schools to invest effort in educating children who may not, when all is said and done, promise much return for that effort. Although from the perspective of educational resource managers, such a policy may seem folly, the *Timothy W.* case emphasizes how radically American special education policy endorses true universality and redefines equality of opportunity.

American special education policy also includes at least two other principles that have proved a chronic irritant to school officials. One is the requirement that parents formally participate in formulating and consent to an individualized educational plan (IEP) for their children. While not a legal contract, the IEP shares important characteristics with contracts. Most fundamentally, IEPs represent a negotiated agreement between parents who wish to lay claim to school resources for their child, and school administrators who manage and who are accountable to the public for the use of these resources. The IEP requirement, therefore, confers on parents an unusual degree of power over how schools respond to children. No tradition of schooling or other law so explicitly and so effectively extends to parents the right to modulate the school experiences of their children. Even though it is doubtful that all parents of disabled children take equal advantage of their legal rights, including judicial relief if necessary, enough do so that public school administrators feel challenged and burdened. Beneath their apparent support for the values espoused by inclusionists, administrators also clearly seek greater discretion and control when IEPs are contested by parents.

Another principle enshrined in contemporary American special education policy that can be antagonistic to traditional schooling is the requirement that special education, when provided, should occur in the 'least restrictive environment' (LRE). As a matter of law, the LRE requirement intends to separate questions of educational programme and physical setting. That is, once parents and schools agree on an appropriate programme, it is incumbent upon the school to provide that programme in an environment that is different from regular classrooms and schedules only to the degree necessary. Gradualists have argued that the LRE provision provides and protects precisely what inclu-sionists propose – opportunity to learn in the same education environments as non-disabled children.

There is no disagreement that schools often circumvent the intent of this requirement by failing to acknowledge the possibility of providing some special education in regular classrooms, particularly for students with severe disabili-ties. But the failure in this regard has been a failure of schools not special education policy, a failure consistent with schools' historical reaction to the intrusiveness of special education. Acknowledgement of possibility requires an attempt; and the attempt to provide special education in regular classrooms, as inclusionists are beginning to learn, immediately creates demand for supple-mentation and contingent reconfiguration of resources available to any given class, including the kind of training and consultative support required by teachers. Schools attempting to exchange special education's current regula-tory strictures for a vague inclusion policy will find themselves recreating the very thing they are trying to escape. Ironically, by adopting inclusionist philos-ophy to counter the perceived burden of special education policy without fundamental restructuring, administrators risk conflicts with general classroom teachers who, without adequate support, will resist the increased instructional burden of 'included' students. One hundred years after the first special day classes were instituted, then, schools will have come full circle.

Can schools change?

It really was not until the *Equality of Educational Opportunity (EEO)* report that the belief that public schooling promoted social mobility and was a force for social equality was ever seriously questioned (Coleman *et al.*, 1966; *Harvard Educational Review*, 1969; Mosteller and Moynihan, 1972; Jencks and Brown, 1975; Levine and Bane, 1975). The massive study commissioned by the Office of Civil Rights and produced by Coleman and his colleagues sought only to demonstrate the magnitude of the injustice that almost everyone agreed must exist. Much to everyone's surprise, Coleman's data showed rather small differ-ences in the resource infrastructure that characterized segregated white and black schools.

It is difficult to recapture in 1995 what profound implications seemed to attach to these findings in 1966. Coleman's findings were surprising because they could not demonstrate the expected inequality of resources that hypothetically accounted for achievement inequality. But they were shocking because they offered little evidence that schools, even with massive federal investment, could correct achievement differences in any case. This seemed to contradict precisely the policy course the federal government had already chosen by the time Coleman's data became known. And more darkly, it appeared to support the view that the real cause of unequal achievement was familial and not social (Jencks *et al.*, 1972; Jencks and Brown, 1975; Levine and Bane, 1975).

Coleman's study instigated two decades of vigorous research to refute the politically unacceptable inference that schools sorted but did not really educate children (*Harvard Educational Review*, 1969; Mosteller and Moynihan, 1972; Hodgson, 1975; Rutter, 1983). Ever more sophisticated analytical methods were brought to bear on the general search for an educational production function – that combination of resource inputs that reliably and strongly would predict achievement outputs (Averch *et al.*, 1972; Bridge *et al.*, 1979). But after two decades, the evidence is still ambiguous and forcefully debated (Hanushek, 1989, 1994; Wainer, 1993; Hedges *et al.*, 1994a, b).

Despite differences in analytical strategy, though, most research habitually focuses on average achievement in the school as the proper indicator of school effectiveness or success. Although policy-makers acknowledge that schools might produce more than one outcome, there has been an unwavering conviction that these multiple 'products' of schooling are simply different domains of achievement or growth, estimated as the *average* performance or status within a school.

Such blind faith in the arithmetic average has led us far astray and helped schools avoid recognizing that they 'produce' a distribution of human beings, not average levels of performance. Ignoring the fact that different outcomes are distributed by schools' instructional arrangements for different students causes periodic paroxysms of reform without ever changing traditional approaches to curriculum and instruction. Enshrining average rather than distributed outcomes permits schools to continue their historical treatment of diverse students as tolerably alike in learning characteristics and, therefore, tolerably alike in their responsiveness to a given curriculum or particular instructional method. Student diversity is reduced to a slogan and the organizational and resource implications of disability continue to be avoided or ignored (Gerber, 1989; Gamoran, 1992; Biemiller, 1993a, b; Slavin, 1993).

Questioning the importance of average performance in terms of its underlying distribution also threatens traditional notions of school effectiveness. Do we expect that as a manifestation of some natural law high achieving students will always make the greatest gains? If so, we are actually expressing a preference for a particular achievement outcome, a distribution that is skewed towards already high achieving students. Because low achieving students, including most considered disabled, achieve at a lower rate, more instructional effort is required to obtain more similar (equal) levels of achievement. If we are committed to universal education for *all* students in a world of scarce and limited resources, then we must contend with the fact that effort invested in many disabled students may alter the distribution (narrowing it) while having little or no impact on the mean outcomes of schools (Gerber and Semmel, 1985; Gerber, 1988). This formulation has serious implications for the concept of school effectiveness.

When is a school effective?

The challenge that special education posed to public schooling in the first decade of this century – and still poses – was the insistence that design and deployment of instructional effort within schools could and should be modified to accommodate individual differences rather than expectations for modal students. This insistence implies a value that suggests a non-intuitive definition of school effectiveness. Schools are effective when and if their poorest-performing students demonstrate significant achievement gains.

Very little serious attention has been paid to such an alternative view. Yet, organizational prescriptions drawn from case studies of schools that appear to be effective at the mean (Purkey and Smith, 1983, 1985) are not useful for predicting school effectiveness with their disabled students. Schools that rank high on performance of their modal students do not necessarily rank similarly on performance of their disabled students (Semmel and Gerber, 1995).

Unlike Coleman and related studies, these findings do not mean that instructional efforts by schools are fruitless, only that they are distributed in such a way so as to make the *average* a poor measure of a school's effectiveness (Brown and Saks, 1981). That is, effects of intentionally organizing instructional effort within schools to meet needs of slower-learning, lower-achieving students are not likely to be detected by changes in mean tested achievement. Special education constitutes an institutionalised, explicit pressure for schools to distribute instructional effort in this way.

The next reform

Special education poses difficult technical problems for universal education, but also reveals a challenging view of our real, as opposed to professed, values and commitment to social justice. School effectiveness cannot be meaningfully inferred from an achievement distribution until these values are made explicit. If equality of educational opportunity means equalizing *substantive* opportunity, then school effectiveness can be demonstrated only in one of two ways. Either achievement variance will decrease by increases in achievement in the lower half of the distribution or mean achievement will rise without increases in variance in the higher half of the distribution (i.e. the entire distribution will shift upwards) (Brown and Saks, 1981; Gerber and Semmel, 1985; Gerber, 1988; Bacdayan, 1994). To obtain either of these outcomes in the next reform movement will require not only new resources and new technologies of instruction, but also a fundamentally different structure, economy and culture of schooling to permit and support individually variable programmes of instruction.

Despite prolific reform rhetoric, the achievement of disabled students as an indicator of school effectiveness has been specifically ignored by blue ribbon panels and commissions (Gerber and Semmel, 1995), as well as in state and national assessments of educational progress ('Students excluded from education data', 1991; National Center for Education Statistics, 1995). Such a profound silence regarding an aspect of public policy that schools view as intrusive and expensive seems odd and worrisome.

Moreover, the apparent and formal lack of interest in assessing the progress of disabled and other low-achieving students on a national scale prevents the possibility of understanding school effectiveness as explicit, intentional instructional effort. Instead we can only perpetuate discredited concepts of effectiveness, equality and opportunity that represent a tangled, ambiguous mix of socio-economic and instructional effects. More disturbing, though, if such lack of interest is actually a tacit, consensual policy, one that the public silently embraces, then it is reasonable to infer that school authorities, policy-makers and many reformers consciously or unconsciously reject either the value or cost of a truly universal education as well as the kind of social justice that follow from it. The reform of special education currently advocated or supported thus must be viewed with profound scepticism.

References

Averch, H., Carroll, S., Donaldson, T., Kiesling, H. and Pincus, J. (1972) *How Effective is Schooling? A Critical Review and Synthesis of Research Findings*. Santa Monica, CA: Rand Corporation.

Bacdayan, A.W. (1994) Time-denominated achievement cost curves, learning differences and individualized instruction, *Economics of Education Review*, 13: 43–53.

Bartlett, L. (1989) Disciplining handicapped students: legal issues in light of *Honig v. Doe, Exceptional Children*, 55: 357–66.

Biemiller, A. (1993a) Lake Wobegon revisited: on diversity and education, *Educational Researcher*, 22: 7–12.

Biemiller, A. (1993b) Students differ: so address differences effectively, *Educational Researcher*, 22: 14–15.

Bridge, R.G., Judd, C.M. and Moock, P.R. (1979) *The Determinants of Educational Outcomes*, Cambridge, MA: Ballinger.

Brown, B.W. and Saks, D.H. (1981) The microeconomics of schooling, in D.C. Berliner (ed.) *Review of Research in Education*, vol. 9. Washington, DC: American Educational Research Association.

Catlett, S.M. and Osher, T.W. (1994) *What is Inclusion, Anyway? An Analysis of Organizational Position Statements*. Alexandria, VA: National Association of State Directors of Special Education.

Chaikind, S., Danielson, L.C. and Brauen, M.L. (1993) What do we know about the costs of special education?: a selected review, *The Journal of Special Education*, 26: 344–70.

Cole, T. (1990) The history of special education: social control or humanitarian progress? *British Journal of Special Education*, 17: 101–7.

Coleman, J.S., Campbell, E.Q., Hobson, C.J., McPartland, J., Mood, A.M., Weinfield, F.D. and York, R.L. (1966) *Equality of Educational Opportunity*. Washington, DC: US Department of Health, Education and Welfare.

Committee on Policy for Racial Justice (1989) *Visions of a Better Way. A Black Appraisal of Public Schooling*. Washington, DC: Joint Center for Political Studies Press.

Dunn, L.M. (1968) Special education for the mildly retarded: is much of it justifiable? *Exceptional Children*, 35: 5–22.

Fuchs, D. and Fuchs, L.S. (1994) Inclusive schools movement and the radicalisation of special education reform. *Exceptional Children*, 60: 294–309.

Gamoran, A. (1992) Is ability grouping equitable? *Educational Leadership*, 50: 11–17.

Gartner, A. and Lipsky, D.K. (1987) Beyond special education: toward a quality system for all students, *Harvard Educational Review*, 57: 367–95.

Gerber, M.M. (1988) Tolerance and technology of instruction: implications for special education reform, *Exceptional Children*, 54: 309–14.

Gerber, M.M. (1989) The new 'diversity' and special education: are we going forward or starting again? *Public Schools Forum*, 3: 19–32.

Gerber, M.M. (1994) Postmodernism in special education, *The Journal of Special Education*, 28: 368–78.

Gerber, M.M. (1995) Inclusion at the high-water mark?: some thoughts on Zigmond and Baker's case studies of inclusive educational programs, *The Journal of Special Education*, 29: 181–91.

Gerber, M.M. and Semmel, M.I. (1985) The microeconomics of referral and reintegration: towards a new paradigm of special education evaluation, *Studies in Educational Evaluation*, 11: 13–29.

Gerber, M.M. and Semmel, M.I. (1995) Why do educational reform commissions fail to address special education? In R. Ginsburg and D.N. Plank (eds) *Commissions, Reports, Reforms, and Educational Policy*. Westport, CN: Praeger.

'Governors seek authority to merge IDEA, other money' (1995) *Special Education Report*, 21: 1–2, 9 August.

Hanushek, E.A. (1989) The impact of differential expenditure on school performance, *Educational Researcher*, 18: 45–51, 62.

Hanushek, E.A. (1994) Money might matter somewhere: a response to Hedges, Laine and Greenwald, *Educational Researcher*, 23 (4): 5–8.

Harvard Educational Review (1969) *Equal Educational Opportunity*. Cambridge, MA: Harvard University Press.

Hedges, L.V., Laine, R.D. and Greenwald, R. (1994a) Does money matter? a meta-analysis of studies of the effects of differential school inputs on student outcomes (an exchange: Part 1), *Educational Researcher*, 23 (3): 5–14.

Hedges, L.V., Laine, R.D. and Greenwald, R. (1994b) Money does matter somewhere: a reply to Hanushek, *Educational Researcher*, 23 (4): 9–10.

Heller, K.A., Holtzman, W.H. and Messick, S. (eds) (1982) *Placing Children in Special Education: A Strategy for Equity*. Washington, DC: National Academy Press.

Hendrick, I.G. and MacMillan, D.L. (1989) Selecting children for special education in New York City: William Maxwell, Elizabeth Farrell, and the development of ungraded classes, 1900–1920, *The Journal of Special Education*, 22: 395–417.

Hodgson, G. (1975) Do schools make a difference? In D.M. Levine and M.J. Bane (eds) *The 'Inequality' Controversy: Schooling and Distributive Justice*. New York: Basic Books.

Hoffman, E. (1975) The American public school and the deviant child: the origins of their involvement, *The Journal of Special Education*, 9: 415–23.

'House IDEA draft would lift discipline barrier' (1995) *Special Education Report*, 21: 1–2, 9 August.

Jencks, C. and Brown, M. (1975) The effects of desegregation on student achievement: some new evidence from the Equality of Educational Opportunity Survey, *Sociology of Education*, 48: 126–40.

Jencks, C., Smith, M., Acland, H., Bane, M.J., Cohen, D.K., Gintis, H., Heyns, B. and Michelson, S. (1972) *Inequality: A Reassessment of the Effect of Family and Schooling in America*. New York: Basic Books.

Kauffman, J.M. (1993) How we might achieve radical reform of special education, *Exceptional Children*, 60: 6–16.

Kauffman, J.M. and Hallahan, D.P. (eds) (1995) *The Illusion of Full Inclusion*. Austin, TX: Pro-Ed.

Kauffman, J.M., Gerber, M.M. and Semmel, M.I. (1988) Arguable assumptions underlying the Regular Education Initiative, *Journal of Learning Disabilities*, 21: 6–11.

Levine, D.M. and Bane, M.J. (eds) (1975) *The 'Inequality' Controversy: Schooling and Distributive Justice*. New York: Basic Books.

Madden, N.A. and Slavin, R.E. (1983) Mainstreaming students with mild handicaps: academic and social outcomes, *Review of Educational Research*, 53: 519–69.

Mosteller, R. and Moynihan, D.P. (eds) (1972) *On Equality of Educational Opportunity*. New York: Vintage Books.

National Assocation of State Boards of Education (1992) *The Report of the NASBE Study Group on Special Education*. Alexandria, VA: NASBE.

National Center for Education Statistics (1995) *The Condition of Education*. Washington, DC: US Department of Education.

Purkey, S.C. and Smith, M.S. (1983) Effective schools: a review, *Elementary School Journal*, 83: 427–52.

Purkey, S.C. and Smith, M.S. (1985) School reform: the district policy implications of the effective schools literature, *Elementary School Journal*, 85: 353–89.

Ravitch, E. (1974) *The Great School Wars: New York City, 1805–1973*. New York: Basic Books.

Rutter, M. (1983) School effects on pupil progress: research findings and policy implications, *Child Development*, 54: 1–29.

Sarason, S.B. and Doris, J. (1979) *Educational Handicap, Public Policy, and Social History*. New York: The Free Press.

Semmel, M.I. and Gerber, M.M. (1995) *The School Environments Project*, final report. Santa Barbara, CA: Special Education Research Laboratory, University of California.

Skrtic, T.M. (1991) The special education paradox: equity as the way to excellence, *Harvard Educational Review*, 61: 148–205.

Slavin, R.E. (1993) Students differ: so what? *Educational Researcher*, 22: 13–14.

Stainback, W. and Stainback, S. (1984) A rationale for the merger of special and regular education, *Exceptional Children*, 51: 102–11.

'Students excluded from education data' (1991) *Outcomes*, National Center on Educational Outcomes, University of Minnesota, No. 1.

Tomlinson, S. (1982) *A Sociology of Special Education*. London: Routledge and Kegan Paul.

Trent, J.W. Jr. (1994) *Inventing the Feeble Mind*. Berkeley, CA: University of California Press.

Wainer, H. (1993) Does spending money on education help? A reaction to the Heritage Foundation and the *Wall Street Journal*, *Educational Researcher*, 22: 22–4.

Wang, M.C., Reynolds, M.C. and Walberg, H.J. (1988) Integrating the children of the second system, *Phi Delta Kappan*, 70: 248–51.

Whitted, B.R. (1991) Educational benefits after Timothy W.: where do we go from here? *West's Education Law Reporter*, 68: 549–55.

Will, M. (1986) Educating children with learning problems: a shared responsibility, *Exceptional Children*, 52: 411–15.

Source

This is an edited version of a chapter previously published in C. Christensen and F. Rivzi (eds) *Disability and the Dilemmas of Education and Justice*. 1996. Reproduced by permission of The Open University Press.

Index